THE DISCOVERY OF

GOD

ABRAHAM

and the Birth of

MONOTHEISM

Three Leaves Press

DOUBLEDAY

New York

THE DISCOVERY OF
GOD

David

Klinghoffer

PUBLISHED BY DOUBLEDAY
a division of Random House, Inc.
1745 Broadway, New York, New York 10019

DOUBLEDAY is a registered trademark and THREE LEAVES PRESS and colophon are
trademarks of Random House, Inc.

The Discovery of God was originally published in hardcover by Doubleday,
a division of Random House, Inc., in 2003. This Three Leaves Press
edition is published by special arrangement with Doubleday.

Book design by Dana Leigh Treglia
Map illustration © 2002, Laura Hartman Maestro

The Library of Congress has cataloged the Doubleday hardcover edition as follows:

Klinghoffer, David, 1965–
The discovery of God : Abraham and the birth of monotheism / David Klinghoffer.
p. cm.
Includes bibliographical references.
1. Monotheism—History. 2. Abraham (Biblical patriarch). 3. Bible. O.T.—
History of Biblical events. 4. Judaism—History—To 70 A.D.
5. Jews—History—To 70 A.D. I. Title.

BL 221 .K55 2003
222'.11092—dc21
2002031566

ISBN 0-385-49974-4

October 2004

First Three Leaves Press Edition

1 3 5 7 9 10 8 6 4 2

FOR NIKA & EZRA

ACKNOWLEDGMENTS

In a typically cryptic verse in Genesis, Abraham is said to have planted an *eshel* at Beersheba (21:33). We would be at a loss to say what exactly an *eshel* is—if it's just a kind of tree, as many translators say, who cares that he planted one? But fortunately Jewish tradition steps in to interpret the word. According to one view, that of the Talmudic sage Shmuel, this *eshel* refers to an inn Abraham established in the wilderness, a hospice where he taught wayfarers to acknowledge God for His blessings. The patriarch would give them food then ask them to say grace.

Eliciting gratitude was central to his mission, and so how could the biographer who seeks to tell the story of his life neglect to thank a few of the people who made this book possible?

The idea for a biography of Abraham came out of conversations I had with Bruce Nichols. It was subsequently encouraged by my redoubtable agent and dear friend Mildred Marmur, and shepherded by my formidably intelligent and unfailingly decent editor, Adam Bellow. This is a much better book than it would have been without him. His able assistant, Miriam Abramowitz, made sure the project did not go off the rails.

Accessing the ancient Jewish primary source material that I have relied on here did not come easily to me. For assistance and inspiration in understanding the tradition, time and again I called upon the help of rabbis whose learning I can only stand back and appreciate, never hoping to match. Rabbi Daniel Lapin, as always, has been my friend and mentor. He has shaped my worldview in innumerable ways. Many of his insights appear in my book, and I hope I have properly attributed them all. Rabbi Elisha Paul selflessly labored with me over the text of *Genesis Rabbah* and reviewed my entire manuscript at an early stage. As an adviser and a reader, Rabbi Jacob Neusner shared his vast scholarship, including his outstanding translations, which I often used when stumped. The translators and elucidators of the Artscroll editions of the Talmud, Pentateuch, and Rashi, including my friend Rabbi Nesanel Kasnett, have performed an amazing service. I often checked my understanding of texts against their work and always came away enlightened. Conversations with other modern-day sages were also of great help to me, including Rabbis Jacob J. Schacter, Meir Soloveichik, David Silber, and Yitzchok Adlerstein. Other scholars were generous with their time, including Professors Edward Alexander and Martin S. Jaffee. This is not to say any of these learned individuals will find himself in agreement with what I have written in this book. Any and all failures of learning are attributable to me alone.

As a reader of an initial version of this book, Bennett Schneir offered invaluable comments. Other friends, including Alex Abrams, Michael and Diane Medved, and Mark Miller, gave me different kinds of support and encouragement.

My father, Paul Kaye, provided moral and material aid without which this book certainly never could have been written. Nor, without his help, could I have accomplished half of whatever I have managed to do so far in life. Other parents and parental figures—Arlene Kaye, Harriet Waring, Nina Erastov—were likewise crucially helpful.

My baby boy, Ezra, did not seem particularly interested in this project per se, but nevertheless always gave me his goofiest grin and said "Dah!" or "Yah!" at the appropriate time.

Finally, and above all, my sweet, loving, tireless, tolerant, brilliant, and beautiful wife Nika gave me the main reason I have had to keep working. I hope to make her proud.

Mercer Island, Washington
October 3, 2002

CONTENTS

PREFACE

Iraq — Land of the Bible

his book was originally published on March 18, 2003, one day before a United States–led coalition invaded Iraq— which happens to be the birthplace of the book's subject, the biblical patriarch Abraham. An interesting coincidence, from a publishing perspective. But is that all it was?

In those days, as American troops moved up the Euphrates River valley toward Baghdad, I thought of Carl Jung, the tidy Swiss psychologist who labored to explain the amazing phenomenon of "synchronicity." In Jung's psychology, synchronicity means the tendency of our lives to include many apparently significant coincidences. To illustrate, he writes of a patient who was telling him her dream about an Egyptian scarab—a kind of beetle common in Egyptian art—when suddenly a real, live Swiss scarab flew in through his office window. He observed that such "coincidences" happen too often to be meaningless. In other words, they are not really mere coincidences at all.

On the issue of synchronicity, the Bible takes what one might call a Jungian view. Scriptural Hebrew has no word for "coincidence" at all, suggesting that, as in Jung's psychology, synchronic events only appear to be coincidental. In fact, they have a genuine if concealed meaning. As America's war in Iraq unfolded, followed by the postwar rebuilding effort, odd parallels between current events and biblical history became apparent. Indeed, with America being led by the most Bible-believing White House in modern times, it was no longer an eccentricity to follow the news with a Bible open on your desk. What are we to make of some of the curious "coincidences" linking the drama in today's Middle East with the dramas of biblical antiquity?

Think fast: Which modern nation can most plausibly be called the Land of the Bible? Israel is the obvious answer, but not the only one. The narrative of the Hebrew Bible begins and ends in Iraq. In the story told by its historical books, from Genesis to 2 Kings, the episodes that occur in the land of Israel can be seen merely as an interlude.

The Bible begins with the Garden of Eden, located in proximity to the Tigris and Euphrates Rivers, in the land called Mesopotamia, the very same location now occupied by Iraq. There follows the story of the Tower of Babel—that is, Babylon, a city whose remains lie 60 miles south of today's Baghdad.

Abraham leaves his native Mesopotamia to migrate to the land of Canaan. His son Isaac and grandson Jacob seek wives in Mesopotamia. While their descendants establish residence in Canaan, the Bible's narrative concludes with Nebuchadnezzar of Babylon, who has come to power in Mesopotamia, invading Israel and deporting the children of Abraham back to the old country: Iraq. I mean, Babylon.

Much of the fierce poetry of the Hebrew prophets is likewise concerned with the peril emanating from Babylon. God warns Jeremiah that "from the North"—Babylon was to the north of Israel—"the evil begins upon all the inhabitants of the land."

Meanwhile, America has often seen herself as a new Israel. The Pilgrims were called Separatists, a fair translation of the word "Hebrew" (or *Ivri,* its original form), which literally means "on the other side," because the first Hebrew, Abraham, came from the other side of the Jordan River, from Mesopotamia. As the scholar Michael Novak writes, our national founding was based on "Hebrew metaphysics." Benjamin Franklin recommended as the seal of the United States a portrait of the Israelites crossing the Red Sea. Lincoln called us the "Almost Chosen People." As if reprising Jeremiah's role, President Bush said in the lead-up to the war that the world's "evil"— as he frankly called Saddam's regime—began with Iraq, which is to say, Babylon.

What meaning is there in the fact that, in the conflict between America and Saddam's Iraq, history recalled the ancient tension between Israel and Babylon? Cynics might argue that the president had spent too much time with his nose in the Scriptures, whose fantastical stories drew his attention to Iraq when it should have been on more pressing concerns, like North Korea.

But there is another way of considering the association of America with Israel and Iraq with Babylon—a more compelling way that emerges from a sensitive reading of the Bible.

The Hebrew Bible is full of strangely repetitive motifs. An example is Abraham's flight to Egypt to escape famine, which plays out again in many of the same details when Jacob flees to the same country for the same reason. Secular biblical critics understand such motifs as evidence of the multiple hands that they say participated over centuries in writing the texts that were later woven together into the Bible.

Traditional religious sages have given a deeper explanation. Well aware of these motifs, the great medieval exegete Rabbi Moses ben Nachman explained that the "deeds of the fathers are a portent to the children." In other words, in the Bible, as in Moses ben Nachman's time and in our own, human dramas play out over and over, in much the same details of personality and geography. Scripture sets down paradigms in which we ourselves live our lives.

Anyone who reads the Bible and contemplates the human experience in its light will, I think, see that there is truth in this. The confrontation with Iraq offers an illustration.

Thus, in the course of the war, one persistent biblical resonance came attached to the many media references to the Euphrates River, which along with the Tigris (east of the Euphrates) defines the heart of Babylonia, or

Mesopotamia—meaning, literally, "Between Rivers"—extending from to-day's southern Iraq through Syria and into southern Turkey. Vivid reports told, for example, of how the 3rd Infantry Division managed to get across the Euphrates on its way to Baghdad. The strategy relied on feinted attacks to draw the Republican Guard out into the field to be destroyed.

In researching this book, I made sure to see the Euphrates River, outside of Harran, Turkey, where Abraham first heard God's voice (Gen. 12:1–3). Up there the river is impressive but unbeautiful, broad, calm, brown, banked on either side by desolate flat, dried mud about the same color as the river. You can't help reading what the Bible says about it without thinking that the Euphrates has some very significant meaning.

The Bible lays great emphasis on the land of Israel, but what are that land's borders, specifically its eastern border? If you said Israel is bounded in the east by the Jordan River, as the modern state of Israel is, you could de-fend that answer. But a number of biblical verses give, as the eastern border, not the Jordan but the Euphrates.

God tells Abraham: "To your descendants have I given the land, from the river of Egypt to the great river, the Euphrates River" (Gen. 15:18). Later He tells the Israelites encamped at Mt. Sinai: "Turn yourselves around and journey . . . [to] the land of the Canaanite and the Lebanon, until the great river, the Euphrates River. See I have given the land before you; come and possess the land that the Lord swore to your forefathers, to Abraham, to Isaac, and to Jacob" (Deut. 1:7–8).

Abraham himself is called the first "Hebrew," or *Ivri*, meaning literally "across"—for he came from "across" the Euphrates. The Bible stresses his origins because before he left that land, he lived and worshipped among be-lievers in a false religion. When his descendants, the Israelites, were poised to invade Canaan, God reminded them of the lowly origins of their ances-tors: "They served gods of others. But I took your forefather Abraham from across the river" (Josh. 24:2–3).

A river is an obvious boundary marker. In spiritual terms, the Euphrates marks a boundary between the old false religion and the new religion of monotheism preached by Abraham.

In the Iraq war, the Euphrates similarly marked the border beyond which falsehood reigned. As American troops were on the outskirts of Baghdad, the Iraqi government was denying that American troops were even a hun-dred miles from the capital. The falsehoods propounded by Saddam's regime were astonishing in their pathetic bravado, but the Iraqi people were accustomed to being fed outrageous lies by their government. In the Bible, to found his new religion Abraham had to escape beyond the boundaries of the Euphrates. Scripture is telling us that between truth and falsehood there is a sharp line, as definite as a broad river, however much liars may seek to convince us that all is a gray area.

It's possible that, in seeking war, President Bush was influenced by his scriptural studies. Maybe that's a good thing. If the Bible helps us understand the patterns that drive history, that would mean that in its pages we find not fantasy but reality, by which a wise leader should indeed be guided.

So too in our own lives, which are often in need of guidance and inspiration. Abraham is a figure of the past, but he is also very much of the present. One of the things I find most electrifying in contemplating the stories of the Bible, as they are interpreted and expanded upon by ancient Jewish rabbinic sources, is how often these narratives shed light on the questions and struggles going on in my own life, as if speaking directly to me. This happens so often it can't be a coincidence. Jung would have called it synchronicity.

Mystically, a rabbinic teaching describes biblical tradition as the blueprint on which the Lord, presented as a cosmic architect, gazed as He made the universe. Anyone in possession of the blueprint will understand the finished product, our world, of which the architect's plan offers a schematic model. In this book I present one thread of data from that blueprint, in the form of a narrative of Abraham's life and times. The reader will find meanings here of significance for his or her life. What those meanings will be depends on the reader, but they are there, waiting to be discovered.

INTRODUCTION

Bus No. 160

earing our plans to visit Hebron, on Israel's violently disputed West Bank, a Jerusalem rabbi warned my wife and
me, "If you two are going to go through with this, you'll
have to call the police that morning. Tell them you're an
American journalist and you want to take bus no. 160 from Jerusalem. Ask
if that would be safe to do. They often know if there's going to be a terror-
ist attack on the roads that day. If they say, 'It's not a good day to travel,' then
you'd better listen to them. If they say, 'The roads are open. It's a free country,' then the odds are in your favor. You'll probably come back alive."

It was the winter of 2000, and we had come from Seattle to visit the sites
in Israel and Turkey associated with the patriarch Abraham. Above all, it

seemed imperative to see the place where he was buried, the tomb called Machpelah in Hebron.

To our surprise there were other passengers on the bus: soldiers and civilians, all silent for the forty-minute ride, peering out apprehensively through smudged, barred, reinforced windows at the brown hills, terraced with tumbledown stone walls like broken teeth. Over the dashboard of the bus somebody had pinned a button to the fabric with a little red heart in the middle, reading, "I love the Pacific Northwest." My wife took my hand, which was cold. We were on our way to see Abraham.

Or were we? Who was buried in his tomb, after all, if anyone?

According to surveys, only 1 percent of Americans declare themselves to be atheists or agnostics. The rest of us have some part of our consciousness set aside for whatever faith we adhere to, however tentatively, about God.

There is a mystery here: Whether or not you yourself believe in Him, the fact that most everyone else you know *does* is one whose peculiarity we hardly register because, like water, oxygen, and light, it pervades our lives. Up until a certain point in history, everyone agreed that there must be many gods. By a later point, that view had been abandoned, at least in the West and Near East. Who or what brought about the change? Let me state forthrightly the conclusion I have reached.

There are grounds to believe that Abraham was a genuine historical figure, the strange and wonderful details of whose 175 years on earth are locked and encrypted in the Book of Genesis, to be unlocked by the key called the tradition. Half the world is filled with a powerful if sometimes fleeting awareness of God thanks to the efforts of this man, born around 1812 B.C. in a city named Cuthah near today's Baghdad.

Of course, many sophisticated people, including plenty who are actively involved in churches and synagogues, would dismiss this view as naïve. "Smart" opinion calls Abraham a fiction. Influential fiction, to be sure—which is why thoughtful writers will be found earnestly meditating on the legacy of the patriarch as the three monotheistic faiths depict him, meaning the impact of the *idea* of the man rather than the man himself—but fiction nonetheless.

This book presents Abraham in a radically different light, which should not be confused with biblical literalism. After all, in the Book of Genesis itself one finds no clear indication that Abraham discovered God. It doesn't even say that he was a monotheist. He prayed to the Deity under several different names, and some scholars have said that these appellations refer to various Canaanite gods. In fact, from just a reading of the Bible, Abraham seems in many ways a mundane, unimpressive person. He goes about planting trees, getting into disputes about wells, negotiating real-estate transactions, sacrificing farm animals, receiving the divine promise that he will become the ancestor of a nation. In the Bible *a lot* of people become ancestors of nations. It's quite routine. The past century's most distinguished archaeological historian of the Bible, who unlike academics today believed that Abraham actually existed, summarized his career as that of "the chief traditional representative of the original donkey caravaneers of the 19th century B.C."[1]

There is another Abraham: the patriarch as portrayed in ancient oral tradition, Oral Torah, which, as I will argue, transmits factual data as old as the Hebrew Bible. By tradition's account, remarkably vivid where Scripture's is modest and circumscribed, Abraham was a missionary who converted tens of thousands to monotheism. He was also an occultist, astrologer, healer, and writer of esoteric texts whose home was a regular gathering place for angels. He was an androgynous figure born with an indeterminate sexual anatomy, a man who wrestled with an accusing spiritual force called Satan. He may or may not have done something terrible to his son Isaac on a rock altar on a mountaintop. A thread of tradition hints that the Binding of Isaac, contrary to what the Bible seems to say, did not end happily.

Jewish tradition—conveyed in the Mishnah, Talmud, and Midrash, by ancient and medieval commentators—gives incomparably more detail about Abraham than do its Muslim and Christian counterparts. Along with much else, these sources convey *aggadah*—a generic designation for material that fills in the gaps of the sparse biblical narrative, material dismissed as charming legends by secular scholars but which we will sift for actual history. The Mishnah, comprising Oral Torah in its most highly crystallized form, mostly conveys traditions about Jewish law. The Talmud, which expounds upon the Mishnah, includes a great deal of *aggadah*. The collections of traditions called Midrash concentrate on filling out the narrative with stories not included in the Bible. (A single item of *aggadah* from a midrashic collection is called, generically, a midrash.) The midrashic collection we will lean on most heavily here is *Genesis Rabbah,* which I refer to simply as "the Midrash," devoted to illuminating the first book of the Bible. In their turn, the commentators seek to clarify the more ancient sources.

The question of Abraham's historicity, and the related question of what sources we can use to learn about him, are not merely academic. While orthodox religious folk revere him, the first patriarch is of no less importance for those who don't know quite what to think of the God of Abrahamic monotheism.

Jews, Christians, and Muslims call him their father, and the present world-spanning conflict pitting radical Muslims against Jews and Christians may be explained precisely as a family feud. St. Paul taught that Abraham has descendants by blood and by faith, and that being a descendant by faith, as a Christian, is much more significant than being so by blood. Muslims understand themselves as the children of Abraham through his first son, Ishmael, though they give a positive spin to this identification, whereas the Bible presents Ishmael as a dangerous misfit. Muhammad is said by Muslims to have been a direct descendant of Ishmael, who along with Abraham founded the primordial religion that became Islam.

The God that agnostics and seekers wonder about is also Abraham's God. That Deity is central to our experience as modern people for reasons that go far beyond the fact that even an atheist lives in society with a majority who are believers, and that belief in God has shaped our culture over millennia.

We belong to a highly affluent society, and it is possible to link this prosperity with the very first sentence in Genesis, where God is introduced. Hebrew Scripture begins by defining Him as the Creator par excellence. In this way, the Bible inspires us to be creators ourselves. It cannot be an accident that the vast majority of the wonderful (or fearsome) technologies we associate with modern life have been the inventions of people living amid the civilization of the Bible. After all, one finds nothing about creation in the first verses of the Quran, which begins on an impressive note—"This Book is not to be doubted"—but one less inviting of human creativity. Had no Abraham initiated the religions that became Judaism and Christianity, it seems unlikely that modern life—with its mixed blessings of electricity, telephones, television, Internet, automobiles, jet airplanes, medicine, and the rest—would exist in its present form.[2]

The same conclusion follows from recalling that polytheism means exalting the natural world, with the gods representing forces of nature. Before Christianity had taken hold throughout Europe, the great teacher Epictetus (A.D. 50–138) articulated the fundamentals of Stoicism, amounting to a most eloquent philosophy of nature worship. In the Stoic ideal, the virtuous man accepts with resignation the ultimate authority of nature's order: basically, what *is,* is what *should be.* Thus sickness, poverty, death, natural disasters—all these are to be endured without protest because the universe wills them. This is in contrast to Abrahamic monotheism, which pictures man as God's partner in improving the world. Thus God commands Adam to "fill the earth and subdue it."[3] The Talmud and Midrash, transmitting Jewish oral tradition, lay great stress on this.[4] When Abraham served food to hungry wayfarers, it being nature's way for hungry people to starve to death, and called them to thank God for their nourishment, God credited him as "My partner in the creation of the world."[5] This bending of nature to human will defines the modern world, and we enjoy its fruits every time we take an antibiotic or adjust the temperature in our climate-controlled homes.

A more basic observation is that without the One God, there can be no system of morality worthy of that name. In the world before Abraham, each city or even each person would have its or his own god or gods. At most, a god's authority covered the territory of a single nation. While the god might dictate to his followers certain standards of behavior, these ethical customs were rendered meaningless as soon as a believer crossed into the next country or city, where his god might be amiably tolerated but wasn't viewed as authoritative. Monotheism guarantees that concepts of right and wrong can be translated from person to person, city to city, country to country. No wonder, then, that the monotheist West is the world's most prosperous region. Prosperity requires trade across borders, and it helps if the trader can be confident of finding approximately the same moral culture wherever he goes. That way he doesn't have to wonder if, for instance, the neighboring country also respects contracts.

From churches and synagogues to air conditioners and antibiotics: our world is in many ways Abraham's world. He set in motion an idea that changed human life forever. If you believe he was indeed a man, not a myth, then we are all his children.

Did Abraham live? Did he ever lie in the tomb of Machpelah? I propose to put off giving my reasons for regarding him as a historical character until we have waded a little bit into the story of his life and of his times.

That life may be divided into three portions, like the panels in a triptych.[6] As traditionally laid out, the Torah calls each portion, or *parshah,* by a name taken from its first words. In synagogues, typically one portion is read each Sabbath, successively, so that the entire cycle of the Pentateuch is completed each year. In the first Torah portion of Abraham's scriptural biography, *Lech L'chah* ("Go for Yourself"), Abram, as he was called from birth, founds his mission to convert the world to monotheism. In the second portion, *Vayera* ("He Appeared"), the now renamed patriarch, Abraham, struggles to establish a successor to lead his ministry. At last such a worthy heir appears when his son Isaac is born. In the third, *Chayei Sarah* ("The Life of Sarah"), Abraham's wife dies. Before he joins her, he must ensure that his mission will continue by seeking a wife for Isaac, for the role of patriarch is hereditary. This is the all-encompassing theme of everything Abraham did: the imperative to pass on the knowledge of the One God to future generations.

Even before the opening of *Lech L'chah,* the Torah briefly introduces us to Abram. For he also had a life before his missionary activities commenced. In the *Mishneh Torah,* that great summation of Jewish law and belief completed in Egypt in 1178, Maimonides offers a narrative of the patriarch's youthful career. Three thousand years before the sage wrote, the Near East and all the world had been utterly lost in paganism and ignorance. Then "there was born the pillar of the world, namely our father Abraham."[7]

THE DISCOVERY OF

GOD

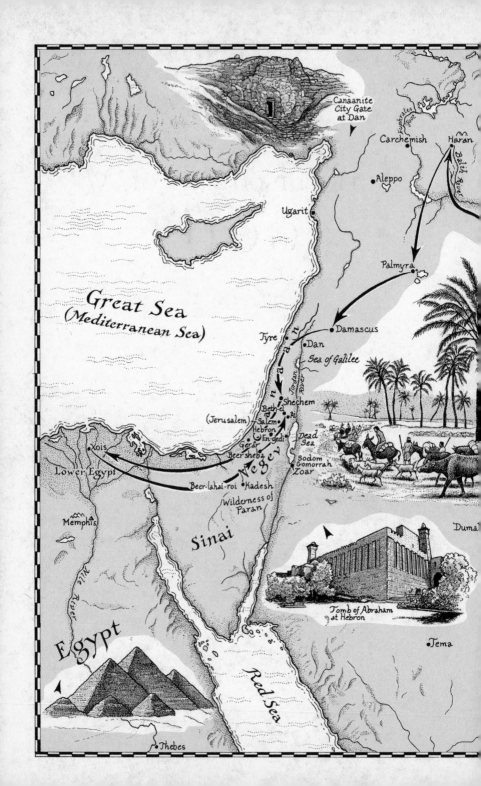

Beehive Houses, Haran

Caspian Sea

Tabriz

Nineveh

Asshur

Nuzi

Euphrates River

Tigris River

Akkad

Babylon

Cuthah

Tigris River

Sumer

Erech

Tigris River

Susa

Ur

Euphrates River

Mesopotamian ziggurat

Lower Sea

N

Abraham's Journeys According to Tradition

Kilometers 0 · · · · 100 · · · · 200 · · · · 300 Km.

Statute Miles 0 · · · · · · 100 · · · · · · 200 · · · · · · 300 Mi.

Map illustration by
Laura Hartman Maestro ©2002

CHAPTER ONE

A Palace in Flames

Reaching us like pulses of ancient light from a star in a distant galaxy, the circumstances of Abraham's birth are obscure. His world—so different from our own, where the worship of one God at most is taken for granted—might as well be a different galaxy. However, this much is clear: no sooner had the child been born than the enemies of God set out to kill him.

In that year, according to tradition, knowledge of the Lord was scarce among men, and certain forces in the Near East wished to keep things that way. Stories collected in medieval times, later published under the title *Ma'a-sei Avraham Avinu* ("Deeds of Abraham Our Father"), recall his birth as being marked by a star rising in the east, consuming other stars.[1] At this fearful wonder, priests at the court of a Mesopotamian tyrant, Nimrod, prophesied that a child was to be born whose descendants would seize the spiritual future of mankind, condemning the old gods to the ashes, to be replaced by the One God. Nimrod trembled at this. Almost alone among his contemporaries, who were ignorant of the Almighty, he knew God and hated Him. The Bible itself mentions Nimrod only in passing, noting that he was "a mighty hunter before the Lord," which the Oral Torah understands to mean that he hunted men's souls, seeking to turn them away from God.[2] So Nimrod, advised by Satan, literally hunted Abraham. The future patriarch was born in a cave suffused with supernatural light, and God sent the angel Gabriel to protect him, causing a black cloud to hide the child from his enemies. The boy was called Abram.

Nimrod sought to bribe the child's father, Terach. If Terach would slay his own son, Nimrod promised great riches. Instead, Terach lied, insisting that the infant had already perished, and kept his boy in the cave until the danger had passed. Thirteen years went by before it was safe for Abram to emerge from hiding.

Details of these stories—the star in the east, the black cloud, the bribe for Terach—not only are dismissed as fiction by modern scholars but are neglected by the greatest medieval sages as well.

However, the sages wholly accept the work called *Pirke d'Rabbi Eliezer* ("Chapters of Rabbi Eliezer"), attributed to the school of Rabbi Eliezer ben Hyrcanus, who lived around A.D. 100.[3] What *Pirke d'Rabbi Eliezer* records about the patriarch's birth is terse. It can be relied on if any midrash, or biblical interpolation transmitted by tradition, can be: "When Abraham our Father was born, all the powerful men in [Nimrod's] kingdom sought to murder him. He was hidden underground for 13 years, during which he saw neither the sun nor the moon. After 13 years had passed, he emerged from underground, speaking the Holy Tongue [Hebrew]. He despised the sacred trees, loathed the idols, and trusted in the shadow of his Creator. He said, 'Lord of Hosts, happy is the man who trusts in you,' " a declaration later enshrined by King David in Psalm 84.[4]

The general location of Abram's birth and early suffering is Mesopotamia, the area between the Tigris and Euphrates Rivers centering on what is today Iraq and extending into southern Turkey. More specifically, Jewish tradition directs our attention to Cuthah, twenty miles northeast of Baghdad, as the city where Abram was born. There, an archaeological mound called

Tell Ibrahim rises from the plain. A tell is an artificial hill comprising layer on layer of debris from a series of collapsed cities that once occupied a site, all interspersed and covered over with dirt. There are lots of them in the Near East. The farther down you dig, the further back in time you go. Since Muslim and Jewish beliefs on the subject of the first patriarch agree on many points, it is unsurprising to learn that the Arabic name "Tell Ibrahim" corresponds with the Jewish tradition that this undistinguished mound hides the ruins of Abram's birthplace.[5] Little is known about Cuthah apart from its having been a center for the grisly cult of Nergal, god of the underworld, on whose account the city was called "the assembly-place of the ghosts."[6]

Admittedly, one reading of Scripture and tradition would suggest that Abram was born not at Cuthah, but farther south at the great metropolis of Ur, or Ur Kasdim, as the Bible calls it. The location of Abram's cave, a place of pivotal importance for his spiritual development, is similarly ambiguous. Islamic tradition offers some speculation. In Turkey close to the Syrian border, a dusty city called Sanliurfa is identified by Muslims with Ur Kasdim. Arabs and Kurds who dwell in the area have built something like an Abraham-related memorial park, containing a cave said to be where Ibrahim was born, presumably also where he was hidden from Nimrod. In the side of a rocky hill, the entrance today is guarded by a one-eyed Muslim in robes who, when I was there, scowled as I purchased a ticket and removed my shoes to enter. Inside is a grotto with water pooled some distance below ground level, barred against entry and almost invisible in the dark.

Those scholars who have been inclined to think Abraham was a real figure have reached no consensus on the year of his birth, on where he fits into the time line of Near Eastern history. Estimates range from 2158 B.C. to as early as 1350. The great twentieth-century archaeologist W. F. Albright set the time of Abraham's migration from Mesopotamia to Canaan as having been between 1900 and 1750 B.C.[7] Most views assign him a birth date somewhere in the Canaanite archaeological framework called the Middle Bronze Age I–II (2000–1650). In this period as well falls the birth year attested by Jewish oral tradition: 1812 B.C.

If tradition is right, then the originator of monotheism was born as the heir to a culture that originated civilization in general. Mesopotamia comprised the lands of Sumer, in the south, and Akkad, in the north. The people of Akkad were Semitic, but those of Sumer came to the region from elsewhere; precisely where is unknown. Before there was a First Dynasty in

Egypt, these Sumerians built Ur. The Sumerian legal system became the basis of the Code of Hammurabi, which in turn preceded Hebrew law by four hundred years. In architecture, Sumerians invented the arch, the dome, and the vault. Abraham may be counted as the greatest of all the gifts to have been bestowed on mankind by Mesopotamian culture.

The Bible says nothing explicitly about what was going on in the Near East at the time Abraham was born. In fact, it says almost nothing about him till he had turned seventy-five years old. But it does tell us what had been happening in his family for the twenty generations that went before him. The story takes us back to Adam and Eve. One notes points of agreement between history and tradition.

It is possible to read the first chapters of Genesis in conjunction with the Oral Torah to suggest that before Adam, there were creatures who looked human and possessed human intelligence but lacked the defining characteristic of true humanity, a soul.[8] If Adam and Eve really did exist, then according to Jewish tradition, they would have been created in the year 3761 B.C. Their original home, the Garden of Eden, is associated in the Bible with four rivers, including the Euphrates and the Tigris. In that period and that place, about 3800 B.C. in southern Mesopotamia, one finds evidence of an unusual people known to historians as the Ubaid culture. They were iconoclasts. In their pottery decorations, they disdained portrayals of humans and animals. At the important site Eridu, they left behind no mother-goddess figurines of the kind so favored by their near contemporaries. To a secular historian, this evidence "indicat[es] a striking difference in religious conceptions" reminiscent of the taboo on figurative art associated with Hebrew teaching.[9] Could these people bear some relationship to the family of Adam and Eve? Some historians theorize that Sumerian civilization as a whole, its origins otherwise mysterious, grew out of Ubaid culture. That would accord with the Bible's narrative, which traces the founding of the civilization of "Shinar," or Sumer, to Adam's descendants.[10]

An outline of earliest religious history is presented by Maimonides— often called Rambam, an acronym of Rabbi Moses ben Maimon (Spanish, 1135–1204). In his *Mishneh Torah,* he writes that Adam and his sons recognized God but that Adam's grandson Enosh strayed, choosing to bow before God's creations—sun and moon, water and fire, the stars above all—through whose worship he thought he could win God's favor. As one generation faded into the next, men began to forget that nature had a single Creator. Temples were set up, sacrifices brought, sacred trees planted, and holy places established on mountaintops. This fits with history. In Mesopotamia, mountaintops were viewed as the principal address of any worthwhile divinity. When the civilization of ancient Sumer began constructing its greatest religious monuments, it fashioned them to resemble a mountain with the god's home at its peak, giving the shape of the classic Mesopotamian step pyramid, or ziggurat.

Rambam explains that at this point "The Rock of Ages [God] was unrecognized by any man, except for certain isolated individuals in the world who knew Him, for example [the biblical figures] Hanoch and Methusaleh, Noah, Shem and Ever."[11] History, too, bears witness to this tenuous transmission.

Modern Bible critics direct our attention to the many similarities between Hebrew and Babylonian myth, the latter having been composed first, notably the Mesopotamian creation epic *Enuma Elish,* which parallels the creation account in Genesis. Writes Professor E. A. Speiser, there is not "the slightest basis in fact for assuming some unidentified ultimate source from which both the Mesopotamians and the Hebrews could have derived their views about creation."[12] In other words, Hebrew "myth" derives from its Mesopotamian counterpart—quite a blow to the prestige of the biblical text—unless there is indeed an "ultimate source."

It would have been more accurate to say that, of such a source, there is no evidence *apart from* the assertion of Jewish teaching that a few of Adam and Eve's descendants preserved a line of tradition concerning the relationship of God to man and to creation. If so, it would not be surprising to discover that from other cultures one hears echoes of the data presented in the opening chapters of Genesis. So, for instance, Mesopotamian myth tells the story of a catastrophic flood and a man who survived it.

Judaism attaches much importance to this figure, called Noah. In the Talmud's tractate *Sanhedrin,* a whole religion, intended for humanity, is outlined: "Noachism" (in Hebrew, "Noah" is "Noach"), a system of moral directives centered on a sublime assertion of God's oneness—traced to Adam, though Noah received a commission from God to spread Noachism to the world. He failed: his tradition was never disseminated beyond his immediate descendants. At age seventy-five, Abraham would meet this line of "Noachides" in the eerie person of Malchizedek. But, growing up in Mesopotamia, he knew nothing of it.

The towering medieval sage Rashi (an acronym of Rabbi Solomon bar Isaac; French, 1040–1105), whose work we will draw on everywhere in this book, comments that since the time of Enosh, the Lord had been God of the heavens, but not God of the earth. "For the inhabitants of the earth did not recognize Him, and His name was unfamiliar in the land."[13] As usual, Rashi conveys a tradition found originally in one of the ancient sources— here a midrash in *Genesis Rabbah*. Any tradition cited by Rashi is likely to be essential to understanding the scriptural text at a most fundamental level. He also notes that "until Abraham" appeared, "the Omnipresent was angry" with humanity.[14]

The Lord was angry, and Abraham's contemporaries continued to pray to their gods.

Today we know details about religion in Mesopotamia that Maimonides did not. We know the names of the gods in its pantheon, who numbered up to four thousand in total, and what they represented. A pair of divine triads stood at the head of this pantheon. Anu (or An in Sumerian) was the god of the heavens, the "father" or "king" of the gods. Enlil was lord of the earth. And Enki was the god of the waters. Those three formed the first triad. The second comprised the gods of the moon, sun, and the planet Venus— respectively Sin, Shamash, and Ishtar.

For Abraham's contemporaries, the spiritual world was not transcendent, but immanent. When Mesopotamians worshiped the sun god or the moon god, it was not, as with Enosh, because they thought nature functioned as a proxy for the creator. Rather, the gods literally were nature. They *were* the idols themselves.[15] Standing in the long chamber at the base of the ziggurat, the god *was* the carved piece of wood adorned with jewelry and gemstones.

The history of Mesopotamian religion may be divided into three parts, each lasting a millennium.[16] In the fourth millennium B.C., man's consciousness focused above all else on the constant danger of death by famine. As in the Rambam's telling, the gods were the forces of nature in quasi-human form, for nature could feed or starve you at will.

Political organization marked the third millennium, as the main danger to human life shifted from nature to other men, in the form of war. The gods were increasingly understood as super-rulers, choosing mortals to serve as their representatives on earth. Hence the novel institution of kingship was established, as history and tradition agree: the sages of the oral tradition call Nimrod history's first king; his ascension, narrated in the Bible ("he began to be mighty in the land"), was a key event in the era immediately preceding Abraham's.[17] Sharing supreme rule, the gods gathered to eat, drink, and issue arbitrary rulings on matters of concern to their human subjects.

In the second millennium, in whose second century Abraham was born, Mesopotamians groped for a more personal relationship to the divine. Man was anxious to believe that the gods were out there listening, feeling concern for him, sharing his worries. Not coincidentally, the centerpiece of second-millennium Mesopotamian literature, the Gilgamesh Epic, is about the prospect of death as the eternal end of all human strivings. The hero, Gilgamesh, goes in search of a way to restore to life his deceased friend Enkidu. Gilgamesh has heard a tale about a mortal who won immortality. This is Utnapishtim, the Mesopotamian Noah, who survived a great flood. But when our protagonist finally has the secret of eternal life in his grasp— it is a certain underwater plant—a serpent suddenly comes along and eats it. The moral of the story is: You are going to die. That will be the end of you.

While some Mesopotamians cheerfully accepted death as a final extinguishing of consciousness, others were oppressed by the terror of mortality. The archaeologist who uncovered the ruins of Ur, C. Leonard Woolley, wrote of Sumerian religion that it was a faith "not of love but of fear, fear whose limits are confined to this present life, fear of Beings all-powerful, capricious, unmoral. Somehow or other virtue does appeal to the gods . . . , but experience shows that mere virtue is not enough to engage and keep their favor; practical religion consists in the sacrifices and the ritual that placate and in the spells that bind them."[18] In the Bible's account, which matches Woolley's, an ancestor of Abraham bears the sinister name Chatzarmavet, or "Courtyard of Death." As the Midrash explains, in his place the people lived in a constant dread of doom.[19]

While acknowledging this doom, it is important that we not discount the weird *reality* of idol worship, of the gods themselves. Since the pagans were not fools, we ought to try to imagine ourselves into their heads. In worshiping the gods, what exactly did a person worship?

Jewish tradition offers surprising answers. One opinion, informed by kabbalah, Judaism's mystical tradition, delicately suggests that what the idolaters worshiped were really aspects of God, pagan religion arising from "the deification by the pagans of cosmic forces corresponding to the various divine attributes."[20] Hence the biblical title given to the Holy One: "God of gods." Another view equates the gods with demons, shadow beings held by the Mishnah to have been created by God shortly after He first breathed a soul into a human body.[21]

A modern rationalistic account of the pagan mind urges us to take seriously what the idolaters of old themselves said about their relationship with the gods. Professor Julian Jaynes, author of *The Origins of Consciousness in the Breakdown of the Bicameral Mind,* taught psychology at Princeton from 1966 to 1990, but he also educated himself in the literatures of the ancient world. He urged that we consider the somewhat hard-to-process fact that idolatry focused literally on the worship of idols.

Ordinary men had their personal gods, accommodated in household shrines. The chief god of a city would have his house in the middle of town, in the religious compound surmounted by the ziggurat. As if the wooden image were truly alive, priests carried him about, served him food and drink, and provided all manner of other services, including sexual ones. The god was clothed in rich garments, and at festival times took trips to visit other gods in their temples. Men were the servants of the gods, who called them the "blackheaded ones." In return for services, the gods spoke to men.

They literally *spoke,* or at least men thought they heard their voices. In Mesopotamia, the voice belonged to the *ili,* the personal god, while in Egypt it belonged to the *ka,* the hard-to-translate lynchpin of all Egyptian thinking about religion and personality, which Jaynes calls the "voice-persona." Essentially the ancients hallucinated the god voices in much the same way that schizophrenics in contemporary times hear voices. The voice was generated in the brain's right temporal lobe. It then traveled across the anterior commissure and was "heard" in the left temporal lobe—heard not, however, as the voice of consciousness we hear today when we think consciously about ourselves, but as a voice from outside, sometimes accompanied by hallucinated visual images. This "bicameral" structure of the pagan mind is to be distinguished from consciousness as we know it, for in fact people then were not "conscious." Jaynes demonstrates convincingly that consciousness is not a prerequisite to learning or to civilization. (Think of the way you drive a car, a complex activity carried out for the most part unconsciously.) When a person needed to make a choice, he heard the voice of his god and obeyed.

The god voices were the main vehicle of social control. Up to a certain level of civilizational complexity, everyone knew his place and his role from the voices. Then, Jaynes argues, writing developed in Mesopotamia around 3000 B.C. This allowed for the recording of divine instructions, or laws, on clay tablets in the medium called cuneiform, a system of some six hundred characters mixing the features of an alphabet with those of pure hieroglyphics, or picture symbols. With these instructions available to be consulted at any time, the need for hallucinations was obviated.

The most celebrated legal code in the ancient world, Hammurabi's, was set down at Babylon about 1750 B.C., within decades of Abraham's birth. By the thirteenth century B.C., the breakdown of the bicameral mind in the Near East had been completed. As recorded in inscriptions, Mesopotamians begin to lament the quieting of the god voices, which had fallen into silence.

However we understand pagan consciousness, it is clear that by the time Abraham was born a major spiritual evolution was under way. His was an era of transformation, and anxiety. From about 3000 B.C., it is as if history was tearing up the soil in the field where the seeds of Abraham's teaching would be planted.

The social and political chaos of the second millennium B.C. played a role in this process, further roiling the Mesopotamian soul. A century or so before Abraham's birth, Sumerian civilization was transformed by the influence of Semitic invaders from the Syrian desert, called Amorites or Martu, meaning "Westerners." It is likely that some of Abraham's ancestors belonged to this group. Cultivated men at Ur detested the Amorite: a nomad "who lives in a tent, exposed to wind and rain; . . . who eats raw foods; who has no home during his lifetime and no tomb at his death," "who does not know grain," these "raiders . . . with animal instincts, like wolves."[22]

The monarchs of Ur fortified their borders against marauding outsiders. However, these defenses were unequal to the strength of the enemy. By the end of the twentieth century B.C., Sumer was completely overwhelmed by Amorites and other foreigners. The last king of the Third Dynasty of Ur was captured and led off in chains. Preserved in cuneiform, a final communication from this monarch, Ibbi-Sin, is a letter like a distress signal from a sinking ocean liner, telling how "all the Martu have penetrated into the interior of the country, seizing the great fortresses one by one."[23]

Gradually the Amorites were tamed, adopting Sumerian culture and religion and setting themselves up as kings of the various Mesopotamian city-states, including Babylon. About the same time that Abraham was born, the first such Babylonian dynasty was established. After an era of violent upheaval, Amorite civilization had emerged; its most brilliant representative would be Hammurabi.

It was the fate of Abraham to be born in the period between the fall of one civilization and the rise of another. Such times are full of danger, but also of promise. The world was ripe for spiritual revolution.

Abram's family resided in the new world politically, the old world spiritually. Though he was born at Cuthah, his relations lived in Haran, an important trading city in northern Mesopotamia. Genesis offers his genealogy, from Noah's son Shem through the patriarch's great-grandfather Serug, grandfather Nachor, and father, Terach. Their names are Amorite and associated specifically with Haran, near which were towns called Sarugi (Serug), Nakhur (Nachor), and Til-turakhi (Terach).[24] Evidently Abram's family was well known in the region. Their spoken tongue would have been Akkadian.

Haran was a center of worship for the moon god Sin, and Terach's name has lunar associations. So do the names of Abram's wife, Sarai, and sister-in-law Milcah.[25] Terach had three sons, each separated in birth by one year; Abram was the oldest, followed by Nachor (named for his father's father), followed by Haran (spelled differently in Hebrew than the name of the city). Not all the boys had the same mother, for Terach had two wives.[26]

He was a merchant in the idol trade, which suggests a couple of observations about the environment in which Abram grew up. First, the father was an educated man, for merchants were among those in Mesopotamian society who needed to be at least somewhat familiar with the cumbersome and difficult cuneiform script in which commercial transactions were recorded.

Second, obviously, Abram would have been intimately aware of the practice of Mesopotamian religion. The clay figures that Terach sold, in human and fantastic animal shapes, often lime-washed and colored in red and black, were of a domestic variety. They were set in the doorway or buried under the threshold of one's home, where they protected the inhabitants from the malign influence of demons and other harmful spirits.[27] They were worshiped in private family chapels and set alongside the family's bodies in the grave. The graves as well as the chapel would have been included in the home. (A well-appointed Mesopotamian house had a brick vault for burials right under the chapel, which gave the living quarters an interesting odor. Periodically, whole quarters of a city had to be cleared out because of the stench.)

Although the pagan background of Terach and the rest of Abraham's family is forthrightly stated elsewhere in the Bible,[28] the idea of a future patriarch going along with his father to bow down to the local lunar deity has troubled some non-Jewish commentators. St. Augustine theorized that a small group including Terach, who passed on his wisdom to Abram, practiced a secret monotheistic religion down through the generations. By contrast the Midrash insists that, in formulating his new beliefs, Abram received no help from his father. Any line of familial transmission had broken down long before he was born, and Maimonides adds that Abram not only learned the faith of his fellow Mesopotamians but "worshipped among them."[29] The Midrash speaks of a "sin" that was in Abram's hands "all those years," the sin of worshiping false gods.[30]

Much has been written about Abram's name, which is attested as authentic to the place and time, the Amorite First Dynasty of Babylon, belonging to a class of names common until the tenth century B.C. but rare afterward.[31] In Torah nomenclature, its key component, *av*, means a father or patriarch, more generally a prototype. Jewish mysticism presents the patriarch as the prototype of a hard-to-define virtue: *chesed,* usually translated as "kindness." What is kindness? Abram entered the world not so much to comfort the afflicted, but to afflict the comfortable, those complacent pagan souls who found satisfying the routine of feeding and placating their gods of clay and wood. That hardly sounds "kind" of him; but a modern sage points to the relationship between the English words "kindness" and "kindred."[32] The profoundest source of true kindness is the perception that all existence is "kin": not simply that all people are part of one human race but that all of creation is united in its one source.

Another meaning of the patriarch's birth name refers to Terach. The *av,* father, of this boy was *ram*, "exalted" or "elevated"—a reference to Terach's position at the court of Nimrod.[33] Besides commercial connections, the old man had government ties. In the Torah's account, the political elite of Mesopotamia is personified in Nimrod, to whom Scripture attributes the building of three Mesopotamian power centers: Erech (or Uruk), Akkad, and Babylon—a précis, in three names, of Near Eastern political history.[34] As some historians argue, the culture of Uruk (not Ubaid) was the seed from which Sumerian society grew, beginning in the fourth millennium B.C. Akkad, under Sargon I, became the leading power in the region about 2340 B.C. And Babylon arose to dominate the land between the rivers beginning about 1750 B.C. Thus the Bible credits Nimrod with holding power over a period of two millennia—indicating that he is to be understood not as one man, but as a succession of rulers who governed Mesopotamia.

At "Nimrod's" court, the leading men of the time felt a rush of dread at the announcement of their colleague Terach's firstborn son. In matters of state, a class of priests called *baru* ("observers"), expert in interpreting omens, read the future through the pseudoscience of hepatoscopy, or liver divination, in which the liver of a slaughtered animal was examined for signs implanted by the god to indicate the shape of future events.[35] Nimrod's *baru* priests must have read in some liver that a boy was to be born to Terach who ultimately, whether by himself or through the influence of his descendants, would overthrow the whole spiritual outlook of their civilization.

It poses no problem to the biblical worldview to suppose that by supernatural means Nimrod foresaw that the boy Abram was dangerous. The Bible does not deny that when idolaters practice occult magical arts, their efforts can be effective. At the time of Moses, the magicians in Pharaoh's court performed genuine if malign miracles. Nimrod must have shared this concern with Terach, who was not averse, if it meant saving himself, to turning his own flesh and blood over to the authorities.

The Talmud hints that, while Abram learned nothing of transcendent worth from his father, he may have absorbed habits of sound reasoning from his mother, whom the Talmud identifies as Amatlai, the daughter of Karnivo.[36] When the oral tradition provides the names of individuals or places that the Bible leaves anonymous, this is not out of a taste for antiquarian trivia. Rather, the names are intended to tell us something about their bearers. In this case, "Amatlai" is built on the Aramaic root *amatla,* meaning "a plausible reason for contradicting a statement." Evidently the young Abram received inspiration from his mother, who supported the youth in the intellectual development that led him to contradict his father's beliefs. Presumably it was not Terach, but the good Amatlai, who kept their son safe underground for thirteen years.

During those years, Abram must have dreamed of the outside world. We may speculate that it is one of his dreams that is collected in *Genesis Rabbah* as a famous parable, that of the burning palace.

Parables have a dreamlike quality, and our dreams are typically parables: symbolic representations of whatever problems we had been grappling with while awake. If Abram did not have precisely this dream, he might as well have. The Midrash sets down the brief narrative by way of explaining his spiritual rebirth as a believer in the One God. Notice the details, which, as in a dream, are not chosen at random.

"A man was passing from place to place, when he saw a palace in flames. He said, 'Is it possible that the palace has no lord?' Then there appeared to him the master of the palace who said to him, 'I am its master.' "[37]

Abram is the subject here, passing "from place to place"—in Hebrew, from *makom* to *makom*. In Torah terminology, a *makom* can be a physical locality, but it can also mean a spiritual or existential framework.[38] My *makom* is the way I understand the universe and my role in it. In idiomatic English, it is "where I'm coming from." Abram was on the verge of a transition between radically different worldviews. The palace, a grand structure hiding more than it shows, is the world. Its owner is God.

And the flames are what? Possibly their light represents spiritual illumination of the kind Abram was destined to experience, and through him, the world. Possibly the fire represents the paradox, demanding explanation, that we live in an exquisitely designed world, suggesting a Creator and Master, but a world where forces of evil and destruction seem to reign, suggesting a world without a Master. Either way, Abram's evolution started in wonder, awe, and questioning.[39]

Was this palace, the universe itself as experienced by a man of the Near East, truly on fire at the time of Abram's birth? In a sense it was. And Abram himself would soon face a trial of fire.

CHAPTER TWO

Let There Be Light

hen Abram was forty-eight years old, murderous Nimrod caught up with him. After dryly noting the patriarch's birth along with that of his brothers, Nachor and Haran, the Bible's first statement in its narration of Abram's life seems strangely irrelevant. It says, "Haran died in the presence of Terach his father in the land of his birth, in Ur Kasdim."[1] What do we care about Haran, who plays no role in the narrative? The verse turns out to be cryptic at various levels, as the Midrash, Talmud, and their decoders make clear.

Since we are still dealing with Genesis 11, before Scripture has begun relating the patriarch's experiences in earnest from age seventy-five, this episode comes down to us exclusively through tradition. In 1764 B.C., the hunter of souls had Abram dragged to an inquisition, which the Talmud locates in Cuthah, in a part of the city called Kasdim.[2] Brought before the tyrant, Abram would have met a man who appeared to be a typical Mesopotamian *lugal*, or "king," wearing a headdress like a cross between a fez and a turban, his face adorned by a long, intricately woven beard falling down his chest and tucked behind his ears. But Nimrod was no typical king.

Upon meeting the prisoner face-to-face, Nimrod spoke with him. Abram still has the mocking, arrogant manner we associate with younger men. Nimrod intended to secure Abram's ascent to paganism, or to punish him with an excruciating death if he refused. There was some preliminary discussion in which Nimrod advised Abram of what he wanted, namely that he acknowledge the animistic forces—like fire and water—that Sumero-Babylonians regarded as embodying gods. Abram responded with contempt.

Outraged, Nimrod demanded that Abram obey immediately: "Bow down to fire!"

But Abram remained cool as a cloud. "Why not bow to water instead," he asked, "for water extinguishes fire?"

"Then bow to water," said Nimrod.

"If so, why not bow to the clouds that carry water as rain?"

"Very well," said the persecutor, "then bow down to the clouds!"

"If so"—and we can sense Abram's enjoyment at this encounter—"let us bow down to the wind which scatters the clouds."

Nimrod had by now entirely lost his temper. "Then bow down to the wind!"

"If so," Abram replied, still serene and unafraid, "let us bow down to a son of man, who endures the wind."

At this, Nimrod erupted. "All you speak are meaningless words!"

An evil idea passed into the tyrant's mind, or perhaps he had been building to this all along. "I myself bow down only to fire [in Hebrew, *ur*]. Behold I shall now cast you into the midst of fire, and let the God you worship rescue you if He can!"[3]

As a form of capital punishment, this would have made sense to Nimrod. In the Mesopotamian mind, when dealing with dangerous magic and ghost forces like the kind represented by Abram's God, the main antidote was fire. We know this from collections of incantations preserved from as far back as the Third Dynasty of Ur, around 2100 B.C. Wizards were burned in effigy to neutralize their power to harm.[4] So now would Abram be burned to neutralize him.

Besides meaning "fire," an *ur* is also any hole in the ground, small or big, from a pit to a valley. Ur Kasdim, literally the "Fire of the Kasdim," is thus not a city, as it seems from a surface-level reading of the biblical text, but rather a fearsome pit of fire.[5] This *kivshan ha'aish,* the Fiery Furnace, as Rashi calls it in his Torah commentary, was prepared. Elsewhere, Rashi suggests what kind of fire it was: a lime kiln.[6] To make limestone burn, it must be heated to a temperature in the neighborhood of one thousand degrees Fahrenheit. The process, conducted in a kiln or furnace, in Hebrew a *kivshan,* decomposes the stone into the two chemical components carbon dioxide and calcium oxide. The latter, called lime, is used in construction and glassmaking and when heated produces a brilliant illumination (limelight).

Nimrod wanted Abram's family, who perhaps shared his unorthodox views, to witness his death. All were assembled, and the stones in the furnace were set afire. When the temperature had reached the point where stone becomes lime and light from the mouth of the kiln glows white, guards brought the prisoner forward.

The traditional sources tell us nothing about what Abram or Terach was thinking at this moment. Only the calculations of the patriarch's brother Haran are specified. Haran was divided in his mind, for he knew his brother was a most unusual person who seemed to have some knowledge of a spiritual force that Haran did not understand. Perhaps this force, this "God," would indeed save him, as the sarcastic Nimrod had suggested. But perhaps Abram would die. As Abram approached the burning furnace, Haran made up his mind. Sort of. If his brother's God saved Abram, then Haran would declare himself loyal to the party of Abram. If God failed to intervene, Haran would declare his loyalty to Nimrod. Haran's resolution would turn out to be as clever as it was brave.

Abram entered, lowered into the flames by Nimrod's attendants.

And a miracle occurred. He felt every one of the one thousand degrees, but only for the smallest moment, enough to demonstrate his just-acquired faith. Just then in Heaven there was an uproar, recounted in the Talmud. The angel Gabriel protested, insisting that he be allowed to take immediate action. "Lord of the universe, let me go down to cool this righteous man and save him from the Fiery Furnace." God replied: "I am unique in my world, and he is unique in his world. It is fitting that the Unique One save the unique one."[7] So God saved Abram, who emerged from the furnace unharmed.

Unharmed yet different. Rashi identifies Ur Kasdim as the place of Abram's, not Haran's, "birth."[8] Some interpreters have understood this to mean that Ur was a city and Abram was born there. But Rashi also identifies Ur Kasdim with the Fiery Furnace.[9] Which is it? The deeper meaning is that in the fire Abram was *reborn* as a man in a relationship with his Creator.

Before this experience, whatever progress he had made toward understanding God had been entirely intellectual. But people do not typically choose to die for the sake of ideas. Not really. They give up their lives for relationships. In wartime diaries, soldiers rarely mention the abstract principles at stake in the conflict. Instead, they speak of other people: family at home, comrades on the battlefield. While occasionally a person will give up his life for the sake of God, he accepts martyrdom not out of loyalty to the idea of God, but because of his relationship with God.

Up till now, Abram had no personal relationship with God. Yet he approached the light of the furnace and entered the torch of a thousand degrees without fear. How is this possible? When the Talmud indicates that God Himself rescued Abram, it means that Abram met God, in person, in the light emanating from the furnace. His first communication from the Deity, in the form of words reproducible on a page, was still years in the future. But you can meet a god, just as you can meet a person, without exchanging words.

All this was lost on poor Haran. He saw the miracle, but for him its meaning had only the practical significance that fate seemed to be on Abram's side. Amid the gasps of horror at Nimrod's court, the king's officers asked him to declare himself. Was he for Abram or for Nimrod?

"I belong to Abram," he replied.[10] Haran's freshly acquired faith in his brother pleased neither the king Nimrod nor the King of Heaven. There is no tradition of Gabriel's seeking to interfere. The court officers cast Haran into the flaming pit and, screaming, he died there "in the presence of Terach his father . . . in Ur Kasdim."

In relating Abram's rebirth, we have skipped over what happened to him in the years between his emergence from the cave at age thirteen and Haran's death thirty-five years later.

The Bible tells nothing directly about Abraham's childhood, education, or other early experiences. For modern scholars, then, the origins of the belief in one God are left completely obscure—which is peculiar when you think about it. For the Bible is of permanent interest to the world only because it provides access to Him.

Giving the details that the Bible lacks, Maimonides writes at length. His narrative, beginning with Abram's early childhood, is worth quoting:

> When this mighty one [Abram] was weaned, he began to philosophize. He was young and commenced pondering day and night and he was amazed at how it was possible that this sphere [of the celestial bodies] moved always and had nothing driving it or causing it to revolve. [In line with medieval thought, Maimonides envisioned the sun, moon, and planets as revolving in a great heavenly sphere.] For [the sphere] could not cause itself to revolve. Abraham had no teacher nor did he have anyone to give him knowledge. . . . His father and his mother and all the people were idolaters and he worshipped among them; but his mind roamed and he sought understanding until he reached the path of truth. . . . And then he knew that there is One God: that He moves the sphere [of the heavens] and He created all and there is no god in existence apart from Him. Furthermore he knew that all the world was in error and that what had caused them to err was their worship of the stars and the idols so that truth had perished in their minds. Abraham was forty years old when he recognized his Creator. When he recognized and knew [Him], he began to exchange views with the people . . . , and to arrange arguments against them, saying, "This is not the way of truth in which you are walking!" He then shattered the idols and he began to teach the people that it is not fit to worship any but the Eternal God, to whom it is right to bow and to sacrifice and offer libations, so that all the men of the future should also recognize Him. And it is fitting to abandon and to break all the idols so all the people should not err because of them like these people who thought there was no god but their idols. When Abraham prevailed over them with

his proofs, the king [of that land] sought to kill him. However a miracle occurred for Abraham and he went out to Haran.[11]

Abraham is depicted here as the first philosopher, in total spiritual isolation, starting from a knowledge base of zero and working his way from there to a preliminary apprehension of God. He harassed his fellow citizens with carefully plotted proofs that their worship of multiple deities was corrupt and false. For this, the local authorities pursued him until he was forced to flee to Haran.

The traditions on which Maimonides draws gloss over the steps in the reasoning process by which Abram began to achieve enlightenment. Recall the story in *Pirke d'Rabbi Eliezer* in which Abram is pictured growing up in a cave where he sees "neither sun nor moon." Perhaps this midrash is trying to impress on us not so much Abram's literal experience of being secreted away underground, but rather the alienation of an individual who feels himself increasingly at odds with the most basic assumptions of the culture around him. For thirteen years, he remains in darkness. Upon emerging into the light at age thirteen, he has already rejected the whole spiritual framework of paganism. In Torah nomenclature, light is always a metaphor for wisdom.

What happened next is disputed in the Talmud and the Midrash. Both record two opinions: one is that Abram recognized the existence of God at the startlingly precocious age of three; the other is that he did so at age forty-eight.[12] Throw in the Rambam's view that the moment of enlightenment happened at age forty.[13] Then there is a further rabbinical opinion that the numbers 3 and 48 are to be understood to mean that a catastrophic event when Abram was forty-eight caused him to retreat from the world for three years of meditation, from which he emerged a monotheist at age fifty-one. Taken together, the disparate views suggest that the process was gradual rather than sudden. Very likely, as a little boy he experienced some intuition of God; but it was only in middle age that the patriarch reached a mature understanding of Him.

Maimonides portrays Abram as engaging from early childhood in philosophical speculation—"roving" or "roaming" in his mind, his attention caught above all by the spectacle of nature which, however inconsistently it may seem to treat man, displays a sublime unity. The world does not seem to be the work of a committee, but of one transcendently great Artist.[14] In the dream of the palace in flames, Abram realized that the palace must have a master, though it burns.

All the time that Abram was coming to believe that there must be only a single deity, the Deity Himself remained silent. This may account for a certain anger attributed to Abram in the traditional sources. The scholar Harold Bloom admirably crystallizes Abram's personality: "The center of his consciousness is a certain discontent, an impatience with things as they are."[15] If the story of his birth in *Pirke d'Rabbi Eliezer* is to be taken at face value, his growing disaffection with popular opinion endangered his life.

On one occasion, Terach left town on business, unwisely leaving his oldest son in charge of his affairs. The Midrash recounts what happened. Abram kept the showroom open but got carried away with his disgust for the merchandise, mocking customers as they attempted to make purchases. When an older gentleman came before him and offered a price for a certain statue, Abram impertinently asked the man his age. Although taken aback, the customer answered that he was sixty years old. Abram asked him what kind of a fool he was, then, bowing down to an object like this that was fresh out of the kiln, just a day old!

Later a pious woman dropped in to offer some flour as a meal to the little clay idols. This gave Abram an idea. Grabbing a hammer, he smashed his father's entire stock into shards. One idol, the biggest, he left untouched but put the hammer in its hand and waited mischievously for Terach. On his return, the merchant demanded to know what madman had been loose in his store. Abram explained that when a woman had come in wanting to offer the statues a meal of flour, he had obliged and set it down for them to eat. "But then," he continued, "this one said 'I will eat first!' and another one said "*I* will eat first!' At which point this biggest fellow among them got up, took a hammer, and broke the rest."

Terach was incredulous. "Do you think you'll fool me? These idols don't know anything."

Bitterly Abram replied, "Do your ears not hear what your mouth has just said?"[16] Terach's response is not recorded. Presumably he was left speechless.

Abram's relationship with Terach grew increasingly strained. Not only did the older man resent his son's scaring pious idol-worshipers away from the family business but the religious authorities also suspected Terach's household of containing seeds of subversion. Rather than risk a late-night knock at his front door, Terach decided to take action. He informed on Abram to a Near Eastern equivalent of the Spanish Inquisition. Nimrod was glad for the pretext, provided by Terach, to arrest and jail a troublemaker.

The Talmud has Abram, thirty-eight years old at the time of his arrest, serving a prison sentence totaling ten years. At first, he was held at Cuthah, in the part of the city called Kasdim. After a few years, his jailers moved him north to Kardu—which an ancient Aramaic translation of the Bible links with the mountains of Little and Great Ararat in today's Kurdistan, where modern Turkey borders on Iran and Armenia.[17] Isolation was the intended effect. At Kardu, Abram was stripped of his belongings and, in the thin air, tortured at length.[18]

In expending such effort on Terach's son, Nimrod sought to avoid turning the man into a martyr—which executing him right away might have done. For the sovereign's main concern was to avoid any significant defections from the God-denying pagan ideology he had established. As the medieval sage Rabbi Moses ben Nachman writes, "He feared that [Abram] would corrupt his land and remove the children of man from their faith [in idols]."[19] (This Spanish exegete and mystic, 1194–1270, is also called Nachmanides or Ramban, not to be confused with Rambam, or Maimonides.) Indeed, Maimonides says that before Nimrod imprisoned him Abram had already begun to speak persuasively with friends and neighbors about the shortcomings of polytheistic worship.[20] Better, thought Nimrod, to let Abram sit in prison and contemplate the wisdom of his conscientious objections. Or perhaps Nimrod waited for certain omens favorable to conducting a trial or punishing Abram, for imprisonment was not a typical mode of dealing with criminals.

In any event, a decade passed, and Abram remained in prison. Finally Nimrod sent for him and he was returned to Cuthah, to Kasdim. Neither Midrash nor Talmud indicates the occasion for the interview with Nimrod, which took place there, but it can only have been the disaster of the Tower of Babel.

Although according to the plain scriptural text, the construction of the Tower of Babel happened before Abram's time, the classical Jewish sages added up the years in the genealogies on either side of the tower story and realized that it must have taken place during the patriarch's life. To be precise, Abram was forty-eight years old. According to one rabbinic view, this was the event that, more than any other, confirmed him in his commitment to monotheism.

There is extant today the ruins of a great ziggurat, a tower of terraces, that was once part of the complex of the temple of the god Marduk at Babylon ("Bavel" in Hebrew). The structure was called Etemenanki, "House of the Foundation of Heaven and Earth." Such towers were being raised up long before Abram was born. Scholars disagree about when this one was built. Some say as early as the twenty-fourth century B.C., others that it was at the time of Hammurabi, still others that it might have been the sixth century B.C. For its part, the Talmud asserts that the name "Babel" or "Babylon" became interchanged with that of nearby Borsippa.[21] This city had its own ziggurat, the Temple of Nebo, which some scholars think is the more likely referent of the biblical narrative.

The project, constructing a tower high enough to reach Heaven and make war on God, was a brainstorm of villainous Nimrod.[22] Or so says tradition. (Interestingly "Borsippa" in Arabic is "Birs Nimrud.")

Nimrod's ultimate intent has been speculated upon, one medieval sage suggesting that his purpose was to unite paganism in falsehood. Up till now, the people had worshiped the forces of nature, under the guise of a pantheon of deities. Rabbi Ovadiah Sforno (Italian, 1470–1550) notes that this state of affairs must have been almost as unacceptable to Nimrod as it was to Abram. After all, since the sun and moon, water and fire are all God's creations, to worship them is in a very broad sense to worship Him. Much better, thought Nimrod in his perversity, to create a single false god to replace all the old ones.[23] In this, he reminds us of Hammurabi, one of whose accomplishments, according to some historians, was to unify and organize the chaotic Mesopotamian pantheon under the personality of the Babylonian city god Marduk. Having gathered mankind in a monumental building project, Nimrod could turn the resulting sense of unity to his own ends. This was the danger to which the story of the tower alludes.

Whatever the location and the intention, as far as Abram was concerned, the builders were committing an unspeakable blasphemy. Publicly he cursed the work that was proceeding: "Consume them, O Lord, and confuse their language," he cried—which the Lord then proceeded to do.[24] When the builders found that they were unable to communicate with each other, for the language they spoke had been shattered into a "Babel" of many different tongues, they abandoned the projected ziggurat. Nimrod was bitterly displeased. To imagine the chronology of these events, we have to use our imagination, but it seems that Abram issued his curse from the mountain prison of Kardu. The language of the builders was scrambled, as the Bible relates, and work on the tower halted. Rumors reached Nimrod that Abram was responsible.

By this point, the patriarch had gone too far to turn back. He had challenged not only his father but the greatest and wickedest ruler in Mesopotamia. The world was on fire and it threatened to catch him up in the inferno. Soon the Fiery Furnace at Kasdim would be lit. Soon Abram would meet God in person in the heat of its flames.

Since we have given the location of the Fiery Furnace as Ur Kasdim, it's necessary to deal with the fact that modern Bible critics interpret those two words in a quite different way. Ur Kasdim is cited by those who wish to demonstrate that Genesis must have been written a millennium or more after the patriarchal period. In fact, those two words may be the most convincing argument the critics offer against the traditional view that attributes the text to God's authorship. Let's follow the critics in breaking the formulation down into its constituent parts, Ur and Kasdim.

First, Ur. A certain Sumerian metropolis was first brought to archaeological attention in 1625 by Pietro della Valle, who found the tell in southern Iraq. The identification with Ur was made two centuries later when the explorer J. E. Taylor uncovered a brick inscribed with the name "Ur." In 1922, Sir Leonard Woolley began to dig up the site, including a well-preserved three-story ziggurat surmounted by a temple of the god Nanna. He announced that he had found Abraham's place of origin. As Woolley's digging confirmed, inhabitation of the city had commenced in the fifth millennium B.C., reaching the heights of urban sophistication in the First and Third Dynasties of Ur but falling markedly in prestige by the time of Abraham. The fortunes of the city kept on this downward course till it was left a ruin, then covered in sand.

The world was fascinated at Woolley's discovery. A famous friend of the archaeologist, mystery writer Agatha Christie, visited him at the dig, bringing back romantic accounts of four-day sandstorms swirling around the ziggurat, "standing up, faintly shadowed, and that wide sea of sand with its lovely pale colours of apricot, rose, blue and mauve changing every minute." Touring the site, Christie even happened upon what she confidently took to be Abraham's own house ("I felt in my mind no doubt whatever").[25]

Now Kasdim. Before it sank into total obscurity after the fifth century B.C., Ur fell into the hands of the people called Kasdim in the Bible, translated "Chaldeans." As an ethnic group of Semitic desert dwellers, the Chaldeans first emerge in recognizable form in southern Mesopotamia, proceeding onto the historical stage around the ninth century B.C. They achieved power over the land of Babylon in the seventh century. According to the scriptural books 2 Kings, Jeremiah, Ezekiel, and 2 Chronicles, it was Chaldeans who conquered the Kingdom of Judah, destroyed the First Temple, and exiled the Jews to Babylon in 587/586 B.C.

The most up-to-date scholarly view thus fixes the writing of Genesis in the seventh century B.C.[26] At that moment in history, it made sense to speak of an "Ur of the Chaldeans," as "Ur Kasdim" is rendered in many Bible translations.

But the hypothesis of the book you are reading suggests that Genesis was produced when the Israelite nation was camped at Mt. Sinai, receiving the Torah from God—seven centuries earlier. This was at a time when the Chaldeans, if they yet existed at all, were in no position to lay claim to the city of Ur.

Maybe, one might speculate, the essential text is old enough to be reliable, but some later scribe added the word "Kasdim" to "Ur" to identify a city with which his contemporary readers may not have been familiar. However, the oral tradition is a stickler about every word in the Pentateuch reflecting God's transmission. If the tradition is wrong about such a basic matter, then it's hard to see why we should trust its testimony at all. We must understand that we are not dealing with the city of Ur or with the people known to history as Chaldeans.

There are anachronisms and anachronisms. If modern historians show the rabbis who convey tradition what the text really means, then there is an evident difficulty with our hypothesis of the text and tradition having been communicated by God. On the other hand, if the tradition explained the apparent glitch long before the skeptical scholars came along, that is quite different. The reference to Ur Kasdim is an anachronism of the latter kind.

Eight centuries ago the medieval Provençal sage Rabbi David Kimchi (called Radak; 1160–1235) addressed the issue.[27] He directs our attention to Genesis 22, where events some 137 years after Abram's birth are narrated. We read that his brother Nachor had twelve sons, one of whom was called Kesed.[28] In the classical Hebrew text, where consonants appear but vowels are absent, the name is spelled with the letters "kof-sin-daled," or KSD. The word "Kasdim" in "Ur Kasdim" is built on the same three-letter root. In Hebrew, the name of a national group can be formed by adding the plural suffix -im to the name of the group's founder. The Kasdim, then, are the descendants of Kesed.

While this kind of analysis, focusing on the roots of Hebrew words, may seem strange, it is standard in Torah exegesis. Any Hebrew word is reducible to a root of three consonants. Once you have identified the root, vistas of meaning open up. As Rabbi Samson Raphael Hirsch (German, 1808–88) made clear in brilliant etymological research, we may have ten different Hebrew words, quite separate in terms of their dictionary definitions, but if they are all built from the same root, then they all share some basic concept. Emphasizing the unique resonances of Hebrew, oral tradition also gives considerable attention to numerology, or *gematria*. The first letter in the alphabet, aleph, equals 1; the second, bet, equals 2; and so on. The numbers add up and hint at deeper meanings.

As Radak makes clear, with this root KSD in mind, there is no real problem with Ur Kasdim. It often happens that the Bible will knowingly employ an anachronism. In the Abraham story alone, we have an allusion to the "territory of the Amalekite," referring to a certain tribe whose eponym was likewise as yet unborn.[29] The city or district of Dan is referred to long before the tribe of Dan (one of the twelve tribes that emerged from Egypt with Moses) has appeared on the scene.[30] Another scene takes place in the "desert of Beersheba"—"Beersheba" meaning "Well of the Oath"—before anyone ever conceived the oath after which the settlement called Beersheba was named.[31] Nowadays we would use a locution like "in the desert that would later be called Beersheba after a nearby town." However, the Pentateuch opts for concision, for it wants us to question the reference.

Questioning this reference to Ur Kasdim, we ask what symbolic meaning the designation "Kasdim" has in biblical language, apart from signifying the much later Chaldeans. In the Bible, ethnic and national groups are closely associated with definite character or philosophical traits, even occupations.[32] Sometimes the occupational name seems to have come first, only to be applied afterward to the people. Or the reverse may be true. "Canaanite" can mean a person descended from one of the peoples of the land of Canaan, or it can mean a peddler of any ethnicity, for Canaanites were evidently associated with an itinerant merchant class.[33] "Ishmaelite" could mean a descendant of Abram's son Ishmael, or it can mean any caravaneer.[34] "Aramean" could mean a member of that ancient Semitic nationality, or it can mean a shepherd.[35]

The people of Kesed looked for guidance in their lives to patterns in nature, as in the heavenly constellations, placing their faith in God's creations, not in God. The word "Kasdim" can thus refer to Chaldeans, or it can mean someone who, like Nimrod, zealously adheres to a type of nature worship.[36]

As we noted earlier, the Talmud indicates that the Fiery Furnace was in a quarter of the city of Cuthah associated with such Kasdim. Ur Kasdim is thus the fire the Kasdim lit to punish the man who preeminently challenged their faith, dealing it a blow from which it never recovered.

Angered and terrified, Nimrod was done with seeking Abram's death—for the moment. The prisoner, he declared, was to be, instead of executed, banished to the farthest reaches of Mesopotamia.

The verse about Haran's death is followed by a verse about Abram and his other brother, Nachor, taking wives, respectively called Yiscah and Milcah. This is followed by Terach's arrival with his family at Haran.

A more filled-out version of the sequence of events, given by tradition, would go as follows. The day of Haran's incineration, we know that his father and oldest brother were present in the sovereign's court. Perhaps his son and daughters were there as well. The Bible identifies Haran's son as Lot, the daughters as Milcah and Yiscah, the latter identified by tradition with Sarai, later to be called Sarah. The whole group thought it wise to leave Cuthah and the wrathful vicinity of Nimrod as quickly as possible. They proceeded to a place that had long been hospitable to Terach's family, Abram's ancestral land in the northwest. The family began to make their way toward Haran, almost five hundred miles up the Euphrates, off a branch of the river Balih.

Tradition offers two key facts about Yiscah. The name "Yiscah" was a kind of honorific, meaning literally "Looker." Her real name was Sarai, which itself means "My Princess." She was a looker first in the sense that her family knew her to have prophetic powers; she "looked" into the future. Second, she was a looker in the vulgar sense. "Everyone gazed at her beauty," says the Talmud.[37] Ten years younger than Abram, and so thirty-eight years old at the time of the journey to Haran, she retained the beauty of a much younger woman, as she did throughout her life.

Accounts of Sarai's loveliness come down to us from antiquity. In the Essene library at the Dead Sea community of Qumran, a scroll was found known as the *Genesis Apocryphon*. Dated to the second century B.C., it takes the form of midrash on part of the Abraham story. Evidently it wasn't considered reliable by the general Jewish population at the time because it was not preserved except by the chance finding of the Dead Sea Scrolls. It contains a passage praising the beauty of Haran's daughter that is worth reproducing.

. . . and beautiful is her face! How . . . fine are the hairs of her head! How lovely are her eyes! How desirable her nose and all the radiance of her countenance. . . . How fair are her breasts and how beautiful all her whiteness! How pleasing are her arms and how perfect her hands, and how [desirable] all the appearance of her hands! How fair are her palms and how long and slender are her fingers! How comely are her feet, how perfect her thighs! No virgin or bride led in to the marriage chamber is more beautiful than she; she is fairer than all other women. Truly, her beauty is greater than theirs. Yet together with all this grace she possesses abundant wisdom, so that whatever she does is perfect.[38]

The canonical Midrash goes further. In each generation, a woman is born who bears the likeness of the first human female, Eve. Eve was the very prototype of womanly beauty. But in beauty, Sarai surpassed Eve.[39]

A bizarre Talmudic statement complicates this image. The third-century-A.D. sage Rabbi Ami received the scandalous tradition that Abram and Sarai were "of doubtful sex [tumtumim]."[40] In the Talmud's language, a tumtum is a person whose genitals are hidden inside the body. Determining his or her gender requires a surgery in which the membrane covering the penis or vagina is split open. Presumably such an operation had been performed on Abram and Sarai, for by this point there was no question as to their respective genders. But to both of them there remained a certain androgynous quality.

A modern rabbinical interpreter understands Sarai to have been "essentially sexless," even "mannish."[41] But no "mannish" woman could exceed Eve in beauty. The seventeenth-century Talmudist Rabbi Shlomo Eidel (called Maharsha; Polish, 1555–1632) portrayed her more like a 1990s supermodel: gorgeous—but flat-chested and with a figure lacking feminine curves.[42]

As tumtumim, neither Abram nor Sarai expected to be able to have children. In ancient medicine, the condition was associated with infertility: Scripture says, "And Sarai was barren; she had no child."[43] But what is the point of telling us she had never had a child if you have just said she's barren? The Talmud interprets the Bible's extra phrase as indicating that in Sarah's case the problem was not merely one of infertility. She lacked a womb altogether.[44] All of which accounts for the fact that, at ages forty-eight and thirty-eight, both Abram and she remained unmarried.

Some pious readers will say that the Talmud's data were not intended to be understood in such a crude, literal way. Rather, Abram's being a tumtum and Sarai's missing womb allude to the new genesis that was going on. God's creation of man had disappointed Him. After just a few generations, humanity had rejected its relationship with the Creator. With this man and woman, God wanted to make a new start. So it was only appropriate that, before the patriarch and matriarch conceived their only child together, He needed to refresh and renew their reproductive systems.

Undoubtedly the Talmud apprises us of such intimate details for a good reason, and mere titillation isn't it. But why can't the androgyny of Abram and Sarai be both literally true *and* symbolically meaningful? As for the symbolism of their barrenness, I direct the reader's attention forward in history about 3,500 years. George Washington never had children, evidently because he was infertile. As the Washington biographer Richard Brookhiser suggests, a childless Washington is perfect poetry. As the father of his country, he is the father of all Americans. So, too, with Abram, the father of all monotheists. The fact that he went his first eighty-six years—a full life span—without having a child makes his fatherly role to us *almost* perfect poetry.

When did Abram and Sarai marry? The sequence of scriptural verses suggests that it was between the departure from Ur Kasdim and the arrival at Haran. If the party traveled twenty miles per day, the trip would have taken up to a month—during which time, perhaps, they fell in love. Till now, Abram had been essentially a walking Idea. In Nimrod's Fiery Furnace, his Idea ascended from the realm of intellect to that of action. This—Abram's deeds, not just his thoughts—was surely what Sarai came to love.

They were married in the customary fashion of Mesopotamian society. The couple had a contract written out for them on a clay tablet—called the marriage lines—which stipulated the conditions for dissolving the marriage and what would happen if one spouse was found to be unfaithful. (Hammurabi's Code made adultery a capital offense—for the wife—punishable by drowning in the Euphrates.) The tablet was sealed and they were henceforth man and wife.[45] Sarai would then likely have donned the veil required of married women.[46]

We should note here an alternative scholarly thesis that the trip to Haran was comparatively short. Some interpreters, regarding Ur as a city, say it cannot be the same southern Mesopotamian city of Ur excavated by Woolley, because that Ur was never called Ur of the Chaldeans. More important, in this view, all the scriptural and other historical clues point to Abram's ancestral land being in the north, not the south. And in the north, there appear to have been some other, lesser cities called Ur, probably founded under Ur's Third Dynasty as commercial colonies of the eponymous mother city. Muslim tradition identifies Abram's Ur with the city today called Sanliurfa, twenty miles up the Balih from Haran. Not all of modern scholarly opinion has rejected the identification.[47]

By a long or a short route, the party came to Haran. Its location is undisputed. The area is barren, dry and hellishly hot in summertime, with few trees to break the monotony of the horizon. Arabs and Kurds live there today in beehive-shaped homes constructed of mud brick (but no wood, hence the peculiar dome shape), overshadowed by ruins of a once-great eighth-century Muslim university, including a lonely, remarkably intact tower. Local architectural techniques have changed little in the past four thousand years. Take away the Islamic ruins and you are left with a view of the place much as Abram must have known it: desolate, dusty in the summer, muddy in the winter. When I was there, it was winter, the rainy season, and the site was a giant yellow mud dump with abandoned digs here and there over the tell, a foot or two of exposed stone walls scattered about. As my wife and I clambered around in the empty silence, my sneakers gathered their total volume in sticky mud. We saw exactly two human beings: our jolly taxi driver, who read an unintelligible script about the connections of "Ibrahim prophet" to Haran; and a local youth called, yes, Ibrahim who claimed that an archaeologist had unearthed an authentic shard with Ibrahim prophet's name on it (alas, untrue).

Haran at its height probably boasted a population of twenty thousand people. At the time of Hammurabi, an Amorite prince called Asdi-takim ruled a population of Hurrians. The latter, of whom much is known from the cache of fifteenth- and fourteenth-century cuneiform tablets found at Nuzi near modern Kirkuk, Iraq, were a non-Semitic people. They descended on northern Mesopotamia probably from Armenia or the south Caucasus. By the nineteenth century B.C., Haran was already well established.

For Abram and Sarai, the way of life here was not terribly different from that of southern Mesopotamia. A modern writer has compared their displacement to an American moving from New York to San Francisco.[48] The culture was cosmopolitan. Its name meaning "road" or "caravan" in Akkadian, Haran sat at a major crossroads of trade routes running north-south, between Babylon and Anatolia, and east-west, between Aleppo and Nineveh.[49]

In this worldly atmosphere, where news traveled fast, including south toward Nimrod, Abram at first thought it best to lie low, play the unassuming private citizen. If Nimrod had compatriots in town, there was no sense in antagonizing them or him. But an idea was forming in his mind.

What had got Abram into trouble to begin with was his occasional run-ins with pious idol-worshipers. Reports of Abram's "proofs" as to the truth of monotheism, which his neighbors found hard to answer, drew Nimrod's attention to the idol merchant's son.[50] For five years, he abstained from drawing the local Hurrians into discussions of their religious beliefs. In these parts, the head of the pantheon was the storm god Tesup. Till now, monotheism had been like water carried by one of Nimrod's clouds. Abram was the cloud and, apart from the occasional drop of moisture on an unwary pagan who strayed into Terach's shop, for the most part the conclusions about God that Abram had arrived at he kept to himself. Five years after the Terach party reached Haran, the storm broke and the cloud began to rain down its truth on the people.

Cryptically Genesis credits Abram with having "made souls" at Haran.[51] That is the literal rendering of the phrase. The conventional translation takes this to mean that Abram "acquired" people, that he bought slaves. But the same verse speaks of Abram amassing other sorts of possessions. The verb *asu,* or "make," cannot mean that he "acquired" souls, because then any slave he bought would also be included in the phrase about his getting possessions. Tradition understands the apparent superfluity as a reference to Abram's efforts at evangelization, in which he brought Hurrians "under the wings of the Divine Presence."[52] The Talmud says that a man who teaches another man about the Lord is considered as if he personally had "made" him.[53]

Breaking with his previous reticence, Abram started to preach. Sarai, who had become a believer herself, joined him. He evangelized the men, she the women.[54] According to Maimonides, "He began to stand up and call out in a mighty voice to all the world, making known that there is one God for all the world, and that it is fitting to worship him."[55] Note the parallel with Nimrod. While the latter was a hunter of souls, so too now, in a sense, was Abram—the one seeking to trap them and draw them away from God, the other to minister to their spiritual needs and bring them closer to Him.

He did this out of love for God. The prophet Isaiah bestowed on our patriarch the title of God's "friend" or "lover,"[56] and Muslims apply to Ibrahim the same honorific. Practically speaking, what does it mean to be God's lover? The Talmud says a person who loves God is one who speaks and acts with faith and pleasantness, so that other people come to wish that they, too, knew something about Him.[57] Echoing this idea, Maimonides in his *Sefer Hamitzvot* ("Book of the Commandments") cites our patriarch as the prime example of someone who made Him "beloved of man."[58]

In the Rambam's view, as a seeker and teacher of Truth with no interest in personal reward, Abraham is no less than the very model of a human being.[59] Indeed, without having yet received even the briefest communication from his God indicating that He cared one way or the other about Abram's activities, the patriarch had begun to show his love for Him by causing other people to wish to know Him and to fall in love themselves. This passionate lover must have been an effective evangelist and missionary.

Abraham as "evangelist" and "missionary" may sound strange. It is often said that Judaism, unlike Christianity and Islam, takes a principled stand against seeking converts. This same line of argument might proceed to say that since Abraham was the first Jew, picturing him as a missionary is surely inauthentic. Not so. Torah not only permits seeking converts: it is a *mitzvah,* a commandment to do so. Jews are not commanded to seek converts to Judaism, however, but to monotheism as Torah conceives it (Noachism). In his *Mishneh Torah,* Maimonides lays out the rather aggressive means by which, in ideal circumstances (which wouldn't apply to our own time), Jews are supposed to strive to bring Abrahamic monotheism to non-Jews.[60] This is what's meant by the phrase in the Book of Exodus calling the Israelites a "kingdom of priests." As the classical commentator Sforno explains, being the priestly nation means that Jews must "teach all of mankind to call in unison on the Name of the Lord and to serve Him with one accord."[61] In this, Jews are to act on the model established by Abram.

Tradition declines to tell us what arguments he used in his missionary work among the Hurrians. Obviously he spoke of the greatness of God and the inadequacy of the gods. But the truth is that almost no one is won over to religious faith by "arguments." So-called proofs of God's existence, as in the work of medieval Christian scholastic writers, may sound good to a Thomas Aquinas or to his intellectually driven contemporaries, as they do to some brainy modern folks. To most people, however, they would seem superficial and forced, mere word games.

Rather than proceeding from the brain to the heart, conversions tend to work the other way around, occurring for very personal emotional reasons. This is not to say such conversions are misguided. We have to give up the notion that when it comes to ultimate questions like the existence of God, the only organ that matters is the brain. Without a foundation in tradition, which provides the axioms on which the brain can then work, the intellect can deceive us. Perhaps that is why there are so many mutually contradictory "philosophies" in the world, each claiming to be constructed on a foundation of pure reason.

Sometimes a person needs to hear "proofs" first to open him up to the idea of God, to give him "permission to believe," intellectually speaking.[62] But this is only to assure him that believing in God is not unworthy of a thoughtful man or woman. Highly intelligent people who don't believe in God may have been going about their whole lives with the impression that only the simple-minded can have religious faith. They say, "I wish I *could* believe, but . . . ," meaning: "I'm too smart to believe, which in a way is too bad because it would be nice." People like this would probably see through alleged "proofs" that God exists. What they need is really the experience of meeting other men and women as thoughtful as they are who *do* believe. This provides the experience that may give them "permission." Abram made it his business to give permission to his more skeptical, brainy neighbors, while approaching the simpler souls on their own level.

Undoubtedly Abram had his specific rhetorical strategies, his "arguments," but these varied with his audience. Rambam gives us an idea of this general technique. He taught "each and every person according to his or her personal needs."[63]

Thus we needn't take literally the image of Abram standing up and calling out on behalf of his God, like the characters you see in New York City preaching on the sidewalk. It is amazing to consider that this street-preacher tradition has its roots, however distorted, in our patriarch. I think of the wild-bearded fellow who stations himself each morning at Park Avenue and 50th Street, holding a Bible aloft and shouting to the skies, not a word out of his mouth intelligible. Abram opted for an approach that was wholesale, not retail. He befriended neighbors and transient merchants, getting to know them as individuals. The process was slow. But over the many years of his missionary work, the Rambam records, ultimately "there were gathered unto him thousands and tens of thousands."[64]

An alternative tradition suggests that these tens of thousands were gathered less by argumentation and more by an appeal to supernatural wonder. Look again at the cryptic reference to his "making souls," which may be interpreted literally. The portrait here is of the patriarch as a master occultist. The Talmud asserts that he possessed a book of four hundred chapters detailing the secrets of pagan magic and ritual.[65] He was renowned among the idolaters, and kings from east and west would be found waiting at his door each morning to press him for his astrological predictions. Deep "astrology was in his heart," as the Talmud puts it. He even possessed a certain magic stone with power to heal the sick.[66] While the Torah forbids Jews to engage in black magic, it does allow them to pursue such manipulations of the natural world as can be accomplished through pronouncing and arranging various esoteric names of God. This "practical kabbalah," a kind of white magic, was deployed by rabbis in the era of the Talmud, and tradition ascribes the authorship of a magical work, the *Sefer Yetzirah,* to none other than Abram.[67]

This brief text, all but unintelligible, is said to contain the secret of creating a living being, a golem. The last chapter of *Sefer Yetzirah* records that "when Abraham our father, may he rest in peace, looked, saw, understood, probed, engraved and carved, he was successful in creation, as it is written, 'And the souls they made in Haran. . . .' " All these terms—"looked, saw, understood," and so on—are code for techniques of meditation involving the arrangement of the letters in divine names. In the opinion of some medieval sages, when the Bible says that Abram "made souls," this means he created golems to astound the people of Haran and inspire them to become his students. Once they entered his circle of disciples, he got down to the real business he intended, which was instructing them about God.[68]

Whatever his exact methods, Abram was fifty-two years old when he began his missionary work that would change the world, and the Talmud notes that this was precisely two thousand years after the creation of the first human soul. We would say it was 1760 B.C., or the year 2000 in the Hebrew calendar.

Jewish tradition assigns to the history of human civilization a total duration of six thousand years, each millennium corresponding to one of the days of creation. Just as God rested on the seventh day, the world will rest in its seventh millennium, which will be the epoch of the Messiah.

The first two millennia were a time of spiritual void—signified during the first two days of creation by the predominance of salt water. On creation's third day, God formed dry land and planted the seeds of trees. The Bible elsewhere compares His teachings to a "tree of life."[69] So the Talmud indicates that the two-thousand-year epoch that began in the first year of the third millennium is the epoch of God's teaching, or Torah.[70] Abram presided over the transition from the second to the third day of millennial history, planting the seeds that would become the great monotheistic faiths.

Abram lived at Haran for twenty-seven years, enduring the heat, the mud, the monotonous scenery, perhaps the hostility of some natives to an outlander and a troublemaker. Missionary activity was not his only occupation. Undoubtedly he had a profession. It is hard to picture him in that category of sons of wealthy mercantile fathers who nurture their idealism while living off Dad's fortune. Albright among other scholars has preferred to think of Abram as a caravaneer, presiding over trains of donkeys trekking goods to Aleppo or Nineveh. For Abram's journeys took him along some of the great trading routes of the Near East. On these highways, a top caravaneer might have driven five hundred to six hundred laden donkeys at a time, accompanied by armed retainers. Albright's Abram would have been an imposing figure. However, the Bible is clear on what business Terach's family in Haran pursued. Later in Genesis, Abram's grandson Jacob labored as a shepherd, caring for the sheep and goat flocks of Laban, son of Abram's brother Nachor. Very likely he took up this calling of his Haran relatives, raising small livestock.

Abram with a shepherd's staff also fits the pattern of Hebrew leaders, notably Moses and King David, both veteran animal tenders. It was fine experience for a man destined to shepherd the lives of his followers. Though based at Haran, he would have led an existence halfway between sedentary and nomadic—as residents of Haran still do. Breeders and keepers of such livestock kept in contact with the settled population of a town or city, but otherwise wandered from spring to spring with their flocks, making short journeys that ultimately covered wide geographic areas. Climatologically speaking, the settlements that according to the Bible Abram visited or lived near—Haran, Shechem, Beth-el, Hebron, and Beersheba—were similar, all with an annual rainfall of ten to twenty inches, conditions associated with the raising of sheep and similar livestock.[71]

In the course of his wanderings, Abram the sheepherder pursued his evangelical mission. Maimonides has him "walking and calling and gathering the people from town to town and from country to country."[72] As Abram entered his seventies, there seemed no reason to expect any destiny for himself other than to go on preaching, in Haran and its environs, for the rest of his life.

But this plan was to be disrupted, a disruption that would prove to be a decisive trial. According to the Mishnah's tractate *Pirke Avot* ("Chapters of the Fathers"), Abram's life was marked by ten tests or "trials."[73] Rashi tells us that his first two trials were the experience of the cave and of the Fiery Furnace, both resulting from Nimrod's persecution. In the vocabulary of the Torah's numerological system, the number 10 signifies completion. Thus the Ten Commandments are regarded as a statement, in the most highly crystallized form, of the whole body of commandments found in the Torah, 613 in total, with each of those 613 falling under the heading of one of the Ten Commandments. Similarly the completion of God's work in creating the world required ten statements ("Let there be light," "Let there be a firmament," and so on).[74] In undergoing his ten trials, Abraham was completed as the man he was destined to become.

In his *Guide for the Perplexed,* Maimonides writes that by undergoing a trial, a person becomes an educational model: "Know that the aim and meaning of all the trials mentioned in the Pentateuch is to let people know what they ought to do or what they must believe."[75] Rambam's evidence includes the midrashic reading of a verse found at the end of the story of the Binding of Isaac. When Abraham has completed this test, God says, "now I know you are God-fearing."[76] The Midrash reads the Hebrew phrase meaning "now I know" in a causative sense, as "now I have *made known*."[77] (St. Augustine likewise understood the phrase in this way, observing that "God was not previously ignorant" that Abraham feared Him, thus "now I know" can only mean "now I have made known.")[78]

On the question of what trials accomplish, the later Spanish sage Nachmanides, or Ramban, disputed Rambam. Ramban locates the importance of such suffering in the person of the sufferer. God "commands [the trial in order] to bring forth the deed from the power."[79] That is, when a man endures pain, the experience takes certain potential virtues in him and makes them actual.

However, the Mishnah, while specifying that there were ten trials, does not tell us what those trials were. Thus Rashi identifies Abram's first two trials as the cave and the furnace, while Maimonides disagrees and offers his own, significantly different sequence. As we proceed with our story, I will note which episodes in the patriarch's life correspond to which trials according to Rashi and Maimonides. The two sages differ because Rashi relies on the midrashic collection *Pirke d'Rabbi Eliezer,* which gives a list, while Maimonides thought that the trials, because the Midrash regards them as so significant, must surely all be part of Scripture's exoteric narrative. In the Rambam's view, Abram's first trial was yet to come.

CHAPTER THREE

Did Abraham Live?

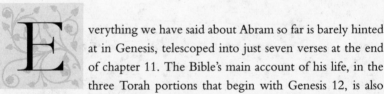verything we have said about Abram so far is barely hinted at in Genesis, telescoped into just seven verses at the end of chapter 11. The Bible's main account of his life, in the three Torah portions that begin with Genesis 12, is also terse in the extreme—fourteen chapters in all—and says nothing about his founding a religion of primordial monotheism. Indeed, on the occasions when he talks to God, the narrative puts in Abraham's mouth a succession of divine names—Hashem[1] (conventionally translated "Lord"), Elohim ("God"), El Shaddai ("God Almighty"), El Elyon ("God Most High")— such that an innocent reader might wonder if Abraham was himself a monotheist. What exactly did Abraham accomplish?

This book is not really a biography. To call it that would imply that there are facts about Abraham that can be definitely ascertained. There are not. As yet, not a single artifact or inscription contemporary with his lifetime has been uncovered that makes even the most oblique reference to the patriarch, his family, or his immediate descendants. Which is a problem: if he lived, where is the evidence? A problem, but not one that proves anything one way or the other, for one cannot make definitive statements based only on the silence of an archaeological record three and a half thousand years old.

Still, in the absence of such evidence, this book offers not a biography, but something different, an interpretive narrative of a biblical life drawing on two resources that don't usually go together: oral tradition and scholarly history. "Tradition," ancient and sacred, not found in the Bible itself, claims to tell us what happened to Abraham and what he did in response. It alludes to the spiritual meanings of the events in his life. "History" tells us what was going on in the Near East in Abraham's time. These resources come to us from sages and from scholars.

The sages are those interpreters of the Bible who regard the book as authoritative and rely on transmitted tradition to fill the gaps in the scriptural narrative. Sages may be Jewish, Muslim, or Christian. Muslim tradition concerning Abraham parallels its Jewish counterpart to an astonishing degree. In the case of Judaism, which offers by far the fullest portrait of our subject, the sages hold that the Torah is cryptic, containing innumerable instances of what appear to be errors, inconsistencies, and editorial blunders. Each is like a pointing finger, urging us to consult the tradition. Called Oral Torah, this explanatory tradition was originally passed down by word of mouth and includes elaborations on the biblical text along with ethical observations, exotic parables, stories of the ancient rabbis, and grammatical and etymological analyses of words and phrases found in the Bible.

While the sages have been around for thousands of years, scholars are a fairly recent phenomenon. Some of them represent the barrier of doubt this book will need to overcome, so I want to introduce their perspective now and begin to suggest how it is by itself inadequate. The scholars are historians and archaeologists. Some of them guardedly endorse Scripture as a helpful document for making educated guesses about history, while others reject the Bible's account of the past almost in its entirety. Among the scholars we may distinguish two subcategories: the skeptics and the supporters. The skeptics trace their intellectual lineage to the German Bible critic Julius Wellhausen

(1844–1918). According to his Documentary Hypothesis, the whole Pentateuch was patched together from older documents, designated by the letters J, E, P, and D, and edited by a Redactor, or R, perhaps nine hundred years after Moses supposedly lived. A theory popular today holds that the Redactor was Ezra the Scribe, who lived in Israel in the fifth century B.C.[2] Wellhausen felt certain that nothing could be said factually about Abraham.

Casting doubt on Wellhausen's skepticism, there arose a group of mostly American historians who sought to support belief in the historicity of the patriarchs by rendering juxtapositions of biblical verses with new archaeological discoveries from the patriarchal period, roughly the middle third of the second millennium B.C. We may call these men, whose earnestness occasionally shaded over into naïveté, the supporters.

William Foxwell Albright (1891–1971), of Johns Hopkins, greatest champion of the Bible-friendly supporters, drew a portrait of an Abraham who was indeed a historical person, if a pedestrian one, who may or may not have been a monotheist. Albright's student Nelson Glueck issued the muscular pronouncement that "no archaeological discovery has ever controverted a Biblical reference."[3]

A skeptical assault on the supporters picked up momentum in the 1970s with books by Thomas L. Thompson (1974) and John Van Seters (1975).[4] One skeptic has reached quasi-celebrity status: Yale's Harold Bloom, in his best-selling *Book of J* (1990), tries to separate the work of the hypothetical author J, an irony-addicted woman in the court of King Solomon's son Rehoboam (tenth century B.C.), from the rest of the Bible.

Today the latest fashion in academic Bible-bashing emphasizes that much material in the Pentateuch points to a geopolitical situation unique to the seventh century B.C. and must therefore have been authored about that time, ruling out historical accuracy. In other words, when a Bible story seems to foretell a time much later than the one the story ostensibly describes, the skeptics automatically rule that the passage must have been authored *after* the situation in question had come to pass. By their lights, there can be no such thing as prophecy. But this begs the question, assuming as fact what cannot be proved.

Outside the universities, in magazines and newspapers, from *Harper's* to the *New York Times,* even from the pulpits of liberal synagogues and churches, the theme is also sounded that the major events in the Hebrew

Bible's narrative could not have happened. These events include the Exodus from Egypt, the wandering of the Israelites in the Sinai desert for forty years, the destruction of Jericho by Joshua's armies, and the flourishing of David and Solomon's kingdom. Little attention is paid to the fact that an independent scholar, David Rohl, has convincingly addressed precisely these questions of historical confirmation. When he looked afresh at the dating of the reigns of the pharaohs as they correspond to what was going on simultaneously in Canaan, he found striking problems with the way scholars have dated the archaeological remains of the ancient Near East. With Rohl's revised chronology, the collapsed walls of Jericho and the ruins of Solomon's kingdom are found just where and when they are supposed to be found. He also offers evidence of an Israelite Exodus from Egypt.

As to the evidence specifically for or against Abraham's existence, three lines of attack go as follows. The Bible speaks of Abraham possessing camels, but during his presumed lifetime these beasts were not yet widely domesticated. It speaks of him interacting with "Philistines," who had not yet arrived in the land of Canaan. And it mentions cities in connection with his wanderings—Beersheba and Ai—which either did not exist or were unoccupied at that time. While the first two of these objections will be dealt with later, the last is easy to answer: the Torah refers to Ai and Beersheba merely as place-names, not as cities.

The skeptics have yet to prove anything about the historicity of the patriarchs, which is why the pendulum of academic opinion is likely before long to swing back from radical skepticism. Even today not all respected scholars dismiss the Bible as history. When Israeli archaeologist Eliezer Oren, who excavated a biblical city where Abraham sojourned (Gerar), was asked recently what grade he would give the Bible "in terms of archaeological accuracy," he replied puckishly, "A plus plus."[5] Still, it has to be stated frankly that for all the labor of the supporters, not a single detail in the story of Abraham has been confirmed.

Yet there are independent grounds for entertaining the possibility that Abraham was a real person and that he did what tradition, properly understood, says he did. First, comprehending Abraham *as a historical character* is the foundation stone of everything that most of us, even if we are not traditionally observant of any particular religion, wish to believe about God. Second, reading the Bible *through the medium of tradition,* which presents

Abraham as a real person cast into sometimes surreal situations, makes more sense than reading it *without tradition.*

As to the first of these two claims, while the sobriety and detachment of the scholars with their professional journals and monographs may numb the reader into forgetting that anything vital is at stake in ancient Near Eastern studies, we should not forget. The Bible is a very assertive book. As the literary critic Erich Auerbach has persuasively argued, "One can perfectly well entertain historical doubts on the subject of the Trojan War or Odysseus' wandering, and still, when reading Homer, feel precisely the effects he sought to produce; but without believing Abraham's sacrifice [of his son Isaac], it is impossible to put the narrative of it to the use for which it was written. Indeed, we must go even further. The Bible's claim to truth is not only far more urgent than Homer's, it is tyrannical—it excludes all other claims."[6]

The Bible offers an either-or choice: either accept the truth of the narrative and the doctrine expressed in it, however those are understood (which is no easy question), or reject both. Of course, we don't have to accept the "tyranny" of the biblical choice. But if we reject it, then we are rejecting the Bible as a source of authoritative teaching. To put it differently, if we reject Abraham, we are rejecting the Bible. If we reject the Bible, then a question asked by the philosopher Abraham Joshua Heschel comes tugging at our sleeve: "It may seem easy to play with the idea that the Bible is a book like many other books," a "fairy tale," but "consider what such denial implies. If Moses and Isaiah have failed to find out what the will of God is, who will? If God is not found in the Bible, where should we seek Him?

"The question about the Bible is the question about the world. It is an ultimate question. If God had nothing to do with the prophets, then He has nothing to do with mankind."[7]

If God had nothing to do with Abraham, then He is not to be found in the Bible at all. If He is not to be found in the Bible, then where should we seek Him? If he never spoke to Abraham, then we are on our own. While we are free to posit some nonbiblical deity, a universal spirit floating in the ether, there is little to say about such a being. He left no record of having communicated anything about himself to anyone. A world in which Abraham never walked is a world without the God so many of us cherish. If this seems too simplistic a formulation, I invite you to offer your own scenario in which God is preserved but Abraham is not.

Now for my second claim, that the Bible makes sense only if read from the perspective of tradition. I am not a fundamentalist—meaning a person who believes you can pick up the Bible, open to any page, read it for yourself as one reads a newspaper, and find all the truth it has to offer. One reason I am not a fundamentalist is that in the Pentateuch, on every page, some places in every passage or even every verse, one finds an apparent blunder: solecisms of grammar or diction, weird spelling variations, needless repetitions, missing words, missing passages, self-contradictions, pointless obscurities, logic-defying transitions, blatant anachronisms, characters introduced without identification then abruptly dropped. I say this as someone who spent ten years as a professional magazine editor: to all appearances, the editing job on the biblical text is so extraordinarily bad as to suggest deliberate sabotage.

That is, unless you have the traditional sources of commentary to explain what's going on. In fact, from the Talmud down to the medieval French exegete Rashi and those who followed him, the classical Jewish commentaries mainly pick up little nettles of apparent sloppiness and explain what subterranean meaning they allude to.

The Pentateuch is a most peculiar book. Imagine a long piece of writing that underwent not just a quick newspaper- or magazine-style editing but an excruciatingly careful *redacting*. In this process, the works of many authors were so skillfully woven together that for a couple thousand years everyone attributed the authorship to Moses (or God). Yet this brilliant editor was so incompetent as to miss sentence upon sentence that screamed out for editing. He must even have introduced glitches of his own, since it is not plausible that all the writers whose works he compiled were as sloppy as he.

Maybe you think that the internal contradictions of the Pentateuch can be accounted for by positing a Redactor too awestruck to change the holy words and eliminate contradictions between the constituent documents. But this doesn't help us with the contradictions that occur from verse to verse in passages attributed to a single source. Admittedly some academics recognize that the Torah leaves out crucial background information, but they give no compelling explanation of why the book was edited that way.[8] Harold Bloom, for instance, writes of an "elliptical" quality in J, though he attributes this to her "virtually Shakespearean" gift for irony.[9] It is unclear what's so "ironic" about this as opposed to being merely confusing.

Though the scholars don't say this outright, their way of thinking leads to the conclusion that the Pentateuch is the editorial work of a bizarre idiot savant. The sages, on the other hand, hold that the biblical text is intentionally cryptic. Because they regard the Five Books of Moses as divinely given, transcendently true, they must also hold that the tradition to which it alludes in a kind of shorthand is also divine and true. In Jewish terminology, both the Written Torah and the Oral Torah that explains it were revealed to Moses at Mt. Sinai in 1312 B.C., then passed down from generation to generation. The oral part was kept oral for a number of reasons: It is too vast to write down in any form that is not hopelessly unwieldy. It is meant to unify those who possess it, which to some extent means excluding outsiders from comprehending its secrets. And finally, writing is an inferior mode of communication compared to orality, the latter requiring more active interface with the words and with other people.

After the destruction of the Second Temple in Jerusalem in A.D. 70, when the Jewish community in the land of Israel was dispersed and its Torah academies disrupted, this chain of transmission began to break down. So the decision was made to commit the Oral Torah to writing. This happened in stages that even today are not yet complete, starting with the Mishnah around A.D. 200, followed a few centuries later by the Talmud, commenting on the Mishnah, and by *Genesis Rabbah,* the chief collection of midrash or biblical interpolation illuminating the text of Genesis. Between 640 and 900, other collections of midrashim appeared, most importantly *Pirkei d'Rabbi Eliezer* ("Chapters of Rabbi Eliezer") and *Midrash Tanchuma* (attributed to Rabbi Tanchuma). When medieval and modern sages comment on the Pentateuch, they draw on these earlier sources, a data stream going back to Moses.[10]

To be sure, the Talmud notes that Moses would be astonished at some of the novel forms the tradition has taken.[11] But the original revelation at Sinai was like an embryo, containing all the genetic information to become one very particular human being. Looking at an embryo, you, too, would be astonished to learn what grown-up person it was destined to become.

Our alternatives, then, are these: the Competent/Incompetent Redactor of the Scholars, or the Cryptic Torah of the Sages. Harold Bloom thinks that attributing much of Genesis to J is "less irrational" than attributing it to Moses. I hope I am beginning to make clear that the Cryptic Torah requires no less of a stretch of the imagination than does believing in J and her editor. To the contrary, as a theory, for all the extraordinary events it records, at least the Torah of the sages is internally coherent.

I am focusing here on Jewish tradition, as opposed to other religious traditions. Why? The Five Books of Moses are code, in a sense, and a code is never created without a key. Only the Jewish sages claim to possess a key that unlocks the Pentateuchal text *at every point* where a seeming error points to an esoteric meaning. No one else even ventures the claim. If the key was preserved, the Jews preserved it. Jewish tradition does a remarkably consistent and coherent, as well as enlightening, job of answering the many questions raised by a sensitive reading of Genesis.

If this tradition is indeed the truest way of understanding the Bible, transmitting data as old as the Bible, then there is apparently something special about it, something quite amazing that would allow it to be maintained intact through the millennia. It would seem we are dealing with a people who possess a unique transmission of information. Given this, we should not dismiss the tradition's governing assumption, everywhere evident, that it conveys genuine historical memories.[12] The scholars give us Abraham as a fiction or fictionalized "composite"; the sages see him as a real person, no myth. It is integral to the latter's entire worldview that they believed they were describing a man who lived in history.

Some professors will tell you that the old rabbis did not think in terms of "history" as we do—that "history" itself is a construct of late vintage. These scholars feel that the rabbis were too naïve to understand that in filling out the details of the patriarchs' lives, they would be understood as giving biographical information. The problem is that the rabbis' words do not read like the naïve imaginings of primitives who cannot understand what fact is. Sometimes they speak in parables, but the parables are usually obvious, exaggerated, and impossible. You only have to read the accounts in the Talmud and Midrash with an open mind to see that what the rabbis teach, they believe to be true.

To restate, in briefest terms, my reasons for thinking the Abraham of tradition was a real person: His existence is not ruled out by history, which lends credibility to tradition on some points. If we wish to know God, Abraham's existence is positively required. Finally, the Bible assumes tradition, tradition assumes an Abraham who lived, and there is something unusual about this tradition that should make us hesitate before rejecting its claims to convey historical truths.

This argument, obviously, is not one you will hear today in university lecture halls. In fact, what I have said could hardly be more divergent from what college students learn from their professors and what readers learn from most contemporary writers on biblical subjects, however earnest and enthusiastic.

Professional scholars cling to the Documentary Hypothesis, and no wonder. Should Wellhausen's theory ever be overturned in favor of an approach that takes seriously the "errors" in the biblical text, then much of modern Bible scholarship would have to be discarded. Instead of studying Wellhausen and his heirs, Bible scholars would have to begin studying Rashi. They would find that the familiar Bible stories read rather differently than they are accustomed to. They would find, too, that the God of the plain, terse, unilluminated biblical text is a different God from the God of the tradition.

It is this latter Deity whom Abraham discovered. However, you needn't be a believer in the God of tradition to entertain the possibility that Genesis is cryptic, that it describes a man who existed in history. You need only have an open mind and be willing to read the Bible sensitively. It is for such readers, rather than for the piously religious, that I set out in this book what there is to be discovered about Abraham in the Jewish sources. Let us then return to his life.

CHAPTER FOUR

The Unknown Land

O ne night Abram lay down to sleep. Perhaps he was in Haran at the time, or by a spring with his flock, wrapped in a cloak against the night cold. Ramban says that Abram had a dream, or a visitation of the Holy Spirit.[1] In any event, it was a prophetic experience, though of a low level as such things are measured.

As Maimonides explains in his *Guide for the Perplexed,* there are two general categories of prophecy: dreams and visions.[2] In the *Mishneh Torah,* he says that a prophet is someone who prepares himself carefully for the experience of being visited by the Divine, which comes only to those possessing very special qualities, both material and physical. The Talmud lists the attributes of the prophet: He must be strong, wise, humble, and physically imposing. He must also be rich![3] In other words, we aren't to picture any prophet as a meek, mild wretch, tormented by poverty, dispossessed in his community. God's intent is that the prophet be someone whom the people around him will find it natural to listen to and respect, which wouldn't be true if he were unimpressive in his person. To be sure, some prophets suffered abuse at the hands of the mighty, but the role of the victim was not natural for the Hebrew prophets. So we should envision Abram not as a man alone in the wilderness tending his poor flock, but as a successful gentleman of commerce and trade, attended by servants, wealthy, and in good health. Also in good cheer. Contrary to what popular culture may have accustomed us to when we think of prophets broadcasting messages of doom, Maimonides draws on Scripture and the oral tradition and finds that prophets entered the prophetic state only when in a "happy, joyous mood." This is because "prophecy cannot rest upon a person amid sadness nor among languidness, but rather [only] amid joy."

Yet, as Maimonides continues, when the spirit at last rests on the prophet, the experience itself can be terrifying. The limbs tremble, the body suddenly loses strength, the physical senses fail. The prophet then enters the spiritual company of a category of angels, the *ishim* (literally "men," a lesser kind of angelic being). At this point, in some sense and not merely a spiritual one, he becomes another person; even the appearance of his face and body may be changed in horrible ways.[4] It sounds like a convulsion or a fit.

All these things now happened to Abram, for the first time and without warning. Notwithstanding all his presumed prophetic cheeriness prior to the event, the moment when it came must have been stressful indeed! And Abram's distress was multiplied because he was about to learn that all the effort he had made toward winning men and women over to the worship of the One God was to be disrupted, perhaps rendered entirely void.

Abram slept and dreamed and the prophetic convulsion came over him. If any of his companions or servants were nearby, or his wife, Sarai, we can imagine their consternation. Afterward when he sat up in bed, or on his blanket spread on the ground by the spring, he knew that in the dream certain words had been conveyed to him. They were, as Genesis states: "Go now, for yourself, from your land and from the place of your birth, from your father's house, to a land which I will show you. I will make you into a great nation and I will bless you and magnify your name and you shall be a blessing. I will bless those who bless you and curse those who curse you and in you shall all the families of the earth be blessed."⁵ That was all he heard.

Though the biblical text informs us that the speaker of these words was the Lord Himself, the message does not identify its source. Like Abram, many of us modern folk believe in a unitary God and occasionally feel His Presence: when observing scenes of natural grandeur, for instance, or at moments of emotional crisis when we instinctively pray for the touch of His hand. But hearing His voice in your dreams is another thing. Most of us would suspect ourselves of incipient dementia.

That is, if what happened to Abram happened to us, we would lack any context apart from madness in which to interpret it. Abram did not suspect that he was going mad because he did have a context, if perhaps a bewildering one. Men and women of his day had their "personal god," the deity bequeathed by their ancestors. This "god of the fathers" was portable, traveling with a shepherd like Abram from place to place, wherever he went. It brought good fortune. Believers interpreted uncanny coincidences as evidence that the deity was at work, as a communication from the supernal realm. If Julian Jaynes is right, men and women in Mesopotamia literally "heard" the voice of their god—emanating, as they, of course, could not know, from the right side of their brain. But Abram had never heard a god voice, or the voice of God, until this night. In Jaynes's terminology, he was "conscious." The only voice in his head was Abram's own voice. Perhaps the history of humanity until Abram, twenty generations as the Bible tells it, may be understood as the genealogy of consciousness, introduced by God when He infused a soul into Adam and Eve. Jaynes's timeline, with consciousness dawning from about 3000 B.C., would support such an interpretation. Unlike the "unconscious" folk around them, the direct descendants of the first couple, beginning with Cain and Abel, were then conscious and heard no voices from their own brains, but only, if they were prophets, the voice of God Himself. To his astonishment, Abram now heard that voice.

The following day, in awe, he pondered the words of God. What was this about a "great nation" descending from him? And about the "blessing" he would become? Abram soon realized that he himself had become a "blessing": a source of blessing, which he could bestow on whomever he chose. The Midrash credits him with acquiring the power to heal the sick and to cause barren women to conceive. This didn't require that he lay hands on the patient, only that the sick or the barren *look* at him, a capacity distinct, it would seem, from the power of the magic stone he possessed that also had some capacity to heal. There are even accounts of ships, about to sink in the Mediterranean, that were saved because Abram looked out to sea and blessed them. Tradition is giving us a portrait not only of a wandering preacher but of an itinerant wonder-worker.[6]

These promises God made were clearly central to whatever mission He had set out for Abraham. Surely, too, the patriarch reasoned, the command to leave Haran had something to do with a mysterious picture of an unknown mountain in an unknown land, the land of Canaan, that had lately become fixed in his mind. Nachmanides suggests that even before Terach and his family arrived at Haran, the outlandish idea of migrating to Canaan had entered Abram's consciousness.[7] Though a major trade highway ran along the coast of the land of Canaan, down through today's Tel Aviv and Gaza, the interior of the land was a barbarous place. Western Semites departed from this hinterland for big cities of the north and east. A man who had tasted the metropolis of Ur or even the lesser but still significant city of Haran did not up and move to Canaan. That is, unless he was gripped by a vision.

We can begin to define our understanding of the idea that had Abram in its grasp. It seems unlikely that Canaan per se was his goal. When there eventually came God's order that he should depart Haran immediately, the commandment was notable for its terrifying vagueness. God did not tell Abram where to go—just that he must get out now. This is what led Maimonides, following Scripture's narrative rather than that of the midrashim, to number this command as Abram's very first trial—making a neat pair with his last, the Akedah (Binding) of Isaac, on which he and Rashi agree. To both trials, the Lord called Abram in exactly the same language: "Go!"

Rashi has Abram, when he departs, heading not for Canaan so much as for a certain mountain in Canaan, a mountain he had never laid eyes on before and whose name and location he did not know.[8] Let us speculate that the vision in Abram's mind was not of a land, but of that mountain.

It was not a large mountain. Probably it didn't count as a real mountain at all, just a flat-topped hill in a region of hills, speckled with pine trees and with deep valleys on its sides. In one valley, to its south, a town had been built next to a spring. Though the rest of the sky was clear and bright, above this single elevation a cloud hung as if tethered. When he closed his eyes and looked closely at the image, Abram thought he could make out, on top of the mountain under the cloud, the ruins of a stone altar. He kept these thoughts from his disciples.

Mental images of lofty, cloud-circled mountains are well and good. But in the quiet of his own soul, which with its terrors and doubts a leader never shares with his followers, Abram also considered a dreadful possibility. What he had accomplished in life so far, the shepherding of his congregation of believers, was being endangered by this great southward exodus from the land of Mesopotamia. Based at Haran, he was an effective spiritual guide. His students knew where to find him with their questions and crises. Word of his teaching traveled beyond the borders of the city, and spiritual pilgrims from elsewhere in Mesopotamia had no trouble finding Abram if they wished to go sit with him and learn. What would happen now? The Talmud emphasizes the material and spiritual costs of travel. Moving from place to place is a traumatic experience, so difficult that God regards it as a kind of trial, an experience of such harsh unpleasantness as to effect repentance and avert the consequences of sin.[9] Abram was subjecting not only himself but his family and faithful to this trial. What would he have to offer his followers in a new land, where their lives would have to begin afresh? God presumably was in favor of Abram's bringing in "converts" to the new faith. Yet what He had commanded could render all of Abram's efforts futile and absurd.

Decades in the future the patriarch would be faced with another trial that likewise threatened to empty all the meaning from the story of his life. However, in the face of absurdity, now and later, Abram had the consolation of God's promise. At Haran, and sixty-two years later at the trial of the Binding of Isaac, God assures the patriarch that through him the families of man will be blessed.[10] It is an assurance not only of physical but of meaningful survival. Not only would the patriarch live through his trials; more important, other people would have the purpose of their own lives clarified and enriched by the record of his deeds.[11]

Abram's dream vision, the commandment to "Go!," occurs in the first verse of the *parshah* of *Lech L'chah*. With those two words, meaning literally "Go for yourself" or "Go unto yourself," God had abruptly overturned Abram's accomplishments as a missionary to date. The challenge now thrust on him at age seventy-five was to journey to a distant land and reestablish his mission in a very different place from Mesopotamia, among a different people, less civilized—indeed, balanced on the edge of barbarism—speaking a different language and practicing a different religion. We must try to imagine how deadly tired we would feel if, after three-quarters of a century of living, we were to be told to uproot ourselves and start our life's work all over again. This was to be the overarching and overwhelming challenge of Abram's next twenty-four years, and the focus of *Lech L'chah*. Would we despair, or would we gamely get up on our shaky old legs and set ourselves out on the road? If we resolved to make the journey and get down to the business of restarting our existence in this faraway place, would we succeed or fail? Having arrived, would we discover that the challenge was simply too much for our exhausted body and mind?

These were Abram's thoughts. Yet after his dream, whatever trepidation he felt, the patriarch immediately gathered up his family and departed Haran, heading southwest. He took Sarai and his disciples, but not his father or mother, for they remained attached to the spiritual paths of their homeland. Many of his disciples also stayed behind. There was a falling-off of their numbers as the vast majority declined to go with their spiritual leader to Canaan. Despite Rambam's claim numbering Abram's followers in the tens of thousands, the thirteenth-century rabbinic work *Sefer Hayashar* preserves a tradition that when Abram ultimately left Haran, it was with a group of only seventy-two adherents. This could not have surprised him. It's one thing to follow a teacher who lives in your town, quite another to follow him through the desert and settle with him among distant barbarians.

Abram also took Lot, who besides being his brother Haran's boy was Sarai's brother. The *Zohar,* principal text of Jewish mysticism, notes that Abram had a feeling about Lot. The younger man was trouble, and would succeed in causing Abram great anxiety in just a short time, placing his uncle in peril of his life. But Abram sensed there was a role his nephew would come to fill, an important role if a painful one.

With the patriarch's flocks in tow, humans and animals, the journey went slowly. The party had to cross the Euphrates, which could be accomplished by taking a barge or by fording across when the water was low.[12] The crossing of the Euphrates must have been a momentous occasion because the word "Hebrew," Ivri, alludes to it. The root means "to cross to the opposite side," for Abram is the ancestor of the Hebrew people who crossed the great river and, metaphorically, came to stand in opposition to the world-view of his contemporaries.

Abram first traveled toward Palmyra, an oasis city above the Syrian Desert, then farther southwest toward Damascus.[13] Along this route, he could count on passing a settlement every twenty miles or so, so supplies of water were never more than a day's journey apart.[14]

Apart from this general picture of his itinerary, we don't know how direct Abram's path was from Haran to Canaan. Nachmanides pictures him wandering from country to country until God at last told him to stop wandering, for he had arrived.[15] There must have been considerable apprehensiveness among his followers, for their leader could not tell them precisely where he was headed.

At last, however, he entered the Holy Land at a narrow, rocky passage between the mountains and the Mediterranean. Called the Ladder of Tyre, it is a series of promontories rising like the steps of a ladder between the coastal cities of Acre and Tyre. None of these peaks were the mountain Abram sought.

Just to the south, toward Acre, is a fertile plain where he was impressed by the local people assiduously tending their fields—oranges or lemons, almonds or figs. An almost contemporary account by an exiled Egyptian official, about 1970 B.C., gives a compelling description of the richness of the land Abram was entering: "Figs were in it, and grapes. It had more wine than water. Plentiful was its honey, abundant its olives. Every [kind of] fruit was on its trees. Barley was there, and emmer. There was no limit to any [kind of] cattle."[16]

Understandably Abram prayed, "May my portion be in this land!"[17]

Who were the industrious farmers Abram met? This was Canaan; and the Bible, in most translations, notes at this point in the narrative that "the Canaanite was then [az] in the land."[18] This is a strange aside, because at the time of Moses, to whom authorship of Genesis is ascribed, the Canaanites were also in the land, and the present verse appears to speak from the perspective of a time when they were no longer there, having been assimilated, driven out, or exterminated. The modern critics leap on this as proof that the Pentateuch was composed long after the supposed lifetime of its alleged author. Actually this is a case where the oral tradition, overlooked by the critics, overlaps with historical research.

The Jewish sages long ago caught the seeming contradiction. Rashi says the verse means that in Abram's time the Canaanites were "in the process of conquering the land of Israel, [taking it] from the offspring of [Noah's son] Shem."[19] The Hebrew word usually translated "then," *az,* would thus mean something more like "by then." In other words, *by this point* the Canaanites had arrived and begun their conquest. Rabbi Abraham Ibn Ezra (Spanish, 1089–1164) comments that either Rashi is right about this or that "there is a secret [here], and the wise one will keep silent." The Bible critics love this little gloss, suggesting, they argue, that even the pious Ibn Ezra realized that a hand other than that of Moses wrote parts of the Pentateuch.

I am not sure what Ibn Ezra did mean, but Rashi is certainly right. Nachmanides elsewhere amplifies the French sage's meaning. At the time described in our verse, a group designated as Canaanites had arrived in the land. In the next chapter of Genesis, they are joined by another group, the Perizzites: " . . . and the Canaanite and Perizzite were then living in the land."[20] Both peoples were seminomadic tent dwellers, driving their cattle from pasture to pasture every year or two.[21] If the Perizzites built permanent settlements at all, these would have been mere unwalled villages; for their name shares a root with the Hebrew word *perazot,* meaning "unfortified settlements." Says Ramban, it was only in years to come that there appeared Amorites and Jebusites, two other biblical ethnic designations. A chapter later in the Bible, the Amorites appear.[22] By the time of Moses, the Pentateuch speaks of seven distinct Canaanite peoples—"Canaanite" being the generic designation as well as the name of a particular ethnic group.[23]

Historians generally accept just such a picture of gradual conquest. Wave upon wave of outsiders entered Canaan and grabbed real estate. At the end of the third millennium, a few centuries before Abram's time, nomadic invaders sacked the cities of the land. The invaders chose to live not in the ruins of these cities, but in the open—in *perazot,* unwalled settlements, just like the Bible's Perizzites. Only in the nineteenth century B.C. did Amorites, nomadic agriculturists, appear on the scene, about the time of Abram's entrance into Canaan—again, a very close approximation to the account of Bible and tradition.[24]

Skeptical scholars lately have questioned whether the Amorites really were invaders of Canaan. More likely, it's said, they were Canaanites by ancestry who moved back and forth between a settled and a nomadic existence. Either way, to the Canaanite folk who stayed settled, Amorite desert nomads in the process of settling down would have *appeared* as invaders. In other words, Scripture gets it right. One skeptic, expressing the view of many colleagues, has sniffed that the Bible demonstrates "substantial ignorance of the ethnic and political situation in pre-Israelite Palestine."[25] In this case, when the text is understood with the aid of oral tradition, the charge of "ignorance" is substantially weakened.

Does the Pentateuch, especially after Genesis, also get it right in its portrayal of the Canaanite peoples as morally decrepit in the extreme? From the moment of Abram's entrance in the land to the day of his death, the patriarch never has any major difficulties with them. The midrash about his finding them virtuously at work in the fields, there by the Ladder of Tyre, is noteworthy. By the time of Moses, God is found warning the Israelite people to guard against imitating Canaanite ways. For the land of Israel, a place of very delicate moral sensibility, has by then become "contaminated" with Canaanite degeneracy and will soon "vomit up" its aboriginal inhabitants.[26]

Today Bible scholars and archaeologists don't go in for passing moral judgment on ancient peoples, so their descriptions of the Canaanites tend to be somewhat anodyne. Of what we know about the aborigines of Canaan, most is drawn from three sources: their pottery shards, such debris being nearly indestructible even over millennia; their graves; and certain religious and bureaucratic texts found at the Syrian tell Ras Shamra, or Ugarit, in 1928. Dating from around 1400 B.C., the Ugaritic material postdates Abram by a few hundred years. But the culture that produced Ugarit certainly existed in his time.

The precise religion reflected in the Ugaritic texts was that of Ugarit, not of Canaan per se. Each Canaanite locality had its own special institutions and customs. But the pantheon of gods, more than thirty deities, was approximately constant up and down the land. At its head was El, the disinterested, ethereal father and creator god who lived at the source of two mythical rivers. Curiously El is reported to have castrated both his own father and himself. His consort was Asherah, and he had a brother called Dagon, who conceived the storm god Baal and Baal's sister, the war goddess Anat. Asherah wanted to seduce her nephew Baal, but failed. Meanwhile Baal and

Anat were quite close and even became lovers. In Canaan, incest was not seen as deeply problematic.[27] Of course, brother-sister relationships like theirs often result in a certain, shall we say, tension. Once, when Anat took on the form of a heifer, Baal proceeded to rape her no fewer than seventy-seven times.[28]

The "Baal epic," a centerpiece of Ugaritic literature, concerns the siblings' death-defying love for each other. Baal gets into a feud with the god of death, Mot, who kills Baal. Distraught, Baal's sister/lover storms the underworld, slays Mot, grinds his body up, scatters his corpse like corn, and restores the dead Baal to life, in the process establishing the myth of the dying and reviving god. The myth was central to the fertility cult of Baal, which draws a parallel between the rejuvenated deity and nature, which revives in the spring. For Anat, the battle with Mot was nothing out of the ordinary. On another occasion, she slaughtered the whole human race (evidently there were survivors): "Then she ties [some human] heads to her back, [some] hands to her girdle, and wades up to her knees . . . in human gore."[29]

It is not an attractive theology, and its practice was no more so. Offerings of sheep and cattle were central, as in the later Temple cult at Jerusalem. Again as at Jerusalem, some sacrifices were rendered as "holocausts" in which the entire animal was consumed in the flames, others as communion offerings, in which only blood and fats and certain organs were offered up while the community ate the rest. The difference between Jewish and Canaanite sacrifice was that in the former the purpose was to draw closer to God, rather than to feed the deity. In Hebrew, the word *korban*, "offering," is derived from the root KRV, "to draw near." Some Canaanite altars can still be seen. Most impressive is the huge oval one at Megiddo in central Israel, six feet high and eight to ten yards in diameter, with seven steps leading up to the top, which was already centuries old in Abram's day.

In visiting it, as I did, one hardly gets a sense of what Canaanite worship would have been like in its gore-dripping drama. Megiddo, also known as Armageddon, is just another perfectly maintained site of the Israeli National Parks Authority, all khaki stones and brown dirt and roped-off viewing platforms with (nowadays, as visits have thinned due to terrorism) the occasional tourist here and there wandering around. You do, however, get a sense of how a typical sacred area would have been laid out in a Canaanite settlement: the altar flanked by three adjoining temples, each on the simple plan of a main hall reached through a porticoed porch. The whole area is identified as a *bamah,* an elevated platform or "high place" of pagan worship, though at Megiddo one actually looks down upon it from a higher station covered by a tent to block out the raging sun. Besides the altar, other religious monuments, memorials to persons or to encounters with gods, were the standing stone *(matzevah)* and the upright wooden pillar *(asherah)* associated, respectively, with the male and female deities.[30]

Overall the function of the Canaanite faith was not to perfect the human being inwardly or outwardly, but to bribe the gods, imagined as possessing all the moral refinement of their human worshipers, to bestow fertility and prosperity. There was no conception of reward in the world to come: the afterlife was anticipated as uniformly drab and depressing for everyone.[31] Morally the cult was not high-toned. Human sacrifice was apparently practiced on certain occasions, when babies were buried alive at the sanctification of a new building. Priests of Baal enjoyed the ritual of engaging in sexual congress with livestock.[32] Ritual prostitutes, male and female, were available in connection with the fertility cult.[33]

As for the ordinary Canaanite in the street, though one can draw few solid conclusions, he could not have gone unaffected by the perversity of his ancestral faith. No wonder the Book of Leviticus introduces its catalog of sexual sins with a warning to the Israelite nation to steer clear of "the practice of the land of Canaan to which I bring you."[34]

However, since some of the above data are taken from the evidence of a time some centuries after Abram, let us assume, as God would later tell the patriarch, that in Abram's day "the iniquity of the Amorite [was] not yet complete."[35] The moral and spiritual civilization of the place had not by this point broken down entirely. In fact, as God directed Abram's steps steadily to the south, far from keeping him away from centers of Canaanite deviancy, their temples and high places, He guided him straight for strategically located cultic sites. At least that is what archaeologists suggest about the two localities to which Abram next arrived, in the heart of Canaan.

The party cut inland till it reached "the place of Shechem,"[36] adjacent to modern Nablus, in a valley between the biblical mountains Ebal and Gerizim—neither of which, one bald, the other full of greenery, was to be Abram's mountain.

An ominous atmosphere fills the valley of Nablus today. The traditional tomb of Joseph, Abram's great-grandson, is on the outskirts of town, and in the late twentieth century the tomb complex housed a Jewish yeshiva guarded by an Israeli garrison—an object of loathing for the local Arab population. My own visit to the tomb required a short trip from an Israeli military base by bulletproof bus. The spare whitewashed interior included a grave marker covered with a simple cloth and shelf with Jewish prayer books and other holy works. Then, in 2000, the Israelis withdrew and a mob of Palestinians burned the yeshiva and garrison buildings, painting the tomb an Islamic green. A rabbi who had taught there came to view the ruins and was abducted, tortured, and murdered, his broken body abandoned in a nearby cave. Not long after, the village built on top of the tell, Balata, a suburb of Nablus, became infamous as the birthplace of a gruesomely violent Palestinian faction, the Al Aksa Martyrs' Brigade, with a specialty of sending suicide bombers to blow up Israeli civilians.

It's all in a day's work for Shechem, a city with an aura so forbidding that, well before the worst of its history, Abram sensed it. At first glance, it must have looked benign enough to him. We see the Shechem valley as it appeared then, seemingly pristine and innocent, in the writing of a nineteenth-century American traveler, John Lloyd Stephens, who visited and wrote: "The valley . . . was, if possible, more beautiful by morning than by evening light, shaded by groves of figs, olives, almonds, and apricots in full bloom, and bound by lofty mountains, with a clear and beautiful stream winding and murmuring through its center." Gerizim and Ebal "tower[ed] like lofty walls." In Joseph's tomb, Stephens found "a white-bearded Israelite, kneeling . . . and teaching a rosy-cheeked boy (his descendant of the fourth generation) the beautiful story of Joseph and his brethren."[37]

But soon Abram felt a chill, an intimation of evil yet to occur. The Talmud records an opinion that Shechem is "a place predestined for punishment." The word for "punishment," *puranut*, is built on the Hebrew root that means "to tear." Time and again in this place, brother was torn from brother, or sister from brothers. The Talmud gives three instances from the Bible. At Shechem, Abram's great-granddaughter Dinah was abducted by the local population and raped by their prince. Her brothers Simon and

Levy, sons of the patriarch Jacob, took revenge on the city. First a tribal alliance of Jacob's family with the people of Shechem was cemented, including the proviso that the male residents of the city be circumcised. Then while the latter were recovering from their surgery, Simon and Levy slaughtered the inhabitants en masse. Not long afterward, Dinah's brother Joseph was in the vicinity when his brothers sought first to kill him, then decided to sell him to slave traders instead. Much later, also at Shechem, the Israelite people disastrously split their royal house in two, becoming the rival states of Judah and Israel.[38]

Abram himself had been torn from his family. More than this, he was troubled by the prophetic intuition that his descendants would suffer terrible sorrows here. He prayed for them.[39] For this, he needed an appropriate sanctuary.

Besides being the man who would be the founder of three monotheistic faiths, Abram was a man of his time. And when such men wished to propitiate their god, they built altars. There were various kinds, natural and manmade. One might simply clear off a rock already in the earth, hew a rock to a desired shape, pile rocks on top of one another, or build a more complex structure. An altar typically formed the center of a sanctuary.[40] Abram wanted to build one for God at Shechem, but he was afraid of the reaction this would prompt.[41]

There were locals hereabouts, Hurrians, another of the groups making up Canaan's ethnically mixed population.[42] Shechem had been occupied for hundreds of years, if not for more than a thousand, but the urban phase of its history was just starting to coalesce. Shechem was probably still unwalled, its most notable feature a built-up platform of earth surmounted by a large building, perhaps a temple. (The cyclopean wall of huge boulders marking the northwest border of Tell Balata, visible today, is from a slightly later period.) It was a significant town in regional politics. The contemporary Egyptian pharaoh Sesostris III knew of "a foreign country of which the name was Sekmem," an apparent reference to Shechem.[43] In contemplating the act of setting up his own altar outside the town, which might appear as a rival to its main sanctuary, Abram must have feared the Middle Bronze Age equivalent of modern Palestinians sacking the tomb of Joseph and lynching its rabbi. He had tested the resistance of Mesopotamians to his radical concept of one God, but Canaanites were an unknown quantity.

Yet these were not the dementedly wicked Canaanites of Moses' time. Abram consulted his soul; and as had not happened since he left Haran, prophecy came to him again. This time the experience was not a dream, as he had had at Haran, but a vision.[44] The Bible says that "the Lord appeared to Abram."[45] We don't know what Abram *saw,* but the words he heard were these: "To your offspring I will give the land."[46] He knew then that if he built an altar, he would not be molested. And something still more wonderful: he, the barren Abram, would have offspring. In a joyful mood, he built the altar and prayed to God.

The company presently continued its southward journey. From Shechem south toward Jerusalem and on to Beersheba on the border of the Negev desert is the land in the Bible depicted as the primary address of the patriarchs. It is where they did most of their wandering. At this time, the mountainous, central region in Canaan was prime territory for seminomads, forested and sparsely peopled. Later nomadic groups chose other areas to wander in.[47]

Not that it was easy country to traverse. Egyptians conducting military campaigns in the thirteenth century B.C. brought back reports of "the peculiar hardships of a campaign in Palestine . . . , the narrow rough passes where chariots had to be dismantled and transported on baggage animals, the rocks which cut the sandals to pieces, the thorns which rip the clothes, and the scrub which harbors hardy guerrillas. The bedouin are constantly pilfering, and night raids are made on the camp."[48]

Ten miles north of the city today called Jerusalem, Abram stopped and pitched camp. It was again a mountain that caught the patriarch's eye. His company had halted on or near an elevation situated between the sites of two cities, both of which archaeologists confirm had been established long before Abram's time. To his west was Beth-el. Between 1927 and 1934, Albright dug up what he believed was Beth-el, today called Tell Beitin, a city first occupied in the twenty-first century B.C.[49]

It had a city wall and a gate. We know something about the feel of such a settlement in the Middle Bronze Age. Houses were rectangular affairs of clay or brick held together with clay mortar, plastered with mud. They were small, usually no longer than the single timber beam that held up the light roofing of wood covered with earth. But it was not the custom to spend much time in the house itself. Housework was done outdoors. When it was cold, a fire might be lit in a hearth. Wealthier dwellings could have an upper story. Houses spread out organically according to no town plan—not that there was much room to spread out in—like tightly twisted bowels. The place probably smelled like bowels, too: there was no drainage, no system for disposal of garbage. Refuse was heaped up outside the houses or outside the town walls to be nosed through by dogs.[50]

To Abram's east was another city, or anyway the ruins of one: called Ai, which had flourished in the previous millennium but was sacked in the twenty-second century and at this time had not been rebuilt. Its somber name in Hebrew means "the heap of ruins."[51]

On the mountaintop between Beth-el and Ai, Abram established another sanctuary, another altar. And he "invoked the Lord by Name"—meaning that he invoked the Name in the hearing of his new neighbors, for either God or Abram chose both Shechem and Beth-el as strategic locales for relaunching Abram's evangelical mission. Both were at principal crossroads where a main road running north-south intersected another main road running east-west, making them well suited to maximize the potential number of spiritually starved Canaanites Abram might reach.[52]

One imagines this as a happy time for him and Sarai. He had God's word that he would conceive children, after all. That God's promise included Sarai as the mother of his "offspring" seemed doubtful. After all, she was sixty-five years old. Abram loved her nonetheless, remaining ever the chivalrous husband. On the verse here stating that Abram "pitched his tent" near Beth-el, Rashi comments that the patriarch was always careful to pitch his wife's tent before his own.[53] In biblical parlance, a "tent" stands euphemistically for a man's physical relationship with his wife. Rashi means that, despite the advanced age of both spouses, Abram was an active and considerate lover, attending to his wife's pleasure before his own.

Whoever was destined to be the mother of Abram's offspring, those descendants would live in the land for which he had prayed to God when he first saw it. So it came to him as a shock when indications began to be felt of an impending disaster, a disaster that would force Abram from the land.

A word began to pass from mouth to mouth among Abram's compatriots. It was a dire word. The word was "famine."

For a person of the Middle Bronze Age, "famine" had the same resonance of terror as "cancer" or "AIDS" today.[54] A modern American can find a twenty-four-hour supermarket packed with food within a ten-minute drive, so he has difficulty imaging the dread evoked in other times and places at the prospect of death by starvation. Abram noted the warning signs. Perhaps the seasonal rains had failed to come to this land of dry, rocky hills and mountains. Or perhaps insects had blighted the crops. Either way, responsible as he was not only for his own wife and brother-in-law but also for his disciples and their families, he resolved to leave the land God had so recently promised him.

This was to be Abram's fourth trial (by Rashi's count; his second by Rambam's). As Rashi states it, God's purpose was "to test [Abram and determine] whether he would question [*y'harher*] the words of the Holy One, Blessed Be He, Who had told him to go to the land of Canaan [in the first place], and now advised him to leave it."[55] Rashi's term meaning "to question" or "to doubt" is built on a two-letter root, "heh-resh," HR, which also means "mountain," *har*. The Hebrew word designating the danger to which this test subjected Abram, namely *hirhur*, or "questioning," can have the additional connotation of immoral fantasy. An unmarried man, says Maimonides in a telling usage, is subject to the danger of *hirhur:* "fantasy," a wandering sexual imagination.[56] On a mountain, a person may fantasize that he has a sort of God's-eye view of the world. Sometimes his vision does indeed coincide with God's view. That is part of the reason that Abram had been seeking the magical mountain whose image was impressed in his mind's eye, but which so far had eluded him. It promised such a divine view. At other times, the view from above is misleading: it makes you think you see things as God does, when really this is an illusion born of your isolation from the rest of the world. What God wanted to test in Abram was the patriarch's faith: whether Abram would imagine himself able to see the world from God's vantage point, when he had not yet been granted that privilege. Did he trust his own intellect, or did he trust God? Abram had just been told by the Lord Himself that this land would belong to his children. Now, indirectly by way of the approaching famine, the Lord was telling him to get out. Had the patriarch second-guessed his Deity, questioning the apparent contradiction, he would have failed the test.

But Abram did not fail. Suppressing his awareness that God had seemingly countermanded Himself, he once more gathered his community together. Their next destination, he announced, was to be the land of Egypt.

CHAPTER FIVE

Into the Spiral

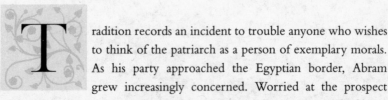radition records an incident to trouble anyone who wishes
to think of the patriarch as a person of exemplary morals.
As his party approached the Egyptian border, Abram
grew increasingly concerned. Worried at the prospect
of the gorgeous Sarai being abducted on entering the country, and of himself being killed so the assailants could get at her, Abram hit upon a two-pronged strategy. Rather than cross into Egypt as husband and wife, they
would identify themselves as brother and sister. No one kills a man to get at
his sister, however radiantly beautiful. Rather, the brother will be feted and
flattered, giving Abram plenty of time to pretend to deliberate in choosing
a suitor for his "sister"—maybe enough time for the famine to dissipate.

Once it was safe to go home, "brother" and "sister" would flee back to Canaan.

Perhaps because he was not entirely confident of this plan, Abram had a second. This was to keep Sarai hidden from Egyptian eyes as long as he could. As the Midrash narrates, the party had a box of some kind with them big enough for a human being to fit into—a coffin, it sounds like. Abram asked Sarai to get in. Against her better judgment she complied, and he shut the top upon her and locked it.

At one of the fortresses along the Wall of the Ruler, perhaps the frontier station called the Way of Horus,[1] the second strategy was put to the test. The Midrash records the ensuing dialogue. A customs officer asked Abram to pay duty on whatever was in that locked box, to which Abram agreed. The officer then initiated a curious game of Twenty Questions. "You've got clothes in there," he said. Abram agreed to pay the tax on clothes. "No," said the official, "I believe you're hiding gold." Abram agreed to pay the tax on gold. The official was now getting suspicious: "Actually, I think it's silk you've got in there." Abram agreed to pay the tax on silk. "Well I bet it's not that at all. It's gemstones!" Finally, exasperated, the officer demanded: "No, all these are impossible. But rather open the box now and show us what's inside!" Abram was in no position to refuse—at which point the lid of the box was lifted, and Sarai stood up. Her loveliness had never been so brilliant as it was at the moment. The Midrash states: "And all the land of Egypt shone with her beauty."[2] Induced by the Lord, it was a supernatural radiance, the first clue to Abram and to us that He intended this sojourn to add up to something more significant than a mere flight from hunger.

Events unfolded swiftly. On hand were certain courtiers of Pharaoh. (At this point in history, the king of Egypt was not yet called Pharaoh, literally "Great House"—an idiomatic expression like calling the American president "the White House," as in "the White House said this morning." The usage became current under the Eighteenth Dynasty, midway between the times of Abram and Moses. Genesis uses it because, by the time it was written, regardless of who you think first wrote the book down, the Egyptian monarch was already called by this familiar title.) These pharaonic dignitaries took Abram by surprise, reporting the strange incident to their king—though he had perceived the luminous glow of Sarai even from miles away in his palace.

In the role of Sarai's "brother," Abram could probably have fended off the advances of any ordinary Egyptian, but he hadn't counted on Pharaoh himself taking an interest. This is just what happened: Sarai was abducted and conveyed to Pharaoh's palace.

In allowing this to happen, Abram had committed a "great sin" against his wife—so says Nachmanides.[3] And his judgment was shared, incidentally, by no less an expert in proper conduct than Queen Victoria. Having been told on her deathbed that she would soon meet Abraham in Heaven, Queen Victoria vigorously denied this; she insisted that Abraham, the scoundrel, would merit no such eternal reward. We need to understand how Abram got into such a morally ambivalent situation.

First of all, why flee specifically to Egypt? Two reasons. First, because the famine that was approaching affected Canaan but not Egypt.[4] But why not go back the way Abram had come, to Mesopotamia? Because it was the established pattern of the time that starving Asiatics repaired to Egypt for sustenance. This was not due to any liberality of spirit among the people of the Nile land. In the twentieth century B.C., Egypt had built a string of fortresses, the Wall of the Ruler, on its eastern border to keep out bedouin and other unwanted tribesmen. But the border was porous. "To keep them alive and to keep their cattle alive," as a frontier official noted, the unwashed hordes were now and then allowed to pass through.[5] So Abram and company took to the road.

Not literally to *the road*. Abram's destination meant passing through the Negev desert. There were two ways to go. One took you by way of the Mediterranean coast. But deep sand drifts there made travel by donkey impossible, and we assume that Abram's party relied on the typical pack animal of their day, the donkey. They opted, then, for the inland desert route.

A top-grade "black donkey" could travel up to twenty-five miles a day. Yet scholars have debated how long it took Abram to reach Egypt. Some say a mere five to eight days; others, weeks or months.[6] The question depends in part on the resources available to the traveler. Abram would have made his way from one desert well to the next. The names of these wells, which are known, conjure the romance of the desert, especially for those who have never experienced such a place except in artistic photographs. From Ain

Quadeis and Ain el-Qudeirat (the biblical Kadesh-Barnea), Abram passed on to Bir Auja, Bir Birein, Bir Reseisiyah, Bir Hafir, Ain Mureifiq, Bir Rekhmeh, Bir Asluj, Bir el-Mishash, and so on: the Way of the Wells.[7] But this makes the journey sound much easier than it was. Travel through any desert on foot or by donkey is deadly serious business, requiring much careful planning. You have to know precisely where you are going and what supplies of food and water you will encounter on the way.

Obviously if there are settlements on your route, so much the better. Albright's student Nelson Glueck used this observation as a way to fix, to his own satisfaction, the narrow window of time during which Abram could have found it possible to travel from Canaan to Egypt. According to his own many years of digging in the Negev, Glueck decided that of all the centuries when Abram might have lived, the only time when there were thriving settlements in the northern and central Negev was the twenty-first through nineteenth centuries B.C. This makes a rough match with the chronology offered by Jewish tradition, which fixes Abram's march to Egypt in the eighteenth century, around the year 1737 B.C. The oral tradition indeed pictures Abram as staying in human habitations along the way.[8]

His company arrived at the frontier, looking like many another mob of "sand people," as the haughty Egyptians called such folk. The famous Beni Hasan mural, found painted on the wall of a tomb on the Nile between Memphis and Thebes, depicts a group like this within a century or two of Abram's time. So the sartorial details are right. This group of Asiatics has come to Egypt to trade black eye cosmetic called stibium, bringing back the staple foodstuffs in which Egypt was rich. Their leader, one might say their patriarch, is identified as Abishar, "Father of Righteousness," a Semitic name built on the same stem as "Abram." They look classically Semitic: dark hair, long noses, the men bearded, the women longhaired, their hair neatly restrained by a band. They wear multicolored woolen frocks, the same for women as for men, though the women's are longer. The men are armed, bearing composite bows, spears, and maces. Altogether they are rather handsome, and we can assume that Abram looked as they do.

The good looks of Semitic travelers in contradistinction to that of the Egyptians forms the background to a shrewd indirect observation in the oral tradition about men and women. We know that Egyptians were darker than Semites: as a modern historian writes, they were "short, slight, long-headed, and dark, a mongrel of Africa, Asia, and the Mediterranean."[9] Still more bracingly insensitive, the Midrash calls them "black and ugly."[10] Observing the scruffy Egyptians and noting the beauty of his wife, Abram became worried. To Sarai he said something peculiar, generally translated as "Behold, now I know that you are a woman of beautiful appearance."[11] Citing the midrashic collection *Tanchuma,* Rashi observes that "until now he had not recognized her [beauty]."[12] Evidently as Abram neared the border, the short, slight, long-headed, and dark Egyptians gawked at the svelte, gorgeous Sarai, and Abram noted their stares. It is a fact about men that they often fail to fully appreciate the beauty of a wife or girlfriend till another man starts making eyes at her.

Around Abram's entrance into Egypt, the tradition depicts an atmosphere of vague disquiet, a threatening disorder. If Abram was concerned that his beautiful wife would be seized, this fear doesn't quite square with our accustomed conception of Egypt, acquired in museum Egyptian Antiquities departments, as an august land of stately, even supernatural orderliness. By the time the patriarch arrived there, Egyptian dynastic civilization was more than a thousand years old. The pyramids were already ancient. In such a place, do they snatch your good-looking wife at the border?

Egypt had fallen into rough times. The country had established its first dynasty around 3100 B.C. The pyramids were constructed under the reign of the Old Kingdom (2700–2200 B.C.), which includes Dynasties 4 to 6. There followed a period of political weakness and disorganization, Dynasties 7 to 11, the First Intermediate Period, from which the land recovered fully under the Twelfth Dynasty, around 1950. By the time of Abram's sojourn, the gloriously stable Twelfth had dissolved into the radioactively unstable Thirteenth Dynasty, its capital in the vicinity of Memphis, later retreating south to Thebes. With the Twelfth Dynasty, it is possible to say which pharaoh ruled when—though, as we noted in Chapter 3, serious questions have been raised about the conventionally accepted chronology of Egyptian history.[13] The Thirteenth, on the other hand, was so chaotic, subject to counterclaims and rivalries of start-up dynasties like the concurrent Fourteenth up north in the Delta region at Xois, that it is impossible even to guess which pharaoh reigned in Abram's day, or which dynastic regime he would have encountered.

It is interesting to observe that all this squabbling among the Egyptians themselves was having the effect of softening up the country for an invasion from Semitic Asia, by the so-called Hyksos (literally "foreign chiefs"), a swarm of Amorites and Canaanites. This cataclysmic event was perceived in antiquity as having occurred almost overnight as the easterners suddenly crossed the border and took over the Nile land, building their capital of Avaris in the Delta area around 1730 B.C.: perhaps less than a decade after Abram's visit. At least this is the account of the disaster given by the ancient historian Josephus. It is an intriguing possibility that what set off the invasion was the same famine that sent Abram fleeing Canaan. After all, a midrash depicts it as the worst famine, indeed the only one worthy of the name, since the creation of humanity.[14]

Certainly, as Abram knew it, Egypt was a country in political, social, and moral decay. A conservative place where, even over millennia, religious beliefs were never exactly discarded but rather piled one on top of the other, new gods continually being added to the old pantheon, Egypt nevertheless wasn't static in its spiritual outlook. Over time the moral temper of the people varied from gross, ritual-obsessed materialism, with physical existence the ultimate value—it seems illustrative that the earliest gods were created by the deity Atum in an act of primordial masturbation—to an almost biblical emphasis on moral uprightness. In one extant text of ethical teachings, a father advises his son, "More acceptable is the character of one upright of heart than the [sacrificial] ox of the evildoer."[15] If, then, the alternating poles of Egyptian moral life are designated as cynicism and idealism, we may say that cynicism played a role in the downfall of the once-idealistic Old Kingdom, which led directly into the First Intermediate Period. In the transition from First Intermediate to the Middle Kingdom, historians detect the shift back to idealism.[16]

It follows that the opening of the Second Intermediate Period, Abram's moment in Egyptian history, was a time of cynicism. In the ethical sphere, darkness was falling swifty. A visitor like Abram with a stunningly attractive wife had reason to be worried.

There was no refusing an Egyptian monarch. Though we are probably talking about one of the minor pharaohs of the obscure Fourteenth Dynasty at Xois, which would have been closer to the border than the synchronous Thirteenth farther south at Memphis, even an obscure pharaoh would insist on the honor owed to his office. For he was a god encased in a man's body, so holy that one did not dare speak to him directly, much less touch his divine person.[17] The god-king was also assumed to be omniscient—though in this instance he was unaware that the story told by the Semite with the delicious sister was a lie, that the sister was really the man's wife.

Thus Sarai was taken. Privately she and Abram prayed to God. "Master of the Universe," cried Abram, "is this what comes of the faith I have placed in You?"[18] Our patriarch wasn't the least bit mistreated. The Bible tells us Pharaoh amply rewarded him for making his "sister" available to the king. And there is an almost contemporary account of what it was like to be royally received by Pharaoh. Two centuries before Abram met Pharaoh, an attendant of the king and servant in the royal harem, called Si-nuhe, returned from a long exile in Canaan. When the king, Sen-Usert I, graciously welcomed him back, Si-nuhe wrote an account of being restored to royal favor, which entailed pampering as only a pharaoh's palace can provide:

I was put into the house of a royal son, in which were splendid things. . . . Clothing of royal linen, myrrh, and prime oil of the king and of the nobles whom he loves were in every room. Every butler was [busy] at his duties. Years were made to pass away from my body. I was plucked, and my hair was combed. A load [of dirt] was given to the desert, and my clothes [to] the Sand-Crossers. I was clad in fine linen and anointed with prime oil. I slept on a bed. I gave up the sand to them who are in it, and wood oil to him who is anointed with it. I was given a house which had a garden, which had been in the possession of a courtier. Many craftsmen built it, and all its wood[work] was newly restored. Meals were brought to me from the palace three or four times a day, . . . without ceasing a moment.[19]

Abram got similar treatment. As Genesis records: "And [Pharaoh] treated Abram well for her sake. He [Abram] received flocks and cattle, donkeys and slaves, maidservants and female donkeys, as well as camels."[20] But on this verse the Talmud offers a surprising comment: "A man should always be careful of his wife's honor, for blessing in a man's home is found only for the sake of his wife."[21] This addendum of tradition has an ironic edge. Far from "honoring" Sarai, Abram had put her in a position of grave danger, abducted by a wicked monarch. Hence his "great sin," as Nachmanides puts it.

Not all traditional Jewish commentators agree with the Spanish sage's (and Victoria's) harsh judgment. Radak, for example, thinks Abram would have been wrong either to stay in Canaan or to tell the border officers the truth. Either way he would have been relying on God to save his life by providing a miracle, and one must not "test" God, as it were, by relying on miracles.[22]

Actually Radak, Nachmanides, and Victoria are all correct. Abram had been placed in a position where no matter what he did, he was bound to do wrong. This condition, Jewish tradition tells us, is the legacy of Adam and Eve's sin in the Garden of Eden, an act whose principal effect was to mix up good and evil for the duration of human history, such that nothing a person does can ever be entirely good. In this case, Abram was being rewarded by his evil hosts for the wrong he had done, however unwillingly. The man's bitterness, his self-recriminations, must have been intense.

As Ramban narrates, Sarai remained silent.[23] She had promised Abram to keep their secret. Courtiers had her brought to the palace, at whose entrance she, like other visitors, would have been made to touch her brow to the ground. They escorted her into the private chamber with its great throne, on which sat Pharaoh. Her radiance filled the residence of the king as it had earlier filled the frontier station and the whole land of Egypt. And, says a midrash in *Pirke d'Rabbi Eliezer*, the king fell in love.

Harold Bloom insists that the biblical text, by the author J, means us to understand that Sarai actually became Pharaoh's concubine—that he succeeded in violating her sexually.[24] Not so, according to tradition, which asserts that he proposed matrimony to Sarai, offering her a marriage contract including gold, silver, slaves, and land.[25] Sarai did not tell him that she was already married. She responded with silence, which Pharaoh understood as consent. He approached her, drew very close, perhaps even lay a hand on her skin.

All at once Pharaoh didn't feel very well at all. His eyes began to tear, snot poured from his nose and spittle from his mouth. He heard a sound at his ear: the buzz of a fly, then another fly, and another.[26] Soon flies were buzzing all around him, gravitating from his head down toward his crotch.

A very great pain seized his genitals, and any thought of consummating his lust instantly fled from his mind.

Pharaoh could not have known that an angel, unseen by him or anyone else but Sarai, had entered the room. It had appeared when he came close to the matriarch, and Sarai knew it would do her bidding. The angel asked if he should strike Pharaoh now with a gruesome affliction called *ratan*—"which would make sex difficult for him," comments Rashi. Sarai assented, and not just the king but his courtiers were struck with this plague; even the walls of the residence were suddenly covered with pulsing plague spots.[27] Ten times the angel asked Sarai whether she would have him strike Pharaoh again, and each time she said yes. Ten times the king of Egypt bent over in agony, as if a great whip had come cracking down on him where a man would feel it most.[28] Everyone in the palace would have heard his screams except that they, too, were clenched in agony, or otherwise distracted by the tumorous malignancies that were spreading across the walls. After the tenth jolt of fiery pain, Pharaoh fled the room, leaving Sarai by herself.

When he had recovered some of his poise, Pharaoh returned to the throne room. Sarai was still there, looking at him without pity. By this point, his attendants came running in to check on their lord. All eyes fell on Abram's wife, the only person unaffected by the sudden attack of—what? Pharaoh questioned her, but, recalling Abram's instructions, she still said nothing. The king had by now figured out what was up between the pair of alleged siblings. The plague centering on his male organ was the giveaway: evidently some god was acting as this married woman's protector. It was precisely to stop him from molesting her sexually that he had been subjected to this agony. Pharaoh called for the "brother" to be summoned.

The courtiers found Abram in his luxurious rooms, and the look on their faces informed him that God had struck. They hustled him before Pharaoh, who repeated the enraged question he must have put to Sarai moments before: "What is this you have done to me? Why did you not tell me she is your wife? Why did you tell me 'She is my sister,' so that I took her myself as a wife? So now here is your wife. Take [her] and go!"[29] Like his wife, the patriarch said nothing.

The abduction of his wife, including this interview with Pharaoh, was his fifth trial, according to Rashi (third, according to Rambam). Abram knew he had done wrong, and the Lord wanted him to accept with meekness whatever came of his wrongdoing: this was the test. Since it was his tongue that had got him and Sarai into trouble in the first place, now he held his tongue.

Sarai was silent, too, but in her case silence followed from a combination of wishing not to disobey Abram, on the one hand, and contempt for Pharaoh on the other.

Impatient that he had yet to hear a word from either Abram or Sarai, Pharaoh decided the best course of action was not merely to let them go but forcibly to *get them out of there* as soon as possible. But as Abram and Sarai were being led out, the king was struck not with another plague, but with an emotion. Of remorse? Maybe fear, that their protector deity might punish him again if the king did not make up for his offense. Or was it love for Sarai?

According to a legal precept known in the Near East at the time, if a man took away another man's wife, even though he had not known she was married, he was bound to pay a fine to the aggrieved party.[30] Perhaps acting from genuine feelings of regret or affection, or perhaps merely as the pawn of a deity unknown to him, Pharaoh now volunteered to Abram a very great fine. First of all, the king announced, he would allow Abram to keep the menagerie of animals and slaves he had already received from Pharaoh's hand. The king granted to Sarai all the money, slaves, and land that he had promised her as a wedding gift. On top of this, in an act that would have ramifications beyond anything the principals could envision that day, he gave a final gift to Sarai. Not a slave either. He called for Hagar to be brought before him.

A young Egyptian woman, attired in royal garb, soon appeared by the side of her father, the king. Pharaoh gestured to her. "Better," he said, "that my daughter be a servant in this house," meaning the house of Abram, "than a lady in another house."[31]

Hagar became a servant of Sarai. When the large group of travelers departed the land of Egypt, as Pharaoh insisted, she was among them. Under ordinary circumstances, Egyptians would have viewed as defilement the idea of handing over an Egyptian princess to Asiatic refugees. Even marrying the king's daughter to a foreign prince would have been out of the question.[32] But when the king has been smitten by *ratan* along with much of his household, and a foreign deity is apparently the cause, it is not an ordinary circumstance.

Pharaoh needed little time to contemplate his stricken body before he arrived at his interpretation. For us, understanding this lurid episode requires deliberation. Various interpreters have used Abram's sojourn in Egypt to illustrate some contradictory lessons.

Believers in the Documentary Hypothesis discern here a confirmation of their belief that various hands composed the Pentateuch many centuries later than the putative lifetime of the patriarch. They point to the so-called wife-sister motif in this story and the presence of camels among the gifts of Pharaoh to Abram.

Before entering Egypt, Abram asked Sarai to tell anyone who inquired that she was not his wife, but his sister. Nachmanides condemned Abram for placing his wife in such a precarious position. Whether or not you agree that Abram was in the wrong, the ruse didn't work out well. But for God's intercession, Sarai would have spent the rest of her life in Pharaoh's harem. So Abram must have come to see that passing his wife off as his sister was poor strategy. Yet twenty-four years later the patriarch would again visit a foreign principality, the city of Gerar, and again ask his wife to masquerade as his sister. Our perplexity is doubled later in Genesis when Isaac, the patriarch's son, engages in the same peculiar game when he and his wife, Rebecca, also pay a visit to Gerar. In each instance, the gambit fails and the wife's true identity is revealed.

Do the men in this family never learn? Since no one thinks the patriarchs were stupid, an explanation of this behavior is required. Bible critics, advocates of the Documentary Hypothesis, have one. In their parlance, an episode that repeats itself in the narrative, with only minor adjustments in setting and principal characters, is called a doublet. A doublet, like the two names of God used variously from the beginning of Genesis onward, Hashem and Elohim, is taken as evidence that two texts by different authors have been woven into the Pentateuchal narrative.[33]

Here we have not merely a doublet, but a triplet. This creates a perplexity because the skeptical scholars have divided up the authorship of the patriarchal stories between two authors, J and E, having as their prime identifying traits the use of one or another of the divine names. J uses Hashem. E uses Elohim. Set aside the difficulty that in E's composition, the episode at Gerar (Genesis 20), we find a verse employing the name associated with J's authorship[34] (a copyist's error, the Bible critics are forced to assert).[35] The real problem is that while according to the Documentary Hypothesis we should indeed expect to find doublets, we should not expect triplets. The critics attribute to J the appearance of the wife-sister motif both in Egypt and in Gerar with Isaac and Rebecca. To E they attribute its earlier appearance in Gerar with Isaac's parents. But if so, we are left with precisely the same difficulty—a doubled episode in the work of one author, in this case J—that was among the considerations that led to the formation of the Documentary Hypothesis in the first place. An explanatory hypothesis that does not explain as it sets out to do needs to be seriously reconsidered.

Why, then, *do* the patriarchs again and again call their wives sisters? Harold Bloom asks how his heroine, the author J, can "retell" such a "damaging . . . story about Abram, the fountainhead of her people's religion, or of the religion that became a people." By way of explaining the paradox, he cites J's alleged belief that the patriarch is as "human-all-too-human" as the Lord Himself.[36] This is assuming you accept Bloom's portrait of J as a basically impious, literary writer who never dreamed that her creation, "God," would become the focus of the religions we know as Judaism, Christianity, and Islam. In J's view, which sounds suspiciously like Harold Bloom's, God is nothing more than a literary character, rascally and very much imperfect, albeit of Shakespearean depth and originality. As the wife-sister episodes demonstrate, Abram is then His moral equal, which isn't saying a lot. (It should be noted that the version of J that Bloom presents at length in his book, as translated by the poet David Rosenberg, in fact doesn't measure up to Shakespeare, not by a long shot.)

One Bible-friendly scholar offered the view that in a certain Near Eastern context, specifically in the realm of Hurrian law as it was observed in Haran, a wife was sometimes "adopted" by her husband, becoming his "sister." Professor E. A. Speiser argued that this was a mark of social prestige: Abram's and Isaac's calling their wives sister was their way of impressing foreigners.[37] Speiser suggested that the authors of these tales had received traditions alluding to the wife-sister relationship of the patriarchs and matriarchs; but by the time the traditions were written down, the community that preserved them had forgotten what such a relationship signified. An interesting idea, but Speiser appears to have been wrong in his reading of two cuneiform documents. It now seems more likely that "wife-sistership," if it existed at all, was associated with low social standing.[38]

Jewish tradition also has its view, or views. One interpretation considers the wife-sister episodes in the context of the patriarchal stories, which it takes all together as a handbook for successful marriage, the relevant lessons being expressed in symbol and parable. The repetition of the motif alludes to the rhythmically repeated period of sexual separation between man and wife, as prescribed by Torah law, each month during the woman's menstruation and for seven days afterward. At that time, husband and wife conduct themselves like brother and sister. Later commentators have drawn out the rationale for this practice. One explanation recognizes that unless periods of separation are built into the relationship, sex between two people will grow stale. This allows the human odometer of arousal to be reset, ensuring that each time the couple comes together after having been apart they will enjoy a night of anticipation and excitement. Abram and Sarai, Isaac and Rebecca, thus offer a recipe for keeping married sex spicy.[39]

This is as good an example as any of the way scholarship uninformed by tradition tends to fly low to the ground, rendering interpretations so mundane that you wonder why anyone bothers reading the Bible—while the sages, ancient and modern, soar above the clouds. The other issue before us, that of Abram's camels, is another example.

The sages don't bother with questions like this one: namely, how is it that Pharaoh gave Abram camels when these beasts were not to be widely domesticated till the twelfth century B.C., six hundred years after Abram met the king of Egypt? One finds this quibble in every scholarly discussion of the Egyptian sojourn, and it is typically understood as pointing to a date of authorship so late as to argue against the historicity of the patriarch. But the matter isn't so simple. In fact, there is scattered evidence of camels, including domesticated camels, in Egypt for periods ranging from the thirteenth century back to the First Dynasty, around 3000 B.C., and beyond. The evidence includes statues, figurines, pictures chipped into rock, as well as camel bones.[40] None of this suggests that camels were common in Egypt, but neither does the biblical text say the beasts were omnipresent as they are today, with tourists posing next to them for a fee at every turn in the road.

The story of Abram and Sarai in Egypt attracts the attention of the sages not for what it says about history, but rather about History. For the Bible has a characteristic understanding of past events that historians typically miss when they read Scripture. It is a commonplace of biblical scholarship that one radical innovation of the biblical worldview in its ancient Near Eastern context has to do with the concept of time. Whereas pagans had viewed the historical process as cyclical, the Israelites invented the idea of linear history. In the idolatrous mind, time itself moved in a circle. The scholar Henri-Charles Puech wrote of Greek thought something that applies equally to its Mesopotamian and Egyptian counterparts: "No event is unique, nothing is enacted but once . . . ; every event has been enacted, is enacted, and will be enacted perpetually; the same individuals have appeared, appear, and will appear at every turn of the circle." The Hebrew Bible is supposed to have contributed the idea that, rather than circle endlessly like a mechanical hawk, history instead moves toward a certain goal. The idea of "progress" is thus said to be initially Jewish.

In traditional commentary on Abram's visit to Egypt, however, we find the first articulation of what is in fact the authentic biblical view: that history is neither a circle nor a straight line. A few lines in Genesis serve Nachmanides as the occasion for his exposition of the doctrine called *ma'asei avot siman la'banim*: the deeds of the Fathers are a sign unto the children. It turns out that when our low-flying scholars notice "doublets" and "triplets" in the Pentateuch, they are really just catching the faintest hint of a great principle of biblical exposition. In the Bible's view, to adapt Puech, nothing important is enacted just once.

Nachmanides observes that Abram's Egyptian sojourn is replayed on a wider scale two centuries later when Abram's descendants go down to Egypt.[41] In the latter case, the Israelites—seventy members of the household of Abram's grandson Jacob—go down just as Abram did, because a famine threatens to decimate their land. As with Abram, the Egyptians oppress them and try to steal their women. (This explains Pharaoh's command that Israelite boys be murdered at birth, while Israelite girls were kept alive, to be given over to the lust of Egyptian males.)[42] As with Abram, the Lord sent terrible plagues, inducing the Egyptians to free the Jews. As with Abram, the Egyptians finally conceded and sent their captives out forcibly.[43] But first, likewise as with Abram, the Jews received silver, gold, and other valuables.[44]

In this way, Torah seeks to teach the lesson that its "paradigms" (to employ Jacob Neusner's term) are eternal. The concept of redemption from servitude finds its ideal expression in the liberation of the Hebrews from

Egyptian slavery. The paradigm works in this way: Whenever we seek redemption from the many forms of slavery that afflict even twenty-first-century Americans—slavery to fear, anger, addiction, and all sorts of other intolerable yet seemingly inescapable life conditions—we must look for guidance to the paradigm of Egypt. For in a sense, a person in the grip of, let's say, an addiction to drugs or alcohol *is himself in Egypt, enslaved to Pharaoh.* His personal history has circled backward, joining the history of eternal Israel. He is walking in the sand by the Nile where the Israelites left their footprints, as Abram left his.

All of which so far seems a perfect reiteration of the pagan outlook—history as eternal return—that Hebraic thought is supposed to have vanquished. But the Abram story quickly moves to correct our impression. It does so in the person of Abram's nephew, Sarai's brother, Lot, the son of Haran. Although the Bible doesn't mention it, Rashi assumes that Lot was present with Abram and Sarai in their confrontation with Pharaoh. His role was passive, as an onlooker, but we'll see that the situation was more complex than would have appeared on the surface. Lot's relationship to Abram is ambiguous: his nephew and his brother-in-law, a follower and an opponent of the patriarch. Before returning to our historical speculations, we must understand the character of this man.

Abram made the cross-desert journey back to Canaan, being careful to stay in the same desert lodgings in which he had stayed on the journey down, emphasizing the point that he was cutting a track in history that could be followed by himself or by others later on.[45] He and his party arrived at Beth-el, where he had pursued his ministry in the land of the Canaanites not long before. The text notes, with ironic casualness, "Also Lot, who went with Abram, had flocks and cattle, and tents."[46] This is no mere throwaway line, as it seems at first glance. The shepherds of Lot soon fell to arguing over grazing rights with the shepherds of Abram, and so Lot's flocks and cattle became a subject of dissension between nephew and uncle themselves. Lot and Abram agreed to part ways, and Lot headed southeast toward the region of what is today called the Dead Sea. Though the Bible gives us barely a hint of what was really going on, in these few spare verses we are witnessing Lot's moral dissolution.

Tradition depicts that dissolution, from the young relative back in Haran, tagging along as his uncle the great man departed for parts unknown, to a mature adult who almost loses his life in the overthrow of wicked Sodom because of corrupt decisions he has made. A nineteenth-century rabbinic sage, Meir Leibush ben Yechiel Michael (called Malbim; Russian, 1809–79), notes the verse in Genesis (12:4) that says, "and Lot went with him [*ito*]" from Haran. When Abram left Egypt, the Bible indicates (13:1) that Lot was also "with him," but here the Hebrew preposition is not *ito* but *imo*. Keeping in mind that the Bible doesn't go in for "elegant variation" (the habit of thesaurus-addicted writers who feel compelled to make sure they never use the same word twice in proximity), Malbim teaches that when the Bible varies its words, it's for a reason. The former expression (*ito*) implies subservience; the latter (*imo*), a perception of equality. Thus when the party left Haran for Canaan, Lot followed Abram meekly. By the time they left Egypt, he had come to feel that he was his uncle's peer.

In the meantime, Lot had grown wealthy, returning to Canaan with his great herds of cattle and other livestock, evidently from the same source that had enriched Abram: Pharaoh.[47] But Pharaoh had enriched Abram because he sought access to the man's beautiful "sister." Though Lot happened to be Sarai's genuine brother, the king evidently did not recognize him as such. So Lot had nothing to offer Pharaoh.

He did have something to offer Abram, at least initially in their Egyptian sojourn: his silence. Lot was in a position to expose Sarai as Abram's wife.[48] The Bible's testimony to his new wealth on their departure from Egypt suggests that he used this power over his uncle to wrest away some of the other man's riches. Lot appears to have successfully blackmailed Abram. But this corroded his soul and he became a mocker of Abram's religious earnestness.[49] Tradition depicts his household as a place where the future of Abram's mission was an object of scorn. Lot's servants derided the patriarch as a "barren mule" whose ministry would come to nothing because the older man was unable to produce an heir as a spiritual successor, thus forcing him to leave his estate to Lot while the leadership of nascent monotheism went vacant.[50] Nothing arouses cynicism in a person more than does his own guilt. Mocking is the natural reflex of a conscience that knows it has done wrong.

What had been an intimate friendship between the two men began to unravel. Earlier they must have been very close, for Rashi tells us that people often mistook one for the other: there was a family resemblance, but this was enhanced by the filial role Lot had played to the childless Abram. Says Rashi, Lot imitated the manners, expressions, and demeanor of his uncle so perfectly that the two were indistinguishable.[51] That's why, after they had left Egypt, a dispute between their shepherds degenerated into a feud between Lot and Abram so bitter as to require them to part ways. Lot's shepherds were trespassing on Canaanite lands where he and Abram had no permission to graze their flocks, and Abram was concerned that the blame would be pinned on him, for the locals tended not to distinguish carefully between Abram and Lot.[52]

In the context of the ancient Near East, where the oldest brother in a family exercised significant authority over nieces and nephews, Abram was responsible for Lot.[53] He assured the younger man that he could be counted on to come to the rescue if Lot got into a scrape.[54] But, Abram said, uncle and nephew must take their own paths: "Let there not be strife between me and you, between my shepherds and your shepherds, for we are brothers. Is not all the land before you? Please separate now from me: if you go to the left then I will go to the right, and if to the right then I will go to the left."[55] Lot agreed.

He thought about what he would do with his new freedom. Abram's community had returned to the mountain between Beth-el and Ai. From this height, where today one can see much of the land of Israel spread out, Lot "lifted his eyes" and looked about.[56] The Bible associates the sense of sight with sinful temptation—in contrast to the faculty of hearing, which it links with morally healthful instruction.[57] Lot's temptation was to go east toward the plain of the Jordan River, from which he had heard rumors of moral abandon in a city called Sodom. With his flocks and shepherds, he made his way toward that sinister place, unafraid that living in close quarters to such people might quicken his slide toward dissolution.[58]

What all this has to do with the direction of history won't be immediately clear. But a closer look at the sources reveals that Lot's departure acts as a philosophical counterweight to the episode in Egypt.

Our first clue is Scripture's reference to Sodom as a locality approaching in lushness the greenery of the "Garden of the Lord," namely Eden.[59] It is not that way anymore. Modern visitors to the Dead Sea wilderness, under whose salt-thickened water the ruins of Sodom must lie, would have difficulty thinking of a more desolate spot: the khaki-brownish color of soil leached of all moisture, except for a great swatch of eerie deep blue, the Dead Sea. But there is reason to think the area was more verdant once, particularly in the vicinity of what is today called the Lisan peninsula.[60] In any event, the reference to Eden is telling, as is the problematic notice that Lot traveled toward Sodom *mi-kedem,* literally "from the east,"[61] since Beth-el and Ai are situated to the northwest of Sodom. Thus to get there from Beth-el and Ai, one travels not from the east, but *from the west* (or from the north-west).

Was the author unaware of the region's geography? (If the Redactor was Ezra the Scribe, as some scholars say, he presumably lived nearby in Jerusalem.) Rashi explains that *kedem,* literally "east," has an additional meaning, preserved here by the oral tradition. The direction "east" is where the sun *first* appears on the horizon. The root of the word, "kuf-daled-mem," KDM, thus has the essential meaning of "first" or "oldest." Hence one of God's appellations is Kadmon shel Olam, the "Ancient One of the World," *kadmon* simply being a variation on the root, KDM, from which we get *kedem.* When the Bible says Lot traveled away from *kedem,* it means that he "caused himself to travel away from" the Lord. For he said, "I want neither Abram nor his God."[62]

Our second clue is that the same peculiar expression, *mi-kedem,* occurs at the beginning of Genesis in the story of Adam and Eve's expulsion from the Garden. "And [the Lord God] drove the man out and stationed, *mi-kedem* to the Garden of Eden, the cherubs and the fiery ever-turning sword to guard the way to the Tree of Life."[63] This makes no sense: He stationed the cherub angels "from the east" to the Garden? But then apply Rashi's interpretation. The cherubs were placed at the entrance of the Garden to keep mankind from entering; for through their sin, Adam and Eve, like Lot, had distanced themselves from the Kadmon, from God.

Lot was traveling away from God, and yet, he believed, back to the primeval Garden. His quest was doomed because while history circles back upon itself it simultaneously moves in a certain direction toward a certain goal. There is no going back to the Garden. Anyone who seeks to return will suc-ceed, rather, in alienating himself from his Creator.

Lot also did something else, with ramifications beyond his power to imagine. Unwittingly he was setting in motion the process that would lead to the redemption of the world, the culmination of history.

The Midrash cites a verse from Psalms that speaks in the voice of God. "I have found David My servant," He says, and the Midrash comments: "Where have I found him? In Sodom."[64] Had Lot stayed with Abram and never pitched his tent near Sodom, the seeds that became the lineage of King David, later of David's descendant the King Messiah, would never have been sown. History moves in a certain direction, toward the Days of the Messiah when the experience of mankind will be radically, permanently transformed,[65] and Lot took the first step toward the first of those days.

History is cyclical, returning us again and again to the experiences of Abram and all his ancestors as we find them in the Bible. Yet it has a purpose and gravitates toward a definite end point. Can we reconcile the apparent contradiction? We can. The geometric figure described by the concept of history as Scripture and tradition present it not as a loop or a line. It is a spiral, a shape combining direction with repetition. This is the real contribution of Hebrew thought to our understanding of where the tides of history are gradually and imperceptibly conveying mankind.

Abram laid down the first track in history. Yet when I find myself in need of redemption from Egyptian servitude, whether each year at Passover or in my own personal trials, my experience is not exactly the experience Abram had. Because history moves both around and upward toward its millennial end, the nature of spiritual servitude and redemption evolve and change.

Meanwhile the patriarch was still being conveyed on the tide of his own personal history. On the mountain between Beth-el and Ai, he now received another prophecy from God: "Rise and walk about the land through its length and its breadth, for to you I will give it."[66] He had been preaching and evangelizing there on the mountain, living with and instructing his followers and slowly rebuilding the fellowship of disciples he'd had at Haran, whose total number of 72 when he left Mesopotamia climbed before long to 318. Understanding this latest divine message as a command to move his operation elsewhere, he took his community south to the place called Mamre, in the vicinity of Hebron. There he built another sanctuary with its altar and resumed his mission of proselytizing. His heart pained him, for he missed his nephew and worried that something terrible was bound to happen to Lot in the land of Sodom.

He waited for the bad news until one day it came.

CHAPTER SIX

The Fugitive

bram was at Mamre when the Fugitive arrived. At this site just north of modern Hebron in central Israel, there is nothing to be seen today but Roman and Byzantine ruins and an oak tree said by the first-century historian Josephus to be one of a grove that Abram knew. The trees gave the place its name, Eloneh Mamre, the Oak Grove of Mamre.[1] Though the Bible makes no mention of this, we know from tradition that under the trees Abram had a sort of academy.[2] There he and a lieutenant, Eliezer of Damascus, taught 318 disciples, among whom were numbered three prominent Amorites: Mamre (who owned the grove), Eshcol, and Aner. These 318 followers were called the Masters of the Covenant of Abram.[3] While Abram was indisputably the leader of the Covenant group, Eliezer was in charge of conveying his master's teachings. The latter would "draw water [that is, knowledge from Abram] and give [them] to drink."[4] Eliezer was Abram's foremost disciple and a kind of surrogate son. Later he would ensure the continuity of Abram's mission by seeking a bride for his master's true son, Isaac. Without him, there could have been no larger body of students learning Abram's tradition. The system was like the one employed centuries later by Moses in the Sinai wilderness, when he would teach his brother, Aaron, who would teach the elders, who in turn would teach the people Israel. When not learning, the Masters of the Covenant of Abram worshiped at the altar Abram had built.

It was a peaceful existence until Og of the Rephaim showed up. Though the biblical text refers to him mysteriously as "the Fugitive," giving no proper name, the oral tradition tells us who he was.

We may imagine Abram's students sitting one day under the oak trees listening to Eliezer, who stood while the master sat nearby. Without warning, a chill crept through them. Someone turned around and his heart felt as if it had died.[5] This is always what happened when you caught sight of a man of the nation of Repha. The Ugaritic texts indicate that there was indeed a historical nation called the Rephaim and even mention a legendary king, Daniel, "the man of Repha."[6] But nothing from Ugarit gives us the tradition's picture of a people so horribly fierce that the sight of them caused other men to blanch with terror. The name "Rephaim" means literally "Ghosts," and when you met them, it was as if you had seen dreadful phantoms. Og, a giant of a man, was the worst of all. The Book of Deuteronomy notes that centuries after Abram's time, Og's bed was still on display for people to gawk at—thirteen feet in length—a symbol of stature, strength, and also of sexual power.[7]

However, Og looked at this moment like he had seen death itself.

It is possible that Abram had previously met this behemoth on the journey from Haran to Canaan. There were two routes from the north down through Canaan. Abram had entered the land between Tyre and Acco on the Mediterranean, so we know he had taken the Way of the Sea. There was also the King's Highway, which ran down from Damascus parallel to the Jordan but twenty-five miles east. Og's city, called Ashtarot or Ashtarot-Karnaim, was the next important city on that route south of Damascus, in the land of Bashan. We don't know for certain if Abram met Og then.

Maybe it was in Damascus, to which Abram had made a detour and where he presumably met Eliezer of Damascus.

In any event the Midrash indicates that Og did not come to Abram's community by chance, for he had cast a desirous eye on the patriarch's wife.

Like Eve, Sarai was the object of lustful stares that were threatening in a way that most such stares are not. In the Garden of Eden, a mysterious natural force, the serpent, had seen Eve naked, unashamedly engaging in sexual intercourse with Adam, and it conceived a plan to bring about Adam's death so that it could have Eve for itself.[8] Hence the Bible's story of Eve and the serpent and the forbidden fruit. Pharaoh had sought to steal Sarai from Abram, and this was to be a pattern in Abram's life. Og had looked at Sarai and Abram the way the serpent had looked at Eve and Adam. When the giant appeared at Mamre, then, Abram's first thought must have been, "He's here to kill me and take Sarai."

But if Og was armed, he drew no weapon. Instead, he announced that he had come to report on a war that was under way in Canaan, and that touched directly on Abram's interests.

His own people, the Rephaim, had been slaughtered. Four armies from the east, from Mesopotamia, had come down the Transjordanian highway to Ashtarot and butchered everyone. Possibly Og himself was taken prisoner and escaped after traveling with the armies for some time; otherwise it is hard to see how he came to know all the details of this incursion, which he related to Abram.

As Og explained, the armies belonged to four kings: Amraphel of Shinar, Arioch of Ellasar, Chedorlaomer of Elam, and Tidal of Goiim. Although these names are mostly still unknown from historical accounts outside the Bible, they have an authentic ring. Amraphel may be Amorite or Akkadian, Chedorlaomer is apparently an Elamite name, Arioch is a Hurrian name that fell out of use after the sixteenth century B.C., and Tidal is a variation on the name of five different Hittite kings of the early second millennium.[9] None have the feel of a mythological character made up by a writer in, say, seventh-century Judea. These kings had been in a vassal-client relationship to five much weaker, local city rulers of the Dead Sea region: Bera of Sodom, Birsha of Gomorrah, Shinab of Admah, Shemeber of Zeboiim, and the ruler of another locality, the city of Bela, whom Og for some reason did not identify. The four stronger kings had forced a treaty of subservience on their five counterparts. For twelve years, the five had served the four. Then the five city chiefs renounced the treaty and their servile status. For thirteen years, the four eastern kings allowed this state of affairs to persist, but in the fourteenth they resolved to make war on their rebellious clients.[10]

Modern scholars have speculated on what type of service the five local city rulers had promised in their treaty to render to the four more powerful rulers. One possibility is that the royal four had an interest in the copper-mining industry south of the Dead Sea, and the rebellious five had cut off the copper supply.[11] What doesn't make sense, either in scholarly treatments of the episode or in the plain text of the Bible, is what Og related next. Instead of moving immediately to punish the five Dead Sea chieftains, the four kings embarked on a campaign of general destruction. The Bible plots their course down the length of the King's Highway, through Ashtarot-Karnaim, completely bypassing their rebellious client-rulers, and then onward, all the way to the Plain of Paran, a wilderness more than a hundred miles south of the Dead Sea. Only then did they turn north, reaching Kadesh in the Negev and, at last after a long detour, making their way to the shore of the Dead Sea at Hazazon-Tamar, the oasis today called En-gedi.[12] Everywhere they went they pillaged, their fury so insatiable that in the twentieth century A.D. Nelson Glueck was able to trace the physical remains of their invasion. He uncovered the ruins of a series of towns along the King's Highway that had all been destroyed about the same time—he thought in the nineteenth century B.C.—most never to be rebuilt.[13]

Whatever the pretext of the assault, the four eastern kings were not merely after copper. Nor was it their only goal to discipline the Dead Sea Five. The route they took is too bizarrely circuitous for that. To update their itinerary, we may imagine a driver trying to reach New York City's Central Park from north of the city. He gets on the West Side Highway going south. But instead of exiting at West 72nd Street as you would expect and driving a few blocks to the park, he stays on the highway and keeps going all the way to the southern tip of Manhattan, where he goes east to the FDR Drive, heads back north up the east side of town, and finally enters the park at *East* 72nd. Either this driver is new to the city and doesn't know his way around, or from the start he had something in mind other than reaching Central Park.

Og was still telling his story when Abram realized what the four kings had in mind. He was unsurprised when the Fugitive related that after touching the Dead Sea shore at En-gedi the four only then turned on Sodom and

Gomorrah, where they had captured Abram's nephew Lot. They locked him in a cage and dragged the cage along with them as a trophy.[14]

Abram saw it all in a flash of clarity: the four invading armies had been *searching for something*—or rather, *someone*. They were looking for Abram.

Amraphel was none other than a nickname of the patriarch's old enemy Nimrod. A midrash explains the name "Amraphel" as a pun on the words *amar* and *pol;* for he said (*amar*), "Fall [*pol*] into the Fiery Furnace!"[15] Evidently Nimrod had been seeking an occasion to come after Abram, who had humiliated him, and who, Nimrod was aware, had gone to live somewhere in the backwater of Canaan. The armies of the four kings searched the land till they found, right in Sodom itself, a man whom Nimrod recognized immediately. Lot, you will remember, closely resembled his uncle. Terrified, the nephew must have protested that they had the wrong man.

Abram also saw through Og's pretense of "warning" him about the danger to his nephew. This wounded monster had not come all the way to Mamre to do him a good turn. His intention was to lead Abram to Lot. Og wanted to see the army of the four punished, for they had slaughtered his people. If Abram could accomplish that, well and good. If Abram himself was killed in battle with the four, that, too, would be fine with Og, who would then take Sarai down on his thirteen-foot bed.[16] The latter outcome seemed the more likely. Although it would not have been unusual for a livestock merchant like Abram to have armed troops in his entourage along with his gentle disciples, the Bible indicates that he had, besides himself and his wife, only those 318 students.[17] He was in no position to challenge one army, much less four.

Despite all this, Abram resolved to do whatever was necessary to rescue Lot. He was unafraid because he bore in mind a principle later articulated in rabbinic literature. A psalm contains the verse "Of evil tidings he will have no fear. His heart is steadfast, trusting in the Lord."[18] The Midrash applies the verse to Abram in his confrontation with the four kings, and the Talmud further expands on it.[19] The two statements in the verse are a sort of "if-then" construction and can be read either in the order we find in the Bible or reversed: "His heart is steadfast, trusting in the Lord. Of evil tidings he will have no fear." In other words, says the biblical verse as we find it in the text: if a person receives no evil tidings, he will trust in the Lord. It is easy for a person who has had a tranquil life to trust in divine providence. Taken back-to-front, however, the verse offers some startling advice: if a person trusts in the Lord, he will receive no evil tidings. Trusting in God *protects* you from evil. For "evil" means any condition or action unwilled by God. Of course, men and women of faith suffer calamities, but they understand that nothing can happen to them unless God Himself allows it. However inscrutable His reasoning, God brings upon them, and everyone else in the world, only what is ultimately good for us. Hence there is nothing to fear.

A corollary is that if you want to avoid fear, act as if there is nothing to be afraid of. This shows your trust in God, and for that He rewards you with heightened confidence. In other words, your feelings will follow your actions. To illustrate, the Talmud tells the story of a rabbi, Hillel the Elder, returning from a journey and entering his hometown, from which he suddenly hears screams. He says, "I trust that this is not [from] my house," and proceeds calmly.

He speaks confidently, and so he *is* confident. Abram probably said something similar, whether aloud or to himself: "I trust that I will return alive." Notice that the Talmud speaks of Hillel *hearing* the screams. The Bible relates that Abram likewise "heard" what Og had to say, but it says nothing about his expressing any fear.[20] Instead, he immediately began preparing himself for war, as if there was nothing to worry about. For this reason he felt no fear. By Rashi's count, it was his sixth trial (his fourth by Rambam's), and in a sense he had already passed the test.

Were his students similarly confident? Evidently not, which brings us to what is perhaps the main theme of this episode.

We will miss it if we pay too much attention to the scholars. The Bible's account of Abram's war with the kings from the east puzzles them. Believers in the Documentary Hypothesis admit that Genesis 14, where the story appears, doesn't fit into any of their source-critical rubrics. The chapter isn't by J or E, they concede. Also, some of its vocabulary is strange. It uses one word, *hanichim* (traditionally understood as referring to Abram's disciples), that Albright dates as a very old word, traced to Egypt in the fifteenth to seventeenth centuries B.C. And it uses another, *rechush* ("possessions," as in Lot's possessions which the four kings took along with Lot himself), which they date as very new, from the time when (as they say) the whole Pentateuch was edited by the Redactor.[21] E. A. Speiser has argued that Genesis 14 is a Hebrew translation of a text originally composed in Akkadian by a non-Jewish writer who knew of the historical Abram. Hence it would be the closest thing we have to a "direct epigraphic witness" to the patriarch's life.

Speiser's best evidence is the first word in the chapter, *vayehi,* "And it happened," whose syntax he thinks is the result of an awkward translation from the original language.[22] But the same syntax is found in the first verse of the Book of Esther, which nobody thinks was translated from Akkadian.

You need to turn to the oral tradition to get to the real heart of the narrative, which is about the relative strengths of the two ways in which we may initiate a relationship with God.

Abram came to know Him by rejecting the beliefs he had received from his father and pursuing knowledge on his own, primarily by applying his intellect to the data provided by his observations of the world around him. Abram's disciples learned about Him by accepting the new tradition from Abram. Broadly speaking, this is the distinction between two kinds of individuals. On one hand, there is the convert to a particular faith, or someone who was born into that faith but never learned about it from his parents and only came to accept it on his own later in life. On the other hand, there is the person who was born and raised in that faith and never wandered from it.

About the grounds on which a relationship with God properly stands, Jewish philosophy is of two minds. The medieval work *Kuzari* by Rabbi Yehudah Halevi (Spanish, c. 1080–1145), seeking to explain religion in philosophical terms, stresses the concept of tradition: the unbroken chain of transmission extending back to the giving of the two Torahs, written and oral, at Mt. Sinai. This is the position corresponding to the experience of Abram's students. They had discovered nothing for themselves, but relied entirely on what they had been told by this man who personally experienced God.

Writing just a little later, Maimonides articulates a different though complementary view. In his mind, one comes to love God not primarily through the passive experience of hearing others—one's parents or teachers—relate their experiences of Him or the experiences of their distant ancestors, but by active contemplation in the manner of Abram. He writes: "When a man intensely meditates on [God's] awesome works and His creations and His wonders, and discerns His wisdom, which is eternal and infinite, immediately he will love and praise and glorify [Him] and desire with a great desire to know the Great Name [of God]."[23] For this reason, "it is necessary for a man to seclude himself in order to comprehend and to discern such wisdom and understanding as will make known to him his Master."[24] The Rambam hardly denies the importance of tradition, but he places emphasis on the individual in isolation from others, working out the Truth in a struggle that ultimately involves himself and his Creator alone. The epithet given to Abram here, Ivri, "Hebrew," alludes to this quality of being alone. Genesis says the Fugitive arrived to bring news to "Abram the Hebrew." The word means "one who stands on the other side." While at the simplest level it alludes to the fact that Abram came to the land of Canaan from the "other side" of the great Euphrates River, more important it reminds us that it was in solitude from other people that Abram arrived at his Truth.[25]

To keep things simple, let us give names to these two models for knowing God. They are the Native and the Convert.

The Natives, Abram's students, had received their learning from their master and from their master's servant, Eliezer.[26] Their spiritual instruction seems to have been not even direct from the source, Abram, but received secondhand from Eliezer, who in turn received it from Abram: the idea of tradition exactly. On the other hand, Abram is the quintessential Convert, who learned nothing from his father and utterly rejected the tradition of his family. What he learned, he learned only by applying himself to the ultimate questions of human existence. He was like many modern-day spiritual seekers, who likewise grew up feeling that their parents could tell them nothing of substance about such questions and so were forced to go in search of the Truth, relying on their own instincts and judgments. Later we will discover what the biblical tradition wants us to understand about the relative strengths of Natives and Converts.

The Talmud faults Abram for pressing his scholarly initiates to go to war, though if he was to rescue Lot, it is hard to see what alternative he had.[27] When the Natives heard they were to accompany Abram into the battle, they were alarmed. Their faces whitened, and someone yelled, "The five [Dead Sea] rulers were unable to stand up against them. So shall *we* then stand up against them?" In the end, Abram had to entice them with bribes of pearls and precious stones. He then armed them and the party set out.[28]

They marched in the general direction of Mesopotamia, where the four armies had come from, and it was not long before Abram's troops began to express further misgivings. When they reached the northern limits of what would later be the land of Israel, Abram had compassion on them. Such kindness was his greatest personal virtue, though here it seems mad. His plan had been to divide the force in half in a sort of pincer move, for there were signs that they had caught up with the four withdrawing armies and were on the verge of overtaking them. But Abram hesitated.

It was to be one of the worst nights of his life. They had reached the locality identified here in the Bible as Dan, though this geographical name is an obvious anachronism. In Abram's day, it was called Laish, a prosperous settlement surrounded by earthen ramparts and a newly built mud-brick gate. The biblical personality Dan was one of Jacob's sons, thus Abram's great-grandson, eponym of the tribe of Dan, which conquered Laish in the twelfth century B.C. and renamed it. The city of Dan was uncovered in the north of Israel in 1966. One may visit it today: a nature reserve at the foot of Mt. Hermon near the source of the Jordan River, shaded everywhere by Syrian ash trees and Mediterranean laurels, with little brooks running through it and lovely Israelite ruins of a gate and altar in reddish basalt rock. It is among the pleasantest spots in the whole country.

However, when Abram and his companions reached there, he was suddenly overcome by dread. He had felt this way before, arriving at a certain place when all at once the blackest possible mood descended on him. That was at Shechem. He understood then that on that spot, the nation God had promised he would father would someday suffer a terrible tragedy. The Talmud reports that on this occasion all his bodily strength suddenly vanished, for the place was also haunted by an event that had not yet happened.[29] Eight hundred years later his descendants would choose this location to utterly reject Abram's vision of the One God. Here Israel's King Jeroboam would set up one of two Golden Calves (the other was at Beth-el), declaring, "Behold your gods, O Israel, which brought you up from the land of Egypt!"[30] Jeroboam's ritual site is still there, picturesquely sheltered in a grove of trees.

Abram's poor deluded children! He was overcome by a swooning love for them that, after he had recovered, made him reconsider his plan to take his students into battle.

As a midrash reports it, he made a speech just like the one God would later command the high priest to make to Israelite soldiers before they went out to war, allowing any fearful souls in the troops a last-minute honorable discharge. "Who is the man that is afraid because of his sins? Who is faint-hearted because of the evil deeds he has done? Let him go and return to his home."[31] The implication was that there were individuals among his students who worried that God would not extend His protection to them.

As soon as he said this, the students began, one by one, to stand and turn away. Gradually they deserted their master, 318 in all. Finally Abram was left with a lone comrade-in-arms, Eliezer—whose name, if you add up the value of the Hebrew letters, equals 318.[32] As far as Abram cared, loyal Eliezer was equal to them all. Aner, Eshcol, and Mamre seem not to have abandoned Abram, but were excused from fighting with him. They agreed to guard his baggage instead.[33]

By any rational calculation, the initiative to save Lot was always hopeless: hopeless with 318 men and hopeless with two. If Abram had been willing to take on the four kings with his little band of followers, he reasoned that there was no reason to give up now that the force was reduced to himself and Eliezer. Acting unafraid, indeed utterly fearless, so they were in reality. They would split up, just as Abram had planned, and pursue the armies.

There was no need to carry on the chase long, for God worked a miracle. In the first half of the night, Abram destroyed the armies of the four kings and rescued Lot and many other captives besides, along with their belongings. The Talmud relates the supernatural manner of his victory. Abram and Eliezer confronted the enemy, which then turned upon them in fury. The army of the four was stopped, however, when Abram and Eliezer threw dust and straw into the air. From this debris, there materialized hosts of angels bearing swords and shooting arrows.[34] In this way, humility (dust and straw) triumphed over arrogance. The arrogant invaders, led by Nimrod, were vanquished.

Key to understanding this miracle is its timing, before the middle of the night had passed. A midrash states that instead of allowing Abram to chase after the four all night long, God arranged it so that the patriarch caught up to them by midnight.

The biblical text hints at this. The Hebrew here is a blatant oddity of grammar and syntax that the Redactor ought to have noticed. The relevant sentence is translated in various ways—such as, "Abram and his followers surrounded the enemy by night, attacked them and pursued them"—none of them satisfactory. What the Hebrew literally says is this: "And the night was divided upon them, [upon] him and his servants, and he struck them and pursued them."[35] One peculiarity is that the second part of the verse switches from plural ("him and his servants") to singular ("he struck them and pursued them"). The oral tradition explains that at the start of the night there was a plurality of attackers; at the end, it was just Abram backed up by Eliezer. But what about the night being "divided"? The sentence simply *does not say* that Abram and his force divided up so as to surround the enemy. Although that reading, found in most translations, is drawn out by the oral tradition, so is an additional meaning: that the night itself was divided. The oral tradition does surprising things with the concept of time. Tonight, God chose to treat time like a loaf of bread and cut it down the middle, placing one half on the table and the other in the freezer for later. According to *Pirke d'Rabbi Eliezer*, He stored up its second half for the night of redemption when the Israelites left Egypt, an event heralded by the plague in which He slew all the firstborn of the land.[36] As we find in the Book of Exodus, "And so it was, *at the half [point] of the night,* that the Lord struck all the first born of the land of Egypt." Something about that night was special, carrying the potential for powerful redemption. Its power still remains available to those who celebrate the festival of Passover, in which Jews relive the experience of their ancestors, the redemption that occurred in Egypt and, before that, in Canaan when Abram rescued Lot.

Is this history? Or myth? It's both. It is a *siman,* which is history in the form of myth, a sign to the future generations. The two redemptive events, at Dan and in Egypt, separated by four centuries, both prefigure the redemption to end all redemptions. In its sidelong way, the oral tradition is telling us: it will happen this way. At the End of Days, the Messiah will deal just such a stunning, total defeat to his adversaries. Or to be more precise, as in these two ancient episodes, God will deliver the blow on the Messiah's behalf.

In the narrative, both the Messianic theme and our theme of Natives and Converts culminate when Abram returns south toward home. They do so in Abram's meeting with the mysterious figure of Malchizedek.

After the battle, when he must have expected to feel relieved, Abram was struck by a deep remorse. We don't know how many people he killed when his dust and straw turned to an army of consuming angels, but it must have been plenty. Most had been wicked, no doubt, but he said, "Is it possible that I have killed all this host and there was among them not even one righteous man?"[37] Abram was afraid that, miracle or no miracle, he had endangered the divine favor that up till then he seemed to enjoy.

As he was thinking these gloomy thoughts, word arrived that the Canaanite rulers whose land he had liberated wished to pay homage to him. They called him to meet them at the Valley of Shaveh, also known as the Valley of the King.

When he arrived—although I can find no source for this in the oral tradition, it must be right—an earthquake of recognition rocked him. The Valley of the King appears elsewhere in Scripture as the spot where David's rebellious son, Absalom, built a monument for himself, saying, "I have no son; [I erect this monument] so that my name should be remembered."[38] The structure, called the Hand of Absalom (Yad Avshalom), is placed by tradition in what is today called the Kidron Valley, just under the eastern wall of the Old City of Jerusalem. It is a desolate place, an ancient graveyard. One of its features is this so-called Yad Avshalom, a peculiar object like an upturned funnel, called Pharaoh's Hat by the Arabs—a tomb dated, however, nine hundred years after Absalom lived. Still, this seems to be the place where Absalom built his memorial to the sad condition of being a man without a son.

Rashi says that Abram had entered Canaan in the first place by making his way toward a mountain he had never seen before, Mt. Moriah. When he reached the Valley of the King, he looked up and there it was, the peak of his mind's imagining. There were two ridges, eastern and western, guarded by the Judean mountains on one side and the Judean desert, sloping down to the Dead Sea, on the other. On the eastern ridge sat a little settlement, barely fifteen acres in all, the home of about a thousand souls.[39] The modest limestone summit, Mt. Moriah, would later be known as the Temple Mount, the elevation on which King Solomon built his Temple, to be destroyed by the Babylonians, again by the Romans, and restored by the Messiah. The town was occupied by Jebusites, and their "king" was called Malchizedek.

Strangely, in a book that rarely stints on genealogical data for significant personages, the Bible gives no indication of Malchizedek's ancestry. He is identified merely as the "King of Salem," which city we learn elsewhere is to be identified with Jerusalem, and as "priest of God, Most High."[40] The oral tradition, though, is clear about his identity: he is Noah's eldest son, Shem (who was quite elderly at this point, having lived 465 of his 600-year lifetime!). Along with the King of Sodom, he went out to greet Abram after the victory.[41]

When the Sodomite offered Abram a payment for saving him from the invaders, saying, "Give me the people [the rescued captives] and take the possessions for yourself," Abram briskly rejected the gift, accepting only a payment for his porters, Aner, Eshcol, and Mamre.[42] We tend to think of villainous individuals like the king of Sodom as materialists who care only for amassing treasure; but good people have no monopoly on spirituality, if "spiritual" is defined in the neutral sense of anything that exists but that has no physical manifestation. The truth is that the worst people in the world—the Stalins and Hitlers—often have no interest in wealth, but primarily seek the allegiance of other human beings, which is a spiritual commodity: "Give me the people and take the possessions for yourself."

Malchizedek, however, wanted only to worship. A midrash describes the scene. "Shem the son of Noah went out to meet [Abram], having seen all the deed he had done and all the possessions he had returned, and he was very amazed in his heart. He began to praise and laud and glorify the name of his Creator. . . . Abram [then] stood and prayed before the Holy One Blessed Be He: 'Master of the Universe, not by the strength of my hand have I done all this, but by the strength of Your Right Hand, by which you have shielded me in this world and will do so in the world to come.' "[43] The Bible recounts the rest of the day's action. Malchizedek gave the tired warrior bread and wine. He then blessed Abram, and Abram responded by paying a tithe to this priest, a tenth of all Abram's belongings.

None of which makes sense without the oral tradition. Why? The scholars point to the name of the deity invoked by Malchizedek, translated "God, Most High, Master of Heaven and Earth." The Hebrew phrase "God, Most High," "El Elyon," sounds like the title of a Canaanite god, "El the Most High," El being the name of the chief god of the Canaanite pantheon.[44] Other scholars see here the name of two separate gods welded into one: El, the earth god, and Elyon, the sky god.[45] Either way, the implication is that Abram accepted a blessing from a god other than the God of Israel, which makes him less than a pure monotheist. But a great deal rides on our accepting the tradition that the patriarch worshiped the One God alone. To put it simply, if Abram wasn't a monotheist, and if we want to be consistent, we must give up any faith in the religions that arise from the Bible. Those religions rest on a foundation stone, which is Abram/Abraham the monotheist. Remove the stone and they collapse. The collapse of biblical faith may be acceptable to some scholars. The rest of us, for help in clarifying what this episode is about, must turn to tradition.

So Malchizedek invoked the same God that Abram was coming to know. In biblical Hebrew, the word *el* (plural: *elim*) is a generic designation for a being or force of great power. When the Israelites crossed the Sea of Reeds before Pharaoh's army, they celebrated by singing an ecstatic hymn to the Lord: "Who is like you among the *elim, Lord?*"[46] Nachmanides writes that there were priests at the time of Abram who served the *elim,* meaning the host of natural forces that God controls but to which idolaters typically attribute independent will.[47] The Canaanites called their chief deity El because in their language, West Semitic, which is a close relative of Hebrew, the name "El" simply means "God."

In calling his and Abram's God the highest (*elyon*) of these forces, Malchizedek was speaking the language of philosophers. God is the cause of all causes. The point is emphasized when he blesses Abram in the name of "God Most High, *Master of Heaven and Earth.*" The word I have translated as "Master," *Koneh,* literally means "he who acquires or purchases"—the point being that God acquired the universe by making it.[48] It's all His, and so in creation there is nothing independent of Him. Nothing in nature has its ultimate cause in nature, though it may appear that it does.[49] One might say that there is no such thing as "nature" in the sense of anything being "natural," which is to say doing what it does simply because "that's nature." Everything in the world does what it does only because God wills it or because (in the case of humans) He allows it a will of its own.

No, Malchizedek did not serve the Canaanite god El. But his service of Abram's God was not the same as Abram's. What was the nature of his service? As it happens, Christians and Jews see the question quite differently. Hidden in these few seemingly obscure biblical verses is a flashpoint of controversy between the two faiths.

The key to the dispute lies in a verse from Psalms. Christians translate it, "You are a priest forever, in the succession of Malchizedek," and take the priestly reference as an allusion to Jesus, God's eternal high priest.[50] That is, Jesus succeeds Malchizedek. Starting with St. Paul, Christian Bible interpreters have sometimes discovered momentous doctrines, the kind that overturn centuries of previous thinking about God and man, in apparently throwaway lines in the Book of Psalms or the prophets. Here the psalm in question, no. 110, isn't about Malchizedek. It merely mentions him. Nevertheless, the author of the New Testament's Letter to the Hebrews uses the mysterious figure to prove that God has rejected the Jewish priesthood descended from Moses' brother, Aaron. Abram represents that outmoded cultic system, whereas Malchizedek stands in relation to Christ, for like Christ "he has no father, no mother, no lineage; his years have no beginning, his life no end. He is like the Son of God: he remains a priest for all time."[51] What clinches the case? It is the fact that Abram receives a blessing from Malchizedek, "and beyond all dispute the lesser is always blessed by the greater."[52] But if you read the rest of Malchizedek's blessing, the problem with the Letter to the Hebrews emerges: after blessing Abram he proceeds to bless God Most High. Does this mean that Malchizedek trumps not only Abram but the Lord Himself?

Drawn from oral tradition, the Jewish reading of the encounter notices this order of the blessings. As priest of God Most High, Malchizedek had carried on a line of transmission that originated with Adam, who passed on his knowledge of God down through an order of righteous ancestors. The Talmud lays out the chain of students and disciples: Adam taught Methusaleh, who taught Shem, who is Malchizedek.[53] It was natural that Abram should honor this man, even, as he proceeded to do, grant him a tithe just as the Israelites were later commanded by God to give a tithe to the Temple priests.

God had considered establishing the Temple priesthood from the sons of Shem, but the meeting with Abram demonstrated that the spiritual outlook represented by Shem/Malchizedek was better suited to another role. Elsewhere the Talmud zeroes in on the fact that the priest blessed Abram first, and only afterward blessed God. Taken aback, his concern for God's honor offended, Abram said to himself, "Does one bless a servant before blessing his Owner?" Malchizedek had violated the principle later formulated in the Second Commandment, which instructs us never to place anything or anyone before God. In a priest, no virtue is more important than a crystalline understanding of this principle. So the Lord withdrew the priesthood from Shem and gave it instead to the descendants of Abram.[54] The line from

Psalms is thus understood to be addressing Abram and his descendant King David (to whom the psalm is dedicated): "You shall be a priest forever because of the statement [al-dibarti] of Malchizedek."

But Malchizedek represents something more than a noble failure. His priestly line was indeed cut off. On the other hand, his tradition was not. A great nineteenth-century Italian sage, Rabbi Elijah Benamozegh (1823–1900), devoted his life to instructing Jews and others about Noachism: that is, the commandments given to Noah by God as the foundation of a religion for mankind. The Noachide commandments are extensively discussed in the Talmud's tractate *Sanhedrin*. They include basic moral strictures, seven in all with manifold ramifications, at the heart of which is the affirmation of God's Oneness. In this future religion, the Jewish people, Abraham's seed, will be a "kingdom of priests,"[55] ministering to the spiritual needs of all the world's other nations, who will fill the role of the laity in a great Universal "Church." This Noachide "Church" will be established after the coming of the Messiah, when God's name will be unified, his Name called One by all peoples. In the meantime, Noachism operates, and has always done so, as an esoteric faith, taught as a kind of gentile kabbalah. Noachides, as the followers of Noah are called, are to be found (whether they think of themselves in such terms or not) among the followers of all the world's religions, not least in Christianity and Islam, who understand God's Oneness and uphold His vision of righteous behavior. Benamozegh speculated that even the pagan religious establishments in Egypt and Greece included enlightened individuals who secretly passed down the teachings of Noah.

As we noted, Malchizedek, or Shem, was Noah's son. In *Pirke d'Rabbi Eliezer,* we find the story of a supernatural staff, created at dusk between the sixth and seventh days of creation, with God's Holy Name written upon it. The staff represents this tradition that preceded Abraham. It also represents spiritual leadership, for a shepherd leads his flock by directing the creatures this way or that with his staff. Adam carried it first, then bequeathed it to his grandson Hanoch, who bequeathed it to Noah. Shem/Malchizedek received it from Noah and gave it to Abram, here at their first meeting. The staff would later pass into the hands of a non-Jew, the Midianite priest Jethro, who was to be the father-in-law of Moses. Jethro planted the staff in his garden, where it radiated a spiritual force that prevented any mortal from approaching it. Before the Exodus from Egypt, Moses appeared at Jethro's home, entered the garden, grasped and pulled it from the earth. Jethro exclaimed that surely this was the man to liberate the Jewish people from Egyptian slavery, and to marry his daughter.[56] In this way, the midrash indicates the existence of a pre-Abrahamic tradition, of which Noah was not even the originator. Adam was, so to speak, the first Noachide, having received a preliminary revelation of God's plans for humanity before Noah received the fuller version.

When Abram encountered Malchizedek at Salem, or Jerusalem, he was encountering that tradition for the first time. Benamozegh writes: "In the very story of Abraham, a certain remarkable, nearly enigmatic person makes a brief appearance, but what light he sheds! From the shadowy depths of the pagan world, from the heart of that corruption and error which already prevailed everywhere, here, in the person of Malchizedek, is an unmistakable trace in heathendom of an ancient and honorable institution, a worship, a monotheistic priesthood."[57] A midrash suggests that Malchizedek, while keeping his priesthood more or less secret, did teach certain select initiates,[58] an underground Noachide movement—which, however, Abram never knew about until now, when he received the teaching from Shem/ Malchizedek, symbolized by the staff of Adam. Tradition records that Shem ran his academy along with his great-grandson Eber. It may have occupied different locations over the years. In the mystical city of Sefat, in northern Israel, a small cave next to a Sephardic synagogue can still be visited, identified by legend as one site of the Academy of Shem and Eber. Certain famous figures from the Bible studied there, notably Abram's grandson Jacob, who was there for fourteen years[59]—but we are getting far ahead of our story.

Abram had approached this august, ancient person in a spirit of considerable apprehension. After all, he had just slaughtered hundreds or thousands of soldiers and he knew that among them were descendants of Shem. The people of Elam, under their king Chedorlaomer, were children of Elam, Shem's firstborn son.[60] Shem himself was similarly mortified, having fathered descendants so wicked as to invade another land, seeking to kidnap Abram. The Midrash says, "This one was afraid of this one, and this one was afraid of this one. [Abram] said, 'Perhaps Shem has some [enmity] for me in his heart, for I have killed his children.' And this one [Shem] feared this one saying, 'Perhaps Abraham has some [enmity] for me in his heart because I have raised up wicked men.'"[61]

This mutual distrust between the old and the new guard brings us back to our theme of Natives and Converts. The Bible is telling us something here about the gifts and the vulnerabilities each brings to Abram's project of drawing the world closer to its Maker. Shem has tradition, the spiritual data meticulously guarded and transferred from one generation to the next. According to one midrash, he taught Abram spiritual truths that would later be employed by the latter's descendants in the Jerusalem Temple. According to another, Shem also revealed to him some portion of the whole divine teaching, called Torah, made known to a wider public at Sinai.[62] Thus the bread and wine he brought out to Abram signify the Temple sacrifices; or they signify Torah wisdom generally, which the Bible compares to bread and wine.[63]

But for all these virtues as a guardian of Truth, the Native is incomplete as a model of the godly life. For all his wisdom, unlike Abram, Shem was unable or unwilling to excite many other people with the prospect of knowing God. Besides having few disciples, he evidently had no children who were willing to carry on the mission of preserving God's Truth. The Elamites certainly weren't interested in Torah. And it is meaningful that the encounter between Shem and Abram took place in the Valley of the King, a site associated with fathers grieving for the loss or lack of sons. Shem, of course, was in mourning for Elam. Abram was only here in the first place because the closest thing he had to a son, Lot, had gone astray after the lurid neon of Sodom. Here Absalom built his monument recalling his sadness at being a father without sons. And later, after seeking his father David's overthrow, Absalom himself became the focus of David grief's when the young man was slain by his father's servants, causing David to utter his heartrending cry, "My son! Absalom, Absalom, my son, my son!" Perhaps the greatest vulnerability of the Native is how often he loses his children—not to premature death, as in Absalom's case, but to unbelief.

This has been the pattern in Jewish life: the grandfather, a believer, somehow fails to pass on the flame of religious passion to his son, who becomes a cynic. This man in turn has children but teaches them little or nothing about their tradition. These innocents grow up not as cynics, but as ignoramuses, and join the legion of other ignoramuses produced the same way. The generation is saved by the passion of the Convert, who may have been born a Jew, raised as an ignoramus, but who rebels against his ignorance; or he may be a convert in the literal sense of a born-gentile who joins the Jewish people. The Natives, in short, need the Converts periodically to revive their community. But the Converts, too, need the Natives, without whom they have no access to the tradition. The same pattern of mutual dependence, Abram and Malchizedek embracing in the Valley of the King, holds in other faiths no less than in Judaism.

The ultimate embrace, the final resolution of such dichotomies, will be the Messianic age, to which the story of Abram's war against the four kings has been building. Judaism also shares with Christianity the perception that in the meeting with Malchizedek we see an allusion to the Messiah King. A figure like Abram can establish patterns in time which men and women thousands of years afterward are bound to follow. His struggle with the four kings is taken this way, as a sign to future generations of Jews who will suffer under the tyranny of four kingdoms (Babylon, Persia, Greece, Rome) before the end of time when (like Lot) they will be redeemed by a Messianic figure (like Abram).[64] This figure will be recognized by the nations of the world, bad and good alike (here represented by the king of Sodom and by Malchizedek, respectively).

The Midrash even hints that this great redemption could have taken place, or at least gotten started, right here at the Valley of the King. Abram had arrived in the shadow of the mountain he had been seeking, the mountain of the Temple that tradition says the Messiah is destined to rebuild; but he chose not to climb to its summit. Instead, he stayed in the valley and drank Malchizedek's wine. Though the Bible doesn't advocate teetotaling, when in its narratives a person guzzles wine, this hints to us that he is letting down his guard and will soon either commit a trespass or a trespass will be committed against him. The millennia-long process of redemption, beginning with the Exodus from Egypt and the conquest of the land of Israel, could have commenced now.[65] Abram simply had to build on the strength and renown he had achieved and gone on to secure the entire land of Canaan for his children. But he did not. The wine he accepted from Malchizedek was like the drink one has at the end of a day's hard work: a signal to the mind that the body can now relax.

Abram relaxed. Sometimes the doors of history open for a day, or an hour, even a minute, then close not to open again for millennia to come. An opportunity for momentous change passes in a moment.

CHAPTER SEVEN

What the Stars Said

bram was seventy-five when in fairly quick succession he left Haran, entered Canaan, fled before the famine to a refuge in Egypt, returned to Canaan, parted with Lot, heard the news of Lot's kidnapping, and went out to do battle with his nephew's captors. The Bible next informs us of his age when he is eighty-six years old and begets a son with his maidservant Hagar. While this decade was consumed with teaching his disciples and making new ones, the only event the Bible records is a very strange prophetic experience described in Genesis 15. As Harold Bloom says well, "Nothing even in J is weirder than the ceremony that celebrates the covenant that has been cut between Abram and [the Lord]."[1]

This event, the Covenant Between the Parts, takes its name from the only real action in the chapter. In the course of a prophetic visitation, God speaks to Abram, assures him he will have numerous offspring, and shows him a vision of the stars whose number is uncountable, as the number of Abram's descendants will be. Man and God then make a covenant. By way of ratifying it, Abram slices in half some livestock between whose neatly separated "parts" passes a divine fire. God tells him that his descendants will be exiled, oppressed, and impoverished for four hundred years in Egypt, after which they will go out with wealth and take possession of the land of Canaan, dispossessing its native peoples.

The "covenant," then, has two parts, both of them promises that God makes. First, He will give Abram offspring. Second, He will settle those offspring in the land of Canaan. The vision ends and we hear nothing further of Abram's activities till his eighty-sixth year.

Let us back up and try to understand what this experience was all about.

Abram was eighty-two years old at the time of the Covenant Between the Parts, living at Mamre and going through what today we would call a personal crisis. The Bible doesn't say any of that, but we'll see later how to infer his age, and we also may judge that Abram was under the pressure of considerable anxiety. Consider the assurance he receives from God immediately upon entering the prophetic state. God says, "Fear not, Abram, I am a shield to you; your reward shall be very great."[2] We have here one of those apparent editorial glitches that believers in the Documentary Hypothesis have a hard time explaining, for immediately prior to God's assurance, nothing has been said to suggest that Abram was in fear to begin with. On the contrary, this was seven years after the war with the four kings, so you would expect him to be feeling rather confident about himself. He had defeated his enemies in great numbers! What was Abram afraid of?

The oral tradition suggests a number of answers, for the patriarch appears by nature to have been a worrier.[3] A man of exquisite moral sensitivity, he feared that among his slain foes there might have been even one righteous person. He feared that the sons of the four kings would come after him, seeking revenge. Despite his earlier warm meeting with Malchizedek, Abram feared the other man's anger, for the king of Salem was also the principal ancestor of the Elamite nation, many of whom were killed in the war. He feared that he would prove unworthy of God's previous assurance that he would beget children. Or perhaps he feared that he would have children only in the sense that disciples are regarded as their master's children, and even so, he worried that they would not adhere to his teachings past his death. Abram also feared that, due to the sins of his descendants if he indeed had any, the special covenantal relationship he had established with God would be superseded by another, new, covenant, with some other people.

To such concerns God wished to respond. Comforting the patriarch, He communicated with him in a vision. It was broad daylight, unlike Abram's previous such experiences, which had occurred at night.[4] Otherwise the symptoms of impending prophecy were the same. Abram had been concentrating his attention, meditating, preparing himself to hear the words of his God. He had sought this encounter. He secluded himself and sleep overcame him, for prophecy happens in sleep. His body shook. Though his mind was acutely aware of what was happening, his senses were temporarily stopped: he heard nothing of the natural world, smelled nothing, felt nothing of a material nature. His soul mingled with the angels called *ishim,* and if any of his compatriots had been present, they would have noticed the features of Abram's face and body altering, to indicate that the spirit of God had rested on him. As Maimonides writes in the *Mishneh Torah* in his detailed description of the prophetic phenomenon, a vision is given to a prophet in the form of an allegory, but the meaning of the allegory is not withheld from him for even a moment. Instead, "in the prophetic vision, the interpretation of the allegory is immediately imprinted on his heart and he knows its [meaning]."[5]

God said, "Fear not, Abram, I am a shield to you; your reward shall be very great." The vision would soon proceed with extravagant images of stars and sacrifices, but for now the Lord simply offered this assurance, its meaning multifaceted. Abram instantly knew the meaning. But since the Bible doesn't make it clear, we as readers need to consult the oral tradition.

At one level of interpretation, we find that God was assuring Abram that His relationship to the patriarch's descendants would never be superseded as a consequence of their sins. They would be forgiven their trespasses. For, among other reasons, a mechanism of forgiveness is built into God's promise to Abram, crystallized in the word "shield." The Midrash reveals the hidden significance of the shield He offered. That significance hinges on a strange doctrine in the Talmud according to which "the death of the righteous atones for [the sins] of Israel."[6]

As the Midrash reports: "The Holy One Blessed Be He said to

[Abram], '. . . When your children will enter into the hands of sin and of evil deeds, I will discern one righteous [man] among them . . . who will be able to say to [My] Attribute of Justice, "Enough!" I shall take him and atone for [their sins].' " By "take him," the Lord meant "take his life." What's hinted at is the mystic unity of the Jewish people, which is not merely a family or nation of individuals but something more like a single organism. Just as a blow to a part of the body of one individual can atone for that person's whole self, so the suffering of a supremely good individual within the Jewish organism can atone for his entire generation, providing them a "shield" against misfortune. This doctrine sounds Christian, for Christians view the death of their Lord as effecting atonement. But it's noteworthy here that the doctrine is articulated in a context where the main point (that the covenant with the Jews is eternal) stands in contrast with a Christian belief (that the covenant with the Jews was superseded).

Rashi, the greatest of the traditional Bible commentators, identifies another level of meaning. As he often does, he puts his finger on the explanation that speaks most directly to people not only of his day but also of our own. After the war, Abram thought, "Perhaps I have already received [all the] reward [I am going to get] for all my righteous deeds."[7] To this, God responded, "Your reward shall be very great."[8]

Rashi has hit on a psychological paradox. After achieving something important and positive, we fret that for whatever good we've done, we have already been given our reward. If we should happen to receive additional, undeserved blessing, we assume we will have to pay for it later on in suffering. But the lesson of Abram's fear and the Lord's response is that God is good. He is not some niggardly cosmic accountant, keeping punishments in store in case we somehow get more than we deserve.

God and the patriarch now entered into a dialogue. To the Lord's promise of a "reward," Abram responded that no reward could be meaningful to him if he had no child to pass it on to when he died. He said, "My Lord God, what can you give me seeing that I go childless and the steward of my house is Eliezer of Damascus?"[9] Under the law in Abram's native land, a barren couple typically "adopted" a slave who on their death inherited their estate.

In Abram's case, Eliezer would be his heir. By law, if unexpectedly the couple then had a child, the servant lost his inheritance.[10] But Abram saw no indications that at eighty-two and seventy-two, respectively, he and Sarai were likely to become parents. He said, "Behold, you have given me no seed, and behold my steward will inherit me."[11] Of course, the inheritance Abram spoke of was not only material but spiritual. It seemed that when Abram died, Eliezer would become the leader of the nascent monotheistic movement.

By nature men are strongly inclined to seek an inheritor—of their wealth *and* their ideas—who is like them in values and beliefs, as Eliezer was like Abram, and also one who is their blood descendant. In no small part, this accounts for the delight and excitement a father feels when he looks at his son's face and sees that the boy *looks like him:* the physical resemblance is the guarantee of their biological relationship.

God promised, as He had done before, that Abram would have a real son. He said, "That one [Eliezer] will not be your heir, but rather the one who comes forth from your loins, *he* will be your heir."[12]

Next the vision itself, a succession of visual images, began. The scriptural text has God taking Abram "outside"—the reader assumes this means outside his tent—and saying, "Look, please, at the heavens and count the stars if you can count them. So shall your offspring be."[13]

However, the reference here to stars, suggesting nighttime, creates a problem. Only a few verses later Scripture refers to the sun being "about to set."[14] The sun doesn't set at night! It would appear, then, say the Bible critics, that we have here two texts by different authors that have been inexpertly knitted together.

The Talmud and Midrash resolve the difficulty by giving an esoteric meaning to Abram's vision of the stars in daylight. It is not by chance that, in Torah nomenclature, pagans are classed under the heading "worshipers of stars." The glowing constellations of night are a stumbling block for the intellect. Abram himself was a learned astrologer, and he felt oppressed by what he had read in the constellations: that whatever God had promised to the contrary, he was destined to produce no heir.[15] In the aspect of a man's fate that dictates whether he will have a child to inherit all that belongs to him, Abram regarded the will of nature, represented by the stars, as supreme.

If astrology is understood as being simply the way the ancient world expressed its faith in the primacy of the natural over the supernatural, then we modern folk can well understand Abram's concern. We may smirk at the astrological charts in down-market magazines and newspapers, but many educated people still believe that impersonal natural forces determine our individual fates: not the stellar constellations, but a constellation of biological, psychological, and other factors (for example, a person's genes).

In the biblical worldview, there are two models for understanding what gives direction to the events in the life of a nation or of a person. We can believe that direction is given by divine providence, or we can believe it is given by chance. Both the ancients with their faith in astrology and we moderns with our faith in nature come down on the side of chance. How the stars are aligned at your birth and what you have in your DNA are seemingly both the result of dumb luck. When it came to his own private existence, Abram still believed in chance. The prophetic event here in Genesis 15 had as part of its purpose to correct his misunderstanding.

If it was daytime, taking Abram "outside" his tent into the sunlight wouldn't facilitate his being able to see the stars. In fact, says Rashi, Abram was able to see the stars because God took him "outside" the whole universe by a kind of astral projection, into the vacuum in which creation hangs.[16] From this vantage, he looked down on the universe pulsing with stars. God had made them and what they represent submit themselves to His providence. With the stars at his feet, Abram could see the universe from a perspective as close to God's as a human being has ever been privileged to do.

God then spoke to the patriarch, who was still floating in the ether: "Abandon your astrology, by which you have seen in the zodiacal constellations that you are not destined to have a son." It is true, said God, that the man called Abram will have no heir. Nor will the woman called Sarai. "But *Abraham* will have a son and similarly . . . *Sarah* will give birth. I will call you by another name and the Zodiac will change [for you]."[17]

According to the Jewish concept of repentance, an unfavorable decree placed by God on a sinner can be annulled by the sinner's changing his name.[18] This idea is not to be understood simplemindedly. Rather, a change of name signals that the sinner has changed himself inwardly. If he corrects the error of his distorted, sinful outlook, he in a sense no longer exists. He has assumed another identity, symbolically represented in the act of taking a new name. Under this new identity, he is no longer subject to whatever undesirable fate God had earlier assigned to him.

In the vision of the stars, God told Abram that he was destined to revise his faulty understanding of personal fate. Symbolically and literally he and his wife would in the future assume new names: Abraham and Sarah. (The actual command to change his name had not come just yet.) In their previous existence, encumbered by the myth of a universe governed by chance instead of by providence, the couple had not merited an heir. In their new existence, they would merit so many heirs that counting them all would be like counting the stars.

Abram believed God's promise of an heir, says the text, "and He [God] reckoned it to him as righteousness." What does this mean?

In the verse just quoted (Gen. 15:6), I have followed the conventional translation by capitalizing the "He" in "and He reckoned." Normally we capitalize the pronoun when it refers to God, but nothing in this verse indicates that the referent *is* God. *Who* really "reckons it" to *whom* as "righteousness"? What is the "it" that is being reckoned? And what is "righteousness," or *tzedakah* in Hebrew, anyway?

Here is a case where Christians and Jews find in the same cryptic verse the same question being addressed, but where the two faiths discover opposite answers. St. Paul boasted of having studied in Jewish religious academies. If so, then perhaps he learned from his rabbis that Gen. 15:6 touches on the issue of grace versus earned merit. Grace is the favor of the Deity when it is bestowed without regard to merit. In Hebrew, "grace" is *tzedakah,* often, as here, mistranslated "righteousness"; whereas reward based on merit is called *mishpat,* or "justice." We have already said that one lesson behind God's assurances to the fearful Abram is that God is good: He often conducts Himself in accordance with His attribute of grace, or *tzedakah.* The understanding of Judaism introduced by Paul, however, is the understanding of the Jewish God as niggardly cosmic accountant. This is actually a tragic misunderstanding of what Jews have always thought about God. Paul uses verse 15:6 to show that, contrary to the claim of "Judaism," God doesn't in fact care about merit in the sense of a person's keeping the commandments found in the Torah. Instead, He cares only about faith: "Look at Abraham: he put his faith in God, and that faith was counted to him as righteousness."[19]

But Paul's reading is problematic. For we need to do something with the next verse in Genesis (15:7): "And He said to him, 'I am the Lord who brought you out of Ur Kasdim to give you this land to inherit it." If all that the previous verse means to do is praise Abram for his faith, what, then, immediately prompts God to identify himself this way? As Paul understands 15:6, there is no logic to the flow of verses.

Jewish tradition provides the webbing that connects 15:6 with 15:7 and makes sense of 15:8 as well. A summary of the tradition as it pertains to these verses is found in the commentary of the Malbim.[20] In 15:6, Abram is seen "trusting" in the Lord, having rejected his astrological speculations. He believes that God will indeed give him progeny. But because Abram doubts his own merits, he ascribed it to Him—not God to Abram—as *tzedakah*. The referent of the pronoun "he" in "he reckoned it" is Abram. In other words, because he felt he didn't *deserve* the blessing of having children, he assumed that God intended to bless him purely as a matter of grace. To this, God responded, "I am the Lord Who brought you out of Ur Kasdim," thus reminding Abram of his greatest merit to date: what the patriarch had done at Ur Kasdim, stepping into the flames for his belief in the One God. Modest Abram was prepared to accept that if the Lord thought he merited progeny, then it must be true.

But what of the land of Canaan, later called Israel, which is the other blessing that God promised at the Covenant Between the Parts? In 15:8, we find Abram asking, "My Lord God, whereby shall I know that I am to inherit it [the land]?" In other words, by what merit would Abram secure that blessing? The question was a good one. Most of the rest of Genesis 15 is taken up with God's answer.

The Lord agreed to provide a sign that the promise of land would be fulfilled.

Since Abram had fallen into this prophetic state, he had heard God's words spoken to him and seen mystic visions. There was, however, nothing for him actually to do. Now he received an order to take three young cows, three goats, three rams, a turtledove, which is a kind of pigeon, and a young dove. Having slaughtered all the animals in turn, he set to work sawing them in half, each one neatly down the center from head to tail, except for the two birds, which he left alone. The oral tradition tells us nothing about the cinematic aspects of this procedure beyond the bare description in the Bible. It doesn't dwell on the Technicolor gore, blood and entrails everywhere, flies buzzing around the carcasses, and the sweat-pouring labor required for an eighty-two-year-old to saw a cow in half, never mind three cows and six other good-sized farm animals. Instead, the Midrash and Talmud want us to understand the meaning of the "sacrifice."

First of all, it is not a true sacrifice because we find none of the hallmarks of sacrifice: there is no mention of an altar, no blood is poured out in a ritual fashion, the "parts" aren't laid on a fire.[21] It is instead the ratification of a covenant. God had promised Abram land and offspring. The slaughter of these animals, at the simplest level, was intended to symbolize the bond of God's promise.

As elsewhere in the Bible, God chose to effect this ratification by employing the symbolic language that would have been familiar to Abram from his contact with other religions of the ancient Near East. In Hebrew, one speaks of "cutting" a covenant, and the idea that establishing a covenant requires "cutting" something is also found in the religious thinking of the Hurrians and Amorites, ethnic groups Abram knew well. The former established a covenant by cutting in half a bull, an ass, and ten sheep, while the latter would deploy only an ass.[22] (Rashi is aware that God borrowed this process of "cutting" from other cultures.)[23] The purpose of this sympathetic magic was to obligate the two parties, who passed through the halved animal parts. The party who violated the agreement would suffer the same fate as the animals. God was here obligating Himself, for the supernatural fire that would in a moment pass through the parts signified His Presence.[24]

At a second level, also in symbolic terms, here was the answer to Abram's question, "My Lord God, whereby shall I know that I am to inherit [the land of Israel]?" As we noted earlier, the patriarch really was asking: By what merit can my descendants be assured that You will keep this promise? What if they fail to keep the commandments You give them? This is how the Talmud says we should understand Abram's question. It goes on to teach that the Lord answered reassuringly: in general, he would settle Abram's descendants in this land whether or not they observed all His commandments. There was, however, one condition, one merit on which the inheritance of the land depended. According to Jewish tradition, the animals—three calves, three goats, and three rams—represent the Temple sacrifices as commanded by God in the Torah. For by this rite, God was telling Abram that if the patriarch's descendants should wish to hold on to the land they inherit from him, then if the great Jerusalem Temple, first built by King Solomon, is standing, they must perform the sacrifices.

The Talmud recounts Abram's conversation with God. "Abram said before the Holy One Blessed Be He: 'Master of the universe! Perhaps, God forbid, Israel will sin before you and you will do to them as you did to the generation of the Flood [of which Noah's family were the sole survivors] and the generation of the Dispersion [punished by dispersion for the sacrilege of building the Tower of Babel]. [God] said, 'No!' [Abram] said before Him: 'Master of the universe, *whereby shall I know?*' " God then commanded him to perform the rite of the Covenant Between the Parts.

But what if the Temple was destroyed, as indeed it was twice in Jewish history, most recently in A.D. 70 by the Romans? Abram "said before Him, 'Master of the universe, that's well and good for as long as there is a Temple in existence. But when there is no Temple in existence, what [remedy] will there be for them? [God] said to him: 'I have already established for them the Order of Sacrifices [describing the Temple rites, as found in the Jewish prayer book, the Siddur]. Whenever they study them, I will consider it as if they had offered sacrifices before Me and I will forgive all their sins.' "[25] So it is to this day, when there is no Temple, that before morning prayers, Jews traditionally read passages from the Written and Oral Torahs describing the Temple rituals.

A third and final level of interpretation is obscure and mystical. We noted the attribution to Abram's authorship of a magical text, the *Sefer Yetzirah*. This book contains the first reference in kabbalistic literature to the Ten Sefirot, the emanations of God by which He created the world. Traditionally the Sefirot are laid out in a chart as three vertical columns: on the left, a column of three; in the middle, a column of four; on the right, a column of three. In the opinion of a modern sage, Abram was diagramming the Sefirot. Five animals, when divided in half, give a total of ten halves, which Abram arranged as vertical columns: on the left, a column of three (cow, goat, ram); in the middle, a column of four (the two birds, considered as halved); on the right, a column of three (cow, goat, ram).[26] Pictured this way, the Covenant

Between the Parts gives a schematic representation of God's relationship to the created universe.

All this fuss about butchering farm animals? If the idea of animal sacrifice strikes the modern mind as barbaric or simply pointless, that is because we fail to understand its true meaning. Indeed, in his *Guide for the Perplexed,* Maimonides suggests that the Temple sacrifices were a compromise God allowed to the Jews, who, being people of their time and place, could only comprehend a religious system that included butchering livestock. The implication seems to be that in the future, when the Messiah appears and rebuilds the Temple, Jewish worship will include no slaughtering. But Maimonides cannot mean that. He wrote his *Guide* in Arabic, the vernacular of his neighbors, not the sacred tongue, Hebrew, because he intended it for a class of doubting or "perplexed" intellectuals of his day. For these sophisticates, he offered the unthreatening suggestion that the rites of Temple sacrifice would never be restored. These readers were unready to hear the truth. But in his monumental work meant for those who believe as he did, the *Mishneh Torah,* composed in Hebrew to indicate its holy status, Maimonides makes plain that sacrifice is indeed to be a feature of Jewish worship in the Temple when someday the Messiah rebuilds it. The *Mishneh Torah* includes pages and pages of description of the sacrifices, which he obviously meant to be consulted someday for practical purposes.

This is in keeping with the picture of the future that we find elsewhere in rabbinic literature. The Talmud goes so far as to say that it is only for the sake of the covenant that God established now with Abram—and the sacrifices that, in the course of ratifying the covenant, He urged on his descendants—that He maintains in existence the heavens and the earth.[27] This sounds like madness. But as the Malbim explains, it is no coincidence that Genesis 15 links Abram's intended self-sacrifice at Ur Kasdim with the ritual of animal sacrifice practiced in the Temple. In the merit of one, Abram was granted progeny. In the merit of the other, his progeny were granted an eternal inheritance, the land of Israel. *For animal sacrifice is nothing more than a proxy for self-sacrifice.* The person who brings an animal offering in the Temple should regard it as if he were offering himself to the flames. And the person who studies the sacrifices should reflect on the logic of self-sacrifice.[28]

This logic says that there is no value in the universe independent of God. Nothing is good or evil, beautiful or ugly, except because He defines it that way. The value we have the hardest time relinquishing as an independent good is the value of our own life. Meditating on the logic of sacrificing one's self—either through offering an animal and imagining that one's own blood was being dashed against the altar or by studying the laws of animal sacrifice—reminds us that everything but perfectly transcendent God is of worth strictly in relationship to Him.

This is the meaning, or part of it, of animal sacrifice for the Jews. These rituals may appear to overlap with the rites of the pagans, but their inner significance is completely different. The deities of the pagans were not transcendent at all. In the idolater's mind, the gods simply were hungry and needed to be fed. Man's role, as the gods' servant, was to feed them. In return he received benefits: safety, prosperity.

Though I don't intend to speculate here on what purpose God had in mind in creating the universe, it must contradict that purpose if His created beings entertain the conceit that there are goods or values independent of Himself. When we embrace the truth in this matter, we affirm His purpose in the creation. So it really is the case, if poetically expressed, that the heavens and earth exist for the sake of sacrificial offerings. When Jews in particular embrace this truth, the Lord forgives their sins and settles them in their land.

Settling the Jews in the land of Israel entails protecting them from enemies. For how can Jews be truly settled if they are under siege by foes, from within or without? As Abram was absorbing the message of the sacrifice God had led him to make, the mood of the prophecy he was experiencing began to darken. A shadow in the sky caught the patriarch's attention: it was a bird of prey wheeling in the heavens. Other birds appeared. The shadows swooped and plunged until the birds were upon him, or upon the animal carcasses laid out neatly, split in half and waiting for the continuation of the prophecy. Abram tried to drive them off with the staff he carried, swinging at the creatures as they dove and climbed, but each time he swung at a bird, he missed.

Finally, desperate, he prayed and repented for thinking that he could triumph over tormentors by relying on his physical strength alone. The Midrash records that when he asked God's forgiveness for this hubris, his enemies fled from him: the birds flew away and disappeared.[29] Symbolically they are Israel's enemies, always circling, ready to plunge on their prey when the Jewish people are weakened and divided into factions like the halved animal parts in Abram's vision, unified by neither belief or affection, but by quarreling with and accusing each other (not unlike the situation in the Jewish world today, and in the State of Israel in particular). At such times, the Midrash tells us, Israel is protected not by arms, whether a man's two arms wielding a staff or the arms of jets and tanks, but by its relationship with God. The surest defense is repentance. Needless to say, this isn't a midrash one hears cited very often by those militant Zionists who indeed place their faith in arms alone.

The birds no longer darkened the sky, yet Abram noticed that the light of the sun was dimming. It was late afternoon, turning into evening. The nature of Abram's prophecy changed now to a lower variety that occurs in dreams by night.[30] As the sun was touching the horizon, God caused a deeper sleep to enfold him, deeper than the slumber in which this divine communication had begun. Abram felt something sweep over him that he had not experienced yet in this prophecy: a terrible "dread."[31]

So far what he had heard from the Lord was good news: that he would have offspring, that they would inherit the land of Canaan. Now came the bad news: the people Israel would be exiled from their land and subjugated politically, a condition that has prevailed until this very day.

For the "sacrifice" had an additional significance. Abram understood that God had asked him to take three of each of the varieties of livestock (young cows, rams, goats) to indicate the first three kingdoms that would overpower the land and the people of Israel in history: first Babylon, then Persia, then Greece.[32] Each of these kingdoms would in turn be overthrown: hacked up by conquerors, slaughtered and ruined like the animals in Abram's vision. There was, however, to be a fourth kingdom, the longest and most painful subjugation: Rome. The Midrash indicates that the "dread" (eimah) Abram felt was a foretaste of this exile of the Jewish people, beginning with the destruction of Jerusalem and the Temple by Rome almost two thousand years after Abram's birth.[33] As the Torah conceptualizes history, the Jewish people are still in this "Roman" exile—an exile that persists under the civilization of the West, which traces its roots to Rome. It is said this exile will persist until the Messiah builds the Third Temple, when a Jewish commonwealth, as the Torah defines it, takes root.[34]

The Roman exile forms the background of Abram's nighttime vision, his dream state which was becoming a nightmare. In the foreground, however, was a different exile.

Still enclosed in heaviest slumber, Abram learned that the land was not to be inherited in his lifetime. God said, "Know with certainly that your seed shall be a stranger in a land that is not theirs, and they [the Egyptians] will enslave and afflict them, for 400 years."[35] After this, "the fourth generation will return here, for until then the iniquity of the Amorites will not be complete."[36] And that is just what happened after Moses led the Jews out of Egyptian slavery and set them under the leadership of Joshua, who conducted the invasion of Canaan.

However, this figure of 400 years poses a serious problem for those who regard the Bible as authoritative. It is not so clear how long Abram's descendants spent as strangers and slaves before being liberated from Egyptian servitude. Scripture and tradition supply three divergent answers to the question. Here in Genesis 15 we read that it was 400 years. In Exodus, the Bible says the period was 430 years in length.[37] The Midrash, however, finds that the Jews could not have spent four centuries as slaves in Egypt. It sets the length of their enslavement at only 210 years.[38]

Is this more editorial carelessness? No, say the rabbis, who supply various resolutions. A minority view, that of the medieval commentator Ibn Ezra, is elegant and makes the most sense. He says the 400 years began with the Covenant Between the Parts.[39] During this time, Abram and his children were "strangers": first in Canaan, later in Egypt. However, in the Book of Exodus, when the Bible looks back on pre-Jewish history to date, it sees the process that ended with the Exodus as starting with Abram's leaving Cuthah after the trial of Ur Kasdim, heading for Haran. This was 430 years before the Exodus.

We know from the Talmud that Abram was fifty-two when he began collecting and converting souls at Haran.[40] Thus began the count of 430 years. Thirty years later Abram was eighty-two years old. Thus began the count of 400 years. At the Covenant Between the Parts, then, Abram was eighty-two years old—which, judging from the sequence of events in the biblical text, is just about how old we should expect him to be.

In Hebrew, the place of servitude God spoke of to Abram is called Mitzrayim, translated as "Egypt." The liberation from Egyptian slavery is still celebrated at the festival of Passover. But we need to understand what "Mitzrayim" really means.

Let's try to liberate ourselves from the idea, imposed by mapmakers, that Mitzrayim is only a physical locality. It is also an experience. In the geographic sense, Mitzrayim is the narrow strip of habitable land on either side of the Nile, bounded by deserts. But the Jewish people lived in *that* place for only 210 years. So when the Book of Exodus says that the Israelites dwelled "in Mitzrayim" for more than 400 years, what does this suggest?[41] "Mitzrayim" is the name given to the land of Egypt, the "narrow land" (the root of the Hebrew word means "a narrow place"). But metaphorically and experientially Mitzrayim is another still narrower place: the birth canal through which the Jewish people passed on their way to emerging into the world.

That process, beginning in the lifetime of Abram, is one of conception and birth. In human terms, conception implies sexual intercourse. The Bible records, "So it happened. The sun set, and it was very dark. Behold, there was a smoky furnace and a torch of fire which passed between these pieces. On that day the Lord made a covenant with Abram, saying 'To your descendants have I given this land. . . .' "[42] The sexual imagery of the covenant with its slaughter strikes this reader as evident. Abram's knife passes through red meat, which parts for him and splits in two. The biblical text speaks of a "furnace" and a "torch" lifted up in the air and moving as if carried by unseen hands, passing through the split parts. In this way, the eternal Father of the Jewish people, symbolized by the divine fire, enters between the parts. This marks the very conception of the people Israel.

Human gestation is a time of confinement, at the end of which the baby moves into the narrowest passage a person ever experiences. We can only guess that after the tranquillity of the womb, this tight squeeze makes for a very traumatic few hours of labor, just as the enslavement in the land of Egypt was among the most traumatic times in Jewish history. Water breaks, signaling that birth is near. For the Jews, water broke literally in half at the Sea of Reeds, which the escaped slaves crossed on dry land between the piled-up walls of water, their former slave masters in pursuit. The actual moment of birth occurred shortly afterward at Mt. Sinai when Moses received the Torah, which gave the Jews their license to exist. The whole four centuries leading up to Sinai are thus called Mitzrayim, which might be translated as the "Birthing Process."

At the Covenant Between the Parts, God previewed for Abram the whole course of Mitzrayim. But the prophecy culminated now in a still grander and more terrifying vision.

As the Midrash recounts, God granted to the prophet the understanding that the two flames represented something in addition to His Presence. They stood for two sets of future possibilities for Abram's children, who would ultimately face a fork in the road of their history, a choice with eternal ramifications. One road they could take led to Hell and the Four Kingdoms (Babylon, Persia, Greece, and Rome) that would someday rule over the Jewish people. This was the road of alienation from God, of chastisement and destruction. The other flame stood for Torah study and the Temple. The meaning was that the latter two fend off the former two. If the Jewish people take the path that leads to study and sacrifice, they will be spared punishment in this world (the Kingdoms) and the next (Hell). Or they may choose the other way. As Abram watched the procession of the flames, God said to him, "All the time that your children involve themselves with these [latter] two they will be saved from the other [former] two. When they abandon the [latter] two they will be judged [and punished] by [the former] two."[43]

Abram perceived that in time his descendants would fail to take advantage of these two defenses, Torah and Temple. As a result they would suffer either the flames of Hell or the torture of being subjected to cruel tyrants. God then offered him a choice. The Midrash quotes Him as saying, "Which do you prefer? That your children should go down to Hell or that they should be [oppressed by the Four] Kingdoms?"

It was full nighttime now, the sun had already set, and Scripture emphasizes how dark it was. In the dark, the impenetrable loneliness that comes with being compelled to make such a terrible decision, Abram sat down to ponder the choice. For a day, he wondered what he should do, in unspeakable pain because whichever choice he made would mean torment for his children. He said to himself, "How can I choose between Hell and the Kingdoms?"

The Midrash presents the rest of the story in two different versions.

When twenty-four hours had passed, God pressed him to decide without further delay. Abram then told God that he would opt for the Kingdoms over Hell. Alternatively, when twenty-four hours had passed, Abram had still failed to make a decision and God made it for him, choosing the Kingdoms over Hell. In either event, the course of Jewish history, with its agonizing periods of exile and domination by foreign powers, was thus set before there was ever a Jewish people.

The Midrash concludes its exposition of Genesis 15 with a dispute among several sages. One rabbi says that, as the prophecy of the Covenant Between the Parts drew to an end, God proceeded to show Abram the details of future events in the life of Israel up to the time of the Exodus from Egypt. Another says He previewed history up to the coming of the Messiah. A third says He portrayed the entire sweep of history up to and beyond the Messiah, all the way to the end of history and the beginning of the World to Come.[44] In this last stage of human existence, the Hebrew prophets say the Presence of God will be revealed in glory.

According to Maimonides, this preview was Abram's seventh trial. According to Rashi, the Covenant Between the Parts was no trial at all. We must conclude that Rashi accepts the third view, that God showed Abram the World to Come—but that Rambam accepts either the first or second view. History that stops anywhere short of its predetermined goal is absurd history, meaningless history: struggle, violence, and suffering which lead only to more struggle, violence, and suffering.

If Abram's preview stopped either with the Exodus or with the days leading up to the Messiah's appearance, the vision must have been crushing to him: a trial indeed. If his vision went further and demonstrated the very meaning of human existence, that history has a goal toward which all our actions—however absurd they may appear to us—are marching, it was one of the great blessings of the patriarch's life.

Then it was over. At last, God released Abram from the prophecy, perhaps a day and a half after it had first come upon him. One assumes that during the time he was seeing visions and hearing the Lord's voice, he hadn't eaten a meal. He was left spent, exhausted, hungry. He had seen terrible things, heard awful portents of the future. Yet, whether or not this was a trial, he must also have been elated: he knew now what direction history was taking, where his mission and his descendants fit into the wide scope of the passing centuries and millennia. He knew a great deal more about the meaning of his own life than he had known two days earlier. Such knowledge must, I think, fill a man with joy. Perhaps to ordinary people like you and me it is granted when we die. God let Abram go, but the vision itself gripped the patriarch, we may assume, for the rest of his life.

CHAPTER EIGHT

The Handmaiden's Tale

We have all heard of families that were unsettled by the introduction into the household of an attractive young woman. This newcomer may be a live-in nanny, personal assistant, exchange student, or perhaps a cousin from out of town trying to establish herself in a new city. At first, everyone finds her presence delightfully refreshing. But gradually a tension begins to be felt as the wife finds her husband looking a bit too long at the boarder, or the boarder speaking to him in tones that are increasingly flirtatious. If their marriage is not to be undermined, the young woman must be sent off to find a new place to live.

By the time Abram was eighty-five years old, ten years after the arrival of his party in Canaan, certain tensions were beginning to be felt in the patriarch's household. We find indications of domestic discomfort in the biblical text. But the real anxiety of that home, its sources and ultimate outcome, is made clear only by the oral tradition, whose focus here is on the person of Hagar, handmaiden of Sarai. We must try to imagine what kind of person Hagar was and what kind of home she had entered.

According to the Midrash, she was a daughter of Pharaoh, but the king of Egypt had multiple wives and it seems unlikely that he would have given away to a foreigner, however notable, a daughter by his principal wife. When the royal father gave Hagar to Abram and Sarai, the king had said, "Better that my daughter be a servant in this house, than a lady in another house." But we have no evidence that Hagar herself accepted the transition from lady to servant as cheerfully as her father seemed to do. It seems likely that she did not.

For she was a purebred in every sense. The Midrash relates that Near Eastern mores were not particular about keeping young girls from being taken advantage of sexually—though technical virginity was prized. (Anal intercourse was thus a favorite.)[1] In contrast to the ways of other girls in her circumstance, Hagar had never been intimate with a man.[2] One pictures her as a rather proud woman, if perhaps not beautiful. Neither the Bible nor the oral tradition stints in its praise of female beauty, consistently alerting us if a woman is good-looking. But in this vein nothing is said of Hagar.

By now, she had been with Abram and Sarai for a decade, and she had noticed certain contradictions in the atmosphere of their home. On one hand, it was a very spiritually elevated environment. The commentator Sforno contrasts Abram's home, a "holy place and a house of righteous individuals," with that of Hagar's father, "a sinful place and a house of wicked individuals."[3] In contrast to Albright's comically pedestrian characterization of Abram as merely a distinguished donkey-caravaneer, mixing with other merchants of the desert highways, the Midrash has him frequently entertaining angels—and not only "unawares," as the author of the Letter to the Hebrews famously put it. We have observed that Sarai's other name, Yiscah, means "Looker" or "Seer" because she had the prophetic gift of being able to perceive supernatural realities beyond what most mortals are aware of. She communicated some of this power to the rest of her household. Merely by treading in the matriarch's home, her servants were infused with exquisite spiritual sensitivity, so that Hagar found she could see angels when they manifested themselves to Abram.[4] According to Maimonides, these ministering forces, messengers of God, can appear as men or as some other, inhuman creature, "fearful and terrible," or in the form of an unearthly fire. The more exalted a person's capacity for spiritual vision, the more likely it was that angels would come to him in the humble guise of ordinary men.[5] So presumably Hagar with her relatively small and derivative gifts had not seen *exactly* what her master and mistress did. But compared to serving girls in other homes, she had seen a great deal.

Yet for all the angels hanging around the living room, the mood of the house had grown dark. When Abram and his company left Haran in the patriarch's seventy-fifth year, God had promised to make of Abram the father of "a great nation," but He had said nothing of Sarai as that nation's mother.[6] Ten years later husband and wife were beginning to think, to their pained surprise, that Sarai was not the intended "matriarch" of this promised people. The reader will remember that both Abram and Sarai had good reason (namely, their congenital condition as sexually indeterminate *tumtumim*) to doubt they would ever reproduce. Yet they had assumed that on departing Haran and entering holy Canaan, they would be cured of any reproductive disability, notwithstanding that they were both quite elderly. For God plainly intended to work a miracle. And the Talmud confirms that living in the land of Israel improves fertility—King David, after all, praised his country as the "Land of Life."[7] According to Jewish law, if a childless couple reside in the Holy Land for ten years and still find themselves unable to conceive, they must conclude that they will never have children together because "he [the husband] did not merit to build [a family] through her."[8]

It seemed, then, that the problem lay in the matching of Abram with Sarai. Since God Himself had promised descendants to Abram, those descendants would have to come through another woman. As the years wore on, Abram and Sarai often looked at each other with sad eyes. Friends urged medicines and charms on the unfortunate couple, but the patriarch and his wife chose to rely on God for their help.[9] They prayed, and among His purposes in afflicting them was precisely to call forth their prayers. "The Holy One Blessed Be He desires the heart," says the Talmud.[10] Passion, as expressed in prayer, is a human faculty that He particularly prizes. One may also speculate, in line with the Midrash, that He wanted to preserve Sarai's youthful appearance and beauty, despite her advanced age.[11] Giving birth typically signals the end of girlish glamour, and God needed Sarai to remain beautiful. Justly or unjustly, leaders who are women are judged by their looks, even by other women, to an extent their male counterparts never are. Sarai's role in Abram's missionary activity was no less than his, and it helped that she didn't look like a woman in her seventies. In fact, for her first ninety years, Sarai remained as lovely as "a bride under her bridal canopy."[12] So the Lord heard their prayers, but as yet he chose not to answer them.

The biblical text informs us that "at the end of ten years of Abram's dwelling in the land of Canaan," Sarai resolved to take action. (The phrase "at the end" demonstrates that he and Sarai waited precisely ten years, from which the Talmud derives its lesson for barren couples in Israel.)[13] In Mesopotamia, monogamy was the rule, though a man might also take a concubine, which was a sort of second-class wife, not altogether unlike a prostitute but bound by law to him alone.[14] In Nuzi, however, there were specific laws and customs to guide a husband whose wife was barren. Thanks to the huge cache of cuneiform tablets discovered there, Nuzi is the second-millennium society about which we know more than we do about almost any other. Because it was in the general vicinity of Abram's precise homeland, and because the predominant ethnicity was Hurrian, as it was at Haran, we can assume that the customs of Nuzi were familiar to the patriarch. Skeptical scholars like Thomas L. Thompson who doubt that Nuzi has any relevance to Abram point out that the practices of other Near Eastern societies, later than Nuzi, also seem to be reflected in the patriarchal narratives. But the point that Thompson and his colleagues miss is that no ancient society with which we are familiar matches the biblical text in more ways than does Nuzi.[15]

At Nuzi, the rule was clear. If a wife proved unable to conceive (and the problem was typically, unfairly attributed to the wife), she was obliged to provide her husband a second wife with whom he could have another go at begetting children. The requirement was chiseled into the clay tablet of a binding legal document, as in this example whereby a man by the name of Shennima married a woman called Kelim-ninu: "If Kelim-ninu bears [children], Shennima shall not take another wife. But if Kelim-ninu does not bear [children], Kelim-ninu shall acquire a woman of the land of Lullu [a place where the most desirable slaves were found] as wife for Shennima, and Kelim-ninu may not send the offspring [of her husband and the slave from Lullu] away."[16]

There were other reasons that a wife presumed barren would be glad to give her husband a child in this way. According to Hurrian customs, the child produced by the union of husband with slave-turned-second-wife became the adopted child of the first wife.[17] As Sarai said to Abram, "Behold now, the Lord has closed me up from delivering. Go then to my handmaiden. Perhaps I will be built up from her."[18] A woman in Sarai's position would also have pondered the folk wisdom of her time, which said that adoption was conducive to fertility.[19] Not only might Sarai gain a child indirectly through the handmaiden: by this method her own infertility problem might be cured so that she would give birth to a child of her very own. (According to modern science, this item of wisdom turns out to be well founded. Women who have trouble conceiving and who then adopt a child often become pregnant sometime afterward, perhaps because the anxiety of trying and failing to get pregnant itself impeded conception and, with the adoption, this anxiety is relieved.)[20]

And so Sarai recalled her duty as a wife as she had learned it from the customs of her native land. The choice of a second wife for her husband seemed obvious. She would give him the finest slave she owned: Hagar, the pharaoh's own daughter. Abram doubted the wisdom of the strategy. But he figured that of the two of them, Sarai was the superior prophet, so she knew best, "and Abram listened to the voice of Sarai"—the voice of the Holy Spirit which he believed that he heard in his wife.[21] With the vision of hindsight, and having read what comes next in the Bible's narrative and what the oral tradition has to say, we know that the plan was ill conceived. Its disastrous results have been felt down through the millennia.

Sarai was a more gifted prophet than Abram, but his instincts here were correct. We find in Maimonides' discussions of prophecy that the gift of knowledge through the Holy Spirit is given to a man or woman only under particular circumstances: "All of the prophets may not prophesy at any time they wish. Instead they must concentrate their mind and attain a state of joy and a cheerful heart and [then] seclude themselves. For prophecy cannot rest amid sadness nor amid languidness, but rather amid joy."[22] And the heart of Sarai was neither joyful nor cheerful. The Midrash indeed offers her as a case study in being "languid": the kind of woman who gets into funks of depression from which, time and again, she needs to be revived by her husband.[23] So it stands to reason that her prophetic powers were not operating at peak capacity.

She had cause to be sad. After all, with each month that passed it seemed a little more likely that whatever plans God had for Abram, they did not include Sarai as the birth mother of his children. Perhaps Abram no longer found himself able to snap his wife out of her moods. Perhaps he had stopped trying. Perhaps along with her moodiness, her impatience for a child marred her powers of spiritual vision. For impatience is at the root of much, if not all, sin. In His teachings, God allows us almost everything that our heart desires—food, sex, sleep, material luxuries. He asks only that we enjoy these pleasures in accordance with the regulations He sets down, and often this means deferring gratification.

So Sarai became convinced that the best course of action was to follow the custom of Nuzi, and Abram agreed to go along with the plan. Note that the decision was hers, not his. The picture we get from the oral tradition is of a patriarch who in certain respects allowed his wife to wear the pants in the family. Sarai did not shrink from ruling over husband.[24]

It remained for her to seek the consent of Hagar. Sarai's somewhat haughty and off-putting speech to the handmaiden is recorded in *Genesis Rabbah*: "How fortunate you will be to cleave to this holy body [of my husband]!"[25] Hagar agreed.

From the beginning, the project was marred by ill feeling. Perhaps the roots of the enmity that grew between the two women can be traced to their first meeting back in Egypt. Sarai associated Hagar with her humiliation at the hand of Pharaoh when the king had abducted her and Abram had neither said nor done anything to stop him. Every time she saw Hagar she must have recalled the experience of being captive in Pharaoh's palace. If she ever resented Abram for this, some of that resentment may have rubbed off on Hagar.[26]

So Abram went to bed with his wife's servant, and their "marriage" was consummated. Maimonides numbers this episode, "taking Hagar as his wife after he had despaired of having children with Sarai," as the fifth of Abram's trials.[27] Sarai was his life's love, and to be denied the privilege of producing new life with the woman you love would indeed be a trial.

Imagine the impact on Sarai a month or two later when it developed not only that Hagar was pregnant but that, as Rashi notes, she had been impregnated on her first act of intercourse.[28] This was amazing, for the Talmud says that "a woman cannot become pregnant from her first sexual act," and presumably medical wisdom at the time held the same view.[29] The Talmud's point is not to contradict modern medicine, which can adduce cases of women becoming pregnant in just this way, but rather to suggest that when it happens, it seems miraculous. Sarai had been with Abram for decades and produced no child. Now this slave conceived on her wedding night. Hagar was proud of herself, and the intensity of her pride was matched by the intensity of Sarai's feelings. The latter, though, were mixed, being composed equally of gratification at giving her husband a child and humiliation at the comparisons between herself and Hagar that her household must now be inclined to draw.

Whatever affection had remained between Sarai and Hagar quickly soured. According to the Midrash, when other ladies came to visit Sarai, she directed them to stop in and see Hagar as well, saying, "Go and inquire too of the welfare of that poor, wretched one"—meaning Hagar, who was having a difficult time of her pregnancy. Sarai's compassion for Hagar has about it an exquisite ambivalence. Sarai seems genuinely to care that being pregnant has physically weakened her cowife; but we detect condescension in her reference to "that poor, wretched one," as in her comments to Hagar about the handmaiden's being joined to the "holy body" of Abram.

The seed of antagonism sprang up from the ground and produced a spreading tree of hatred. Hagar turned proud and bitter. To her visitors, she said, "What my mistress Sarai hides is not like what she reveals. She appears to be righteous, but she is not righteous! If she were indeed righteous—why, see how many years she did not become pregnant. But I became pregnant in one night!"[30]

The deteriorating relationship between Sarai and Hagar brings us up against a tricky question on which, at first glance, the rabbis who transmitted the Oral Torah seem to have been divided. This is the question of whether our matriarch and patriarch were saints—or rather, individuals who consistently behaved in a saintly fashion. Rashi indicates that they were indeed almost perfect. "The years of Sarah's life," he says, "were all equal in terms of good-ness." Even at one hundred years of age, Abraham and Sarah both remained "without sin," as innocent as children.[31]

Writing a bit more than a century later, Nachmanides appears to dis-agree. We have already observed that he wrote of Abram's behavior in Egypt that it constituted a "great sin" against Sarai. In the matter of Hagar, he wrote that Abram and Sarai ultimately came to sin so egregiously that the repercussions continue to be felt. For Hagar gave birth to Ishmael, whose descendants, the Arabic peoples, have assaulted "the seed of Abraham and Sarah with all manners of affliction."[32]

Torah is an organic whole. We need to understand the opinions of Rashi and Ramban not separately, as if one commentator were right and the other wrong, but together. Where the classical rabbinic or Talmudic authorities appear to diverge, it is not exactly a disagreement but rather a *machloket,* a very special kind of disagreement in which each view reflects a portion of the truth. (The word *machloket* is derived from the Hebrew root that means "portion.") Comprehended simultaneously, Rashi and Ramban really are saying as follows. If miraculously you and I were to be conveyed back in time to Mamre in the land of Canaan in the year 1727 B.C., we would ob-serve no terrible "sin" being committed by Abram or Sarai. But there is a general rule in Torah thought that God judges people with rigor or laxity depending on how much of Himself He has manifested to them. The more they know about Him, the more He expects. This explains why through His judgment the Jewish nation has suffered as it has for millennia. If like Abram you were the person chosen to reintroduce God to His world; if like Sarai you had been granted an unusually close relationship with the Deity; then your behavior, too, would be evaluated according to extraordinarily rigor-ous standards. He expected more of Abram and Sarai than He does of us. And in His eyes, they sinned.[33]

What did they do that was so bad? Abram didn't *do* anything, which was the problem. Sarai had a right to Hagar's respect. The spirit of Near Eastern law was on the matriarch's side. The young lady of Nuzi we met a few pages ago, Kelim-ninu, received as a marriage gift the handmaiden Yalampa, who was required "as long as she is alive" to "revere" Kelim-ninu.[34] The Code of Hammurabi formally set down laws whose provisions mirror the situation of Sarai and Hagar almost perfectly. If a socially elevated mistress (actually a priestess) gave her slave to her husband; and if this childbearing slave subsequently "claimed equality with her mistress because she bore children, [then] her mistress . . . may mark her with the slave-mark and count her among the slaves."[35] In other words, the mistress was entitled to punish the other woman by demoting her to her former, exclusively servile, station. An earlier legal code, that of Ur-Nammu, founder of the Third Dynasty of the metropolis of Ur, was still in force—or anyway still being copied out onto clay tablets at Ur to be found by archaeologists—during exactly the period that Sarai was fussing with Hagar. Ur-Nammu offered another remedy: "If a man's slave-woman, comparing herself to her mistress, speaks insolently to her (or him), her mouth shall be scoured with 1 quart of salt."[36] Abram might have averted all this trouble by chastising Hagar; or he might have punished her himself; but his *chesed,* his kindness, got the better of him. He remained silent.

"My injustice is upon you," cried his wife, meaning that the injustice done to Sarai was Abram's fault. "Let the Lord judge between me and you." She called on God to take Abram to task for his hurtful silence, and to punish him accordingly.[37]

The sins and errors of this husband and wife—again, relative to their status as prophets of God—had started to pile up. Both the Midrash and Talmud condemn Sarai for demanding that God judge her husband. In *Genesis Rabbah,* we find that for this, Sarai died thirty-eight years before her time.[38] The Talmud's tractate *Rosh Hashanah* tells of "three things [that] cause a person's sins to be recalled [in Heaven]," including "submitting judgment of one's fellow to Heaven," and offers Sarai's words as a prime example.[39] The tractate *Baba Kamma* says, "He who calls to judgment his fellow man—he will be punished first," and once again Sarai provides the proof text.[40] But in *Baba Kamma,* it is said that the stricture against submitting someone else to judgment—which is really about the peril of having too much confidence in one's own righteousness—and its associated punishment apply only if there are judicial avenues available to set things right. If the law offers no remedy, you may submit your case to God. The Talmud must then be aware that Sarai had a good legal case against Hagar, which she neglected to pursue.

Abram bowed to his wife's anger, granting her the freedom to punish Hagar as she saw fit: "Behold, your handmaiden is in your hand. Do to her that which is good in your eyes."[41]

The Bible says that Sarai proceeded to "afflict" Hagar; but what exactly this means, the text in typical fashion leaves unclear. The Hebrew root of the word meaning "to afflict," spelled "ayin-nun-heh," appears later in the Pentateuch when God explains to Moses how on each Yom Kippur, in the process of atoning for their sins, the people of Israel shall "afflict" themselves. As the oral tradition specifies, the "afflictions" of Yom Kippur included five types of self-chastisement, the purpose being to deprive the body of its customary sources of pleasure and dignity. Thus the soul is directed to contemplate itself and God from a perspective of maximum spiritual purity. For twenty-five hours, a Jew must refrain from eating, bathing, sex, anointing himself with oil, and wearing good shoes. Sarai's afflictive strategies correspond to two of these activities. According to the Midrash, she denied Hagar the conjugal bed of their husband, Abram, and she removed Hagar's slipper and slapped her with it. She also compelled the other woman to perform menial tasks in public—like walking behind her mistress, carrying Sarai's towels and water buckets for her bath.[42] This last humiliation was later made the object of a Torah prohibition: the sin of working a slave in such a way that his or her slave status is made known to all. Deriving this from a verse in Leviticus, Rashi gives the example of one who orders his servant to "carry his belongings behind him to the bathhouse."[43]

Punishing a miscreant is one thing. Though Sarai's intent was pedagogical, her purpose being to encourage Hagar to repent of her bad attitude, it is not the place of one human being to impose a Yom Kippur on her fellow. That right is reserved to God alone. It would have been better if she had washed out Hagar's mouth with a quart of salt.

As the Ramban explains, it was Abram's inaction in the first place and Sarai's afflictions in the second that initiated the chain of events leading to the birth of the child Ishmael. The baby that Hagar carried now was not, however, that child. Had the fetus in her womb, Abram's first-conceived child, actually been born, we don't know who it would have grown up to be. Instead, it became a victim of the *ayin ha'rah*.

This Hebrew phrase is literally translated "evil eye." Thus superstitious Jews will sometimes be found wearing amulets to ward off the *ayin ha'rah*, which they take to mean some demonic force that strikes people especially when they have experienced good fortune. Actually the *ayin ha'rah* is something different. Jewish mysticism holds that there is indeed a destructive moral power that is unleashed under circumstances connected with good fortune. But contrary to what the amulet wearers believe, that force is no demon or devil. Rather, when a person receives a blessing, such as a baby in a woman's womb, which the woman allows to aggrieve others who have not been similarly blessed, then her smugness triggers a spiritual mechanism, set in place by God, that can result in her blessing being taken away from her.

As Rashi explains, that is what happened to Hagar.[44] Maybe she was carrying Sarai's bath togs along behind the matriarch—feeling humiliated yet at the same time proud that she had conceived by Abram while Sarai never had—when the *ayin ha'rah* caused a spontaneous abortion. We are free to imagine her groans of despair.

The scriptural text notes simply that Hagar "fled" from Sarai.[45] It was a flight not of fear, but of mad grief. When a woman miscarries her baby, especially her first baby, the loss can almost equal losing a child that has already been born. In this case, Hagar's distress was multiplied by the fact that all of her self-regard had been hanging on the birth of that child. Here she was a daughter of Pharaoh, reduced to servitude. She must have been aware that a great destiny was in store for Abram. Her own sense of nobility depended on her having a role in his destiny. That chance had now been washed away in uterine blood.

With hardly enough time to pack provisions, she dashed from the house, intending to return to her father.[46] In the Bible, we next encounter her on the road heading toward Shur, the Wall of the Ruler that protected Egypt from Asiatic invaders. This road, a major caravan route, crossed the northern Sinai, but Hagar had not yet reached that awful desert. She was "between Kadesh and Bered," two localities that were apparently in the western Negev wilderness. Kadesh lies on the border of the Negev and the Sinai. Bered, whose name is obscure, may according to one ancient Aramaic translation be identical with Chalutzah, southwest of Beersheba.[47] If so, then we can trace a line between Kadesh and Bered and find its midpoint where the line intersects the road to Shur, which likely ran nearby modern Israel's

Route 211. There by a spring of water, some fifteen miles east of today's Egyptian-Israeli border, Hagar encountered an angel.

A word on Hebrew angelology is in order. Scattered cryptic references to angels are found in the Talmud and Midrash, expanding on bare and still more cryptic references in the Bible. The Talmud warns that this field of study—called *Ma'aseh Merkavah* ("Work of the Chariot"), referring to chapter 1 of the Book of Ezekiel with its esoteric vision of the Lord's chariot— is to be taught only to students individually, rather than to groups of people.[48] Evidently it is subject to misunderstanding and thus, lest the student lead himself astray, requires deep contemplation, even apprenticeship to a master sage—something that cannot be conveyed by listening to a lecture or reading a book. Maimonides warns, "You know very well how difficult it is for men to form a notion of anything immaterial and entirely devoid of corporeality, except after considerable training."[49] Nevertheless, later sages, including the Rambam himself and Rabbi Moshe Chayim Luzzatto (also called Ramchal; Italian, 1707–46), sought to systematize the major points of the topic in an accessible fashion.

A key to understanding angels may be found in a peculiarity about the way that they appear in the Bible itself. At times they seem to be entities separate from God, while at other times they speak in His voice as manifestations of Him. In Hagar's meeting with an angel in the desert, the supernatural being is repeatedly called "an angel of the Lord." But then Scripture has the angel promise her, "I will indeed increase your offspring," as if the angel were God. In the next verse, it reverts to speaking of God in the third person, as the angel assures her that "the Lord has heard your prayer." The typical approach of biblical source critics would be to insist either that we have here a textual corruption or that two sources have been knitted together. A more sensitive modern scholar points out that the "apparent interchangeability" of the angel and the Lord "cannot be resolved by assuming a clumsy merging of two traditional stories. The same ambiguity occurs in many narratives (e.g., Gen. 21:15–21; 22:11–12; 31:11–13; Exod. 3:2–6; Judg. 6:11–24)"—so often that it must be intentional and meaningful.[50] The scholar goes on to say that the most likely explanation is that the author wants us to experience a paradox: that angels participate in God's will in a much more direct way than people do. The identity of will is so close that they both are and are not to be identified with Him. For while the Lord is indeed somehow present when the angel is present, at the same time humans are not permitted to have an unmediated encounter with Him.

This paradox offers a point of entry to the Rambam's and Ramchal's descriptions. Angels are creations. They are not to be identified with God. However, God uses them as agents to drive all the natural and supernatural forces in the world. They are how His will operates in the world. The Midrash says, "There is no blade of grass down below that does not have an angel on high that strikes it and tells it to grow."[51] We experience His will through their agency.

Ramchal begins his systematic philosophical treatment of all Judaism, *The Way of God,* with the statement "Creation in general consists of two basic parts: the physical and the spiritual."[52] While we are accustomed to thinking of the spiritual realm as overwhelmingly a positive thing, while the physical is subject to corruption and wickedness, biblical tradition sees matters differently. Neither good nor bad, the spiritual is simply anything that is not physical. There are purely physical beings (animals), and there are purely spiritual beings (angels), while humans mix in their essence the physical and the spiritual. At certain times, a person can encounter the purely spiritual, as in prophetic dreams and even in ordinary ones, when he or she may meet angels and demons. As Luzzatto summarizes the angelic role, "God had thus willed and organized things so that His decrees should be translated into action through angels, each in its own appointed area of influence. . . . Thus, for example, there is a directing angel associated with trees, and its task is to strive to sustain these trees."[53] As the Midrash relates, an angel has one task to accomplish, never more than that.[54] Thus all of causation, the unfathomably complex chain of effects that links all actions in the universe, is carried out by angels. One angel causes an effect, which can be understood as being represented by another angel and so on in an endless web of causation.

We can make certain statements about angels, drawn from the Talmud and other rabbinic literature, that may or may not be informative. Angels were created before man was, either on the second or the fifth day of creation (man was created on the sixth).[55] They carry up our prayers to Heaven.[56] Every person has two angels to accompany him at all times, which record his deeds to be evaluated later by a heavenly tribunal.[57] Angels are organized into ten distinct categories, including *serafim,* angels that burn with love of God, and *keruvim,* or cherubs, a lower variety pictured as children in a rare artistic representation of angels in ancient Judaism: the two cherubs that guarded the Ark of the Covenant in the Temple. The *ishim* are the lowest type of angel, the kind that typically interact with human beings, including prophets.[58] These would be the sort of angel that Abraham regularly had as guests in his home.

Another function that angels have is to guard the interests of the world's nations. Each nation has its own ministering angel, which shares its fate. Thus when the Israelites made their Exodus from Egypt and were pursued to the Sea of Reeds by Pharaoh's army, the Torah says the Jews looked up and saw "Egypt" pursuing them: meaning they saw the guardian angel of Egypt descending from Heaven to join ranks with the Egyptian charioteers.[59] When God drowned the Egyptian soldiers, He also reduced the angel of Egypt to a debilitated condition, and thus the nation as a whole must begin to sink permanently in its fortunes. (Indeed, history confirms this. If the Exodus occurred, per tradition, in 1312 B.C., that would place it in the Eighteenth Dynasty. Thanks to war and invasion, the Nineteenth and Twentieth Dynasties initiated a remarkable decline from which Egyptian power never recovered.)

Israel's guardian angel is Michael, who will later announce to Abraham's wife, Sarah, that she is to give birth to Isaac, progenitor of the nation Israel. With this in mind, we may speculate that the angel Hagar met now was the guardian angel of the Ishmaelite nations, the Arab peoples, whose own progenitor would soon be born.

This angel may have taken the shape of a flame or maybe of some dread inhuman creature. Either way, Hagar was unafraid. Scripture says nothing at all of her reaction, which is how we know that she was accustomed to seeing angels in Abram's home.[60] Actually the language of Genesis is strangely repetitive, the phrase "And an angel of the Lord said to her" being said several times in succession, from which the Midrash understands that not one but four or five angels met her by the spring.[61]

They directed her to return to Sarai, submitting herself to her mistress's will, and announced that she would once again conceive. "And an angel of the Lord said to her: 'Behold, you will conceive and bear a son and shall call his name Ishmael [meaning "God Has Heard"], for the Lord has heard of your affliction. And he [Ishmael] will be a wild ass of a man, his hand will be against everyone and everyone's hand will be against him; and he will dwell in the face of his brothers.' "⁶²

The ancient and medieval rabbinic commentaries on these prophetic verses about Ishmael and his Arabic descendants read like notes for a newspaper editorial about the relations of the Arab world with Israel and the West even as I write this. The first-century-A.D. Aramaic translation of Onkelos interprets, "And he will be rebellious among mankind. He will be in need of everyone else, and at the same time mankind will be in need of him."⁶³ On the phrase "and the hand of everyone will be against him," Rashi says, "All will hate him and attack him."⁶⁴ As for his "dwell[ing] in the face of his brothers," the idiom is up-to-the-minute modern.

We noted in the preface that, regarding the details of Abraham's life, Muslim tradition tracks its Jewish counterpart to a remarkable extent. Represented in the collections of reports traced to Muhammad, the *hadith* literature, this tradition fills in blanks in the narrative left by the Quran just as Jewish tradition does for the Bible. Indeed, many *hadith* reports appear to have drawn considerably from the Talmud and Midrash, if indirectly. There is even agreement with Jewish sources on such an obscure point as Ibrahim's birthplace, which several *hadith* reports likewise give as Cuthah. Of course, there is eventually a point where Islam must break off from Judaism and set its own course on these matters, with Abraham becoming the first Muslim, founder of the primordial faith which Muhammad later expounded. We would expect the annunciation of Ishmael's birth to be that point, for Muslims join Jews and Christians in regarding Ishmael as Muhammad's ancestor—but it is not.

The Quran actually says little about Ishmael, other than to praise his trustworthiness: ". . . you shall tell of Ishmael: he, too, was a man of his word, an apostle, and a prophet. He enjoined prayer and almsgiving on his people, and his Lord was pleased with him."⁶⁵ The *hadith* literature does not go far beyond this, though it does tell amusing tales about Ishmael taking his qualities of patience and reliability to extremes. Versions of the story tell of a person who made an appointment with Ishmael to meet at a certain time and place, but who then forgot. Ishmael waited all day, or in other versions for three days, or even for a whole year! When the fellow at last showed up, he said, "You did not leave!" Ishmael replied, "No." The man said, "But I forgot!" Ishmael: "I would not leave until you came."

Possibly the traditions are scanty simply because the Quran says so little, indicating there cannot be much to tell; or possibly because the Jewish sources from which Muslim sages drew paint a fairly negative picture of Ishmael, which would be unacceptable in Muslim eyes. Still, a few points of interest stand out. One Muslim rendition notes that Abram and Sarai waited twenty years while living in the Holy Land, not ten as Jewish tradition records, before Sarai figured she could not become pregnant herself and turned Hagar over to Abram. But Hagar was proud and antagonized Sarai, who caused her to flee from their home. An angel found Hagar at the well and promised her she would give birth to a line of mighty rulers, namely, Muhammad and those who followed him. Another account identifies the angel of the annunciation, Gabriel, and says that when Ishmael was born, his face shone with holy luminescence, like the moon, a hint of his great descendant the prophet Muhammad.[66]

Wearily, after calling the spring where she stood Beer-lahai-roi, or "Well of the Living One Who Appeared to Me," Hagar turned her steps toward Abram's home and returned, repentant, to her mistress.

She once again slept with her master, though now, Ramban explains, in the reduced role of concubine rather than wife.[67] When, just as the angel promised, she conceived and bore a son, the baby was duly named Ishmael. Strangely, though, Rashi says that the parent who named him was not Hagar, but Abram: "Although Abram had not heard the words of the angel who said 'And you shall call his name Ishmael,' the Holy Spirit rested upon him and he called him 'Ishmael.' "[68] But hadn't Hagar told him of her experience in the desert? Evidently they made love in silence and remained silent thereafter. Somehow, either from an excess of passion or from the coldness of alienation, Hagar neglected to tell Abram that the Lord himself had named the child. So the Lord, through the Holy Spirit, was obliged to tell Abram this Himself.

I would suggest that it was passion, not coldness, that made Hagar keep quiet; that they rushed to be together without speaking first because their desire for each other was so heated. Seemingly it has to be one or the other: fire or ice. And Abram as an icy character, devoid of feeling, doesn't match the quality of *chesed,* kindness, an overabundance of human warmth, that the tradition identifies as his main personality trait.

It is in their mutual silence that we find a first clue to solving a conundrum posed by the Bible critics: that of the "doublets" in the Abraham story. Supposing that there was a passion between Abram and Hagar helps explain the overall structure of the narrative. We have already observed this phenomenon of strands of motif. Depending on how you count, the patriarch's story may include five such pairs, each composed of one strand by one author, the other by a different author. You would *expect* these to fall at random, wherever our Redactor happened to work them in. Yet as the scholar Devora Steinmetz lays out in detail, the doublets exhibit an unexpectedly tidy pattern.[69]

Here are four doubled motifs: (A) Abram pretends that Sarai is his sister, once in Egypt (Genesis 12) and again in Gerar (Genesis 20); (B) Lot departs from Abram or otherwise rejects his company, once when the two first split up (Genesis 13) and again after the overthrow of Sodom (Genesis 19); (C) Lot's life is endangered, once during the war of the kings (Genesis 14), again at the overthrow of Sodom (Genesis 18); (D) God makes a new covenant, once at the Covenant Between the Parts (Genesis 15), again at the Covenant of Circumcision (Genesis 17).

In each doublet, the first component comes before Genesis 16, while its repetition comes after. What's more, the paired motifs are disposed in a precise forward-backward arrangement: ABCD followed by DCBA. In the exact middle falls Genesis 16. That chapter—Hagar's pregnancies, the birth of Ishmael—is the pivot on which Abram's life turns.

With Ishmael's birth, perhaps even earlier in the sexual relationship with Hagar, something changed in Abram. In the first strand in each of our four motifs, he focuses on the welfare of his Mesopotamian family—Lot and Sarai. But after Ishmael's birth, he seems focused on his Egyptian family—Hagar and Ishmael—or on individuals unrelated to him. For example, in Genesis 14 (Lot Endangered), he goes to war to save Lot. But in Genesis 18, he tries to save Sodom, not Lot. In Genesis 15 (New Covenant), when

Abram is promised descendants, they presumably will come through Sarai. But in Genesis 17, he begs God to carry on his destiny through Hagar's son.

After Ishmael enters the world, Abram is supposed to understand that the Destiny Child has still not been born. It is not Ishmael. But the spiritual vision that had sustained him up to this point is suddenly dimmed. He loved Sarai passionately, and it tore his heart that they seemed unable to have children together. But he would also come to love Ishmael. That he loved Hagar is, I think, also a definite possibility—loved her enough partly to blind him to the future that God had set out for him

I have suggested that Abram's future also contained a certain mountain, which he knew to be of key importance. From the moment he entered Canaan, Abram was looking for a mysterious peak where he sensed that a culmination of his life would take place. This mountain was also part of his vision. As we explore the next four biblical chapters, you will hear nothing more about this mountain—that is, until the mountain he had once envisioned and the Destiny Child about whom he now forgot come together.

CHAPTER NINE

The Kindest Cut

bram was still living at Hebron. At age ninety-nine, he received a vision from the Lord giving the old man a new name, Abraham. In the vision, God also called on him to circumcise himself and every male among his followers and servants, including even his thirteen-year-old son, Ishmael. Despite wanting to be prompt in carrying out the commandment upon his own body, the patriarch worried that if he was circumcised first, then due to his advanced age, he might be unable to assist in the circumcision of everyone else. So Ishmael and the rest went before him. Ramban suggests that rather than carry out each surgery by himself, an arduous task, Abraham may have sought the assistance of other men trained in the art of foreskin amputation.[1]

These would have been Canaanites who knew the technique from their own traditions. As late as the fifteenth century A.D., a stone in a small cave at Mamre was preserved, said to be the stone on which Abraham circumcised himself and his household. As each male was cut, his foreskin was placed in a little pile of other amputated foreskins.[2] The flesh began to decay and the smell ascended to God, Who was pleased.

The blood must have flowed for hours, as one man after another was brought forward. It is not like clipping your fingernails. In Mamre's palace among the grove of oak trees, the patriarch's son, servants, and disciples lay round about him in various states of physical distress, for, of course, there were no anesthetics at the time. At last, everyone had been cut but Abraham. He said to God, "And who will circumcise me?"

God answered, "You yourself."

Abraham then lifted up a knife and took his foreskin, withered and loose, in his hand. Because he was so elderly, he felt afraid. God took compassion on him. Says the Midrash, "What did the Holy One Blessed Be He do? He sent forth His own hand and took hold [of Abraham's foreskin] with him, and then Abraham cut [himself]."[3]

Never mind the tradition's image of the Master of the Universe holding in His hand the desiccated member of the aged prophet. The whole picture of a mass circumcision is strange enough by itself, and would seem still more so if we were not Americans, citizens of a country where circumcision is common among non-Jews as well as Jews. We need to understand why God insisted on this painful mutilation, for Abram and every Jewish male who has followed him down through the ages. Let us, then, back up and consider God's communication that led to the pile of foreskins sending up their stink to Heaven.

For this communication, the Bible uses an expression, "and the Lord appeared to Abram," known to designate an event called a *mareh,* or "vision," which falls short of prophecy per se, or perhaps refers to a relatively low-level prophetic experience.[4] In any event, the two messages God proceeded to impart to the patriarch were not at all of a low or common variety.

The first words Abram heard from his creator on this occasion were not unlike words he had heard previously from the same source. Said God: "I am El Shaddai. Walk before me and be perfect. And I shall set my covenant between me and between you and I shall multiply you most exceedingly."[5] Upon hearing this, Abram bowed down, setting his face in the dust. He was overcome with awe and gratitude. But why? After all, the content of God's assurance was no news to him. The Lord had promised Abram a covenant and offspring seventeen years earlier at the Covenant Between the Parts. The vision continued as God elaborated:

> As for me, behold this is my covenant with you. You shall be a father of a multitude of nations, and no longer shall your name be called Abram. Your name shall be Abraham, for I have made you father of a multitude of nations. And I will make you exceedingly fruitful and I will make of you nations; and kings shall go out from you. And I will set my covenant between me and you and your offspring after you for your generations as an eternal covenant, to be a God to you and to your offspring after you. And I will give to you and to your offspring after you the land of your sojourns—even all the land of Canaan—as an eternal possession; and I will be a god to them.[6]

Why did God repeat more or less the same promise He had made almost two decades ago, and why did Abram—now called Abraham—act as if he were hearing all this for the first time?

Believers in the Documentary Hypothesis assert that Genesis 15 (where the Covenant Between the Parts is to be found) and Genesis 17 (where the present divine assurance occurs) are the work of different authors, J and P, respectively. There was a tradition that told of a covenant, a tradition that preceded J and P and on which both J and P drew, each in turn giving his own spin and interpretation. From Genesis 15 to Genesis 17, there is, then, no logical progression but instead only random variation, which the Redactor failed to properly edit.

There are two problems with this explanation. First, while brilliant enough to edit the most influential book ever, our Redactor neglects an elementary editing rule, which is to eliminate pointless repetition. Second, the rendition of the covenant here in Genesis 17 is attributed to P, whose work is marked by its use of the divine names "Elohim" ("God") and "El Shaddai" ("God Almighty"). But 17:1 employs the tetragrammaton, as "the Lord" appears to Abram. This is a "scribal error," an "exception," a "slip," we are assured by the critic E. A. Speiser.[7] Untroubled by circular reasoning, believers in the Documentary Hypothesis say, in effect, "Because we have identified this chapter as the work of P (or J), any indications that it might be by J (or P, or some other author) must by definition be an error, an exception, a slip."

Alternatively, if we are prepared to entertain the hypothesis that Genesis was composed by one hand or Hand, then we should look for an underlying structure that gives order to the whole narrative of Abraham's life. I have suggested one possible structure, identified by the scholar Devora Steinmetz. That structure pivots on the story in Genesis 16 about the birth of Ishmael. Before Genesis 16, Abraham's mind is focused on his Mesopotamian wife, Sarai (soon to be renamed Sarah). After Genesis 16, he is focused on his Egyptian wife, Hagar, and her son. We should then expect to find that a key difference between the presentation of a new covenant in Genesis 15 and the renewed covenant here in Genesis 17 is that in the latter Abraham shows evidence of a preoccupation with his son Ishmael. Thus (although this is getting a little ahead of ourselves) we can observe that later in Genesis 17 God will feel the need to remind Abraham that Sarah's as-yet-unborn son is, even more than Ishmael, destined for greatness. Says the Lord, "I will bless [Sarah] and I will give to you, through her, a son; and I will bless her. And she shall become nations; and kings of peoples shall come from her."[8] Abraham understands this to mean that Ishmael has been edged out of the running to be his spiritual heir: either because the lad, now thirteen years old, has proved himself unworthy or because he is destined to die young.[9] Abraham pleads with God both that Ishmael should be virtuous and that he should not die: "Oh, would that Ishmael live before you!"[10] (To live *before* God means not only remaining alive but remaining in His good graces.) Abraham's plea is in vain, at least partly. God answers that Ishmael will indeed live—but not before God. The boy will receive a blessing and become the ancestor of a great nation (traditionally, the Arabic people). "But I will establish My covenant with Isaac whom Sarah will bear to you at this season next year."[11] In his intense desire that Hagar's son succeed him in his spiritual mission, Abraham has been gently rebuked.

But the Ramban detects another structure in the Abraham narrative. We have so far noted two promises, one of them seemingly redundant, which God makes to the patriarch. But Nachmanides finds a total of four promises (including these two). Now, *that's* redundant—or is it?

The promises are as follows. Ramban focuses on God's assurance, in each case, that Abraham's divine blessings will include possession of the land of Israel. When he entered the land, at age seventy-five, and made his way to the city of Shechem, God offered the vague promise "To your offspring I will give the land."[12] Precisely what land He was referring to—its precise borders—was unspecified. Abraham wondered about the size, shape, and location of his real-estate gift only for a short time—less than a year—until he returned with his company from Egypt and came to worship at the altar he had set up previously between Beth-el and Ai. There he received a prophecy in which God showed him, not visually but spiritually, the total extent of the country, saying, "All the land that you see I will give to you and to your offspring for eternity."[13] Both these promises are given in the future tense. By the time, at age eighty-two, of the Covenant Between the Parts, the promised gift of the land has already taken place. Abraham's act of possession was no longer in the future. Hence the promise here is given in the past tense. Also the eastern and western borders of the land are given. "On that day the Lord made a covenant with Abram, saying 'To your offspring I have given this land, from the river of Egypt to the great river, the river Euphrates.' "[14]

Finally, in Genesis 17, the land is promised to Abraham a fourth time—but with God's language now, oddly, reverting to the future tense. "And I will give to you and to your offspring after you the land of your sojourns—even all the land of Canaan—as an eternal possession; and I will be a god to them."[15] What information does this add to the three promises that precede it? It is, says Ramban, a cryptic reference to future travail and redemption. If the descendants of Abraham are ever exiled from the land, then God promises to return them to their home; for their possession of it is "eternal."[16] Of course, the offspring of Abraham, the Jewish people, have been twice exiled from the land of Israel—once by the Babylonians, again by the Romans. From the Babylonian exile, they returned to Israel within a matter of decades. From the Roman exile, they began to return en masse around 1948. God, it would seem, keeps His promises.

Devora Steinmetz and Rabbi Moshe ben Nachman give us the alternative to the outlook of the Bible critics. Either this twin structure is merely the imagining of traditional Bible interpreters—for the Redactor was too sloppy to have intended it, or too unwilling to edit the imprecise traditions set down by other writers—or the structure was intended from the start by a very careful Author.

In this *mareh* vision, God not only restated old promises but also issued new commands. There was, first of all, the new names He assigned to Abram and Sarai. Some scholars explain "Abraham" as merely a dialectal variation on "Abram." Depending on whether the language of origin is Akkadian or Aramaic, they say both names mean something like "Love the Father" or "the Father Is Exalted."[17] It is unclear what either name has to do with the character of the patriarch. These scholars dismiss the biblical tradition's own etymology of the name. As usual, we are compelled to choose between the skeptical-scholarly viewpoint and the traditional one of the sages, from which infinite vistas open up.

As the Bible itself explains, both the patriarch's and the matriarch's new names allude first of all to the universalization of their mission. That is, before the name change, their spiritual constituency of followers and potential followers was limited to the narrow Near Eastern context of their physical wanderings. As of this moment, God was expanding the field of their endeavors to include the entire world. Whereas "Avram" could be understood as meaning "Av Aram," "Father of Aram," a name for his native land in Mesopotamia, "Avraham" is a contraction of "Av Ham[on Goi'im]," "Father of a Multitude of Nations."[18] The Midrash adds the nuance that the name serves not so much as a personal designation as it does a royal title, like pharaoh—or king or president. We would speak of a man, when he assumes the throne of Egypt, *becoming* pharaoh. If he wins the highest elected office in America, he *becomes* president. In this sense, Abram *became* Abraham. Later his son Isaac held the same title.[19] He, too, became the Father of a Multitude of Nations.

Sarai's name, meanwhile, which means "My Princess," was now changed to *Sarah,* which means simply "Princess." Previously her influence had been limited to Abram, who called her his princess, and to his circle of disciples and students. Henceforth she would become princess of all those who, in millennia to come, would ever believe in the One God—indeed, says the Midrash, "to all the people of the world."[20] Whatever doubts have been raised about the derivation of these names, the traditional understanding has on its side the testimony of the history of world religion. The names "Abraham" and "Sarah" were prophetic in a way that the author P, whose work the skeptics say was edited in the eighth century B.C., could not have foreseen. Abraham did go on to become the spiritual father of monotheists all over the world, as Sarah became their spiritual queen.

The means by which they assumed their respective offices was to be through a son whose birth God now promised to Abraham. Abraham and Sarah personally could not bring the news of the One God to the world, but they could do so through their descendants, their "seed."[21] Because the word "seed" in Hebrew is in the singular instead of the plural, St. Paul and Christian thinking after him have interpreted it as referring to a single "seed," Jesus Christ.[22] Those who accept Christ's message join him in the status of being called Abraham's "seed." But in biblical Hebrew, the word *zera,* or "seed," typically denotes offspring in the plural, which is why the Jewish people have understood the reference as pointing to themselves.

At the news that Sarah would give birth, Abraham again bowed with his face to the dust—and laughed. It was a laugh of joy and of faith. Abraham did not doubt that, however strange it might seem, the ninety-year-old woman Sarah would give him a son. When God heard Abraham's laughter, he decided that the boy should be called Isaac—in Hebrew, Yitzchak. The name, of a typical Amorite construction, is formed from a verb in the imperfect tense: "He Laughs."[23]

So Sarah was to be healed, as Abraham had already been healed, of her barrenness. But the healing of the patriarchal couple's infertility problem was not the only precondition before Abraham's beloved first wife could bear a child to him. The other requirement was that Abraham cut off the flesh of his own foreskin. This was to be a sign of the new covenant, as well as, strangely, being somehow the covenant itself. Said God: "This is my covenant, which you shall guard, between me and between you and between your offspring after you: circumcise yourselves, every male. You shall circumcise the flesh of your foreskin and it shall be a sign of the covenant between me and you. At the age of eight days there shall be circumcised among you every male for all generations, both the boy born in your house and the one bought with money. And so shall my covenant be in your flesh as an eternal covenant."[24]

What happened next? On this the Pentateuch is, as usual, uninformative. We read that once God had finished speaking with Abraham, the patriarch gathered the males of his household, circumcised them, then did the same to himself. We are left to ponder such obvious questions as, How did Abraham react on hearing this bizarre commandment? Having resolved to carry out the divine command, how did he introduce the subject to his comrades and loved ones? Did he offer a rationale for the proposed act of mass sexual mutilation? Is there indeed any convincing reason why every Jewish male should have his foreskin snipped off? Working with a manuscript composed by a mortal, any alert editor would have insisted that the author fill in some of the maddening holes in his narrative.

The historical context is relevant here. Neither Abraham nor his descendants introduced circumcision to the world. The surgery may have originated either in Egypt or in upper Mesopotamia—not far from Abraham's ancestral home at Haran but considerably earlier than his lifetime. Egyptian mummies from as early as 4000 B.C. have been scanned by X ray and found to have been circumcised. A funerary bas-relief from the 2400 B.C. tomb of Ankhmahor at Saqqara shows mortuary priests doing the deed to young men, some of whom have to be restrained to keep them from fainting or running away. Under one scene, a caption has the patient coaching the surgeon to "thoroughly rub off what is there," to which the doctor reassures him, "I will cause it to heal."[25] It may be that circumcisions were conducted upon groups of young men as a ceremony of initiation and purification. One can imagine the distress that ran through the crowd as flint knives were drawn and priests approached. A self-identified "commoner of repute" called Uha testified in a stela erected to his memory at Naga ed-Der in Egypt that he had been circumcised, around the twenty-third century B.C., along with 120 other men. These gentlemen were able to steel themselves against the pain to such an extent that, says Uha, "there was none thereof who hit out, there was none thereof who was hit, there was none thereof who scratched, there was none thereof who was scratched."[26] The question of how Abraham was able to induce the consent of the men of his community is thus underlined.

The Greek historian Herodotus—looking back from the great historical distance of the fifth century B.C.—asserted that the first culture to embrace circumcision was indeed that of the Egyptians. But some modern scholars think the Egyptians adopted the practice from northern Syria, from whose Amuq Valley brass figurines have been unearthed, dated to about 2800 B.C., depicting unclothed, anatomically correct warriors bearing spears, maces, and a clearly depicted circumcision.[27]

None of this, however, should lead us to assume that the Hebrew people merely picked up circumcision from their Near Eastern neighbors. In several key details, the surgery as practiced by Abraham's offspring is set apart. For one thing, as God's commandment to the patriarch makes clear, circumcision for the Jews was to be universal: "At the age of eight days there shall be circumcised among you every male for all generations." This was not true of the Egyptians, who practiced it selectively. Moreover, Abraham was instructed that he and his descendants should circumcise their sons on the eighth day of life. Other cultures circumcised adults only. The surgery itself was different as it was performed by the Hebrew people. Egyptians merely slit open the foreskin so as to allow the glans penis to hang free, while the Jews amputate the flap of skin altogether. Most important, while scholars think that Egyptians circumcised as a sanitary measure, the Jewish people regard it as a sign of their covenant with God, not as a procedure offering medical benefits. The physician and sage Maimonides stated the Jewish view when he wrote, "No one . . . should circumcise himself or his son for any other reason but pure faith."[28] (Indeed, current medical opinion holds that, from a strictly physiological perspective weighing risks against benefits, the net advantage of circumcision is close to nil.)[29]

In short, we know that circumcision had been practiced in the Near East for a thousand years or more before Abraham was born. A widely traveled man who had come into contact with all sorts of people, the patriarch by age ninety-nine was surely familiar with the surgery. So he wasn't shocked by the commandment when it came.

He was, however, concerned about the impact of the institution of circumcision on his missionary work. The Midrash notes that God had delayed giving him the instruction till now in part so as not to "shut the door in the face of converts" who might balk at being circumcised.[30] (St. Paul, facing the same problem in seeking to win gentile converts to his religion, struggled with other leaders of the early Church who insisted that new Christians be circumcised. Paul won the battle, and the practice was discarded.) On hearing God's will, the patriarch gingerly questioned the Lord: "Until now [potential converts] have come and joined themselves to me [to know You]. Do You say that, once I have been circumcised [and it is known that my followers must do likewise], they [will continue] to come and join themselves to me?"

To this, God offered a cryptic response alluded to in his name El Shaddai. Rashi explains the divine title "Shaddai" as deriving from the Hebrew word *dai,* meaning "enough" or "sufficient." Said God, "Abraham, it is sufficient *[dai]* for you that I should be your God. It is enough for you that I should be your patron. And furthermore it is sufficient not [merely] for you but for my [entire] world that I should be its God. It is sufficient for my world that I should be its patron."[31] In other words, Abraham was directed not to worry about the possible negative effects on his ability to attract converts. It should be "enough" that he himself had established an intimate relationship with the Lord. Here perhaps we find the seeds of the classical Jewish attitude to the winning of converts. Sincere converts have almost always been welcomed but almost never actively sought. It is "enough" for the Jewish people that they themselves maintain and deepen their relationship with God. Whether the number of Jews grows or stays the same, it will be "enough."

Satisfied with this response, however, Abraham made the surprising decision to ask some of his friends for their advice. The Midrash finds this indicated in a superfluous expression a chapter later in Genesis when Abraham is already recovering from his surgery at "Elone Mamre," where he receives a delegation of angelic visitors.[32] Mamre was one of the Masters of the Covenant of Abram. He had two comrades, Aner and Eshcol. "Elone Mamre" is variously explained as the Plain of Mamre, the Oak Grove of Mamre, and the Palace of Mamre.[33] Why does the text bother to tell us that the visitation occurred on the property of Mamre? Because unlike Aner and Eshcol, Mamre passed a test that Abraham set.

The patriarch had already decided to circumcise himself and his household. Before going ahead, he wanted to know which of his three chief disciples (after Eliezer) understood the kind of relationship with God that

Abraham sought to model for them. He would find this out by telling them about his vision and then asking each what he thought Abraham should do. When the patriarch visited Aner and told him what he proposed to do, the other man upbraided him. "Do you wish to make a cripple of yourself?! Then the relatives of the kings you killed [the four kings who had invaded Canaan and kidnapped Lot] will come and [seek to] kill you! Then you will be unable to flee before them."

Abraham went to speak with Eshcol, who said to him, "You are an old man! If you circumcise yourself, you will lose a great deal of blood. You won't be able to withstand this [blood loss], and you will die."

Finally Abraham came to Mamre. He told him what God had commanded, to which Mamre replied incredulously, "Do you then seek advice in this matter?! Did [the Lord] not save you from the Fiery Furnace and perform for you all the [other] miracles and save you from the [four] Kings? And were it not for his strength and power, they [the kings] would have killed you. He saved [all of] your 248 body parts. And about the tip of one body part you now seek advice? Do what he has commanded!"[34]

Abraham resolved to perform the circumcision on Mamre's property and to spend some days there afterward to recuperate. He would be well taken care of.[35]

It remained to introduce the subject to the male members of his household. The text says, "Then Abraham took [va'yikach] Ishmael his son and all the lads of his household and those purchased with money, even all the male members of the house of Abraham."[36] On the word va'yikach, "and he took," Rashi elsewhere comments that it has the connotation of "taking" someone by persuading him with words of comfort and reason.[37] A man can endure pain as long as it has meaning to him. It is absurd pain that is unendurable. Abraham needed to explain to Ishmael and the rest that the agony they were about to experience had a profound spiritual significance. We don't know precisely what Abraham said, but because Jewish tradition has reflected extensively on the meaning of circumcision, and because presumably some of these reflections originated with the man who originated it, we can speculate.

What does this "ritual," called *brit milah* (Covenant of Circumcision), really signify to Abraham's progeny? In reality, there are no rituals in Judaism—if we define a ritual as a formalized act you do just because God wants it. Every Jewish religious practice is meant to be an object of meditation. One hopes to understand its meaning at deeper and deeper levels, but it is not enough just to read about the thing in a book. You have to *do* it, or in the case of circumcision, have it done *to* you. The meanings are multiple.

As treated in the Talmud and Midrash, circumcision points first to the need for sexual self-control. We find this in Rashi's comment that Abraham made certain that his own circumcision was performed in public and in daylight.[38] Traditionally, too, *brit milah* is performed in public, in daylight. The reason is that what a man does with his penis is not just *his* business. It is everyone's business. At the very beginning of life, a Jewish male's sex organ is exposed before his community and cut, signifying that the community has an interest in his sexual future. Rambam adds that when the foreskin is amputated, sexual pleasure for the man is diminished. The membrane of the glans penis is left exposed to the wide world, with the consequence that a degree of sensitivity is lost. For uncircumcised men, sex is even better than for their circumcised fellows. Sexual moderation is thus encouraged.[39]

According to Maimonides, another purpose has to do with national solidarity. It is a sign of unity with other men of your nation, and "there is much mutual love and assistance among people that are united by the same sign when they consider it as [the symbol of] a covenant."[40] The sign reminds them of the values they share. In this connection, it is significant that America is the only nation that practices circumcision on its infant males anywhere near as consistently as the Jewish nation, Israel, does: the figure is 60 percent. (Muslims also circumcise their males but not at birth.) That day on which the patriarch Abraham took himself in hand, he was not alone. He also circumcised all the members of the budding religious movement that grew into organized monotheism, for he recognized that a household must be joined by common values, and the values of his household were represented in the mark of *brit milah*. But only Abraham's own descendants, through his son Isaac and grandson Jacob, became Jews. The children of his friends, students, and soldiers remained gentiles. What this says about America—the circumcised gentile nation—is a question we shall touch on at the end of this book.

Circumcision also has to do with forgiveness. Like Christianity, Torah does not lack a concept of atonement through shed human blood. The Midrash relates that the smell of the foreskins that Abraham amputated rose to Heaven like the scent of a sacrifice from the Temple altar.[41] The Lord has given to the sense of smell a power, unrivaled by the rest of the senses, to evoke memory. When a baby boy is circumcised and his foreskin begins to decay, the tiny aroma that is released also rises to Heaven and recalls to God's mind the memory of Abraham's great act. God recalls the merit of Abraham, and as a result grants forgiveness to the patriarch's spiritual descendants.

Finally, along with the Sabbath, circumcision is understood by the Midrash as an acknowledgment of God's sovereignty.[42] Abstaining from creativity one day a week reminds us of His lordship of the macro-world of human interaction and striving, while chipping off this bit of a prized organ calls to mind His mastery of the more personal micro-world. This may be the fundamental significance of *brit milah*.

But the Midrash implicitly raises a difficulty. Abraham observed the commandment of circumcision, thus acknowledging God's lordship of the micro-world of his body. Rashi notes on the *gematria* value of his new name, Avraham, that the letters that compose it—when understood as numbers rather than letters—add up to 248. This is traditionally regarded as the number of independent parts in a man's body. His old name, Avram, added up to only 243, five short of 248: before his circumcision Abraham had experienced some difficulty in controlling five of his body parts: his two eyes, two ears, and one male organ.[43] (These are indeed among the most wayward parts of the human anatomy.) Evidently the commandment of circumcision was given to him after a century of moral struggle. At last, he had achieved something like perfect physical self-control. The name "Avraham" and the sign of circumcision both celebrate his victory over himself.

But here is the difficulty. There is no explicit indication in the Bible that Abraham observed the Sabbath. Did he, then, not acknowledge God's sovereignty over the universe apart from over his own individual self?

We come now to the heart of the ideological struggle, waged for almost two thousand years, between Judaism and Christianity for the soul of Abraham. Jewish tradition, in fact, teaches that Abraham observed the Sabbath. And not only that: he observed every commandment in the Torah, whether (as in the case of circumcision) given in his own time or (as in the overwhelming majority of commandments) given formally only to Moses in the

Sinai wilderness. The Talmud and Midrash find this extraordinary fact hinted at in a verse from a speech made by God to Abraham's son Isaac after the first patriarch had died: "Because Abraham obeyed my voice and observed my safeguards, my commandments, my ordinances, and my Torahs."[44] If God only wished to praise Abraham for his obedience, He need only have said, "Because Abraham obeyed my voice." Each seemingly extraneous word is understood as a reference to some aspect of written, oral, even rabbinic law (that is, Torah law expounded by the rabbis) which Abraham anticipated and observed. The final word in the sentence, *Torot*, literally "Torahs," denotes the two separate Torahs, Written and Oral.

Torah in general can be compared to the point of matter that preexisted our universe, and that, in the moment of the Big Bang, exploded to become every material object that will ever be.[45] Just as at that moment, all of matter existed in a potential form, before the moment of revelation at Mt. Sinai all of Torah also existed in potential form. Long before Moses, a spirit and an intellect of sufficient greatness were capable of seeing all of Torah even in a small point of God's teaching. This is what the first patriarch did. That small point, given now to the great spirit and intellect we call Abraham, must have been the commandment of circumcision. For circumcision is the only Torah commandment that God ever explicitly revealed to him.

By contrast, Paul formulated the classic Christian understanding of circumcision: that because Abraham was considered righteous before God even before he went under the knife, circumcision is therefore no prerequisite to being righteous, whether you are a Jew or a gentile. For this reason, Abraham "is the father of all who have faith when uncircumcised."[46] As one historian has observed, "Oddly, Abraham, the first to be circumcised, became the vehicle for the inclusion of the uncircumcised."[47] In the work of later Christian thinkers, Paul's indifference to this sign of God's covenant with the Jews deepened to an outright hostility. No commandment bothered them as much as circumcision. Not unlike the rabbis of the Midrash and Talmud, they found in it the seed of all the rest of Jewish law—or anyway that part of Jewish law that was not explicitly about ethics, that is the so-called ritual laws. But precisely because Paul's followers saw it as the keystone of the rest of "ritual" law, they made circumcision the focus of their critique of Torah as understood by Abraham's descendants. As the second-century apologist St. Justin Martyr wrote: "If circumcision was not required before the time of Abraham, and before Moses there was no need of sabbaths, festivals and sacrifices, they are not needed now."[48]

The patriarch shared some of these meanings of the rite of circumcision with his household on the day he "took" them to be circumcised. By Rashi's count, it was to be Abraham's sixth trial—or his eighth, according to Rambam—and part of the trial lay precisely in putting so many loved ones to such pain. We have no record of anyone hitting or being hit, scratching or being scratched, fainting or running away. So presumably his words of encouragement and explanation brought out the courage of these men and boys. They submitted to him and to his God.

In doing so, they demonstrated how well Abraham had succeeded in overcoming what had been up till now the greatest challenge to his life's mission. We said in the preface that the patriarch's life, as the Torah gives it to us, forms a drama in three acts. In the first (the *parshah* of *Lech L'chah*), his mission has been to establish the nascent movement for the worship of one God in the unique land of God's choosing, Canaan. Abraham, or Abram, had already built a monotheistic community at Haran. Everything he accomplished there might have been erased by the migration, at the Lord's insistence, to Canaan. Despite further hardships, though—Sarah's kidnapping, Lot's kidnapping, the war with the eastern kings—Abraham found at age ninety-nine that his achievement was intact. He was the leader of a community of believers whose devotion to him and his God was so strong that the men were willing to be mutilated (so it must have seemed to outsiders) in their sexual organs, a most agonizing test of loyalty.

Even so, this would amount to nothing if Abraham had no one in whose hands he could leave the leadership of his movement. Monotheism would die with him. Now, as the *parshah* of *Vayera* opens, God had promised that Sarah would give birth to a son, Abraham's true heir. But Sarah was eighty-nine years old, as depleted by age as her husband. Could she really become a mother? There was Ishmael to be concerned about as well. In a part of his soul, Abraham wished that Ishmael could assume the role of patriarch. For tradition leaves no doubt that, for all the Bible's disparaging of Ishmael, his father loved him. Then again, if another son was indeed given to Abraham through Sarah, and if God confirmed this other boy as his successor, would Ishmael accept his younger half brother as his spiritual master? As the Bible will later repeatedly show, rivalry between brothers can be deadly business. (Genesis has this as one of its great themes: one thinks of Jacob and his brother, Esau, and of Joseph and his brothers. In each case, murder, no less, is only narrowly averted.)

Tremors of worry assailed the patriarch even now. In time, the tremors would become earthquakes, reaching a pitch of violence—of despair seeking to dash all hope—on a lonely mountain peak in the Judean wilderness.

CHAPTER TEN

Annunciation

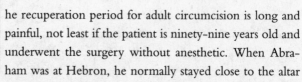he recuperation period for adult circumcision is long and painful, not least if the patient is ninety-nine years old and underwent the surgery without anesthetic. When Abraham was at Hebron, he normally stayed close to the altar he had built there almost a quarter century before.[1] However, for the three days since he had operated on himself, he was found elsewhere, availing himself of the comfort and hospitality of his friend Mamre.[2] There he recuperated and waited impatiently to return to his main occupation: ministering to, and seeking to convert, weary travelers.

Hebron was situated on the important route called Derech Ephratah, literally "the Way to Ephratah" (and points beyond), Ephratah being identical with Bethlehem.[3] One traveled this road to get from the area of Jerusalem down to Bethlehem and on south to Hebron. It wasn't the four-lane highway of today, but something more like a well-beaten trail of three to four feet in width.[4] Having traced the spine of the Judean mountains, at Hebron Derech Ephratah branched into three roads: one running southwest toward the Negev, another west toward the Mediterranean coast, and another winding southeast gradually downward to the Dead Sea. In that direction, at Sodom, near the shore of the sea, lived Abraham's nephew Lot. We don't know if Lot was a frequent visitor to his uncle's home, but a large portion of the travelers to whom Abraham demonstrated his hospitality were the seedy denizens of Sodom.[5] His missionary interests were as catholic as could be.

Abraham had pitched his and Sarah's tents by Mamre's oak grove. He should have been inside resting his weakened old body, but the patriarch waited up for whatever spiritually parched Sodomites might come along.

He was disappointed in this. Since the Lord wanted Abraham to heal and this required rest, He discouraged the usual Sodomite traffic that would today be passing through Hebron. Derech Ephratah was empty, because God had ratcheted up the ambient temperature to a distinctly uncomfortable—indeed literally hellish—level. It was only springtime, which is normally quite bearable in the Holy Land. But a midrash states that God drilled a hole through the earth down to Hell itself and heat billowed up from below: the ultimate global warming.[6]

Interestingly, Muslim tradition likewise portrays Ibrahim as sitting by the entrance of his tent waiting for guests to come along.[7] (Young Ishmael must have been otherwise occupied.) In this version of the narrative, the road is also empty for no fewer than fifteen days, but Abraham is not recovering from circumcision, so it's hard to see why God has arranged to keep him unoccupied as a host. Muslim traditions tend to pick up the Abraham story from right about now in his life. They often give the impression that someone has taken the Bible and Midrash and cut out and displaced elements for reasons of his own. Muslims would reply that it is biblical tradition that distorts the facts, which are passed down faithfully in the *hadith* literature of authoritative prophetic traditions.[8]

Besides wanting Abraham to rest, God also wished to deliver certain information to him—or rather to his wife. Prophecy does not usually come to those who are ill; and even under the most propitious circumstance, before it comes it requires meticulous preparation of one's self and his environment.

In the present instance, Abraham was both ill and unprepared for new divine instruction.⁹ But one of the benefits of his having been circumcised was a heightened level of prophetic susceptibility: perhaps because the foreskin represents an excessive attachment to the material realm which, when removed, increases one's sensitivity to the spiritual.¹⁰

God would gladly have appeared to Abraham on the old man's sickbed. But because he had chosen to go outside, it was outside in the brutal noontime haze that God chose to manifest Himself. The biblical verse says, "God appeared to him at Elone Mamre when he was sitting at the entrance of his tent in the heat of day. He lifted his eyes and *he saw*, and behold three men were standing over him. And *he saw*, and he ran to greet them from the entrance of his tent and bowed toward the ground [emphasis added]."¹¹ Focusing on the seemingly pointless repetition of the verb "he saw," commentators from the Talmud down to modern times have found much complexity packed into those two verses.

Specifically there seem to have been not one but three separate divine manifestations. Abraham had directed his old servant Eliezer to venture out in search of wayfarers. Eliezer returned empty-handed, but Abraham said, "I don't believe you," for he suspected that Eliezer wished to spare him the trouble of attending to guests.¹² Retying his bandages, Abraham walked forth from the tent's entrance when—suddenly—the Presence of the Lord was upon him. God Himself touched the patriarch—wordlessly at first, for nothing was communicated now—the first manifestation. The Lord was at that moment simply visiting a sick friend.¹³

As we have noted earlier, one of God's vehicles for communicating with mortals is the divine messengers called angels. He was preparing to communicate with Abraham by this method. Angels take various forms, none of which represent their essence but which instead allow them to be observed by human beings. Soaring in the sky above Abraham, there presently appeared a shimmering angelic *something*.¹⁴ There is no way to describe the experience of angels in the form they take to be discernible to the prophetic eye. This was the second manifestation.

Perhaps because both Abraham's body and his prophetic powers were still recuperating, God then reconfigured the angelic visitation. Rather than have the messengers speak to Abraham from the midst of an exalted spiritual state, He chose to give them a material form, which could be seen even by a person who is not a prophet. And so in a third manifestation there appeared to the patriarch's eyes, in the distance, three men. One imagines them blurry in the heat. Nachmanides writes of a phenomenon he terms *malbush,* when purely spiritual beings, angels, assume a husk of material existence, a sort of clothing. What this actually means, the sage finds impossible to say. "I cannot explain," he pleads.[15] In any event, no one would have guessed that the three were angels; nor did Abraham.

In the Quran, this ambiguity is preserved. God's "messengers" come to Abraham, bearing "good news." They greet him with cries of "Peace," which he returns. But after bringing them roast calf, he becomes suspicious, not realizing they are angels: "He saw their hands being withheld from him, he mistrusted them and was afraid of them. They said, 'Have no fear. We are sent forth to the people of Lot.' "[16]

In Jewish tradition's account, Abraham was aware of something supernatural afoot. But as far as he knew, it was simply that God was preparing to speak to Him through the shimmering sky. The patriarch, however, was not ready to be spoken to. He now diverted his attention to the matter that was uppermost in his mind: the distress of three apparently ordinary travelers making their way down the Derech Ephratah in this heat. He addressed God: "My Lord, if indeed I have found favor in your eyes, do not pass away from your servant."[17] In other words, "Wait here, I'll be right back." His devotion to other human beings was such that he was willing to put his Creator on hold. For God can wait—He has all eternity—but a human being cannot. The elderly patriarch ran to greet the mysterious figures.

They walked to meet him. They were dressed in bedouin fashion, so he assumed they were *aravim,* desert nomads.[18] But as old man and three angels came within a few feet of each other, the angels noted that Abraham was in pain and that it was only to greet them that he had emerged from his tent. Part of their *malbush* was to behave in the manner of men, and proper courteous bedouin would not trouble a stranger who was plainly too ill to be a host. One of them said, "It is not the way of the land [that is, good manners] that we should remain here," and they sought to bid him farewell.[19]

But Abraham was undaunted. He pursued his quarry, crying out to the three, "Let there be brought a little water, then wash your feet and recline under the tree. I will fetch a bit of bread and you shall get sustenance for yourselves, after which you shall go on [your way] for indeed you have passed by your servant."

One of the *aravim* said, "So shall you do, as you have said."[20] The three visitors followed Abraham back to his tent.

As he walked, a strange thing happened. To his amazement, Abraham found that he had been healed. Not only of the wound in his groin, the pain of which lifted in an instant. He also felt a sudden rush of *youth* surging through his limbs. Twice in the Abraham narrative the text notes that Abraham was "old"—once in the context of this angelic visitation, again thirty-seven years later at the death of Sarah.[21] The Midrash explains the apparent redundancy: at age ninety-nine Abraham was indeed old, but in that year, just now in his encounter with the three travelers, he was restored "to the days of his youth."[22] Over the ensuing decades, he aged *again,* and by the time his wife died he was once more "old."

This explains the frenzy of activity that ensued after the strangers had agreed to accept sustenance from their host. In three verses, the biblical text describes Abraham's preparations in terms that suggest a manic rush of energy: he first "hastened," then "ran," "took," "gave," "prepared," "took," "prepared," "placed," and only then "stood" to watch his guests eat. Abraham rushed to his wife Sarah's tent and was so excited he could barely form a complete sentence: "Hurry up! Three seah-measures of meal, fine flour! Knead and make cakes!"[23] A seah in biblical times was the equivalent of about thirteen liters: in other words, fixings for a great deal of cake.[24]

The rest of the meal was similarly extravagant. The Bible mentions as the main course only one calf, "tender and good," plus yogurt and milk. (Having intuited the laws of *kashrut,* of permitted and forbidden foods and food combinations, Abraham did not eat dairy products with meat. However, one may eat dairy *before* meat, even immediately before, so he must have served the yogurt and milk as an appetizer.) But the Talmud indicates that after Abraham placed before his guests one roasted calf, cooked with special emphasis on the tongue, which he served with the ancient Near Eastern equivalent of the finest mustard, he set out another and another for a total of three calves. All of this is by way of illustrating an aspect of refined behavior that Abraham exemplified. The Talmudic sage Rabbi Eliezer is quoted as saying, "The righteous say little and do much. The wicked say much but fail to do even a little."[25] Abraham had promised a snack but delivered a banquet.

The biblical text mentions a "lad" who assisted Abraham, and Rashi notes that this was Ishmael, who at thirteen years of age was now being trained by his father in the path of righteousness.[26] (Did Ishmael, one wonders, cook up a nice mustard-based gravy for the calves in the famous saucepan of the prophet Ibrahim? According to Ishmael's Islamic descendants, this item can be found today among other Muslim relics, such as beard hairs of the prophet Muhammad, in the treasury room of the great Ottoman palace, Topkapi, in Istanbul. I saw it myself: a stoneware vessel, prominently labeled, that looked somewhat less than the 3,700 years old it would have to be if it were authentic.) At some point in the cooking process, a mishap occurred.

Some Islamic traditions depict Ishmael as a bumbler. In their account of Abraham and Ishmael building the Ka'bah, the revered cubic structure in the middle of the Great Mosque at Mecca, Ishmael keeps messing up the works, to Abraham's annoyance. He can't find a cornerstone, or he finds one but Abraham says it's no good, or he arrives after it's too late. Finally Abraham bawls him out: "God would not entrust such a thing to you, my boy!"[27] In the present context, Abraham gave each calf to the "lad" for preparation. A midrash, however, adds that one of the calves escaped, and Abraham had to dash after it. Perhaps the butterfingers Ishmael wasn't paying attention and it ran away.

If Mamre's property, where all this action was taking place, is situated in relationship to modern Hebron where the ancient historian Josephus indicates, then the calf ran a couple of miles before Abraham caught up. It dashed into a small valley between hills. The patriarch must have been following along close behind, or otherwise he would never have found the little animal, cowering, in a cave in a field.

Abraham recognized the field as belonging to the family of Tzohar, who had a son called Ephron. He saw the calf dart into the cave's narrow entrance. Abraham followed it, figuring that the animal couldn't run much farther; at least from the outside, the cave appeared to be very small. But once he had squeezed his way some distance under the ground—still not finding the calf—the space suddenly opened up into a round chamber, not a natural cave, but a carved room. He was in the place called, since the writing of the Bible and no doubt before, the Cave of Machpelah. It is in Hebron, concealed for the past two thousand years under the great edifice built by King Herod in the first century B.C.

Today the cave itself is inaccessible, since its Muslim keepers fear the otherworldly consequences of violating a tomb. However, in 1981 a secret nocturnal expedition conducted by members of the local Jewish community penetrated Machpelah. The explorers describe a double cave: a narrow passage leading to a carved round room, then an entrance to another, smaller cave. As other, earlier visitors had done, they reported a wind emerging from somewhere under the earth, up through the cave, though it is far from clear what might cause air to gust about in a cave open at only one end.

Abraham felt that strange wind on his face. He found the calf in the cave, but he discovered something much more wondrous as well. From the first cave, a passage led down into a second. In a photo from 1981, the opening looks vaguely esophageal and triangular, though the corners of the triangle are rounded. Abraham caught a smell emanating from the throat of the second cave. It was like the smell of Paradise.

Actually it *was* the smell of Paradise. A midrash in *Pirke d'Rabbi Eliezer* narrates Abraham's discovery: "The calf entered the Cave of Machpelah and [Abraham] entered after it. There he found Adam and Eve lying on biers and sleeping. Candles burned round about them and a good smell was upon them, a pleasant smell."[28] Another tradition, found in the *Zohar,* states that Abraham had stumbled on the very entrance to the Garden of Eden.

Were Adam and Eve entombed in the second cave, or perhaps another, unknown chamber? The midrash doesn't specify. But wherever the patriarch found them, from that point on he wanted to possess the cave as an eternal resting place for himself and Sarah.

It had been a strange afternoon, and Abraham's visitors hadn't even sat down to eat, much less performed their assigned tasks. Each was on a separate mission. When they had first appeared to the patriarch, they stood in a row, shoulder-to-shoulder. In the middle was the angel sent to carry out the most important mission: Michael, who would announce to Sarah that she was destined to give birth to Isaac. To his right was Gabriel, sent to overthrow Sodom and Gomorrah. And to Michael's left was Raphael, the angel of healing and rescue, assigned to heal Abraham and rescue Lot from the doomed city of Sodom.[29]

From the biblical text, it is unclear whether Abraham ever recognized his visitors as heavenly deputies, or whether from start to finish he believed they were simply desert nomads. Rashi asserts that up through the moment when he parted with them, Abraham remained under the illusion that they were as they appeared, mortal men.[30] Ramban insists that he recognized them as angels right away. However, both opinions are problematic. If Rashi is right, then upon the angel Michael's annunciation to Sarah, did her husband not perceive that there must be something supernatural about the trio? Or if Ramban is right, how are we to reconcile the fact that Abraham knew they were angels with one of the morals of the story, which is that we should emulate the patriarch's hospitality? Playing host to angels, if you know they are angels, reflects no special merit. Maimonides bypasses the whole question by insisting that the episode was entirely a prophetic vision on Abraham's part. "Do not imagine," he warns us, "that an angel is seen or his word heard otherwise than in a prophetic vision or prophetic dream."[31] But Rambam must be mistaken, Ramban thunders back, and it is "forbidden to listen" to him. For if angels didn't really visit Abraham at Mamre, then who are the angels, in the Bible's narration, who proceed onward to overthrow Sodom in Genesis 19? Are they also no more than figures of Abraham's prophetic imagination?[32]

The truth probably falls somewhere between the approach of Rashi and that of Ramban. Surely when the calf darted off down the hill toward Ephron's property and Abraham pursued it into the burial cave of Adam and Eve, the patriarch must have begun to suspect that the hand of God was directing the afternoon's events.

Sarah also soon perceived that she was in the grip of the supernatural. As Abraham carried the calf back to Mamre's place, Sarah was in her tent, kneading flour for bread, when a most peculiar sensation overcame her. The very cells of her body, down to the level of molecules and atoms, were at that moment being manipulated and revived by a force whose existence she sensed only as the most subtle tickle one can imagine, everywhere at once all over her body. First she felt the same rush of youthfulness that her husband had experienced. Though eighty-nine years old, she suddenly had the impression that she was a young girl. Perhaps she looked up through an aperture in the tent toward the three strange "men" whom her husband had invited to lunch. One of them, Raphael, was looking straight at her, as if he had been waiting for her to look up.

Then a feeling she had not had in forty years or more interrupted the ela-
tion of the moment. It came from between her thighs: something warm
emerging, beginning to trickle downward. She had experienced this before.
When? Her memory grasped back to the time when her body had passed
the threshold that marks the onset of elderliness. Sarah realized—bizarre as
it seemed, but undeniable—that the sensation was the beginning of a menstrual flow.[33]

The Lord had started to revive her body, but with the return of her
monthly cycle there immediately returned also the discomfort of a woman's
first menstrual day. A pain twisted underneath her stomach and nausea
stirred. When Abraham returned, having given over the delinquent calf to
Ishmael to be slaughtered and roasted, he entered his wife's tent and found
her, to his astonishment, in the grip of menstrual sickness.

The bread she had been kneading, in that case, would have to go un-
eaten. The Bible states clearly that Abraham had called for bread to be
served. But it makes no mention of his placing it before his guests along with
the rest of lunch, whose contents are specified. Readers of the biblical text
who don't consult the oral tradition will have to conclude that the author
(who is J, say the scholars) has been nodding again and forgotten to mention
the bread along with the other components of the meal. The Midrash, on
the other hand, figures that if the bread wasn't served, it must be for a reason other than authorial or editorial incompetence. Abraham, we learn, anticipated along with all the Torah's commandments certain ritual stringencies
of his pious descendants, such as that bread that has been handled by a men-
struating woman is not to be eaten. (The logic of the custom, which is not
observed today, has to do with separating life from death. Bread is nourishment par excellence, a foundation of life, whereas the sloughing off of an un-
fertilized human egg from the wall of the uterus represents the extinction of
a potential life.) Sarah's husband first made certain that his wife was as comfortable as she could be, then served the rest of the meal. The matriarch remained in her tent.[34]

The angels ate—or did they? Can incorporeal beings consume yogurt
and calf's tongue? The Talmud states that they only appeared to eat, and the
Midrash suggests that before the food touched their "lips" it was burned up
by a holy fire.[35] This was out of consideration for their host, who had gone
to a lot of trouble on their behalf. But in the sense that Torah defines
"bread" not as stuff made from flour and water, but as whatever "nourishes

the heart," as Rashi says, then we can affirm that they really did eat Abraham's "bread."[36] While human beings are sustained by bread in the literal sense of the word, angels are sustained by deeds of loving kindness: such deeds are their "food." In rushing to extend hospitality to the trio, Abraham created powerful angelic nourishment.[37]

After they had finished eating, it was time for the annunciation. This caught Sarah off guard. We may wonder why, unlike her husband, she did not realize the visitors were angels; and, second, why the news they bore was news to *her*. She was called Yiscah, the Seer, after all. But prophecy does not come to the sick, and Sarah had been rendered unwell. A trickier question is why this annunciation was necessary in the first place when the good news Michael bore had already been announced to Abraham by God when He commanded him to circumcise himself. God had said, "I will establish My covenant with Isaac whom Sarah will bear to you at this season next year." Abraham did not share this information with Sarah. Why? Probably it was because he doubted her faith. He suspected that if he told her that God had told him that she was destined to bear a child, she would have laughed at him.

After lunch, the "visitor" Michael said, "Where is Sarah, your wife?"

Abraham said, "Behold, in the tent!"

Michael then spoke in the name and voice of the Lord, for an angel is nothing more than an extension of God's will. He said, "I will surely return to you at this season [and there will be] life. For behold a son shall be born to Sarah your wife." He meant that Isaac would be born at what we know today as the season of Passover, for it was that time of year even now.[38] (In fact, the bread Sarah had been preparing was to be matzoh.)

The angel was standing with his back to the tent. When Sarah heard her name, she moved to the entrance and looked out. Though it was still daytime, the light around the table suddenly brightened. The supernal, incandescent light of Sarah's youthful beauty had been restored along with her menstrual cycle, and even the outdoor scene was illuminated by the glow that emanated from the tent door where she stood.[39] But Sarah was unaware of the fullness of the change that had come over her. She thought to herself,

"Is it possible that these innards will bear offspring? That these breasts which have contracted will give milk?"[40] And so she laughed, not as Abraham had done, a laugh of pure joy, but rather a laugh of disbelief. The angel was speaking for God—that was clear to everyone present, the disguise of wandering *avarim* was off now—but Sarah lacked faith. We laugh when the laws of custom or nature are broken. Abraham had laughed because he saw that God was about to void the law of nature that states that a ninety-nine-year-old man and his eighty-nine-year-old wife cannot have children. Sarah laughed because, as she saw it, the angel had broken the regulation of custom that says that one does not make statements that are clearly untrue.

In the midst of her laughter, she spoke again to herself. "After I have withered, shall I have clear, lustrous skin [*ednah*]? And my lord [Abraham] is old [as well]!"[41] The notion struck her as deeply absurd. The obscure Hebrew word *ednah,* which, following Rashi, I have translated as "clear, lustrous skin," shares a three-letter root with the word "Eden," where the primordial Garden lay from which Adam and Eve were expelled.[42] The text hints at an idea that the story of the tomb of the first man and woman also alludes to. Abraham and Sarah were being granted the opportunity to reinvent Eden. For Sarah, the impossibility of this notion was crystallized by what she took to be the impossibility of her formerly perfect skin being rejuvenated. If she had a compact mirror handy, she would have seen that the impossible had already come to pass. She was already Eve.

Someone then spoke to Abraham and reprimanded him for Sarah's impertinence, saying, "Why does this one, Sarah, laugh?"[43] The text appears to state that the speaker was God, but it seems rather that Michael was speaking again in God's voice.[44] (The scholar E. A. Speiser follows the view of some, who reject the oral tradition and thus says that one of the three "men" wasn't an angel at all but rather God Himself in human form. Speiser doesn't explain why the text then goes on to say that after the men had already passed onward in the direction of Sodom, Abraham was "still standing before the Lord."[45] The Redactor didn't notice he had left God in two places at once: on His way to Sodom, and back in Hebron with Abraham.)

Whoever had reprimanded him, Abraham didn't reply. Sarah did. She was sufficiently frightened, having been challenged by God or His spokesman, as to choose to lie. "I did not laugh," she said, to which He replied ominously, "No, but you did laugh."

Michael was almost done with his assigned task. He gestured to Mamre's palace, beside whose walls Abraham had pitched his and his wife's tents. Where he had pointed, there appeared a deep scratch in the wall, lit by the rays of the sun, which he intended as a kind of astronomical bookmark. He restated the promise he had made earlier. "At this season I will return to you. It shall be a time of life, and Sarah shall have a son."[46] He explained that when at this time of day the sun returned to precisely this spot on Mamre's wall, it would be a year later and Sarah, who would have conceived in the meantime, would be due to give birth.

The angel Michael had brought news of life, but the attention of his colleagues was now turned toward death, toward Sodom and its intended destruction. When the meal was concluded, Abraham continued in the role of the consummate host and escorted his guests a distance in the continuation of their journey. They followed the road that led from Hebron down to the plain of the Jordan River, where Lot lived. At some point, Michael, who had no business with Sodom, ascended to Heaven.

The two remaining angels passed onward from Abraham's custodianship, and the patriarch was left alone with God. The Lord thought to Himself, "Shall I conceal from Abraham that which I am about to do, now that Abraham is to be a great, mighty nation, and the nations of the earth will bless themselves by him?"[47] Surely it would be wrong not to tell this father of peoples that one group of wicked people, the residents of Sodom and four other cities, were to be wiped off the face of the land for their sins. Picking up the thread of the encounter they had begun when the angels first turned up outside Abraham's tent, God informed him of His plans. Abraham's argument with God, seeking to dissuade Him, is so famous that it has entered the realm of cliché, with ill-informed would-be commentators habitually employing it to insist that questioning the Creator's will is a central feature of Judaism—which, very much to the contrary, it is not. This encounter between man and God has in fact become so buried in trite interpretation, on a level with the bumper sticker one sees smugly ordering us to "Question Authority," that I don't propose to try to dig it out. To regain some of its freshness and vigor, this biblical scene may need to be left alone for a generation or two.

Still, regarding the dispute that includes Abraham's pained protest, "Will You also stamp out the righteous with the wicked?," two quick points need to be made. First, the answer to Abraham's shockingly bold question is an equally shocking yes. It is in the nature of the world God has made that when the wicked act up and are punished, the innocent are also often lost in the ensuing conflagration. As the Talmud puts it, "When permission is given for destruction, no distinction is made between the righteous and the wicked."[48] The point has been borne out often in Jewish history. This serves as a warning to good people not to be satisfied with their own goodness but to seek to correct the wayward.

Second, we should notice that when Abraham argues with God that He should take pity on Sodom, he omits any reference to Lot, Sarah's brother, who was living in Sodom at the time. The omission is striking. A quarter century earlier he had literally gone to war, against seemingly hopeless odds, to save his nephew. Now he will not so much as utter the man's name. This is further evidence that Devora Steinmetz is correct when she says that with the birth of Ishmael, Abraham lost some of his concern for his Mesopotamian family.

While Abraham talked with God, Gabriel and Raphael continued their journey. The distance they needed to traverse was forty miles, about two days on foot, which is just how long it took them. Do angels walk? In an instant, God could have materialized the two outside the gates of Sodom. But rather than do so, which would have hastened the fate toward which Sodom and other cities of the plain were spiraling, He gave their residents forty-eight hours to reflect on their deeds. As the Midrash puts it, "the Omnipresent opened for them the Door of Repentance."[49] Perhaps during those two days all the people of the plain felt a certain unfamiliar tug in their hearts, the still, small voice of conscience. The Sodomites had only to step through the Door.

They did not. When the angels reached the top of one of the Judean hills that looked down over the city, Raphael and Gabriel "gazed" down at Sodom.[50] The word Scripture uses here, *va'yashkifu,* has a sinister connotation. As Rashi explains, in biblical usage one only "gazes" upon an object for the sake of "bad"—that is, when the object of one's gaze is destined for a bad end.[51] The people of Sodom were about to find out just how bad their end was destined to be.

CHAPTER ELEVEN

Sin Cities

t the very moment that Abraham concluded his unsuc-
cessful defense of Sodom, the angels arrived by night at
the city gate. The Midrash points out that this is the way
juridical custom operates. In modern terms, as long as the
judge is willing to listen, the defense attorney pleads his case. But when the
judge stands up, indicating that he has heard enough, the defense must fall
silent. Immediately the prosecutor, who also acts as the executioner, goes
forth to perform his dark duty.[1]

In the Middle Bronze Age, the gate of a walled city was more than just
an archway. It was often a large structure comprising two or three subsidiary
gates at an angle to one another, thus allowing no direct entrance to the city,

and it was flanked by towers. There was plenty of room for the governmental functions that typically went on there. In our period, it was the practice of a town's judges and elders to sit under the town gate and hear cases. Lot, it happened, was a judge. This evening, after everyone else had gone home for the day, he was still hanging around his "office."

Suddenly the two glorious beings stood before him.

To Abraham, Gabriel and Raphael had appeared as men. But that was a function of Abraham's spiritual stature: the extraordinary came to him in the guise of the ordinary. To Lot, they appeared as the awesome creatures they were.[2] He immediately bowed with his face to the ground in the manner that was customary when one was confronted with lords and kings.

Lot knew the local law about harboring visitors, that in Sodomite eyes such hospitality was the ultimate offense. He was himself an officer of the law, after all, and one of his own daughters had suffered capital punishment for extending charity to a stranger. Yet he chose not to worry about that now. Was he going to turn away a pair of obvious deputies of Heaven? Lot knew that the wrath of God was to be feared more even than that of his fellow citizens. He offered the angels the courtesy he had been taught by Abraham: "Behold now my lords, turn about please into the house of your servant and spend the night. Wash your feet, and then get up early and go on your way."[3] At first, they demurred, saying they would spend the night in the town square, but eventually the angels agreed to accompany him.

Lot wasn't a typical Sodomite. The Bible says of him that when he first settled there, he pitched his tent "up to" Sodom.[4] Literally this seems to mean that initially he didn't live inside the city proper but, because the place was wicked, stayed just outside the wall. In terms of religious sociology, one might call him a traditionalist. In religious communities, one often meets such people. They may not believe in the truth of the faith they avow. On the other hand, they refuse to give up its practices. This is because doing so would alienate them from the social life of the community, or because they don't know any other way to live, or because in some quiet part of their souls they are not entirely sure that God isn't watching them. Yet when they practice their faith, they do so without conviction. They do the minimum required, or a bit less, and take comfort that they remain in contact with the old ways. They pitch their tents up to the walls of Sodom, but never inside.

Though he had parted ways with his teacher, Abraham, and thus given up a direct link to God, Lot would not give up the traditions. He had married a Sodomite woman, named Idit, but had done his best to impart to his five daughters an appreciation for the customs of his uncle.[5] Indeed, they believed in God to the extent their father did.[6] Thus he practiced the Abrahamic virtue of hospitality—even when, as tonight, doing so put his life in danger.[7] As we will see, he even followed Abraham in eating matzoh at the Passover season.[8]

Yet for all his traditionalism, he was accepted by the populace as one of their own, a prominent citizen. The very day the angels entered the city, he had been elevated to the position of chief municipal judge.[9] His home, figuratively and literally, was now in Sodom itself.

The meaning of Sodom is widely misapprehended. The English word "sodomite," when defined as "homosexual," gives a false impression of what made Sodom unbearable to God. We need to understand the city better, starting with its geography, which is not irrelevant to comprehending its moral character.

What had the angels seen when they caught their first view of the Jordan valley, called here the Valley of Siddim? Modern travelers to the region would not recognize the place as it was then. The Dead Sea sits in the basin of the lowest spot on earth, 1,290 feet below sea level. Today it is a blasted wilderness, a gorgeous but lonely desert whose solitude is disrupted only by an anomalous cluster of huge luxury hotels. As one drives the twisting Route 31 down from Arad, the eye is dazzled by a poisonous blue lake, its waters so densely salty that bathers are warned against swallowing even a mouthful. The salinity is 25 percent, higher than any other natural body of water. This is why you float in it.

The Bible, however, preserves the memory of a valley famous for lush vegetation, "like the Garden of the Lord," meaning Eden.[10] The Roman historian Tacitus agrees that the sunken plain, also called the Ghor, was indeed a place of greenery and populous towns. Probably the flora was like that around the Sea of Galilee today—connected to the Dead Sea by the Jordan, which feeds both. The Galilee region is the most verdant in Israel.

One scholar has attributed the decimation of the Valley of Siddim to the work of nature: "a great earthquake, concomitant explosions, ignition of natural gas, and [a] general conflagration."[11] As biblical tradition notes, the lush plant life of the fertile Ghor concealed an array of naturally occurring bitumen pits. Bitumen is a viscous, tarlike black or brown substance distilled from petroleum. Still found by the Dead Sea, where government-posted signs admonish visitors to beware of hidden pits, it is highly flammable. This modern hypothesis suggests that a great earthquake, accompanied (as earthquakes sometimes are) by lightning, ignited the local bitumen supply and set the whole valley aflame.[12]

Nearby, archaeologists have found the remains of five Early Bronze Age towns which they say ceased to exist a bit too early to have been concurrent with Abraham. But three of these settlements were clearly destroyed by fire. Thus a tentative match has been made between them and the cities of the plain whose chieftains did battle with the four kings who invaded from the east under the orders of Nimrod, looking for Abraham: Sodom, Gomorrah, Admah, Zeboiim, and Zoar. Two of the ruined cites have been proposed as the possible locations of the famous Sodom. Both lie on wadis (streambeds) leading down from the hills of present-day Jordan to the edge of the Ghor. One, east of the Dead Sea, is called Numeira; the other, to the south, is Feifa.

What if the cities were not, however, in the hills but on the valley floor where the lower embayment of the Dead Sea is today? In the millennia since about 2000 B.C.,[13] this area has been covered by water, hiding any man-made structures that might have existed there in Abraham's time. Very recently the level of the Dead Sea has fallen back again as Israel diverted water that would have entered southward from the Jordan, revealing land that was once above-water. No ruined Sodom or Gomorrah has yet emerged from the depths.[14] But as we'll see, this does not mean the cities were *not* in the basin of the Ghor.

Blessed amid its green oasis, Sodom had provoked the Lord beyond His endurance. The rabbis of the Talmud teach, "The people of Sodom became arrogant only because of the bounty that the Holy One Blessed Be He bestowed upon them."[15] They were the spoiled brats of the ancient Near East. Indulgent parents think that by giving their young ones everything and requiring nothing of them, they will thereby purchase their children's love.

But the opposite is true: children who have been given all the bounty of their parents' wealth without being required, for instance, to do any chores around the house come not infrequently to despise their mother and father. So it was with the Sodomites, whose fertile valley resembled an earthly Paradise.

Sodomites sinned not because they failed to master their impulses (as most of us do), but rather on principle. The Bible says that they were "wicked and sinful toward the Lord, exceedingly."[16] On the extra modifier "exceedingly," the Talmud comments that they first concentrated their minds on the sin and only then committed it. In other words, they sinned *for the sake of sinning.*

In its tractate *Sanhedrin,* the Talmud includes a lengthy exposition of Sodomite depravity, prefaced with a dispute among the rabbis touching on the question of which is a graver violation of God's will: sins involving sex or sins involving money.[17] In other words, which is worse: having sex with another man or cheating in business?

The Sodomites engaged in acts of both kinds, and the Bible for its part refers to both as "abominations." Though the Talmud leaves the question open, its telling of various shameful episodes in Sodomite history leaves a definite impression that sins involving commerce, property, and the like are the more egregious, perhaps because they involve an offense against God and man alike. For all the sins of Sodom that the Talmud highlights have precisely to do with the unjust disposition of wealth. The essence of a true Sodomitic character was an intense selfishness. Sexual "sodomy"—gratification of the body that provides pleasure but no possibility of giving life to another person—is only a subsidiary variation on this theme.

Harold Bloom has it close to right when he explains, about the author J's portrayal of Sodom, "Sin is not one of J's concepts: contempt is. Sodom is not destroyed because of its sin but because of its contempt: for [the Lord], for strangers, for women, for Lot, for all who are not Sodomites."[18] The main theme of their wickedness is a deep antisociability. The Torah stresses the importance of developing and maintaining good relationships with friends and strangers, achieved primarily through communication. To this value it applies the word *chen,* generally mistranslated as "grace." That is why Jewish tradition views commerce not as a necessary evil, as socialism views it, but as a positive good. Having to earn a living, facing every day the prospect of losing your job or your customers, forces people *to act* as if they like each other. And on both sides of a relationship that was once only outwardly friendly, acting with *chen,* graceful sociability, often leads to genuine warm feelings.

The Sodomites represent the negation of *chen* as well as the negation of the value most characteristic of Abraham: *chesed,* or kindness. Thus we find that they undertook to harass any foreigner who entered the city, especially if he came to trade. They entered into a "gentleman's" agreement that if any stranger came to town, they would first sodomize (in the conventional English sense of the word) then rob him.[19] The locals are depicted as howling like dogs, such was their lust for wealth won by theft. They cast a particularly malignant eye on traveling merchants. Seeing that in this wealthy land the "very dust is gold," the Sodomites said among themselves, "What do we need with wayfarers, who come to us only to deprive us of our money? Come, let us cause the very idea of wayfaring to be forgotten in our land."[20] Traveling salesmen happen to be the very epitome of *chen:* for wherever they go they bring the gifts of commerce and sociability. Before communication traveled electronically, it traveled with itinerant merchants.

The Torah regards currency as a godsend, a guarantor of *chen:* it crystallizes the faith and goodwill that merchants share with customers. Indeed, accepting small pieces of green paper in return for goods and services may be the commonest act of faith there is: only his faith guarantees to the merchant that he will be able to exchange this paper for other goods.[21] So it's not surprising that, as a consequence of the Sodomites' contempt for *chen,* currency in Sodom lost its value. The Talmud relates that if a pauper came to town and asked for sustenance, they all gave him coins but refused to sell him bread. When eventually he starved to death, they gathered around the corpse and took their money back.

They went so far as to outlaw generosity of any kind, and this was the immediate cause of their downfall. The Pentateuch alludes to this in a grammatically curious expression attributed to God. "And the Lord said, 'Because the outcry of Sodom and Gomorrah has grown great and because their sin has become very grave, I will descend and see. If they acted in accordance with its outcry which has come to me—[then] destruction! And if not, I will know.' "[22] The single Hebrew word translated here as "if . . . in accordance with its outcry" [hak'tza'akatah] literally means "if . . . in accordance with *her* outcry." But if it were translated that way, the referent of the pronominal suffix meaning "her" would be uncertain. Who is "she" whose "outcry" God wishes to investigate?

The Bible critics are forced to discover here an anomalous "archaic feminine suffix without possessive," to be translated as if there were no referent: "whether . . . in accordance with *the* outcry."[23] Or maybe what we have is yet another "scribal error." The midrashic accounts, on the other hand, find the 911 call that brought God to the scene of wickedness.

The "outcry" belonged to a girl, Plotit, Lot's daughter. A law was passed in Sodom decreeing death by fire upon anyone who ventured to offer food to a poor person or any wayfarer or stranger. Plotit was married to one of the leading men in town and so in her defense could hardly plead ignorance. She met a pauper inside the city gates and took pity on him. Every day when she went to draw water for her family she put food in her bucket and, on her way to the wadi or the well, surreptitiously passed the food to the poor man. The authorities noticed that the impoverished fellow persisted in not dying, and they figured that some criminal must be sustaining him with charity. Plotit's illegal deeds were discovered and she was taken out to be burned. Before she perished, she cried out to Heaven, "Lord of the Universe, exact justice and judgment from the men of Sodom!"[24] God heard her voice and said, "I will descend and see whether they act in accordance with *her* outcry which has come to me."

The story of the destruction of Sodom sounds at first like a case study in divine wrath, so it is unexpected to find throughout the story, as we do, the name of God associated with the attribute of divine mercy: the ineffable four-letter name, the tetragrammaton. (This has led the critics to attribute authorship of the Sodom narrative to J, whose hypothetical work is noted for employing this divine name—notwithstanding that verse 19:29, toward the end of the story, twice employs the divine name "Elohim," linked to the author E.) The point is that the destruction of Sodom was really an exercise in compassion for the innocent Plotit.

When Lot got home with the two visitors, Plotit's mother, Idit, was incredulous. Did he not know that he endangered the whole family by taking in these strangers? When Abraham received the angels in his home, he had the support of his wife and son, who assisted him in preparing the meal. The Bible's language here—"He [Lot] prepared a feast for them and baked unleavened bread [for it was Passover] and they ate"—indicates that Lot received no help from Idit.[25] On the contrary, she fought him from the moment they entered the house until he subjected her to the final indignity, which led to her own destruction: salt.

The party sat down to the meal. Or rather Lot sat down to it, for angels only give the appearance of eating while not actually ingesting anything. Indeed, the medieval commentator Sforno points out that the text has Lot preparing a complete "feast," in Hebrew a *mishteh,* from the root meaning "to drink": literally a "drinking party." Never mind that his guests couldn't eat or drink, this was as an occasion for Lot to indulge a love of alcohol— which was to get him into trouble on an occasion soon to follow.[26] Another sage, Rabbi Chaim ben Attar (called the Or HaChaim; Italian, 1696–1743), also notes the oddity of preparing a feast for angels but explains that Lot did so with better intentions than Sforno attributes to him. The purpose was to honor the angels, celebrate their presence under his roof, since feasting is associated with celebration even if the honorees aren't hungry (or thirsty).[27]

Before the festive event could really get under way, Lot looked about for salt—by Jewish custom, an essential accompaniment to a meal—but found none. He asked his wife if there was any in the house: not a good question. At this simple request, she exploded: "Do you also propose to teach *this* wicked and reprehensible practice here [in our house]?"[28] It was bad enough to invite guests into the house. How much worse to enhance their enjoyment by flavoring the food with salt! She, unlike Lot, evidently did not know the visitors were angels. Idit shouted something about going around to the neighbors and asking if *they* had any salt, and out the door she went. At each neighbor's home, she asked, "Can you give me any salt? We have guests."[29] And, just as she intended, very shortly the whole town knew that Lot had violated the sacred antihospitality law. Lot's wife had deliberately put his life in jeopardy.

The reader must be wondering what it was about salt that so distressed Idit. Lot had called for salt not only to bring out the flavor of the flavorless matzoh he had served. He was also imitating the ways of his uncle Abraham, who had anticipated the Jewish practice of salting the bread at a ritual meal, as on the Sabbath. Jews salt their bread as a remembrance of the sacrifices that were brought in the Temple at Jerusalem, which as per biblical law were salted. In the context of the Sabbath, a meal is a form of worship, a Temple sacrifice in miniature. Salt was crucial to the Temple rites because its presence meant that every category of God's material creation was included in the service. In the Torah's understanding, there are four such categories that together constitute everything physical that exists in our world: mineral (for instance, salt), vegetable, animal, and human. Idit objected to worshiping the Lord, as any good Sodomite would, and she knew what salt meant. When her husband asked for the condiment, she judged him worthy of death.

So did the rest of the Sodomite population. Word spread fast, and soon every man in town had gathered outside the home of Lot and Idit. As Rashi comments, they came "from one end of the city to the other end, for there was no one to stay their hand, for there was not even one righteous person among them."[30] Sodom was thoroughly wicked. There was no longer any hope of saving it.

Rudely interrupting the drinking party, Lot's neighbors called on him to give up his guests so they could sodomize and rob them. Terrified, he refused, and in his desperation he even calculated that it would be better to purchase the safety of his visitors by offering up his own daughters to the pleasure of the mob. He stepped outside and said, "See now I have two daughters who have never known a man [sexually]. Let me then bring them out to you and you may do to them whatever is good in your eyes. Only do nothing to these men inasmuch as they have come under the shadow of my roof."[31]

His motivation must have been one of a hysterical, irrational sort of pity on the people of the town. He understood that the "men" were not men but angels, so there was nothing the ugly crowd could do to them against their will. But should the Sodomites splinter his door and seek to gang-rape the visitors, Lot knew it would be all over for the town and its residents. Gabriel had not yet told him precisely what the Lord intended, but Lot suspected. According to the Midrash, he had spent the entire evening up till this point begging the angels to spare Sodom. Now he thought to himself, If only I can forestall the assault on these heavenly beings, even if that means giving the crowd my two virgin daughters, then there is some chance of winning the angels' sympathy and rescuing Sodom from its fate.

Over dinner, Gabriel and Raphael had seemed to consider the merits of

Lot's defense, just as God had considered Abraham's. But now they stepped to the door and revealed their majesty, blinding the Sodomites, sending them groping back to their homes. The angels ordered Lot to say no more on the subject: "Until now you had permission [from us] to speak in their defense. From now on you have no permission."[32]

They confessed to Lot that they indeed had been sent to overthrow the city. If he wanted his family to escape the conflagration, they had better do it now. Of Lot's surviving daughters, two were married and two betrothed.[33] The latter two lived at home. In the hour or two before dawn, Lot visited his two married daughters and their husbands and the two young men who were engaged to marry his other two daughters. He warned them all, "Get up! Get out of this place for the Lord is about to destroy the city."[34] But they were sure that Lot was pulling their leg. Sodom was a rollicking place after dark, full of reveling. Tonight the usual noise of laughter and music had subsided during the assault on Lot's home and for a short time after till the mob regained its vision. Now everybody had recovered, forgotten about the strange encounter with the visitors, and gotten back to rejoicing. Lot, his sons-in-law concluded, was acting in the spirit of the evening and engaging in a practical joke. When he persisted and their amusement began to fade, one of the young men pointed out that the city was engaged in merrymaking just as it always was around 4 A.M. Was it possible that such a city could be on the brink of destruction? No, he concluded, there was no danger.[35]

Lot returned to his home, deeply depressed, to find that the angels had become still more insistent. He must right now, without delay, get his wife and two unmarried daughters out of Sodom, "lest you be swept away because of the iniquity of the city."[36] Dawn was then rising. According to the Talmud, the red in the sky at the first light of day is reflected from the roses in the Garden of Eden, while the red of sunset reflects the fires of Hell. We may imagine the crimson horizon that morning taking on more of a hellish than a paradisiacal hue.

Yet, despite all he had heard and seen, Lot hesitated. He believed that the angels were about to incinerate the cities of the plain. But the mad, grasping character of Sodom had infected him. He began to try to gather his valuables from around the house. In Rashi's phrase, he "took pity on his money"[37] and was heard muttering to himself, "How much will be lost in silver and gold, precious stones and pearls?"[38] King Solomon in his wisdom would later say, "There is a sickening evil I have seen under the sun: wealth hoarded by its owner to his misfortune."[39] The Torah takes a dim view of those individuals who spend too much energy guarding their physical resources. There's nothing to object to in prudent saving, but it is spending money, not guarding it at all costs, that leads to the communication and relationship-building that are the essence of *chen*. At this point, Raphael had to forcibly take Lot by the hand, along with Idit and the girls, and *make* them leave.

Once the family was outside Sodom, the angel gave Lot one last item of stern advice. He said, "Do not look behind you and do not stop anywhere in all the plain. But rather flee to the mountain lest you be swept away."[40]

This was easy for an angel to say. According to the Midrash, when they assume the shape of a human being, angels lack one feature of the human anatomy: they have no necks.[41] The lesson is that angels don't look back on their actions, wondering if they did the right thing. In the heavenly realm, there is no hindsight. It's one of the frailties of men that we constantly second-guess ourselves. Raphael was telling Lot and his family not to worry if they had been correct to abandon their friends and loved ones in Sodom. They would be better off in this respect if they could emulate the angels.

Idit was the least angelic of the four humans that escaped Sodom. Out of compassion for the two married daughters she had left behind to die, or perhaps because she simply wanted to indulge the human impulse to see others in distress, she turned around and beheld the city in flames. God metes out punishments according to a rule of what might be called poetic correspondence. The punishment fits the crime. Because Idit had sinned against her husband in the matter of the salt he had asked her to fetch, now she was punished accordingly: before the eyes of her horrified family, she became a pillar of salt.

Near the southern extreme of the west side of the Dead Sea one may still see the forty-foot Jebel Usdum ("Mt. Sodom"), a rough cylinder composed of salt except at the top where it is carbonate of lime, said since ancient times to be the remains of Lot's wife. Modern geologists have speculated that the formation arose from the ground as semiliquid salt was thrust upward. They also say it is far too old to be a relic from Abraham's time, dating instead from the far more antique Mesozoic or Paleozoic age.[42] We needn't hesitate in granting that the scientists may be right: nothing in the Bible's account indicates that the salted bones of Idit were to be an eternal memorial. But the geologists' observations give us an image of Idit's last moments, the salt rising up from the ground at her feet as a semiliquid, quickly covering her legs, her torso, finally closing over her screaming mouth.

At first glance, Raphael's instruction that Lot flee to "the mountain" is a problem. The definite article implies that some particular mountain is meant, but the biblical text doesn't say which. If the narrative chooses to speak of a mountain without noting its name or location, that can only mean the mountain has already been referred to explicitly. Rashi points out that in the Abraham narrative, "the mountain" that has already been mentioned is the one between Beth-el and Ai ("the mountain east of Beth-el") where Abraham had established a worship site shortly after entering Canaan and which he'd visited again after returning to the land from Egypt.[43] Thus when the angel directed Lot to flee to that mountain, it must have been to seek refuge with his uncle. Though Abraham's primary residence was at Hebron, he had many homes, one of which was between Beth-el and Ai. The angel knew that when the patriarch had parted ways with his heavenly guests, he had traveled from there not back to Hebron, but north to "the mountain." According to the Midrash, the first time Abraham had prayed at that altar he had begged the Lord to have mercy on a group of Israelites who, in the time of the conquest of Canaan under Joshua, he perceived by prophecy were destined to be slaughtered thereabouts.[44] The patriarch returned there now in the hope that the altar between Beth-el and Ai was a place from which God was especially inclined to accept prayers for mercy on doomed mortals: in this case, the population of Sodom and her sister cities.

Lot, however, was disinclined to reunite with his uncle. The Bible quotes him as saying enigmatically, "But I am unable to flee to the mountain lest the evil attach itself to me and I die."[45] As Rashi explains, he intended to say, "When I [lived] in proximity to the people of Sodom, the Holy One Blessed Be He looked upon my deeds and the deeds of the people of the city, and [in context] I appeared as a righteous man and worthy of being saved. But should I come into proximity to the righteous one [Abraham], I will be [in God's eyes] like a wicked man." In other words, when he was a Sodomite, he was good by comparison with his neighbors. If he fled to his uncle, once he was there, the "evil" of Sodom would follow and swallow him up. The angels saw his point. They allowed him to flee to Zoar, the least wicked of the five cities of the plain, which Gabriel then temporarily spared from the fate of the other four.

As Lot was seeking to put as much distance as he could between himself and Abraham, as he had done once before a quarter century earlier after they had returned from Egypt, the uncle was rising from sleep. Abraham got up early this morning, as was his custom, to pray. He is credited with initiating the morning worship service in Jewish tradition called Shacharit.[46] He had created that special place in time, just after sunrise, when morning prayer is most propitious, just as he had created the special place on earth where he now prayed, the altar on "the mountain." From this vantage point, he saw the flames that engulfed Sodom now ascending from the basin of the Ghor: for "behold, the smoke of the earth rose like the smoke of a lime pit."[47] As Harold Bloom rightly points out, the sight would have reminded him of the fiery, smoking covenant he himself had made with God at the Covenant Between the Parts.[48] He noticed that as the sun rose, the moon was still visible—a sign to those idolaters who regarded the sun or moon as divine that both "gods" were powerless to save the wicked cities.[49]

There is no indication in either Scripture or tradition that Abraham grieved at what he must have presumed to be Lot's funeral pyre. This is in contrast to the patriarch's urgent concern for his nephew's welfare when the younger man was kidnapped by the four kings: more evidence that Abraham's Egyptian family (Hagar, Ishmael) had to some extent displaced his Mesopotamian family (Sarah, Lot) as the main concern in his life.

The oral tradition explains that the destruction of Sodom and her fellows was accomplished by a combination of fire and water.[50] The disaster began innocently enough as ordinary rain. The rain became sulfur and fire.[51] Once the incineration had been accomplished, the Bible says that God "overturned these cities and the entire plain."[52] The Hebrew verb in that sentence, *va'yahafoch,* can mean either "He destroyed" or, more literally, "He overturned" in the sense of turning an object upside down. The Midrash reports a tradition that the latter meaning is intended. The five cities sat on a plain of bedrock which the angel Gabriel lifted up and flipped over on top of itself, forever hiding the remains of Sodom and Gomorrah from archaeological investigations.[53] Water then covered the overturned valley floor, leaving the configuration of the Dead Sea in relationship to the Ghor that we see today.

An angel changing the geography of the Holy Land in such a manner doesn't sound like something for which we should hope to find geological confirmation. But in fact, the same historian who attributed the destruction of the plain to an earthquake suggests the cataclysm effected a "faulting or slipping of the rock strata." This "may have first allowed the water to escape from the very deep northern part of the Dead Sea into the shallow depression south of [the Lisan peninsula, which extends into the sea from the east]."[54] His account is close to that of the Midrash, allowing us to entertain the possibility that Sodom and the other four cities really do lie under the Valley of Siddim.

We still need to clarify what the destruction of Sodom has to do with Abraham. Why does the Pentateuch devote a good part of its narrative concerning the patriarch to an episode that didn't directly affect him?

If Scripture is merely a collection of loosely edited tall tales, then we needn't bother with such questions. There is no saying why the Redactor included some stories and left out others.

If on the other hand the Torah is a communication from the divine realm, then every event it narrates should advance some purpose of the book. One purpose of the Bible's narration of the life of Abraham is to explain how the Jewish people got its start. The purpose of the Bible's narration of the formative history of the Jewish people is to explain by what vehicle God's Truth, in the form of the written and oral teaching called Torah, entered the world. Where, then, does Sodom fit in?

The history of humanity is a process in which man gets to know God. This education of mankind has been accomplished through the spreading, in one form or another, of Torah. For not only the people Israel but also the nations espousing Christianity and Islam have access to all or part of the Torah and devote more or less energy to disseminating its truth. The process of dissemination, which began with the career of Abraham, is not open-ended. No one knows precisely when it will draw to a close; but when it does, the oral tradition suggests that the end time will be presided over by a figure called Messiah, a descendant of King David.

With this in mind, we return to Lot and his two surviving daughters. The devastation of the region where they had lived was enough to convince the three of them that not only the cities of the plain but all of Canaan had been consumed. This evaluation sprang from their own moral decrepitude, for the wicked person and the cynic tend to assume that all the world is as wicked and cynical as they are. So naturally if the Lord got sick enough of Lot's town to destroy it, then no doubt he destroyed all the other towns, which were just as bad.

After spending some time in Zoar, they at last fled to "the mountain," having decided after all to seek refuge with Abraham.[55] They figured that he, at least, must have survived. But when they reached the vicinity of Beth-el and Ai, Abraham was no longer there. They took refuge in a cave. The older daughter said to her sister, "Our father is old and there is no [other] man in the land to come to us in the manner of all the earth [that is, to impregnate and give us children]. Come, let us feed our father wine and lay with him, that we may give life to offspring through our father."[56] No bolder plan was ever conceived.

These were the two daughters that Lot had offered to the Sodomite crowd, so neither held him particularly in awe. Lot had told the mob that both girls were virgins, which was true and posed a slight challenge, because the two assumed that a woman is less likely to conceive the first time she engages in intercourse. This apparently had something to do with the need to break the hymen. The blood or the trauma could interfere with conception. The daughters resolved to maximize their chances of getting pregnant through an act of self-mutilation, reasoning that if they plucked out their own hymens first, that would do the trick. They proceeded to do so.[57] As for Lot the tippler, glad to forget the decimation of life he had witnessed, he drank heartily. Later that night both girls fought down any moral scruples they felt and were intimate with their father. From this, two children were conceived: Moab, from whom the biblical nation of Moab was descended, and Ben-Ammit, ancestor of the biblical nation of Ammon.

Moab and Ammon were located just on the other side and to the southeast of the Dead Sea, in what is today Jordan. It happens that throughout much of the ninth to seventh centuries B.C., their relations with the Hebrew kingdoms of Israel and Judah were unfriendly. This fact has led some scholars to claim that the story of Lot and his daughters was composed around the seventh century, its purpose being to mock the ancestry of Ammon and

Moab.[58] In other words, the story amounts to nothing more than a juvenile ethnic insult from long ago.

If the Bible is not a bigoted fraud masquerading as a divine document, what is the meaning of the episode? A hint is found in Lot's wine. Did the father and his daughters bring it from Sodom? The scholarly skeptics don't ask questions like that, because they don't expect the Bible to be logical. The oral tradition, however, does ask, and it has an answer. No, Lot didn't carry a case of wine on his shoulder as he ran for his life, fire and sulfur falling around him. God prepared and placed it in the cave, for He intended the girls to become pregnant by their father.[59]

The Midrash points out that when the older daughter hatches her plan, proposing that they "give life to offspring through our father," the word "offspring" is curiously vague. Why not say "a son" or "children" instead? Because the "offspring" she meant, by unconscious prophecy, was not the two boys that were born to Lot and his daughters, but some other "offspring" whose genetic line was initiated that night in the cave, who would be descended from either Moab or Ammon. That offspring, says the Midrash, is "King Messiah."[60] For from Moab there arose a woman called Ruth, a convert to the Hebrew religion, who was the great-grandmother of King David. Her story is told, her genealogy specified, in the Book of Ruth. And David's descendant will be King Messiah, illustrating the principle of Torah thought that a drama hidden in all God's interactions with the world is the discovery and extraction of the good locked in the heart of evil. On this, the Midrash comments by quoting a line from Psalms: " 'I have found my servant David.' Where did I find him? In Sodom."[61]

Thus, in the narrative of Abraham's life, which tells how God began to establish a relationship with the human race, we find very appropriately the birth of a child whose line of genetic descent leads straight to the climax of that relationship, to the end of history. The seed of the end is planted in the field of the beginning.

CHAPTER TWELVE

Thy Neighbor's Wife

braham had seen the smoke rising from the ruins of Sodom, and he felt the impact of the disaster soon after. As an evangelist for monotheism, he preferred to target those men and women who seemed the most alienated from their Creator, and none were more so than the residents of Sodom. When they stopped passing through Hebron on their way to or from home, the main purpose of his being in that place was extinguished.[1]

So he moved, first to the northern Sinai peninsula, by the road called Derech Shur, "the Way to Shur," Shur being identical with the Wall of the Ruler that marked the border of Egypt. He figured on encountering travelers to or from Egypt, a place notable for licentiousness, who would likely be in need of his ministrations. But the volume of passersby must have been low. Soon he headed back north to the uppermost border of the Negev wilderness, to Gerar. The residents of this city posed a different kind of challenge from what he had gotten used to when dealing with the Sodomite and Egyptian traffic.

We know something about the character of the Gerarites, and so presumably did Abraham. What the oral tradition tells is hinted at in the biblical text, for we have come to the second of the "wife-sister" episodes in the Abraham narrative. The first was on his visit to Egypt twenty-four years earlier. Now Abraham directed his wife, as he had done before, to tell anyone who asked that she was his sister. The scholars explain that the first episode came from the pen of J and this one from the pen of E—notwithstanding that the divine name associated with J's work appears in the present story at verse 20:18 (yet another "copyist's error," we are assured).[2] A more satisfying explanation is that the two incidents illuminate the respective situations at the places where they occurred. Each is like a candle held up in a dark room: the same candle, moved from room to room, will show different furniture and wallpaper depending on where you take it. Here the furniture and wallpaper were the moral conditions of Egypt and Gerar, respectively.

In Egypt, Sarah was abducted by the king, and when he found out that the Lord of the Universe had an interest in reuniting her with her husband, Pharaoh commanded Abraham in the most urgent terms: *"Kach va'lech!,"* meaning "Take [her] and go!" Pharaoh was in a panic, as Rashi explains, because he could not guarantee Sarah's safety if she remained in the land. This was because the "Egyptians were steeped in lewdness."[3]

It was not so at Gerar. The classical Jewish commentators, drawing on the oral tradition, depict that city as in the grip of a culture that modern folk would recognize. It was a civilized place that was, however, deficient in the quality called *yirat Hashem,* a phrase often mistranslated as "fear of the Lord." The word *yirah* means something more like "awe" and shares a root construction with the Hebrew verb meaning "to see." That is, someone who has *yirat Hashem* behaves as if he could see God, so to speak, standing before him. A country where the citizens behave themselves according to generally accepted rules of good conduct, but where they don't believe that God stands before them—such a country is capable of anything. The medieval sage Radak makes this point in his commentary on the episode in Gerar.[4] The later commentator Malbim, writing in the nineteenth century, explains that a civilization that has no faith in divine providence, however proper its "ethical" standards, can't be trusted not to take a sudden turn into barbarism.[5] In this manner, Weimar Germany became, almost overnight, Nazi Germany.

Abraham worried about what would happen to his wife in Gerar if he presented her as his wife. The Talmud suggests that there was an element of prophecy in his concern, a premonition of danger.[6] So he compelled Sarah to resume their previous lie. In Egypt, he had asked her permission for this, but now he literally forced her to consent. Even Rashi, who generally defends the conduct of the patriarch, draws on the Midrash and speaks of his acting "against her will, not for her own good, for she had already been taken into the house of Pharaoh by the same [ruse]."[7]

Thus a worried Abraham and an unwilling Sarah entered the ramparts of Gerar. In the Middle East today, attractive women who walk around cities are accustomed to being assaulted by the attention of innumerable men. The men stare; sometimes they grab or pinch. It was the same way thousands of years ago. Sarah, who tradition presents as being remarkably attractive despite her advanced age, immediately felt herself under a siege of lust. To give further definition to our picture of the matriarch, we may envision her adorned as a typical woman of her time and station would have been. She would have worn earrings, nose rings, neck pendants, bracelets, her eyes set off by the cosmetic kohl, her face colored, her body smelling of sweet-scented oil. When she walked, her anklets tinkled.[8] Yet there was an imposing dignity, even a severity, about her.

The men of Gerar, among whom there were no proper gentlemen, were not intimidated. This doesn't mean they cared nothing for propriety. They preferred not to engage in adultery. Amid the fumes of a morality whose basis their ancestors had forgotten, this much they could discern: that one doesn't sleep with another man's wife. In Egypt, where adultery was also seen as problematic, a husband might be killed so that the crowd could enjoy the favors of his widow. Here the people weren't lawless. Some entirely legal way would be found to separate the man from his wife; it would be done in court, under the eyes of a judge. If the husband resisted the will of the court, *then* he would be killed. It was a civilized place, but as the Bible intends to teach here, the distinction between a "civilization" where there is no fear of God and a jungle where total moral degradation rules is a distinction that in the end makes little difference. So while in a godlier city one

would expect the locals to greet a visitor with offers of food and shelter—
did the stranger know someone hereabouts who would take care of him?—
in Gerar the first question put to Abraham was, "Is she your wife or your
sister?"[9] Abraham said, "She is my sister."[10]

Who exactly were these unappealing Gerarites? The ruins of the place, extensively explored in the 1980s, can, like most other archaeological sites in
the region, illuminate only such matters as the local taste in architecture and
pottery. Gerar was no insignificant hamlet but a city of forty acres, which in
the Middle Bronze Age made it one of the biggest urban settlements in
southern Canaan.[11] Abraham found there a less austere landscape than that of
the rocky Judean mountains around Hebron. Today, identified with Tell
Haror, halfway between Beersheba and Gaza, the remains of Gerar lie in flat
farming country on the bank of the Wadi Gerar. Not knowing what was underneath, the Israelis some decades ago tried to turn the tell into a public
park, complete with planted eucalyptus trees and a jungle gym.

As Abraham approached from the south, the first thing he would have
seen was the big sloping earthen ramparts with a sort of moat or "fosse" at
the bottom and topped by strong walls. It was a design intended to protect
the fortifications from assault by battering rams, which could find no foot-
ing on the ramparts. This typical defensive strategy of the Middle Bronze
Age Canaanite city-state gave to Gerar, seen from a distance, the classic sil-
houette of such a place, which Abraham encountered many times in his travels in the land.[12] From afar, he might have seen the shape of a tower, or
migdal, rising above the walls.[13]

Abraham was familiar with Gerar's culture, if not because he had visited
it himself, then from reports of acquaintances who had done so. Its king was
called Avimelech, meaning literally "My Father [was also] the King"—a
thronal rather than a personal name, like "Pharaoh." Later in Genesis, Avimelech's rule is associated with "the land of the Philistines."[14] Still later, when
Abraham's son Isaac visits Gerar, we are informed that the Avimelech of that
day was "king of the Philistines."[15]

This identification presents a difficulty because most historians who have
written on the subject tell us there were no Philistines in Canaan at the time.

These writers assume that the Bible intends to link Avimelech to the Philistines who were among the Sea Peoples that famously migrated from the vicinity of the Aegean Sea (which separates modern Greece from Turkey) and sought to invade Egypt about 1190 B.C. They were subsequently cast out by Pharaoh Rameses III, who settled what remained of them on the southern Canaanite coast. In other words, the Philistines who are best known to history did not arrive in Canaan till more than five hundred years after Abraham's visit to Gerar. The fact that the Bible speaks unambiguously of there being Philistines there during the lifetime of Isaac is, to most scholarly commentators, proof that the account must have been written long after the supposed patriarchal period. Those who assert that the Abraham narrative was written in the eighth or seventh century B.C. point out that around that same time Gerar was a major Assyrian stronghold, thus "an obvious landmark" which the author would naturally want to include in his story.[16] This doesn't explain why the place is identified as a *Philistine,* not an Assyrian, city.

The period of Philistine flourishing in Canaan was short, only a couple hundred years, between 1200 and 1000 B.C. By the ninth century, the Philistines had been more or less absorbed into the non-Philistine culture around them.[17] So another problem with the scholarly-skeptical viewpoint is that the author(s) of the Abraham narrative portrays these Philistines in a far less threatening light than do such later books as 1 Samuel, which contains the story of David's defeat of the Philistine giant Goliath, and the Book of Judges. If the authors of the Abraham story as well as those of 1 Samuel and Judges all had in mind the same Philistines who were their neighbors between 1200 and 1000, as the skeptics insist, why don't the Genesis authors E and J depict the Philistines in equally dark terms?

The most attractive hypothesis, a minority view among the scholars, is that what we are dealing with in the patriarchal encounter with "Philistines" is not the Sea People who invaded Egypt but rather some relatives of their ancestors: an early colony of traders from the Aegean or Mediterranean. The Bible links the Philistines with the island of Caphtor, of which they are said to be "remnants" or "survivors," and which in turn is identified either with Crete or Cyprus.[18] As it turns out, Cypriot pottery from the Middle Bronze Age has been found in small quantities in the ruins of Canaanite settlements (much more of it was imported in the Late Bronze Age).[19] Perhaps the "Philistines" of Isaac's day were merchants sharing an ethnically Cypriot background; while only much later, with the entrance of the Sea People in the Early Iron Age, did Philistines become a major presence in Canaan.[20] The difference between the early and later stages of Philistine immigration would then be something like that between the early and later stages of European immigration to the Americas. Norsemen turned up in eastern Canada around A.D. 1000 but left no substantial evidence of having been there. Probably the Native Americans of the time didn't view them as much of a threat. After Europeans started to arrive en masse after 1492, the Indians took a different view of white men. Still it's noteworthy that the Bible's Abraham narrative does not directly identify the Avimelech who ruled Gerar in Abraham's day as a Philistine. Though the Abraham narrative does refer to "the land of the Philistines," this may speak from the later historical viewpoint of Moses, in whose time tradition says the text was composed. It might be that in the year that Sodom was destroyed and Abraham left Hebron, about 1713 B.C., the Aegeans were still some decades short of establishing a presence in Canaan.

Of course, such speculation, informed by archaeology, says nothing about the actual character of ancient peoples. Their pottery and their ruined buildings are mute. Even such fragmentary written documents as are unearthed— internal government correspondence, merchant records, tales of the gods—cannot be relied on to indicate the moral spirit of the culture. They tell us no more than shreds of a transcript of debates in Congress, a Microsoft annual report, or a Gideon's Bible from a motel room will tell future generations about the true nature of American society in our own day. From such documents, one could draw any number of quite misleading conclusions about what Americans were actually like. For an intimate understanding of the heart of Gerar, we must rely on tradition, which concerns itself with intimate matters. Let us then return to what tradition has to say.

The heart of the city was its king, and no one in Gerar was more woman-crazy than Avimelech. Never did a new female pass through the gates of the city without her being greedily appraised by him. It would seem he had first dibs on such visitors. On seeing Sarah, aglow with beauty despite her age, he decided he must have her.

Yet Avimelech hesitated. He asked the customary question, "Is she your wife or your sister?" Abraham said, "She is my sister." The king even asked the woman herself, and she said, "He is my brother."[21] Still, something made him doubt the story. The couple had with them a company of slaves, camel drivers and donkey drivers. In the Midrash's telling, each one of these individuals Avimelech confronted and asked the same question: "Is she his wife or his sister?" Each one said, "She is his sister," for they had been advised by Abraham to say this. The king knew somewhere in his heart that he was about to sin, yet he felt a need to assure himself ahead of time that it was really all right. No one, not even a very wicked person, wants to think of himself as a wrongdoer. Man is the self-deceiving animal.

When Avimelech was satisfied, he directed his henchmen to seize Abraham's "sister" and bring her to the palace. He then prepared himself to take her as his own, in the way it was done, says Maimonides, before the spread of Abrahamic teaching: through sexual intercourse.[22] The Bible gracefully elides here the action of that night. Between Avimelech's "taking" Sarah and God's warning him not to try anything further, the text gives no information at all. But something must have happened, otherwise how to explain God's terrifying words?

The oral tradition steps in to clarify. There are different views as to how long Sarah spent in the palace. The Midrash says just one night, whereas Nachmanides says it was many days.[23] Perhaps it was one night that *felt* like a whole month or more. Whatever the duration, it was not only Avimelech who was straining impatiently for the evening's main event, the sexual violation of the matriarch. A whole crowd of men had seen Sarah enter Gerar and had lusted for her. News of the king's prize had spread across town, and everyone wanted to take part, if only as voyeurs. Avimelech was not averse to this and allowed his subjects to gather outside the palace.

Sarah, meanwhile, had spent the hours leading up to this in desperate prayer. She felt that God had abused her trust. Lying on the ground with her face in the dust, she pleaded, "Lord of Eternity, Abraham went out [from his homeland] with a promise [from You that he would be rewarded]. But I went out [from my homeland only] with faith [for You spoke to him, but not to me]. Now Abraham is outside of this prison, but I am myself in the prison." Her virtue was greater than her husband's, she argued, yet for a reward it seemed she was about to be raped!

To this, the Lord answered her enigmatically, "All that I am about to do,

I do for you." It didn't seem that way to Sarah, as the crowd grew increasingly impatient. They taunted Avimelech, says the Midrash, daring him to remove the woman's shoe, for a start. The fact that *this* was their challenge indicates that the king and everyone else were in some way aware that violating this particular woman was a weightier undertaking than it had been to violate any other they had known. To approach even her shoe was awesome. But this Avimelech did. His trepidation as great as his arousal, he knelt at the side of the praying woman, reached out a hand, loosened the shoe, and revealed the shapely foot before his subjects. Then something terrible happened.

When Pharaoh had imprisoned Sarah, an angel had rescued her, striking Pharaoh with a heavenly whip. Another mystic being now appeared at Gerar with a whip in *his* hand. Only Sarah could see him, and for the rest of the night he consulted her, asking whether she willed that he strike Avimelech. If she said "Strike!" he would do so. If she said "Desist!"[24] he would do that instead. The Bible, and even the Midrash and Talmud, are reticent about what it was that Avimelech actually felt when he was struck. The Bible speaks of all the "wombs" in the royal household being "shut."[25] But this punishment, of women being unable to give birth, would not have been apparent for months, and would not save the matriarch from the menacing crowd of lustful men. Rashi explains that the closing of wombs here refers to the blockage of *all* bodily orifices, of men and women: "of semen, urine and excrement, ears and nose."[26] But this fails to satisfy as well. Being unable to pass waste or to ejaculate is a handicap that would not have been apparent to Avimelech at least for a few minutes, till he had already molested Sarah. Or did he indeed molest her? When he later converses with the angry Deity, the king will protest his own innocence, that he did whatever he did with Sarah "in the simplicity of my heart and in the purity of my hands." To which God replies that He knows the king did it "in the simplicity of your heart," conspicuously not repeating Avimelech's phrase about "the purity of [his] hands."[27] For the king's hands were *not* pure, having removed Sarah's shoe.

Rumors would persist among those who knew Abraham and Sarah that he did much worse, that she had indeed been raped. But the tradition hints at another answer to our problem. Rashi states unambiguously that Avimelech laid no hand on Sarah's flesh (though he did touch her shoe).[28] To this pair of seemingly contradictory claims—first, that Avimelech knew right away, upon being struck by the angel, that his orifices had been closed, and second, that he never touched Sarah's—there is a possible resolution: that the king was a premature ejaculator. In his arousal at the sight of Sarah's naked foot, he climaxed—or felt as if he was about to do so. At that moment, the angel sealed his urethra, and the royal seed had nowhere to go. Any man will be able to imagine how excruciatingly painful this would be.

Even once he had recovered, Avimelech decided to give it another go. He approached Sarah, gazed at the gorgeous toes, the splendid sole, and—if the previously noted interpretation is right—was about to climax again when, on Sarah's order, the angel blocked him up once more. Judging from the language of the Midrash, this may have happened several times in succession. In the end, increasingly alarmed, the king gave up and the crowd went home.

That night in Gerar no one slept easily, for not only Avimelech but every person who had witnessed the dismaying event and cheered it on was afflicted with the same supernatural condition, as became clear, at the latest, when they sought to relieve themselves before bed.

We may wonder at the symbolism of a body-wide blockage of one's orifices. A clue to its meaning is found in the homeliest benediction in all of Jewish tradition, the prayer Asher Yatzar. Traditionally when a Jew exits the bathroom, he praises God for the miracle of having been given a body whose insides work properly. The text of the prayer reads in full: "Blessed are you Lord our God, King of the universe, Who has fashioned man with wisdom, and created within him various openings and cavities. It is revealed and known before the throne of Your glory, that if one of them were ruptured, or one of them were blocked, it would be impossible to rise and stand before You. Blessed are You, Healer of all flesh, He who does wonders." In other words, every time we relieve ourselves, a miracle has taken place: the exquisitely complicated network of organs in our body has done its job. This is an appropriate moment to acknowledge that our bodies are God's creation. As we noted earlier, the people of Gerar were basically civilized (except in how they treated women!), but lacking in their culture any element of God-awareness. Before Sarah came to town, they attributed the miracle of a functioning body and its orifices to nature. They now saw that what we call nature is simply the pattern of miracles that we are accustomed to. God can change this pattern at will, initiating what in more common usage is called a miracle, and sometimes He does so precisely to remind us that he is the Creator. The people of Gerar needed to be reminded, and God thought that stopping up their orifices would do just that.

That night the king and his subjects were troubled by dreams. The Midrash says that the people of Gerar saw the smoke of Sodom.[29] Literally this is impossible. Sodom was too far away. Perhaps they saw the smoke in their dreams, and their intuition alerted them to the point of similarity between the two cities. Sodom was destroyed for the horrendous way it treated strangers, and Gerar had treated one pair of strangers, Abraham and Sarah, very badly indeed. In their sleep, they saw the smoke, didn't know what it meant, but sensed the danger. When they woke up, the Gerarites were overcome by the eerie, frightening sensation one sometimes gets at night, without exactly knowing why, of some ill thing crouching on the horizon, a shadowy threat you can't define.

As for Avimelech, "God came to [him] in a dream by night and said to him, 'Behold, you are to die, because of the woman whom you took, for she is a married woman.' "[30] Still dreaming, the king protested his own innocence, pointing out that Abraham and Sarah had told him they were brother and sister. To which the Lord answered that that was why "I held you back from sinning against Me, and therefore I did not allow you to touch her. So now return the man's wife, for he is a prophet and he will pray for you."[31]

That morning, Avimelech and all the people of Gerar were terrified—Avimelech because he had initiated the crime, the people not only because they had cheered him on but also because God holds a nation responsible for the sins of its leader. Immediately Abraham was hustled before the king, who demanded an explanation of his behavior: "What have you done to us? How did I sin against you that you have brought upon me and my kingdom a great sin? Deeds that should not be done you have done to me!"[32]

Abraham's spluttered response, a twofold self-defense, is revealing, suggesting he felt that neither explanation really justified the danger in which he had placed his wife and the temptation to which he had subjected the people of Gerar. Two-pronged self-defenses are like that, scented with guilt. First he blamed the deceit on Gerar, saying that if he had introduced Sarah as his wife, he doubted he would have been left alive. Then he pointed out that in a sense she *was* his sister, "my father's daughter, though not my mother's daughter; and she became my wife."[33] Abraham's father, Terach, was not literally Sarah's father. Her father was Haran, Abraham's brother. Thus she was Terach's granddaughter. But as Rashi notes, a man's grandchildren are in a sense like his own children, making Sarah in effect a daughter of Terach—though by a different mother. (Terach had two wives: one was Abraham's mother, the other Haran's.) Thus the patriarch had married his half niece rather than his half sister.

But there was no need to make the distinction for Avimelech's benefit; all the king would have been concerned about was that the couple did not share a mother. As Rashi also points out, the concept of fatherhood, as we know it today, was unknown in the society of Gerar.[34] While the Gerarites understood there was such a thing as *biological* fatherhood, fatherhood in its deepest sense is a spiritual relationship. The link between mother and child is unavoidable: a mother is seen to give birth to her child. But it is possible for a man to impregnate a woman and then walk away; or for a woman to have sex with many men and for the identity of her child's father to remain unknown. If a man chooses to claim a child as his own, and help raise the child, he does so not out of biological necessity, but for spiritual—that is to say, nonmaterial, nonbiological—reasons. In a society that has no relationship with the ultimate spiritual reality, this kind of relationship will be rare. Hence at Gerar the natural aversion to incest would have ruled out a marriage between two children of the same mother, but there was no objection to marriage between children of one father. In this encounter with Avimelech, we are witnessing the birth of fatherhood in the sense it is known to the monotheistic world. Every person who enjoys such a relationship with his father in our time can attribute it to the victory of the Abrahamic model of fatherhood over that of Gerar.

Though Abraham was not guilty of incest, he did feel morally compromised for another reason. He said now to Avimelech, "And so it was when God caused me to stray from the house of my father, I said to her, 'Let this be your kindness that you do to me—that to whatever place we come, say of me, He is my brother.'"[35] Commentators have focused on the Hebrew word that means "caused [me] to stray," *hitu*. We find the same verb stem elsewhere in the Abraham narrative, when Hagar "strays" from Abraham's house into the desert of Beersheba. Rashi understands this as indicating that the Egyptian handmaiden "strayed" morally as well as geographically: "She returned to the idols of the house of her father."[36] Did Abraham in some manner "stray" from the house of his heavenly Father?

Nachmanides would say that the patriarch had committed the same "great sin" he had committed twenty-four years earlier when he and his wife entered Egypt, endangering his wife by placing her in such an unprotected position.[37] Sarah herself had gone along with the wife-sister ruse once again only because Abraham made her do so. What's more, he had no excuse. As Devora Steinmetz argues, Abraham had lost his way, spiritually and morally speaking. Unlike when they had gone down to Egypt, there was no need to subject his wife to the danger of visiting such a place. There was no famine in the land, as there had been when they went to Egypt.[38] But the woman who had given him a child, Hagar, had distracted Abraham's conscience. Yet again he had neglected the woman who was destined to produce the child who, unlike Hagar's boy, Ishmael, would carry on Abraham's spiritual legacy. In his admission that he had "strayed," we find the first sign that Abraham was beginning to recover his moral compass and rediscover the mission God had assigned him, a mission that could not go forward until Sarah gave him a child.

In Abraham's prayer for the healing of Avimelech's household, we find another indication that the patriarch was reviewing the way his soul had strayed. As God had promised the king, Abraham beseeched Him, "and God healed Avimelech, and his wife, and his maids, and they were relieved."[39] The word used here to describe Abraham's prayer to God, va'yitpalel, is remarkable. Its grammatical form is reflexive, meaning that it denotes something that the subject of the verb does to himself. The root, "peh-lamed-lamed," means "to judge." In other words, "to pray" in the way Abraham did now means literally "to judge yourself." As the Midrash comments, "From the beginning of the Book [of Genesis] until now, there is no such language as this. When our father Abraham prayed, this knot was untied."[40] While previously in the Bible people had asked God for things, never had anyone prayed in the way Abraham did now. He prayed in a very special way, one that "untied a knot": allowing others to do so by following his example.

The uniqueness of his prayer was twofold. First, it involved self-judgment: the recognition that he was unworthy of being granted the thing he asked for, that God gives us gifts because He is merciful and gracious. Second, as the Talmud explains, he demonstrated the principle that if you desire something for yourself, the most effective way to win God's blessing is to pray first that it be given to someone else who needs the same thing. We may pray for our own desires, but if we pray for others beforehand, our needs will be addressed more speedily.[41] God wants us to care more for others than for ourselves, and He rewards us for doing so. Avimelech and his wives had been rendered, among other things, unable to have children. Abraham and his wife, of course, had been unable ever to have children. When Abraham prayed for Avimelech, it was Abraham's need that God addressed first.

But Sarah still worried. God willed that the Destiny Child be the spiritual and biological heir of the patriarch, and also that his status as the heir in both respects be firmly established before the world. Sarah had God's promise to her in mind, the promise of a son. But what if the paternity of the son was in doubt, as it might now be if the rumor spread that she had been sexually violated by Avimelech? Just as Pharaoh had sought to appease Abraham with gifts, according to the ancient Near Eastern custom, the Gerarite did likewise, granting him livestock and slaves, as well as permission to settle anywhere on the king's lands that he chose. Though Abraham was satisfied with this, his wife was not. Sarah continued to lacerate the king, reproaching him for the shame to which he had exposed her. She was a tougher customer than her husband, and Nachmanides indicates that we are to understand this as a credit to her.[42]

Finally the three of them arrived at a solution. In addition to the animals and servants, Avimelech would pay Abraham a staggering amount of silver. Said Avimelech, as the Bible quotes him, "Behold I have given to your 'brother' a thousand pieces of silver. Let it be to you an eye-covering before all who are with you; and before all you will be vindicated."[43] By "eye-covering" he meant that Sarah's shame would be concealed from the view of gossipmongers. As Rashi explicates, Avimelech meant to say: All who see you "will cover their eyes, in that they will not belittle you. For if I had returned you [to Abraham] empty-handed, they might have said, 'After he violated her, he returned her.' Now that I have been compelled to squander [all this] wealth to appease you, they will know that it was against my will that I returned you, and by means of a miracle."[44] That last phrase is the key to what is, in the text of the Bible, a typically enigmatic exchange, unintelligible without the oral tradition. Avimelech reasoned that because he gave the couple such an enormous amount of money, anyone who heard about the affair would assume that he did so only because God had forced him. This evidence that God was involved, the same God who promised Sarah a son by Abraham, would confirm that the son was indeed Abraham's: that the Lord's providence had not abandoned Sarah to the lust of the Gerarite king.

Unfortunately when gossips want to believe the worst of someone, they will do so no matter what the facts appear to be. Abraham and Sarah would soon find this out. For as it would soon become clear, the eighty-nine-year-old matriarch was pregnant.

CHAPTER THIRTEEN

Birth of a Nation

From Gerar, Abraham and Sarah relocated to Beersheba. There, after experiencing the miracle of ninety-year-old Sarah giving birth, Abraham underwent the most excruciating test of his life as it had unfolded so far: the expulsion of Ishmael and Hagar. Both Rashi and Rambam number it as his ninth and penultimate trial, though Rambam numbers the expulsion of Hagar as a trial unto itself, his eighth. Abraham gave no prior notice of what he intended. Having heard God's word, the patriarch, this model of chesed, simply got up early in the morning, wrote out a document of divorce to Hagar, gave her and Ishmael what he took to be sufficient provisions, and pushed the bewildered pair out the door.[1] In Jewish tradition, rising early in the morning is connected to accepting one's role as the Lord's servant. Abraham had sub-limated himself totally to his God.

To the frightened travelers, rousted out of their sleep, he gave "bread and a skin of water," which ought to have lasted them till they reached the nearest settlement. But it did not, and why not is hinted at in a verse that has puzzled the critics. The Bible says here, literally, that Abraham "took bread and a skin of water and gave [them] to Hagar, placed [them] on her shoulder [or back], along with the boy, and sent her away."[2] In other words, he placed Ishmael on Hagar's back. This narrative, attributed to E, does not give Ishmael's age; but the text supposedly by J back in Genesis 17 says he was thirteen years old when Abraham was ninety-nine. If Abraham was one hundred when Isaac was born, it follows that when the baby was weaned, Ishmael must have been at least fifteen years old. Does such a lad, indeed a young man, need to be carried on his mother's back? The scholar E. A. Speiser called our present verse "obscure"—an understatement—and lamented that "an acceptable solution has yet to be discovered."[3] The problem of Hagar carrying an almost grown man on her shoulder leaps out from the page.

In the Midrash, the tradition explains that Hagar was forced to carry her son, who was actually seventeen years old by now, because he had become ill with a fierce, debilitating fever.[4] At work was the spiritual force called *ayin ha'rah*. Ishmael's gift was that he was Abraham's firstborn. At the feast where his own half brother Isaac's birth was celebrated, he flaunted his status as the firstborn, and mocked his baby brother, whom the Midrash hints was a puny specimen.[5] Typically the *ayin ha'rah* robs us of precisely the attributes we most glory in: in this case, Ishmael's physical strength as compared to the helpless baby Isaac, and his father's recognition of him as an honored member of the family. When Ishmael and his mother were hustled from Abraham's tent, his immodesty had caught up with him and his body shuddered with a heat that rivaled that of the desert they now entered. He was reduced to a weakened, fatherless child. As best she could, Hagar supported him on her shoulder.

Later, when it was over, she and her son must have recalled the wilderness journey as if it had been one of those nightmares in which nothing makes sense, all is confused yet terrifying, punctuated at the end by supernatural relief and a weird clarity. One may wonder if Ishmael's descendants, the Arabs, carry in their collective unconscious a memory of their forefather's rough treatment by Abraham, who in expelling him made way for Isaac, whose own sons, Jacob and Esau, by tradition are identified respectively as the progenitors of Jewish and Christian civilizations.

The geographical isolation of Beersheba is key to our understanding of what occurred. The next outpost of human life was distant. Though Abraham had given them enough water and clear directions to reach it, he didn't anticipate Ishmael's illness.

Beersheba is thirteen miles southeast of Gerar at the border of the Negev wilderness. Because the city plays such an important role in the lives of Abraham and Isaac, it is worth considering it from a historical perspective before we rewind a bit and approach the disturbing question of what drove kindly Abraham to so endanger the lives of his concubine and his son.

For believers in the historicity of the Bible, Beersheba presents a difficulty that is unique among the localities the Bible links with the career of Abraham. All the rest were certainly occupied in the Middle Bronze Age, but of occupation from that period at Beersheba there is no evidence. A visit to the site today certainly gives a feeling of patriarchal authenticity. The modern city of Beersheba is less than a century old, tacky and gritty and full of immigrants from the former Soviet Union. But city streets fade abruptly into the desert, and a short drive brings you to Tel Beersheba, or Tell es-Saba as the local Arabs called it. Before archaeologists began uncovering the mound in 1969, bedouin buried their dead atop the 2.5-acre mound at the junction of the dry Hebron and Beersheba riverbeds. When my wife and I were there, the immaculately kept National Park site was empty. The sun was sinking in orange over the horizon as a muezzin called out from a nearby Arab village and—an impossibly picturesque touch—a small caravan of camels passed in the distance. A well outside the ancient gates of the city was identified on a sign as Abraham's well (as indeed it has been identified, tentatively, by the archaeologist Yohanan Aharoni, though other authorities find no positive evidence of this and attribute it to a much later date).

The archaeological record so far finds remnants of occupation only from the Chalcolithic period, in the fourth millennium B.C., and from the Iron Age and after. The ruins of the small, neatly planned city one sees there date from the Iron Age, eight hundred years and more after Abraham's time. Does this rule out the patriarch's having lived here, as the scholar John Van Seters would wish us to think?[6] Not at all, for nowhere in the Bible do we find it asserted that Abraham lived here in anything like a formal settlement, certainly not in a city. On the contrary, when Abraham moved to the area, it seems clear that it had no name at all: it was named Beersheba in commemoration of an episode in his life that was to occur sometime after he moved here. If the place had no name, it could hardly have been a city or any type of permanent settlement. Nor is there any indication in the Bible that Abraham or his family founded a city at Beersheba. They were here, but Abraham lived much of his life as a pastoral seminomad, breeding sheep and goats, hopping from spring to spring as dictated by the needs of his flock.[7] Such an individual may have a base of operations in a city, such as Hebron, or he may simply keep in touch with several cities but have no permanent address. That he might regularly pitch his tents at a convenient but unsettled spot by a crossroads, with good soil near the junction of two rivers—a place like Beersheba—is not hard to believe. That such a temporary encampment would have left no trace 3,700 years later is also understandable.

Abraham came here to raise the "flocks and cattle" Avimelech had given him as an appeasement gift.[8] The king ruled over his city and the surrounding countryside, extending as far as the future Beersheba, which historians would call a dimorphic zone. That is, it supported two ways of life, in a symbiotic if often distrustful relationship to one another: that of city or village and that of nomadic pastoralists such as Abraham.[9] The Gerarite had invited Abraham to remain in Gerar itself, but Abraham declined, choosing to encamp at the edge of the king's area of influence.[10] This makes sense. He valued the ruler's protection, but sought to escape the rumors that were circulating among the townfolk about what had happened between his wife and Avimelech.

A wife wrongly suspected of sleeping with a man other than her husband is a figure to whom the Pentateuch directs our sympathy. Typically this would occur if she had been improperly secluded with the other man. She is commanded to appear before the priestly authorities at the Temple and undergo a test intended to vindicate her in her husband's eyes. That such a woman should be oppressed by her husband's suspicions is seen as intolerable. Once she has passed the test, God tenderly promises that as a further sign of her fidelity, "she will bear seed": if she had trouble conceiving or giving birth to the sort of child she most desires, she will no longer have any difficulty.[11] In connection with Sarah's grief at her childlessness and her humiliation at the hands of Avimelech, the Midrash draws our attention to this procedure. Shortly after the patriarchal couple left Gerar, "the Lord remembered Sarah as He had said, and the Lord did for Sarah as He had spoken"—meaning that He caused her to conceive.[12] As the Midrash implies in its reference to the suspected wife: not only did the Gerarites whisper their smirking stories of the king's conquest but perhaps those stories reached Abraham's ears and had some effect on him as well.

If Abraham was uneasy, he must have felt reassured—not to mention awed that God's amazing promise had been fulfilled—when Sarah revealed to him that she was pregnant. The timing of the pregnancy should have reassured him. She had conceived not at Gerar, but three to five months later, in the summer or fall.[13] A view in the Talmud indicates that God "remembered" her specifically at Rosh Hashanah, in the early autumn, which makes sense.[14] In Jewish tradition, on that day God "remembers" us all and sets our fate for the coming year. At each Rosh Hashanah in synagogues, the story of Sarah's remembrance, and of the wondrous birth of her son, is chanted.

The birth was wondrous for her, but equally so for us. With Isaac was born Western civilization. One traditional interpretation of his name in Hebrew, Yitzchak, is as a contraction of *yatzah Chok,* meaning literally the "Law went out" to the world.[15] In other words, Torah, the expression of God's will for humanity, which is sometimes called His Law, or Chok, went out from Him and entered the stream of history. For almost half a century, Abraham had been teaching God's will. But we know that this teaching was carried on into succeeding generations, and taught ultimately to the world in the form of Judaism, Christianity, and Islam, only by the descendants of Isaac. Without the continuity assured by Isaac, Abraham's mission would have been swallowed up by the void where all events go that happened but were forgotten. Though Muslim Arabs claim Ishmael as their ancestor, they affirm that before the rise of Muhammad they were pagans who had received no tradition from Abraham's firstborn son. Knowledge of God first became a mass phenomenon only through the determination and obstinacy of Isaac's family, specifically through his son Jacob, ancestor of the twelve tribes of Israel. Had this transmission, from the Jews to the peoples of Europe and Arabia, failed to take place, then nothing like the civilization we know today could ever have taken root. In the preface, we discussed the debt we owe to these ancient figures.

No wonder, then, that the midrashic tradition depicts Isaac's birth as an event of positively Messianic significance.[16] Many people who had been sick were cured. Many who had been troubled were blessed. Many women who had been barren were "remembered," just like Sarah. The blind and deaf could suddenly see and hear, while the mad became sane. The rays of the sun—which symbolize enlightenment—were magnified. Though the Midrash doesn't say so directly, we can interpret it to mean that these wonders did not occur the very day of Isaac's birth, but as a result of it even millennia later through the gift of science. To give one example, every mother today who in previous generations would have despaired of giving birth—due to age or infertility—but now thanks to the latest reproductive technology holds her own baby in her hands, can trace her joy to the birth of Isaac. The same goes for people with terrible illnesses who, just a decade or two ago, would have died of them, but now can live a long life.

However, that Isaac should be born into the world was not a sufficient condition for the dawning of Western civilization. God was also determined to make clear that the boy was not the adoptive but the natural son of Abraham and Sarah. Doubts as to the parentage of the child swirled about, a rumor even circulating that the elderly matriarch's apparent pregnancy was all a ruse, that she hadn't conceived a child at all but instead went to the *shuk,* the public open-air market, and purchased a foundling.[17] Then as now there was a trade in adoptive children. If anything, adoption was an even more prominent social institution than it is today. In Mesopotamia, people adopted not only children, but also siblings, even parents. (In those Near Eastern societies where it was illegal to sell land outside one's family, land changed hands between nonrelatives by the expedient of the seller "adopting" the purchaser.)

The idea would have sprung easily to the minds of Sarah's contemporaries; it had to be dispelled. Why? A child is the product of his blood as well as of his environment. In Isaac's case, God was determined to leave neither to chance. And by stressing His efforts to demonstrate that Isaac was the natural child of Abraham and Sarah, the tradition is also determined to make clear to us that a person is formed by both nature and environment, with all the lessons that entails for mothers and fathers. Having the most brilliant, spiritually and aesthetically sensitive parents in the world won't mean much if from childhood on, Mommy and Daddy left you in the kind of schools and day-care centers where kids are treated like cattle. Similarly the most extravagantly funded schools can't help a child who lacks the intellectual and other unquantifiable gifts fortunate people inherit at birth.

So God planned every detail of Isaac's early childhood. The birth took place at high noon (on a day that would later be enshrined in the festival of Passover); it was a public event, as it might not have been if it had happened by night. God ensured that the face of the newborn looked remarkably like his father's, to a degree that no child ever before had resembled his dad.[18] On the eighth day, Abraham circumcised the boy—another public event—and he received the name "Isaac," Yitzchak, one of whose meanings is derived from the root TZCHK, "to laugh." We laugh primarily at violations of the normal ways of the world. Among other things, the name reminds us that Isaac's birth was such a violation: very elderly people do not normally become parents. The wonder, the absurdity of it was not to be waved away by suggestions that he had merely been adopted.

When Isaac was two years old, he was weaned and, says the Pentateuch, "Abraham made a great feast on the day that Isaac was weaned."[19] Without the oral tradition, this last detail seems a point of interest only to party planners. The Talmud, however, directs our attention to a seeming typographical error in the text. Sarah declared, "And Who is the One Who said to Abraham, 'Sarah would nurse children'?"[20] She was paying tribute to God—but actually whoever said anything about her nursing "children"? She had only one child in her life.

In fact, while Sarah gave birth to only one child, she nursed many. As we noted before, the word used here for "feast," *mishteh,* literally means a drinking party. Abraham recognized that to disseminate the news of his son's birth as widely as possible, a grassroots approach, informing every common person he knew, would be ineffective. Information spreads most economically by going first of all to a society's leaders, through whose influence the word gets out. So Abraham invited to the weaning feast only the most prominent persons in Canaanite society, including Avimelech and even the patriarch's old comrade from the war with the four kings, Malchizedek.[21] These chieftains brought their wives and children. They also brought the still-circulating rumors about Isaac's paternity. When the moment came for Sarah to nurse Isaac for the last time, the ladies gathered around. It transpired that none of the mothers had remembered to bring their wet nurses, and a miracle took place. Sarah offered to nurse all the children herself. Everyone mocked her, until they saw it for themselves. Says the Talmud, "her breasts were opened like two fountains and she nursed them all."[22] For the future of monotheism, the "drinking party" that ensued was a triumph of public relations.

"There was great cheer in the world" that day, says Rashi, but not for Ishmael.[23] We can imagine his distress, and his building anger. For all his first fourteen years, he had been the center of his father's attention. He must have anticipated that he himself would carry on Abraham's legacy, but this new child, and all the fuss that was being made of him, suggested otherwise. "Fools," he admonished the revelers, "I am the first born! And I will take a double inheritance." At this, Sarah turned to her husband. A woman who saw matters clearly, who could not tolerate ambiguity, certainly not about so central a matter as inheritance, Sarah said, "The son of this slavewoman [Hagar] will not inherit along with my son."[24]

Under biblical law, the firstborn male receives twice the share in his father's estate that any of his siblings do. Ishmael was simply insisting on what he took to be his right—which would have been upheld by the legal system of his father's homeland. The Code of Hammurabi, promulgated a few decades before the episode we are discussing, and based on older Mesopotamian legal traditions, forbids a master from arbitrarily disinheriting a slave's children if the master has acknowledged those children as his own.[25]

However, we may ask whether the dispute really was about a material inheritance—of flocks, gold, and slaves—alone. The biblical critics understand it that way, but why, millennia later, should we be at all interested in a standoff between two long-dead Middle Eastern gentlemen as to which would get his father's sheep when the latter passed on to his reward?

Actually at stake here was not merely Abraham's material wealth but primarily his spiritual wealth. The question was which son would become the ideological heir of his father—which would inherit the teaching mantle, the right to decide what the Abrahamic tradition really means. The issue of Abraham's spiritual estate continues to haunt the Western world, with each religion claiming that it alone truly understands what Abraham meant to teach. The Jewish view of the issue is suggested through the reading by the Talmud and Midrash of a later verse in our story, when God takes Sarah's side and instructs Abraham that "in Isaac [alone] will offspring be called yours."[26] The awkward phrase "in Isaac" is taken to mean that only some of Isaac's descendants will carry on the authentic Abrahamic legacy. For instance, anyone who denies that there are "two worlds"—the earthly world we inhabit along with the world of life after life, of the existence that follows death—is excluded from the category of Abraham's true descendants "in Isaac."[27]

So it wasn't just to deny the young man a lot of goats that Sarah insisted to Abraham that he "drive out this slavewoman and her son!" Her husband, whose kind heart gave him excruciating pain on this point, hesitated. Sarah's was distinctly the tougher personality. But God agreed with her, saying to the father of this unlucky son, "Let the thing not seem evil in your eyes, concerning the lad and the slavewoman. In all that Sarah says to you, heed her voice."[28] So the matter was settled. The voice of Sarah was the voice of prophecy, and Rashi notes that the wife was a superior prophet to her husband.[29]

What precisely had Sarah perceived through her prophetic powers that led to her harsh demand? After all, if it was legally questionable to disinherit Ishmael, expelling him from the household was at least equally dubious. On this, the laws of Nuzi, the principality geographically close to Abraham's family home at Haran about which we know a fair amount from its archives, were unambiguous.[30] (Though another Mesopotamian legal tradition, the Lipit-Ishtar Law Code, compiled in the century of Abraham's birth, allows a slave son to be cast out if he is first granted his freedom.)[31]

The Bible, wanting us to understand that Ishmael was expelled for good reason, notes that Sarah had seen Ishmael being *mitzachek*—a word often translated as "mocking" or "jesting," built on the same root as Isaac's Hebrew name. But if, as the critics are bound to say, this was all she saw in Ishmael's behavior that motivated her to send him and his mother into the wilderness, then we must ascribe to Sarah not prophetic powers, but rather a vengefulness approaching insanity. The critics attribute these passages to the author E, but nowhere else in the narrative does the hypothetical E portray the matriarch as a madwoman. What, then, is going on?

We have already observed that the root TZCHK, figuring in the Hebrew word for "laughter," connotes a rupturing of the norms of expected behavior. According to tradition, when Ishmael engaged in the behavior of being *mitzachek,* he ruptured some basic norms. Specifically he committed the three cardinal sins. He engaged in idolatry, building altars and childishly offering on them some insects he had caught. He committed adultery, ambushing married women and raping them. And he murdered, or at least showed himself willing to do so. He would shoot arrows at Isaac, then claim that he had only been horsing around.[32]

This should make us wonder what Abraham was like as a father. We are talking about a son of the man who initiated the worship of the One God, a deeply inspiring figure to those who knew him. Yet his first son was uninspired. So the question needs to be addressed. The answer may be less than inspiring.

Consider the relations of parents with children in our own time. As this book was being written, America was in the grip of what seemed an epidemic of mass killings. Every ten days, by one estimate, a previously law-abiding American suddenly showed up at the place where he normally spent his days and shot several people in cold blood. Shootings at schools by angry teenagers were particularly disturbing, not least because the students in question tended to be from middle- to upper-middle-class homes where they had been cared for by upstanding parents of conventional sensibilities. The lesson seemed to be that children are not the mere products of their environment. People, unlike animals, have souls. We don't respond as robots to stimuli, the way animals do. If a gorilla at the zoo does something unsociable—bites the person who feeds him, let's say—we can assume that something went wrong in his environment: too much food, too little food, unhealthful air or water, too much taunting from visitors. But when children go bad, even the children of the greatest parents, we must be open to the possibility that the soul of the child alone is at fault.[33]

Abraham loved his son Ishmael, and yet he also hated him. About this Rashi is clear—or, rather, clearly conflicted. When, later in the narrative, God instructs the patriarch to take his son, "whom you love," up to Mt.

Moriah to be sacrificed, Abraham is confused as to which son God has in mind, Isaac or Ishmael. "I love both of them," he responds.[34] But in the present moment, when God instructed him to banish Ishmael and Hagar, Rashi notes that Abraham "hated [the boy] for having gone forth to wicked behavior."[35] It is a paradox of parenting that a father can indeed simultaneously love and hate his own child.

Despite this ambivalence, Abraham felt that Ishmael might reform himself and come to succeed the patriarch in his spiritual mission. He held out the hope that Hagar, rather than Sarah, might be the wife whose child would secure his immortal destiny as the first teacher of monotheism. To correct him once and for all, God was revealed to Abraham in a dream by night, scolding him for his spiritual blindness. Said the Lord, "Abraham, do you not know that Sarah was destined for you as a wife from her mother's womb? She is your [eternal] companion and wife of your youth. Let Hagar [no longer] be called your wife, nor Sarah [in any sense] your concubine. All that Sarah has spoken [to you, insisting that you expel Ishmael and his mother], she has spoken in truth. Let [what she said] concerning the lad and your handmaid not seem evil in your eyes."[36] At last, Abraham surrendered to the divine will. In the context of Hagar's first expulsion, the patriarch had lost his spiritual vision, the true understanding of who the son of his destiny really was. Now at her second expulsion, he had regained that vision. We shall return to this observation and its meaning in the literary pattern that Devora Steinmetz has identified as the key to understanding the structure of the Abraham narrative.

Having been rushed out of her master's house now for the second time, Hagar "strayed in the wilderness of Beersheba" and soon "the water was finished from the skin."[37] As is made clear in the midrashic collection *Pirke d'Rabbi Eliezer,* after she and Ishmael were some distance from Abraham's camp, two things happened. First, in spite at having been scorned by the man she loved, Hagar "strayed," throwing off the monotheistic discipline she had accepted when she joined his community. Some modern renditions portray the patriarchs as tolerating in their homes a diversity of religious opinion. A recent example is the popular novel *The Red Tent,* a multigenerational saga written from the vantage point of the female members of the patriarchs' extended family. Author Anita Diament imagines that while the patriarchs devoted themselves to the God of their fathers, their wives and concubines preferred a variety of colorful Canaanite goddesses. A midrash, however, teaches that Hagar could only worship alien deities when she had left Abraham's company.[38] A woman who falls in love with a man often falls in love with his god as well. If her love is rejected, she may turn to other worship. When the Bible says that she "strayed," *va'teytah,* it means it in the same way that Abraham strayed when he admitted to Avimelech that God had "caused [him] to stray." They had both become spiritually lost.

Second, while Hagar prayed to the old gods of her father's house, Ishmael grew steadily weaker. Sick people drink copiously, and it wasn't long before there was no water left in the skin.[39] In Torah nomenclature, water always stands for divine teaching. Deprived of Abraham's influence, mother and son became spiritually parched to the point of death.

It is here that the Abraham narrative turns around for almost everyone involved. We have seen that the patriarch himself reached a turning point when he overcame his compassion for Ishmael and, more important, his hope that Ishmael would inherit his mantle of leadership. Before this, Abraham had in some spiritual sense been blocked up. We will see that he was due now to become unblocked. But the first signs of recovery for his family occurred in the Beersheba wilderness.

Ishmael was near death, tortured by wasting fever and demonic sun. His grieving mother placed his poor body in the shelter of a lowly bush. She then sat down at a distance from him and they both wept.

But it was Ishmael's voice that God heard, in the sense that He was more inclined to save him than her. For God's mercy is always aroused by the sick.[40] Perhaps this is because an individual sick enough to look death in the face is likely to review his life, seeing clearly his failures and sins, and to repent.

God was about to save Ishmael when the ministering angels protested. They pointed out that if he lived, Ishmael would produce descendants, the Arabs, who would torment those of his brother, Isaac, the Jews. Rashi recounts the deliberations on high. God said to the angels, "What is he now, a righteous person or wicked?" They admitted, "He is righteous," having repented of his earlier crimes. God said, "According to his deeds right now, so do I judge him." It was decided. At that moment, an angel called down from

Heaven, "What troubles you, Hagar? Fear not, for God has heard the voice of the lad where he is, there." In the scriptural phrase, "where he is, there," Rashi finds a proof that God judges everyone "in accordance with the deeds he does now . . . and not in accordance with the deeds he will do in the future."[41]

This is the doctrine, enunciated in the Talmud,[42] that allows a person to repent at Rosh Hashanah for the sins committed over the previous year, or over the course of an entire lifetime up till that day. For this reason, the story of Ishmael in the desert, along with that of Isaac's birth, is read in synagogues each Rosh Hashanah as an encouragement to repentance, a guarantee that as God was merciful to Ishmael, He will be merciful to us.

"Then God opened [Hagar's] eyes"—for she saw spiritual reality in a way she hadn't before—"and she saw a well of water," of spiritual water, of His teaching.[43] Both drank of the water, and their lives were saved and renewed.

Ishmael now exits the Abraham narrative, at least in the Bible's iteration. The text notes that he lived in the desert of Paran, south of Canaan, at the entrance of the Sinai wilderness; and that Hagar married him to an Egyptian woman. Tradition gives the name of his first wife, Isa, as well as that of his second, Fatoma. Normally in Near Eastern society, it would have fallen to his father to marry him off.[44] The fact that Hagar did this suggests that while mother and son had repented and accepted God's sovereignty afresh, Ishmael and Abraham remained alienated from one another.

Pirke d'Rabbi Eliezer indicates that the alienation was not total or everlasting. Even after the young man had set up a household for himself, Abraham would visit, to check up on him, when the son was away from his tent. Three years after their estrangement, Abraham journeyed south, promising Sarah he would not so much as dismount at his destination but would hurry right back. He reached Ishmael's encampment at noon and was met by his daughter-in-law, Isa, whom he had never seen. Presenting himself as a stranger, he asked where Ishmael was. She said, "He has gone with his mother to fetch fruits and dates from the desert." He said to her, "Would you please give me a little water and bread and refreshments, for my spirit is exhausted from traveling the wilderness." Discourteously she lied to him, "There is no bread and no water." When Abraham heard this, he knew that Hagar had picked a poor wife for their son. He said to Isa, still not having identified himself, "When Ishmael returns, tell him [as follows]: 'An old man came from the land of Canaan to see you, and said, "The threshold of your house is unsound." ' " When Ishmael got home and his wife recounted the story, he knew what it meant. He divorced her and sought out a new wife.

Three years later Abraham took another trip to see his son, again promising Sarah that he wouldn't even dismount. Again Ishmael and Hagar were out foraging and again the patriarch asked the young woman, Ishmael's second wife, Fatoma, for food. This time the good-hearted girl generously supplied the needs of the mysterious traveler. In thanks to God, Abraham prayed that Ishmael's house should always be filled with blessing. The girl overheard him pray and later told Ishmael what had happened. The son knew then that his father still loved him.[45]

Ishmael exits the biblical narrative in another sense. It is here that Islamic sources, claiming that the Bible is corrupted, turn most sharply away from the story Genesis tells. As we noted earlier, Abraham is in some ways a more important figure to Muslims even than Muhammad himself. The departure of Ishmael from Sarah's home is the initial act that set Abraham on the road to becoming the first Muslim (though he had been a Muslim, in the sense of being a primordial monotheist, even before this).

Here is what happened. The Quran simply states that Abraham and Ishmael built and dedicated the Ka'bah at Mecca, the stone monolith toward which Muslims pray, but declines to explain the circumstances of their journey there.[46] This elaboration is left to the *hadith* literature, traced to Muhammad. We learn that Sarah was jealous of Hagar and insisted that she and her son be expelled from Abraham's home in Syria. But rather than send them out into the wilderness unescorted, as in the Jewish tradition, the patriarch personally led them to the site of Mecca, which Muslims equate with the Bible's Paran. He left them there, and Ishmael, who was still a baby and not yet weaned, almost perished of thirst, causing Hagar in her desperation to run back and forth between two hills, Safa and Marwa. In other versions of the story, Sarah doesn't enter into the matter. Instead, God or Gabriel initiates the departure from Syria with the express purpose of guiding the prophet to build the Ka'bah, Abraham carrying his family, minus Sarah, on a magical horse called Buraq. The party passes through towns and other attractive locations, and at each Abraham asks if they are there yet, if this is the place to build the Ka'bah. Every time, Gabriel says, "No, keep going!" Finally they arrive at a hill of red clay, which turns out to be Mecca. Abraham again asks if this is the place, and Gabriel says yes.[47]

Despite the change of venue, Judaic parallels persist. God showed Abraham a special spot, marked by a hovering cloud. The Midrash, too, places a cloud above Mt. Moriah when Abraham brings Isaac there.[48] Here Abraham found the remains of a temple built by Adam—much as, in the Jewish version, he would build the altar for the slaughter of Isaac at Moriah upon the location of Adam's place of worship.[49] And here Abraham and Ishmael built the Ka'bah, the son showing little aptitude for construction, which annoyed his father.[50]

When the job was done, Abraham called the world's faithful to emulate him in journeying to Mecca, thus instituting the Hajj, or sacred Pilgrimage, which is one of the Five Pillars of Islam. Abraham first performed all the rites that constitute the Hajj for Muslims today—including a ritual sacrifice, shaving the head, and stoning the devil while repeating the formula *"Allahu akbar,"* "God is most great!" His "call" to the pilgrimage is not to be understood figuratively. Traditions picture him stuffing his fingers in his ears and shouting at a supernaturally enhanced volume. Thus everyone in the world, those alive at the time and those yet unborn, heard his voice[51]—a parallel with the Judaic tradition in which the souls of Jews as yet unborn heard God's voice emanating from Sinai.[52]

The most significant point of agreement between the two faiths is that after Ishmael's departure—from Canaan or Syria, depending—Abraham became the man God had been waiting for him to become. In Islam, he built the Ka'bah and inaugurated the yearly Pilgrimage. In the Torah, Abraham's full emergence as the patriarch is subtler.

The text describing Ishmael's expulsion concludes with two incidents that seem—like much else in the Abraham story without the expositions of the Oral Torah—utterly mundane and pointless. First, Avimelech sought out the patriarch and made a treaty with him, after which Abraham protested that the Gerarite's servants had seized a certain well belonging to Abraham. Avimelech replied in the manner of all weak commanders who decline to take responsibility for the actions of their subordinates: "I do not know who did this thing. What's more, you [never] told me, nor did I hear [about it] until today!"[53] To repair the breach of trust, Abraham gave Avimelech seven ewe lambs, along with other livestock, ratifying an oath of nonaggression between themselves. The spot was thus called Beersheba, meaning "Well of the Seven" or "Well of the Oath."

Second, Abraham planted at Beersheba an *eshel,* conventionally taken as referring to a shrublike little tree, a tamarisk. At the *eshel,* he "called upon the name of the Lord, God of the Universe."[54] That is, he was again preaching his message of the universal lordship of God, His dominion over all peoples—the essence of monotheism.[55]

As usual, the scholars go to work with their tendency to the reductio ad absurdum. In the oath between Abraham and Avimelech, one historian notes "the great emphasis placed upon continuity of water rights." What's "being addressed" here is "the very real problems of herd management in a semiarid, steppe region."[56] To this animal-husbandry angle, another scholar prefers a legal analysis based on Near Eastern precedents, concluding that "the agreement . . . bears all the hallmarks of an ancient parity treaty."[57] Of the tamarisk, a third suggests that Abraham shared with Canaanites of the time a disposition to worship gods "under every leafy tree," as Moses later contemptuously put it.[58] A fourth says he is puzzled that the Redactor tucked into the work of E—whose authorship is indicated through most of Genesis 21 by the name "Elohim" or God—this verse about the sacred tree, clearly authored by J, who calls Him by the ineffable four-letter name, translated "Lord." "One can only guess at the reason why such a brief excerpt from J was inserted at this particular point," he writes, but declines to offer a guess himself.[59]

If we assume the Bible is a book like any other, then we can hardly object to scholarly efforts that so trivialize the text. Maybe the ancient authors really did have uppermost in their minds such unelevating matters as treaty law and water rights! But if we hope the Bible is something greater, then we must look below the surface.

Actually in these two apparently minor incidents we have a puzzle with two main components—Abraham's well and his *eshel*—to which the sages of the Midrash offer the key. But they rely on us to insert the key in the lock and open the door. The sages allude to the significance of the well and the *eshel,* one immediately following the other in the midrashic text.

First, we read that prior to the treaty between Abraham and Avimelech, there had been a dispute between the two men's shepherds over the ownership of a certain well—perhaps the one that can still be seen outside the gates of Beersheba. "Abraham's shepherds said, 'The well is ours!' These [the shepherds of Avimelech] said, 'The well is ours!'" To resolve the dispute, a contest was proposed. "Abraham's shepherds said, 'For whomever the water [of the well] rises up [by itself] to water his flock, the well belongs to him.'" So the miracle occurred, with the Midrash adopting a strange anthropomorphism as if life and intelligence animated the water itself. "When the water *saw* the flock of our Father Abraham, immediately it rose up."[60] The seven ewe lambs the patriarch gave to Avimelech symbolize this larger flock for which the water rose. By accepting the animals, the Gerarite admitted that Abraham dug the well. The water itself, as always in Torah nomenclature, signifies Torah itself. We will see shortly what all this means.

Second, we read that the *eshel* is no simple tamarisk tree but something completely different: an inn for travelers. We have noted already that Abraham's Beersheba sat at a lonely crossroads. Here he established a sort of hospice where exhausted Canaanites found shelter and nourishment. Rashi explains that the word *eshel* is an acrostic. Spelled "aleph-shin-lamed," it stands for three Hebrew words that begin with those letters: *achilah,* eating; *shtiyah,* drinking; and *levayah,* escorting.[61] These are the three principal obligations of a host: giving food and drink to guests and then, when they are satisfied, escorting them safely toward home. Another view is that the letters of the word *eshel* are decoded by reversing them: "lamed-shin-aleph" spells the Hebrew word meaning "ask."[62] Travelers would "ask" Abraham for help and he would give it to them.

The help and nourishment were not only physical but spiritual. The "inn" was a forerunner of today's Salvation Army soup kitchen, where the point is to save lives *and* souls. As the Midrash recounts, Abraham would say to his guests, "Ask for whatever you [wish to] ask: bread, meat, wine, eggs." When they had eaten, he would say, "Now bless." This confused them. They asked, "What shall we say?" Abraham answered that they should say, "Blessed be the God of the Universe from whose [bounty] we have eaten."[63] It was the first instance of people saying grace for their food, and the biblical text refers to this obliquely when it notes that after "planting," or establishing, the *eshel,* Abraham "called upon the Name of the Lord, God of the Universe."[64] The Talmud suggests that the Hebrew word translated here as "called upon" can be understood in a causative sense.[65] He not only "called upon" God's name himself, but caused others to do so. He had found a new way to bring men and women closer to God. It was by the simple expedient of pointing out to them the abundance of nature and asking that they give thanks to its Creator. We noted earlier that the Hebrew word for "thanks," *todah,* shares a root with the word that means "admit." When we thank God, we admit that all we have is ultimately from Him. As a proselytizer, Abraham had reached a new height of brilliance.

Let us, then, simplify the themes we have been working with here. By expelling Ishmael, Abraham decisively acted on his growing awareness that he had strayed from the path of God's will—that the child of his destiny, his spiritual heir, was not Ishmael, but Isaac. When he had done this, the water rose up for him by itself. That is, the source of wisdom, Torah, was released to him in a way it had not been before. And this in turn enhanced the effectiveness of his mission to bring humanity to the recognition of the One God.

It almost sounds as if the Bible's tale of Abraham is over. His narrative has the classic shape of a good story. The hero receives a mission, which he sets out to complete. But some force, either outside or inside himself, opposes him. He almost fails but struggles and overcomes that force. He then goes on to glory. You will find this structure almost every time you read a gripping novel or see an exciting movie. This archetypal narrative appeared in the Bible and its traditional commentaries thousands of years before Hollywood got hold of it. In the terms of the pattern we identified with help from Devora Steinmetz, the second expulsion of Hagar echoes the first such incident, which was the turning point of Abraham's story. In the earlier event, Abraham lost his spiritual vision. Now he regained it.

But actually the classic narrative structure often includes a certain kind of twist. Recall the last good blockbuster movies you saw and you will find this is what invariably happens. After the hero *seems* to have triumphed over the force opposing him, that force will rise up once more to give him a final test, often his toughest. Upon overcoming it this last time, the hero *then* proceeds to claim his reward: safety, money, the beautiful girl. This is the "Will all be lost?" moment. Every well-scripted popular movie has one.

So does the story of Abraham. The patriarch's "all" was his son Isaac, the heir of his life's mission. Thus we arrive at the last and most appalling of Abraham's ten trails: the Binding (in Hebrew, Akedah) of Isaac atop Mt. Moriah.

CHAPTER FOURTEEN

The Slaughter of Isaac

hat happened at the Binding of Isaac can be simply told, its meaning endlessly debated.

Let us visualize Abraham and Isaac as they climbed Moriah, known today as the Har ha'Bait (Temple Mount), site of Solomon's Temple, later enclosed in the walls of Jerusalem's Old City. If one looks down upon this modest elevation from the vantage of Hebrew University's campus, located on Mt. Scopus, the exact shape of the mountain is impossible to discern. It is not the highest point on the ridge of hills of which it forms the southern end. Downtown Jerusalem, a ten-minute walk from the Old City, occupies that higher position. One sees the thirty-four-acre Haram esh-Sharif, as Muslims call the platform of the Temple

Mount now with the burning gold and blue Dome of the Rock, finished in A.D. 691, as its centerpiece. From Solomon's original plan, the platform was massively extended by Herod in the first century B.C. The Dome is not exactly at the center of the platform but a bit to the west. It is positioned over the spot once occupied by the Holy of Holies of the Temple, symbolizing the Muslim belief that Islam has displaced Judaism (and Christianity) as the vehicle of Abraham's mission.

While we can't trace Abraham and Isaac's steps upward on Moriah, it is possible to have the experience of seeing a part of the mountain itself that was hidden for thousands of years. A modern tunnel traces the western edge of the Haram, below street level, its main entrance by the synagogue of the Western Wall. For a few shekels, you can take a tour. As the tunnel descends, you see on your right first the cyclopean stones that hold up the walls around the platform, with characteristic drafted margins in the Herodian style. Then the tunnel plunges into the bedrock, and you actually see where the walls rest on the limestone surface of Mt. Moriah. Water drips from somewhere overhead, and there is the chalky smell of wet stone. On precisely this rock, around on the eastern side, Abraham and Isaac climbed.

About the middle of the tunnel, which at the northern end opens under the Arab *shuk,* there is an arch that has been filled up with brick-shaped stones. When I visited, a girl was sitting on a plastic chair by the wall, reciting psalms. People leave little notes in the cracks between the stones, expressing their prayers to God. A sign marks this as the closest spot to where Abraham and Isaac were now heading—that is, closest within the small portion of the Haram to which Jews have access. Because the Temple stood on the platform overhead, and because by Torah law men and women were allowed into the Temple environs only when their ritual purity could be assured, rabbinic authorities strongly discourage Jewish people from visiting the Haram.

The bricked-up arch once led to a stairway that led to the platform. It is very close to the Dome of the Rock. According to tradition, the Rock is Abraham's rock, where Isaac was bound. It's still to be seen, fifty-nine feet by forty-three feet, a rough contrast to the geometric perfection of the Dome above it. Maimonides and *Pirke d'Rabbi Eliezer* give its history. Here Adam worshiped God, followed by Cain and Abel, and Noah. Abraham built an altar by piling twelve rocks one atop the other. The site on which he built would become the location of the altar of Solomon's Temple. The patriarch's altar itself, however, was subsequently moved by his grandson Jacob, the rocks fusing into the one Rock, which became the Foundation Stone, located in the Holy of Holies, on which the Ark of the Covenant sat.[1] So when Genesis says that Abraham with Isaac "arrived at the place of which God had spoken to him and . . . built *the altar* there,"[2] the text's use of the definite article is not an editor's glitch. If he had simply built an altar where none had been, the text would have said "*an* altar." Rather, he *rebuilt* a *particular* altar on the spot where the ancients had worshiped before him.

One scholar has rightly said that Abraham's actions in the biblical text sound like those of a sleepwalker.[3] After building the altar, he "arranged the wood. He bound Isaac, his son, and placed him on the altar, atop the wood. Abraham stretched out his hand and took the knife. . . ."[4] Isaac could have easily overpowered his father but went willingly to be slaughtered. Nor did he doubt the old man's sanity, but simply accepted that his death must be God's will, though he himself had received no revelation.

The binding of Isaac was hand to foot, hand to foot, so as to fully expose his neck and assure a clear path for the knife.[5] The trance was broken by falling tears—some say Abraham's tears falling into Isaac's eyes, rendering the latter blind in his later years; others say they were the tears of the angels who cried out to God to save Isaac.[6]

At that moment, Abraham heard God's voice through the medium of an angel—reaching, according to Maimonides, the highest level of prophecy he would ever attain.[7] From slicing the knife across Isaac's throat Abraham was not easily dissuaded. He begged at least to be allowed to draw a small quantity of blood, but finally the angelic tears melted the knife in his hand.[8] It would seem that Abraham's greatest fear now, worse even than losing his son, was the fear of absurdity: that he should have come all this way, shown himself ready to murder Isaac, only to have the act called off. That fear was only partly assuaged by God's command to sacrifice a ram in Isaac's place. Abraham found the creature caught by its horns in a thicket of brush behind him.

After the ram had been offered up, God blessed Abraham and his descendants unconditionally, adding, "and all the nations of the earth shall bless themselves by your offspring, because you have listened to my voice."[9]

The Lord had said much the same thing to the patriarch sixty-two years earlier when he left Haran: "and all the families of the earth will be blessed through you."[10] But note the difference in grammatical inflection, from "will *be blessed* through you" to "*shall bless themselves* by your offspring." The progression is from the verb form called *niphal,* the passive, in Hebrew, to that called *hitpalel,* the reflexive. We may speculate that what is being alluded to here is a progression in history. At first, the nations will be blessed by way of Abraham's seed but without fully appreciating the role of that people, Israel, in the world. The development of Christianity and Islam, both of which educated the pagan world in the ways of God, are part of that blessing. However, both faiths have often regarded Jews with contempt, as a stubborn remnant without a positive role to play in history other than to be converted. Later the nations will realize the source of their blessing and "bless themselves."

In this context, one thinks of the many modern Christians who are coming to appreciate the Judaic roots of their faith. The Roman Catholic Church has gone so far as to say, amazingly, that the Jewish wait for the Messiah has not been in vain, a position hard to reconcile with classical Christian doctrine, while the pope prays at Judaism's holiest site, Jerusalem's Western Wall, leaning against the stones.

In America, especially among evangelical Protestants, the philo-Semitic phenomenon is really striking. I know of no comprehensive study of the Judaization of American evangelicalism, but the anecdotal evidence impresses me. Here they not only seek the welfare of the State of Israel but actively want to learn from Judaism the meaning of their own faith. An Orthodox rabbi, Daniel Lapin, has an enthusiastic following among Christians, who mob his public lectures, call upon him to appear as a guest expert on their radio shows, buy his books, and call him "my rabbi." The *mohel,* or ritual circumciser, in a large midwestern city reports that a great proportion of his business comes from Christians, who want their sons not merely to be circumcised but to have the mark of Abraham, the *brit milah,* on them.

In western Washington State, where I live, Christians gather each year at Ocean Shores, a resort city on the Pacific Coast, to observe the festival of Sukkot, complete with dwelling in temporary booths, or *sukkot,* and waving palm branches and citrus fruits as per Jewish tradition. They don't mean to convert any Jews: there are no Jews in Ocean Shores. When I told an investment adviser at my bank in a Seattle suburb that I was researching a biography of Abraham, using Jewish traditional sources, he said, "Oh, you mean the oral tradition." Explaining that the pastor of his nondenominational church had been lecturing about the Oral Torah, he eagerly pressed me for details of what I'd discovered. A scruffy young guy sent to install cable TV in my home volunteers that he has been learning some Hebrew in his prayer group. "Shalom!" he says before departing. And so on. As the commentator Sforno predicted almost five hundred years ago, basing himself on the text of God's blessing from the end of the Akedah, "When all [the nations] call upon the name of the Lord to worship Him together, they will bless [Abraham's] seed [and] imitate them."[11]

When the Akedah was finished, "Abraham returned to his lads, and they rose up and went together to Beersheba."[12] (The elderly Eliezer and the middle-aged Ishmael had accompanied the patriarch and are each called a *na'ar,* a lad, because in Hebrew the word can signify not only a youth but alternatively someone who is lower in status, a subordinate.)[13] The Bible strangely omits any mention of Isaac returning from Moriah, a deeply significant textual oddity.

Among the nations of the earth, from Christians to Muslims to religious skeptics, no episode in the Hebrew Bible has attracted more interpretive energy than the Akedah. St. Paul, St. John, St. Augustine, and others noted parallels between the story of the Akedah and that of the Crucifixion. Jesus was the "lamb" of God, just as Isaac asked Abraham where was the "lamb" they were going to slaughter. Jesus' birth and that of Isaac were both announced by an angel. The ram of the Akedah was caught among thorns just as a circle of thorns would crown Jesus at his death. A donkey accompanied Abraham and Isaac to Mt. Moriah, while on Palm Sunday Jesus rode into Jerusalem on a donkey.[14]

For Muslims, the importance of the event is muted but still present. The Quran presents a brief narrative in which Abraham is given a "gentle son," but then when the boy grows up, the father has a prophetic dream in which he sacrifices him before God. Abraham asks the "son" what he thinks this means, and the "son" replies: "Father, do as you are bidden. God willing, you shall find me steadfast." But at the last minute, the slaughter is called off, and a "noble sacrifice," presumably of a ram, is substituted. A heavenly voice calls out, "Abraham, you have fulfilled your vision" and "Peace be on Abraham!"[15] Tradition places the event chronologically sometime after the construction of the Ka'bah and the call to Pilgrimage. A few details are emphasized that do not appear in Jewish tradition: that God caused a sheet of copper to materialize around the son's throat to protect him from Abraham's knife, at which the father turned the son over on his forehead.

The identity of "the son," however, is left unclear in the text. Is it Isaac—or Ishmael? Later Islamic opinion favors the latter view, but a modern scholar has counted "authoritative statements" in the most venerable Islamic sources and found a dead heat in traditional opinion, with 131 statements identifying the son as Isaac compared to 133 identifying him as Ishmael.[16] The Islamic Akedah became, at any rate, the inspiration for the Feast of the Sacrifice celebrated each year as the climax of the Hajj season. In Mecca, hundreds of thousands of rams or other animals standing in for rams are slaughtered.[17]

Modern views range from the profound to the shallow. Soren Kierkegaard discovered proof in the Akedah that there is something higher than the universal obligation to live "ethically." That "something" is the "absolute" reality of God. As the Lord of the Universe, He transcends the sphere of "ethics," which would have ruled out the sacrifice of an innocent like Isaac. Kierkegaard calls this the "teleological suspension of the ethical," but in more homely terms it is a rejection of the whole idea of a field called ethics, as in "medical ethics" or "business ethics," practiced by professional "ethicists" and meaning the elucidation of morality without God.[18]

Popular opinion has focused on the Akedah as the occasion for mankind's rejection of human sacrifice. This is what you learn in Sunday or Hebrew school. Some scholars, though not all, agree that Canaanite spirituality in the Middle Bronze period included the practice of smothering children, placing them in jars buried in the subsoil, as a "foundation sacrifice" under the corner of a newly built wall.[19] Thus, interestingly, for Canaanites as for Abraham himself, human sacrifice seems to have been associated with beginnings: the beginning of an architectural project, or, in the case of the aborted sacrifice of the Akedah, the true beginning of Isaac's ministry as leader of nascent monotheism. This was the occasion on which his father definitively recognized him as his successor. For pagans in the region, human sacrifice may also have been a way of offering up to the god one's firstborn child—a grotesque distortion of the Jewish idea that the firstborn of humans was originally due to be donated to serve as the priesthood of the Hebrew people. This institution of the priesthood of the firstborn was supplanted, according to tradition, after the sin of the Golden Calf. While Moses was receiving the Torah on Sinai, the Israelites, including the firstborn of their families, constructed and worshiped an idol. As a result, the priesthood of the children of Levy was instituted and the firstborn were deposed from their sacred role, though even today each firstborn male is to be "redeemed" from his obligation by his father giving coins to a Levite.[20]

But this explanation of the Akedah's significance, as a rejection of human sacrifice, renders the event meaningless in our own time, when no one but a lunatic feels the impulse to kill children and bury their bodies under the floor of the garage. What's more, God's very commandment to Abraham, and the latter's willing acceptance of it, suggests that when a person has been commanded by God, being the "absolute" in Kierkegaard's terms, there simply cannot be anything to object to in His commandment, even in human sacrifice. This Absolute defines right and wrong. If the Absolute wills it, it is right no matter what our conscience may object. If the Absolute *ever* willed it, then circumstances could arise where it might be willed again.

Drawing on tradition, I'll offer what I think is the truest understanding of the Akedah. Let's begin by addressing an obvious question: Why did God choose this moment to demand the slaughter? What had happened that, so to speak, put the idea in His mind? The Bible itself is mum: God seems strangely undermotivated. Is this just further editorial incompetence? As tradition tells it, the answer is given in the first words of Genesis 22, the chapter that contains the story of the Akedah. Let us back up to recount the days that lead up to the Akedah in the kind of detail the scriptural text itself doesn't give.

It is the nature of biblical narrative to closely describe an event or series of events in the life of figures such as Abraham, then allow decades to go by without commenting on their activities at all. After time has passed, suddenly the tale is resumed, often with the phrase "And it happened after these things." These are the words we find immediately following Scripture's recounting of the treaty with Avimelech and the establishment of the *eshel,* narrated at the end of Genesis 21: "*And it happened after these things* that God tested Abraham . . ." (22:1). If the Bible were a book like any other, we would assume that this phrase was nothing more than a crude transition, intended to give an illusion of continuity to a disjointed story.

The Talmud and the later sages give several interpretations, hinging on the Hebrew phrase translated as "these things," *ha'devarim ha'eleh*. One reading directs our attention to the role of Satan in Abraham's career.

The word *devarim,* "things," can also mean "words." The Talmud records that the "words" in question here came from the mouth of "the *Satan,*" a Hebrew term meaning literally "the Accuser." After the feast Abraham gave in honor of Isaac's weaning, when the patriarch was 102 years old, Satan accused him of niggardliness. Amid the celebration, which ought to have been focused on thanking God for the gift of a son by Sarah, Abraham sought no opportunity to offer a sacrifice. The *devarim* that Satan spoke were as follows: "Master of the Universe! You have graced this old man, at 100 years of age, with the fruit of the womb. [Yet] from all the feast he made, he offered before you not one turtledove or one young dove." To this, God answered enigmatically: "Did he [make the feast] for any reason other than for his son? If I were to say to him, sacrifice your son before Me, immediately he would sacrifice him." In other words, the Satan had misrepresented the purpose of the feast. The point had been to establish Isaac's paternity before the world. There was a time and a place for Abraham to thank God for Isaac, but this needn't be that time or place. Even so, God at once moved to "test" Abraham.[21]

There are a couple of striking features of this Talmudic interpolation. First, anyone who has read the Book of Job will recognize the motif: Job, a righteous man, was also the object of a challenge to God from Satan, who asserted that Job's righteousness was a function of the comfortable life he lived. Take away the comfort, said the Satan, and you will soon see what the man is really made of. God accepted the challenge and began to assail Job with misfortunes.

Second, we know that Abraham's trial occurred when he was 137 years old.[22] Between his 102nd year and his 137th, his life had not been uneventful. When he was 125, he moved the family from Beersheba back to Hebron. When he was 135, his father, Terach, died at Haran, and Abraham briefly returned to his homeland to mourn the old man (who in the meantime had repented of his idolatrous faith and became a monotheist).[23] So the Satan had waited thirty-five years to make his accusation. Some commentators explain that the lag was needed because Abraham would already have had almost four decades in which to become profoundly attached to the younger man—making the trial a still greater challenge than if it had occurred when Isaac was a toddler. The Accuser, then, held his tongue before God to maximize Abraham's pain.

But that only underlines the obvious difficulty here, also raised by the story of Job: What does the tradition mean in appearing to ascribe an independent authority to Satan such that the Accuser can provoke God Himself into testing the patriarch's devotion? Is the Lord of the Universe so easily manipulated? What *is* Satan, anyway?

In the popular Jewish conception, the Accuser is pictured not as a devil figure with horns presiding over the damned in Hell, but rather as a courtroom official prosecuting sinners before the Heavenly Judge. The source of this notion is the Talmud's definition of him as a threefold threat: "He is the Prosecutor. He is the Inclination [that can lead people to do] Evil [in the first place]. He is the Angel of Death [who brings capital punishment from Heaven down on sinners]."[24] But it is a mistake to think of Satan as an independent entity, a power in opposition to God.

Whenever a tradition conflicts with another aspect of Torah, as it does here—God cannot at once be the Master of the Universe and a Being vulnerable to manipulation—the answer is to look to another source in the oral or written transmission to resolve the contradiction. In this case, we juxtapose the Talmud's interpolation with the one found in *Genesis Rabbah*. The Midrash tells the story a little differently. The "words" that preceded the occasion were actually spoken by Abraham *to himself*. He berated himself, saying, "[At Isaac's feast], I rejoiced and caused others to rejoice. But I did not set aside for the Holy One Blessed Be He even one heifer or one ram." To this, God responded, seeking to comfort him, "If it were told to you that you should offer your own son as a sacrifice before me, you would not hesitate."[25] In this version, "Satan's" accusation comes from Abraham, but it still serves as the catalyst for God's decision to command the patriarch to bind his son for slaughter.

Did Satan make the accusation, or did Abraham accuse himself? The answer is yes. They both did. What Torah is suggesting is that Satan really is an aspect of one's self. Abraham spoke to his own soul in the mode of the Accuser. One of the Satan's favorite strategies is to discourage a person from pursuing the most elevated mission he has been given in life by accusing him of having already failed in lesser ways. The Satan's accusation prompts the person to accuse himself. The implication is, "If you couldn't get that right, an easy thing like remembering to sacrifice a ram at your son's weaning, how can you possibly expect to accomplish anything more challenging? Why even try?" In the human repertoire, this is one of the great excuses for mediocrity.

Abraham's mission was to bring mankind closer to the One God—with the crucial detail that this was to be accomplished ultimately by passing on his mission to Isaac. In the years since he expelled Ishmael and Hagar, however, he had been tempted to think that he wasn't really up to the task. The fact that Abraham had moved back to Hebron from Beersheba, away from the *eshel* hospice that had become the focus of his and Isaac's missionary activities, indicates that he was beginning to succumb to the suggestion. There was never a more grand ambition than to introduce the world to monotheism. Naturally he doubted himself. This is what the Talmud and Midrash tell us.

How comforting it would have been for Abraham to content himself with the minor legacy of a missionary who had tried his best to influence his neighbors in a godly direction, with limited success, and later decided to retire from public life as a noble mediocrity. But how disastrous that would have been for the world! God could not allow Abraham to see himself in this way, if only because it would influence Isaac, robbing the young man of the near-supernatural valor it would require to pass on the Abrahamic mission to his own descendants. So the Lord resolved to test Abraham.

Four days before the Akedah—by coincidence, it seemed—Ishmael had paid a visit to his father, perhaps in the hope of reconciling with the old man. He was staying overnight with the family. In another tent, Abraham was suddenly overcome by the words of God resounding in him. The voice said, "Abraham."

He responded, "Here I am."

The voice said, without introduction or preface, "Please take your son, your only one, whom you love—Isaac—and go to the Land of Moriah. Bring him up as an offering on one of the mountains that I shall tell you."[26]

That was all. (The significance of God's referring to Isaac as Abraham's "only son," when Ishmael was present in the household that night, is a point to which we'll return.)

In line with its cryptic style, the Bible is silent on the question that jumps up first in the reader's mind, the question of Abraham's inner reaction to the commandment. The patriarch was not aware of the exchange between God and Satan. Why did he not at least ask about God's purpose in issuing this demand? We must not allow the fact that we already know the story of the Binding of Isaac to numb us. The Christian liturgical cycle calls for Genesis 22 to be read each Easter time, either on Good Friday or during the Easter Vigil. Jews hear it chanted in the synagogue each Rosh Hashanah. Nobody anymore is surprised by the notion of a God of mercy politely asking his servant to make of his son a holocaust, a wholly consumed sacrificial offering.

Yet it is Abraham's heart—not his actions, but his feelings—on which the meaning of the trial hinges. Before explaining what I mean, let us recall what tradition says it is about "trials" that appeals to God so much that he made Abraham undergo ten of them.

Rambam and Ramban debated the question. Unlike Harold Bloom, who denies that it could even have entered the mind of the writer J that the Lord would put anyone to a "test,"[27] these two great Spanish medieval Bible commentators viewed the meaning of trials as an intensely important matter. As with all authentic traditions about the multifaceted biblical text, one view does not exclude the other. Very likely God sets trials for more than one reason. First, let's focus on the Ramban's conception of the purpose of a trial, that it seeks to actualize a potential in the person on trial. What potential did God seek to actualize in Abraham?

A hint is found in a comment by Rashi on the Ten Commandments. In the Book of Exodus, Moses has just smashed the first pair of tablets, after witnessing the Jews frolicking before the idolatrous Golden Calf. On these tablets had been written, of course, the Ten Commandments. He then prays to God that He should forgive errant Israel "for the sake of Abraham, Isaac, and Jacob."[28] Setting aside Isaac and Jacob, Rashi asks why Moses thought that invoking Abraham would be efficacious in calling down divine mercy. He cites a tradition that at the episode of the calf the people engaged in a whole riot of other sins, breaking all of the Ten Commandments, and that the Ten Commandments bear some kind of relationship to the ten trials of Abraham. In effect, Moses was saying, "Their Father Abraham was tried with ten trials and never received his [full] reward. Give it to him [now], and let ten [trials] go out [and atone] for ten [categories of sin]."[29]

What's interesting is that if we set Rashi's recounting of the ten trials alongside the Ten Commandments, curious parallels emerge. The First Commandment instructs us to affirm God's existence. In his first trial, Abraham recognized God's existence and as a result was persecuted and forced to hide underground. The Second Commandment prohibits idolatry. In his second trial, Abraham met Nimrod, who ordered him to commit idolatry by prostrating himself before the forces of nature. The Third Commandment prohibits vain oaths. In his third trial, Abraham was commanded to leave his homeland. The parallel here is unclear to me. Not so in the case of the Fourth Commandment, which deals with the Sabbath. The most basic challenge of Sabbath observance lies in having faith that if you do no work Saturday, there will still be food to eat and you won't starve. In his fourth trial, Abraham faced starvation, as famine compelled him to move with Sarah down to Egypt. The Fifth Commandment instructs us to honor our parents. Distasteful though this may be to modern attitudes, the Talmud compares the relationship of parent to child with that of husband to wife. A husband is regarded, in a mystical sense, as having given birth to his wife.[30] In his fifth trial, it was precisely through her honoring Abraham, by complying with his instruction to her, that Sarah presented herself as her husband's sister and thus became a prisoner of Pharaoh. The Sixth Commandment prohibits murder. In his sixth trial, rescuing Lot from the four kings, Abraham killed other human beings for the first and last time in his career and feared that he had done wrong. The Seventh Commandment prohibits adultery. In his seventh trial, the Covenant Between the Parts, Abraham foresaw the subjugation of Israel to four historical kingdoms, resulting in the four exiles of the Jews—each of which has resulted in Jewish people being drawn after the gods of those foreign nations and committing "adultery" against their God. Metaphorically, in Torah terms, He is often pictured as the faithful "groom" to Israel's adulterous "bride." The Eighth Commandment prohibits "theft" but, according to the tradition, specifically the theft of one human by another: seizing a person in order to sell him into slavery.[31] The idea is that a human body—whether someone else's or your own—cannot be treated as your property. All persons are the property of God alone. In his eighth trial, Abraham circumcised himself: the ultimate sign that one's body belongs to God, like a divine branding. The Ninth

Commandment prohibits the bearing of false witness. In his ninth trial, Abraham expelled Ishmael and Hagar. As we have seen, in that act Abraham repudiated the hope—a hope as false as any false witness—to which he had devoted himself previously, that Ishmael was to be his successor.

As for the Tenth Commandment, the prohibition of coveting, it stands out from the other nine as does the tenth of Abraham's trials. What's unique about both is that they have to do primarily not with actions or beliefs, but with feelings. To withhold oneself from "coveting" means to sanctify and offer up one's very heart to God. This is the essence of the Akedah. Abraham's love for Isaac was the greatest passion in his heart. God asked him to sacrifice the lad, to offer up his heart.

But the parallel goes deeper. The real challenge lay not in the mechanical process of binding the young man and cutting his throat. If you *knew* that the Maker of Heaven and earth had commanded you *personally* to do something, however outrageous, could you possibly refuse? Abraham's compliance was never in doubt. He had not once in his long life failed to carry out an order from the Deity. True, he had argued with God over the fate of the Sodomites, but in this instance he did not argue because he understood that he was being tested, which had not been the case when he learned that Sodom had been condemned to destruction. What lessons the Akedah seeks to teach us about God is a separate question from that of what God was seeking to teach Abraham about himself, what attributes He sought to actualize by testing him. We shall deal with the former question later on in this chapter. As for the latter, the answer seems to be that God wished to show Abraham not what he could *do,* but what he could *feel.*

When Abraham received the commandment to slaughter Isaac, he knew instantly that he would do it. He also knew that it was a test. I believe he understood what the nature of the test was to be, which is why we do not find him even asking God about its purpose, much less debating Him. Abraham did not know what the course of his emotions would be, but he did know that his inner response was the real point of the trial. This was his beloved son, needless to say. There was no longer any doubt in the patriarch's mind that the son of his destiny was not Ishmael, but Isaac. Yet he also knew that to slay Isaac would mean rendering his whole life's work absurd.[32] Isaac was his intended successor, but now it seemed there would be no successor at all. The Akedah would certainly nullify whatever claim he had to representing the virtue of *chesed,* or kindness.[33] When his students found out what he had done, they would abandon him. And so the old man would die, childless and friendless, his career of 137 years all for nothing—simply because God had got it into His mind to put him to this test.

We circle back to the Satanic challenge that catalyzed the Akedah to begin with. Abraham's self-accusation had to do not with what he did or didn't do. A sacrifice of a heifer or a goat is a small thing. The accusation really was that he served God with imperfect inner devotion. Had Abraham been perfectly devoted, he would have included some easy sacrifice in the celebration of his son's weaning. Abraham doubted his own heart, our most obdurate organ, the hardest there is to conquer.

The Talmud has God pleading with Abraham, "I have tested you in many trials and you have stood fast in them all. Now stand fast for me in this trial, lest people say that there was no value in the preceding [nine trials]."[34] The first nine trials had all been leading up to this one, which validated all the others. Those earlier experiences had tested Abraham's willingness to *act* against his instincts—for self-preservation, for treating others with kindness. What he *felt* wasn't being directly tested. Now it was. In Torah thought, the purpose of performing commandments, doing what God asks, is to train and perfect your inner life. *Doing* leads to *feeling*. So it was here. From his first trial to his penultimate one, he had done the right thing. In acting with his body, he had perfected his soul.

All this is crystallized in the single verse indicating that after his nighttime visitation from the Deity, "he rose up early in the morning."[35] Jewish tradition lays great stress on the virtue of getting up early every day. In the authoritative sixteenth-century legal code the *Shulchan Aruch,* rising up from bed instantly on reaching consciousness and leaping to your feet "like a lion" to serve God is the very first commandment for a Jew. Practically speaking, there is little you can do by jumping out of bed that you could not do if you hit the snooze button a couple of times and *then* rolled out from under the covers. But that headlong leap into the first moments of the day is taken as proof that you love serving God.

Abraham "rose up early" not only because he was prepared to obey but also because he had mastered himself to such an extent that *he did so with joy*. His heart was being tested, and he was finding, to his amazement, that so far his inner spiritual condition was more profoundly correct and true than he had realized. He not only leaped out of bed but hastened to prepare his own transportation, saddling his donkey himself, though normally one of his servants would have done this. "Love," comments the Midrash, in this case Abraham's love of God, "disrupts the natural order of things."[36]

We may find this somewhat eerie. So did Sarah, or at least she would have if she had known what Abraham intended. But he artfully dissembled. When Sarah found him busily preparing for the journey that no one had so much as mentioned till this very morning, he explained that it all had do with making good Isaac's education, which he, Abraham, had neglected till now. The not-so-young man was thirty-seven years old. "You know that when I was three years old I recognized my Creator. But this young man is mature now and has received no such initiation. There is a place somewhat distant [from here] where they bring lads to be educated [in the ways of God]. I shall take [Isaac] there to be educated."

The patriarch did not mean that he had neglected to teach Isaac altogether, but rather that there was a kind of teaching he could not give. There was a place, the academy of Noah's son Shem, also know as Malchizedek, where the primordial monotheism was still preserved, a secret freemasonry with few initiates. The handful of followers of Noah in the world, of whom Abraham, growing up in Mesopotamia, had been unaware, brought their children to Shem to be initiated in what amounted to a mystery cult, in form not unlike the cult of the Eleusinian Mysteries in classical Greece. Abraham's monotheism was self-taught; he wanted Isaac to experience the tradition of the One God as it had been passed down from Adam to Noah and his sons. We saw that there are subtle differences between the tradition of the Convert (Abraham) and that of the Native (Shem/Malchizedek), which complement each other. Missing either element, the tradition is incomplete. Sarah understood this and took it to be Abraham's reasoning. To his announcement, she replied simply, "Go in peace."[37]

He hesitated to tell his wife what God had commanded him because he feared that Sarah would be overwhelmed by the truth. The medieval commentator Radak remarks, "He did not make it known to Sarah, lest she do some evil to herself on account of her love for Isaac."[38] Father and son were aware of a certain instability in the matriarch. A modern sage, Avivah Gottlieb Zornberg, reflecting on this feature of Sarah's personality, contrasts the quality of *chesed,* of kindness, which was Abraham's chief characteristic, with the quality of *mishpat,* or strict judgment, which was Sarah's. What do these mean in practical terms?

It is impossible to get an objective, scientific impression of what Abraham and Sarah would have been like if you had met them in the street. The Talmud and Midrash don't seek to acquaint us with the patriarch and his wife as personalities. But in my reading I have arrived at a more subjective impression. I think Abraham would have been the sort of man who sounded harsh in his public pronouncements against idolatry and immorality, but who in private was a deeply compassionate soul, exquisitely sensitive to the needs of his followers and others: in other words, a softie. Sarah I imagine as less approachable than her husband, a woman who might be quiet in public but whom people found intimidating, even a little scary, when they were in her home.

In philosophical terms, *mishpat* is the application of "pure thought" to the problems one encounters in life. Whereas *chesed* admits of multiple, seemingly contradictory truths, *mishpat* demands clarity and denies paradoxes. This is why it took Sarah's insistence for Abraham finally to accept that, for a spiritual heir, he must choose one of his sons over the other. To the *chesed* personality, such decisions do not come easily. Unfortunately for Sarah, when life is lived at the spiritual heights that she and Abraham inhabited, where God visits in dreams and issues personal commands, paradox is unavoidable. The air is thin, and eventually the *mishpat* personality develops altitude sickness.

Kierkegaard observed that "suicide is the only tolerable existential consequence for pure thought." And Abraham would have said he was afraid that Kierkegaard was right.[39] So he deceived his wife out of concern for her safety.

For assistance along the way, the Bible indicates, Abraham brought "two lads"—who were Ishmael and Abraham's old servant Eliezer, says the Midrash—for a distinguished man like Abraham would always travel with attendants.[40] (The Bible doesn't identify them because their function was not as individuals—their personalities don't really come into play here at all—but instead as instruments, serving the purpose of assuring that Abraham and Isaac reached their destination without hindrance.)

Abraham could not tell any of his traveling companions exactly where he meant to lead them. "Moriah" designated a land, and also the name of a particular mountain in that land. Ramban notes that when God told Abraham, "Bring him up as an offering on one of the mountains that I shall tell you," this meant that Abraham knew the identity of the land but not the precise location of the mountain.[41] Rashi comments that "the Holy One Blessed Be He makes the righteous wait and afterward reveals to them."[42] It is the same way with us, the less righteous. The meaning of events in our lives is typically kept from us by God—sometimes just while the event is happening, more often for some time, even years, after that, and quite commonly for the duration of our existence on earth. After death, when we meet Him, we may hope He will explain all.

According to Genesis, after Abraham had set off, God made him wait for a total of three days. This was the length of time that elapsed between his departure from Hebron and his arrival at Mt. Moriah. The number 3 is significant in Jewish mysticism. It represents the sequence of past, present, future—and Abraham's journey was all about either losing or securing the future of his monothestic movement with either the death or rescue of Isaac from his father's knife. It also represents a strong bond, as between this father and son. "A three-ply cord is not easily severed," King Solomon wrote.[43]

Where precisely was Moriah? Some modern scholars throw up their hands. Writes one, "All attempts to explain the name and identify the place have been futile."[44] Another scholarly view holds that the tradition found elsewhere in the Bible (2 Chron. 3:1) identifying Moriah with Jerusalem is inauthentic, invented to "enhance the prestige of that city as the sole authorized center of the Jewish cult."[45] Other scholars point out that the trip from the south up to Jerusalem would have consumed hardly more than a day's time. And they notice the verse about Abraham placing the wood for the sacrifice on Isaac's shoulder. At the time, there were perfectly good trees in the hill country of Judah. Why bother carrying wood with you unless Moriah was not in Judah but, let us say, farther south, in the treeless waste of the Negev or Sinai—possibly, says Glueck, at Bir Birein, southwest of Beersheba, where the Negev meets the Sinai.[46]

For its part, the Oral Torah indicates unequivocally that Mt. Moriah is indeed the site of Jerusalem, specifically the Temple Mount where Solomon built his sanctuary, now occupied by the Dome of the Rock and bordered by the Western Wall. It was the mountain that Abraham had sensed he was making for from the moment he entered the land of Canaan.

The Jewish sages were aware that to reach Jerusalem from Hebron would not have required three days' journey. Ramban indicates that it took only a day. God had said Isaac was to be offered up "on one of the mountains that I shall tell you." When the party arrived in the land of Moriah, they wandered about for two further days waiting for God to inspire Abraham and clarify for the patriarch the meaning of His enigmatic phrase.[47] As for the wood, on this the Christian and Jewish traditions agree. We said earlier that Christian teachers from Paul onward have found in the Akedah a preview of the Crucifixion. But the Midrash itself notes, without fuss or other comment, that when Abraham placed the wood for the offering on Isaac's shoulder, the patriarch's son was "like one who carries his own cross."[48] To the first Jewish readers of this text, after the orally transmitted material had been committed to writing, the image would have been familiar. During the period of Roman domination of the Holy Land, they had witnessed the ordeal of Jews sentenced to this "most wretched of deaths," as Josephus called the practice of crucifixion. In Roman custom, victims carried at least the transverse beam of the cross from wherever they were imprisoned to wherever they were to die. But crucifixion extends far back in history beyond the Romans at least to the Persians as Herodotus describes them. Other sources report its use in Babylon and even in India.[49] In other words, contrary to the view of some Bible critics, the rabbis of the Midrash did not in some way seek to recover the Akedah from Christian hands by pretending their tradition had been aware all along of the crucifixion reference. That cruel punishment was known to the world long before there were Romans or Christians. It is entirely plausible that the Hebrew Bible itself intends us to find here the reflection of an ancient punishment.

Bearing his cross, Isaac, along with Abraham, Eliezer, and Ishmael, reached the hill country of Moriah. Only a day had elapsed since they had left Hebron. It was, as one may imagine, a time of heightened testing for Abraham. If we rush into a forbidding task, we may forget to fear what is about to happen. Since part of God's purpose was to prove to Abraham that his inner devotion was sterling in quality, the trial would have been incomplete if the patriarch had no time for doubt. God thus gave him two further days for this.

The midrashic collections portray him struggling against the Satan inside him. Of these depictions, *Midrash Tanchuma* gives the most interesting. In the course of the party's wandering, Abraham was taken aback by the sudden apparition of a great river. In the Judean hills around Jerusalem, there are no rivers. The midrash indicates that this one was a creation of Abraham's Satan. Whether it possessed a material reality, or was wholly an illusion, is unclear.

Abraham began to ford the river, wading in up to his knees and calling to his companions to follow him. When they reached the midpoint of the stream, the water had come to the patriarch's shoulders. The midrash says nothing about the shoulders of the other men. Only Abraham, it seems, was on the verge of drowning.

We might say he was out of his depth, or felt that he was. In the nomenclature of Torah, water signifies Torah itself, God's revealed will. The patriarch's Satan, his voice of inner doubt, was telling him that by ignoring its previous intimation of his inadequacy as a servant of the Almighty, and consequently by wading deep in the unfordable stream of divine will, the patriarch had placed his life in imminent danger. He simply was not worthy of this trial. His stubbornness in thinking that he *was* worthy threatened to overwhelm and drown him.

Abraham lifted up his eyes to Heaven. "Master of Eternity," he cried, "you chose me and you taught me and you were revealed to me and said to me, 'I am unique and you are unique. By your hand My Name has been made known in My world. [Now] offer up your son Isaac before me as a wholly consumed offering.' I did not hesitate [to comply]. Behold I am engaged in fulfilling your command. But now water has come [up so high as to extinguish] my soul. If I or my son Isaac drowns, who will [there be left to] uphold Your word? By whom shall Your name be unified? [That is, who will teach the doctrine of the One God?]"

God replied, "By your life [I swear] that by your hand shall my Name be unified in the world." At once He shut up the source of the river. The water disappeared and Abraham found himself standing on dry land.[50]

Jews commemorate this miracle each Rosh Hashanah. On the second day of the festival, they go to a body of water—a river, lake, or ocean—and perform a contemplative exercise called Tashlich. The ten days between Rosh Hashanah and Yom Kippur are devoted to penitence. It is a time when a person may readily succumb, as Abraham nearly did, to the voice of Satan. The voice says, "Why bother pretending that you have 'repented' of your failings? Whatever you did wrong this past year, you will only do again in the coming year. Carrying out the fullness of God's will is too much for you.

You'll drown if you try. Don't be a hypocrite!" The message of Tashlich is one of hope: "Wade in up to your shoulders, till you *think* you will drown. At once God will answer you and you will find the 'water' as you see it now, lapping gently at your feet. Get on with it!"

Abraham got on with it. At the end of the two days of wandering about, the party reached a peak at the northern and highest end of a ridge of hills. Today that ridge is best known for one of its lower heights, the Mount of Olives, immediately east of the Old City of Jerusalem. Abraham and his companions were standing on Mt. Scopus, with a fine view down upon the Temple Mount toward the southwest.[51]

From Scopus, Abraham looked to the southwest and saw something hovering over one of the lower elevations opposite him, something that froze the patriarch in his steps. It was a great cloud, or maybe a pillar of fire.[52] Either way, it was one of the signs that occur in the Bible when God is present in a most concentrated form.

Perhaps still more exciting was the feeling of recognition that overcame the patriarch. This was it! The mountain he had imagined in his mind's eye decades ago when he first set out from Mesopotamia for the land of Canaan. He had seen it once in the intervening years. His encounter with Malchizedek sixty-two years earlier had taken place in the Valley of the King, today's Kidron Valley. Just to the south was the Jebusite settlement over which Malchizedek presided. (So Abraham hadn't exactly lied when he told Sarah he was bringing Isaac to Malchizedek. He had just been slightly off in his geography.) But somehow he must have realized then that his vision was not simply of Mt. Moriah, but of Moriah *on this day,* seen in company with his son and heir. He had been destined to climb this mountain only now, with Isaac.

Isaac, too, felt the Presence. The younger man was gazing wide-eyed at the miraculous image. Eliezer and Ishmael, however, seemed oblivious. A tradition in *Midrash Tanchuma* recounts their conversation. Abraham said to Isaac, "Do you see what I see?"

Isaac said, "I see a mountain, beautiful and praiseworthy, and a cloud as if it were tied [to the mountain]."

Abraham said to the other two men, "Do you see anything?"

They said, "We see nothing but wilderness."

To which Abraham replied, as in the foreshortened scriptural text, "Stay here with the donkey. The lad and I will go up there. We will worship, and we will return to you."[53] For Ishmael and Eliezer had proved themselves, at least for the moment, to be no more spiritually elevated than the donkey, a creature signifying the human propensity to become dominated by material, as opposed to spiritual, considerations. The Hebrew word for "donkey," *chamor*, shares a three-letter root with the word meaning "clay," *chomer*. Thus when the builders of the Tower of Babel sought to unite in their perverse vision, which elevated material reality over the spiritual realm, and to rebel against God, the Bible describes them as reaching for *chomer* before they had even decided what to build.[54] They were not the last group of humans who sought to overthrow a godly vision of goodness by uniting around an ideology of materialism.[55]

Abraham and Isaac, however, were as one in seeing through the veil of gross matter into the heart of reality that is God's Presence. It was clear to the patriarch that the rest of the journey would include himself and Isaac but not Ishmael or Eliezer. We may imagine the latter two feeling a certain relief as the master and his son trudged downward without escort into the valley that separated Scopus from Moriah.

We have returned to our point of departure: Abraham and Isaac's ascent of the mountain on which they met the climax of their destiny as servants of the Almighty. They reached the bottom of the valley and began to climb upward. Isaac said, "Father—"

Abraham replied, "Here I am, my son."

Isaac said, "Here are the fire and the wood, but where is the lamb for the offering?"

Abraham replied enigmatically, "God will see the lamb for Himself for the offering, my son."

The Bible tenderly comments that "the two of them walked on together."[56] In those few words, we find one of the most heartrending scenes in the entire Bible. As one scholar was moved to say, "The short and simple sentence, 'And the two of them walked on together,' covers what is perhaps the most poignant and eloquent silence in all literature."[57] Rashi brings to the surface the submerged meaning that accounts for the power of the scene. Before this exchange, "Abraham, who knew that he was going to slaughter his son, was proceeding with the [same] willingness and [even] joy as did Isaac, who was totally unaware of [what was really going on]." Now Isaac understood his father's intention. Yet the two of them proceeded up the mountain "with an equal heart"—that is, with a perfect unity in their eagerness to carry out God's will.[58] There was no need for further conversation.

For they loved each other. It is noteworthy that Scripture's first use of the verb "to love" occurs in the context of the Akedah, in God's command that Abraham offer up "your son, your only one, whom you love."[59] Since when the Bible employs a word for the first time it does so with the intention of defining the word in its quintessential meaning, the essence of true "love" must somehow be captured in the relationship between Abraham and Isaac. It is this union of two hearts that marks the apogee of Abraham's love for his son, and the son's love for his father. The Bible informs us that love is no matter of simple affection, however passionate, but rather the ultimate fusion of wills; and that it transcends words, in fact finds its greatest fulfillment in silence.

Without the Oral Torah, the meaning of what was about to happen must remain obscure. There is no better example of the way believers in the Documentary Hypothesis seek to compel the evidence to fit their hypothesis. As one notes with amusement, the critics react to the concise and unified narrative of Genesis 22:1–19 by dividing up the credit for it between E and J. The scholars are in a bind. One problem is that the text mixes elements of E and J, employing both of the principal divine names, Elohim and the tetragrammaton. If the text were by E, it should use only the former name. Yet the scholarly consensus is indeed that E wrote our story, while the same consensus admits that the overall narrative style seems more in keeping with J's interest in characterization and psychological nuance. The critics offer solutions, including that (a) the Redactor unaccountably changed God's name in several places; (b) other scribes unaccountably "miswrote" the divine name; (c) E and J were appended to or superimposed on one another, never mind that mixing the work of great writers tends to produce mush.[60]

So let us turn to the oral tradition. The motif that emerges is a weird, totally unexpected time-bending effect, which we find in three places: the fate of Isaac, the identity of the ram, and the salvific effect of the Akedah.

What happened to Isaac? We noted earlier the omission of any mention of Isaac's returning from Mt. Moriah. God had commanded Abraham to bring him up as a sacrifice. Did Abraham do it?

Strange things are reported in the Talmud, midrashim, and other classical sources. In the reign of King David, as punishment for a sin the king had committed, a plague assaulted Jerusalem. The First Book of Chronicles recounts that in the midst of the disaster, "God saw and reconsidered the evil," and He called off the angel of pestilence.[61] What did God "see"? The Talmud passes along a tradition from the sage Shmuel, who lived in Babylon in the third century A.D.: "Shmuel said, 'He saw the ashes of Isaac.' "[62]

Immediately after Jerusalem was saved, David purchased the land on Mt. Moriah where the Akedah took place. Here his son Solomon built the First Temple. When that structure was destroyed by the Babylonians in 586 B.C., the Jewish population of Israel went to exile in Babylon. Upon their return, they set about rebuilding the Temple. But a question arose: where precisely to build the altar? It was imperative that it should occupy the same place it did in Solomon's Temple, and the location was found. The Talmud cites the tradition of a certain Rav Yitzchak Nafcha: "They saw the ashes of Isaac in that place."[63]

Translations of these and similar passages will often dutifully note that what God *really* perceived was the "merit" of Isaac's ashes—that is, the merit of Abraham's *willingness* to sacrifice Isaac. A midrash in *Tanchuma* explains that on Rosh Hashanah the Jewish people blow shofars, the ram's horn, in memory of Isaac's near-sacrifice. "It shall be remembered for you, [namely] the Binding of Isaac, and it shall be considered for you *as if* the ashes of Isaac were piled up on top of the altar, and it shall be forgiven you."[64] But when he cites this midrash, Rashi drops the nuance. After the Akedah event, Abraham named the site Hashem Yireh, meaning "God Will See." "And Abraham called the name of that place 'Hashem Yireh,' as it is said today, on the mountain of the Lord [it] will be seen." And what will be seen? Says Rashi: "the ashes of Isaac still piled up, for atonement."[65] The same idea is repeated each year in the liturgy of Rosh Hashanah, when the person assigned to blow the shofar for the congregation first recites a prayer authored by the kabbalist Isaac Luria. It includes the request: "May You be filled with mercy upon your people, and may You contemplate the ashes of Isaac, our fore-father, that are piled up on the Altar." Rabbi Luria lived in Israel in the sixteenth century. What did *he* see piled up on the Temple Mount?

Needless to say, any notion that Isaac gave up his life on the altar would appear to be refuted by the Bible narrative itself, which proceeds to recount the post-Akedah life of Isaac and his descendants. Still, as late as the twelfth century, the commentator Ibn Ezra felt obliged to offer his rebuttal to a quite different version of the story. On the verse at the end of the Akedah story that reads, "Abraham returned to his lads, and they rose up and went together to Beersheba," Ibn Ezra notes: "And [this verse] omits the mention of Isaac, for he was under [Abraham's] supervision [and thus reckoned as accompanying the Patriarch even if unmentioned]. And he who says that [Abraham] slaughtered [Isaac] and left him [there], but that afterward [Isaac was somehow] revived, speaks contrary to [the plain meaning] of Scripture."[66]

There were indeed sages who said just this. An obscure midrash, *Shibbole HaLeket* by Rabbi Tzidkiyah HaRofei of Rome (c. A.D. 1230–1300), makes the point explicit. "When our Father Isaac was bound on the altar and reduced to ashes and his sacrificial dust was cast onto Mt. Moriah, the Holy One Blessed Be He immediately brought upon him dew and revived him." A rare manuscript of this midrash, preserved at Cambridge University, gives a still more explicit rendition: "When Abraham bound his son Isaac on the altar, and slew him and burned him, [the lad] was reduced to ashes, and his ashes were cast on Mt. Moriah," etc.[67]

This is not simply a matter of two different theories about Isaac's fate. Oral Torah, as it understands itself, doesn't present theories—it presents truth, only truth. Sometimes that truth is too complex to be conveyed through simple declarative sentences: like "Isaac survived" or "Isaac was sacrificed." Not infrequently the only way to convey the truth is through paradox, apparently conflicting statements. This is how we understand the many, many mutually contradictory views given in the Talmud. When sages seem to disagree, it's not the case that one is right and the other wrong. They're both right, if you understand them correctly, and we are challenged to expand our minds to encompass the complexity of God's world. If that were not so, why didn't the Talmud simply give the right "theory" and leave the wrong one out of the text?

Isaac survived, and yet, at one and the same time, he was also sacrificed.

It is as if the stream of time splits in two. In one branch of time, Isaac lives. In the other, he dies. Before considering what all this means, we proceed to a couple of further time-bending phenomena.

Where did the ram come from? The ram that Abraham sacrificed in the end, "caught in a thicket by its horns," is included by the Mishnah, tractate *Pirke Avot,* in a list of wondrous creatures and other items created by God at the end of the week of creation, before the onset of the first Sabbath.[68] In other words, the ram was by now some 2,085 years old. In the context of an already miraculous story, that would be fine except that in Jewish law a ram over the age of two is invalid for sacrifice. One only offers to God an animal in its prime. This may seem an arcane objection, but as we know, the Midrash asserts that Abraham observed all the details of Torah. This has led to the deduction by at least one commentator, the Chassidic sage Rabbi Yehuda Aryeh Leib Alter (called Sfas Emes; 1847–1905), that the ram had somehow been preserved intact and ageless as if in suspended animation, for two millennia.

The salvific effect of Abraham's sacrifice. We have already seen that at Rosh Hashanah Jews blow the ram's horn to commemorate the Akedah, specifically for the purpose of arousing God's compassion. For God, the sound is like Proust's madeleine, bringing Him back to the time when his servant Abraham was prepared to slaughter his beloved son. Skeptics assert that this idea—that the Akedah, which occurred about 1675 B.C., can effect the forgiveness of men and women later in time—has its origins in paganism. Idolaters also thought that the gods reckoned it as a merit to the descendants of a man who slaughtered his own child.[69] But contrary to what the skeptics say, the fact that idolaters or other unbelievers embraced an idea also found in Torah, albeit in a different form, does not mean that the idea had its *origins* in paganism. It could also mean that pagans intuited a certain element of spiritual truth before it was revealed later in its pure form, or that truths received by Adam were disseminated among mankind.

In *Midrash Tanchuma,* God says, "The descendants of Isaac are destined to sin before me, and I shall judge them [each] Rosh Hashanah. But if they wish to seek merit for themselves, that I should remember on their behalf the Binding of Isaac, let them blow upon the shofar of this [ram]."[70] Actually in Jewish liturgy, the Akedah is recalled every day of the year in the morning prayers of Shacharit, by way of beseeching God's mercy. Professor Jacob Neusner has commented on the manner in which time functions in the relationship between the deeds of the patriarchs and the *zchut*, or "merit," that, because of those deeds, accrues to the patriarchs' descendants. It is as if Abraham exists across the span of time, so that his deed saves us today as if it had been performed yesterday—as if his deed and my sin were separated not by 3,678 years, as it would appear, but by no time at all. That the merit of a parent should save his immediate descendants is unsurprising. For instance, imagine the situation of a schoolteacher with a student in her class whose mother or father once did her a good turn. She would have a harder time flunking that student than she would if she had never known the child's parent. Granted that God has a longer memory than we do. But that He should forgive my sins of today because Abraham bound Isaac on the altar greatly stretches the conception of gratitude He planted in us.

Some religious people deal with conundrums like the three we have considered by driving themselves into ecstasies of gassy, fulsome praise for the mysterious Divine. Another approach is to ask what the oral tradition seeks to tell us about the nature of the reality God created. To be sure, He is infinitely great and good. More than our praise, however, He desires our understanding. In the *Mishneh Torah*, that comprehensive summation of Jewish teaching, Maimonides gives as the very first commandment that one should "know" about God. He calls this knowledge "the foundation of foundations and the pillar of wisdom."[71]

Maimonides also wrote that the purpose of trials is to broadcast certain truth to humanity. I think that what the Akedah tells us about God has to do above all with His unity. Rambam gives the knowledge of this unity as the second of all the Torah's commandments. For His unity is unlike any other: "This God is One. . . . Of all the unities that exist in the universe, there is not one that is like his unity."[72]

This is no mere gassy, fulsome praise. Abraham began his journey of discovery with the observation that God has no competitors, that there is only a single Deity—a position that's no big news today. In the post-pagan world, the uniqueness it attributes to God hardly impresses us. After all, the reader of this book is also unique. There never was and never will be a person with your face, your thoughts, your personality. Yet somehow God's unity infinitely surpasses yours. The surprising, time-bending features of the Akedah indicate that His unity extends to encompass universes and realities.

Long before physicists understood that time and space belong to a single continuum, the Torah alluded to the same truth. Rabbi Yehudah Loewe of

Prague (called Maharal; 1526–1609) noted that the Hebrew word *olam* refers both to infinite time ("eternity") and to infinite space (the "universe"). Quantum physics has begun to work out what this means in some detail.

Anticipating modern subatomic physics, Hugh Everett became in 1957 the first scientist to argue for the existence of the "multiverse." But Hebrew thought, crystallized in the word *olam*, beat him to it. In the language of Torah, we speak of an *olam*, describing an infinity linking space and time, as in the eleventh-century hymn "Adon Olam" ("Lord of the Universe"). But we also speak of *olamim,* "universes"—as in Psalm 145, which includes the statement "Your kingdom is a kingdom of all universes *[olamim],*"[73] and as in the divine title "Adon Olamim," "Lord of Universes."[74] The plural noun *olamim* could as well be translated as "multiverse." I am suggesting that the unity of God surpasses the unity of everything else that exists because it encompasses the multiverse. The "reality" of everything apart from Him would then be multiplicitous—shivered and shattered.

If true, this explains a great deal that is mysterious in our encounter with God's creation. Far from being the perfectly unified reflection of the Creator, the world we know is profoundly confusing and seemingly self-contradictory, full of apparent injustice and paradox. As we said in the preface, there are some respects in which a universe ruled by multiple gods makes more intuitive sense than does an uncomplicated rendering of monotheism. Speaking to us from Abraham's time, a pagan might say, "Life as we experience it does not seem to be the handiwork of a single omnipotent, all-just, and all-good Deity. So come worship the gods with me!" Perhaps our answer to him, hinted at by tradition, would be that creation, unlike the Creator, is stabbed by the shards of multiple, infinite realities.

If that is so, then we are now in a position to illuminate the three conundrums of the Akedah. In one universe, Isaac was slaughtered. In another, he lived on. This helps us comprehend the salvific effect of the event. As David Deutsch says, "It is only what really happens that can cause other things really to happen." This observation may not hold true in human experience, where lies and rumors can indeed cause things to happen. But surely it is true in God's experience of reality, or realities. To cause the salvation of those who pray for forgiveness through the merit of Abraham, at least in some reality not only the Binding but the Slaughter of Isaac must really have happened.

We recalled earlier that Jewish tradition includes two approaches to the function of trials. In the Rambam's opinion, trials serve a didactic purpose. In that case, Abraham's mere willingness to slaughter his son was enough. But in the Ramban's view, trials actuate in a person qualities that had been only potential. If the trial was never actually completed, if the slaughter itself remained only potential, it's hard to see how it could actuate anything at all. But this problem disappears if, in some alternative *olam,* the trial was in fact completed. For—as we have seen in the simple case of photons bumping into photons—the *olamim,* while distinct, can sometimes interact with each other.

Nor does the apparent distance in time stop that long-ago event, the Slaughter or Binding, from effecting salvation today. To see why, we must refer to an intriguing corollary of this theory of the multiverse, which deals with time travel. Deutsch says, "Other times are just special cases of other universes." He believes there is no paradox in the idea of finding a "pathway" from one universe to another, each universe having a distinctive time framework. Human technology may or may not find a way to create such a pathway. But since time is like a fourth dimension in addition to the three dimensions of space, there is no theoretical bar to moving from one time to another as one moves from one space to another. The "distinctive aspect" of this movement would be to experience "certain physical objects or processes—'clocks' or 'calendars'—in states that occurred only at past times."[75] This is what *Pirke Avot* tells us that Abraham did. He experienced, and sacrificed, the ram in a state that occurred less than two years after creation. And it is precisely what can render the Slaughter or Binding an event in close enough proximity to our own experience of Rosh Hashanah in the twenty-first century, helping us win divine forgiveness on that day.

Let us put all this as concisely as we can. Abraham *did* and *did not* slaughter Isaac. He *did;* and through God's unity, transcending the whole of the multiverse, or *olamim,* that act affects us today. He *did not;* and through God's unity, transcending the whole of the multiverse, he was able to experience and sacrifice a 2,085-year-old ram as if the creature were less than two years old.

If I'm right about this, then Abraham now comprehended God in a new light. From the Akedah, he came to understand the *olamim* and God's relationship to reality in a way he had not before. His was a more complex sort of monotheism.

The Bible sets up the Akedah as the climax of a process that had begun sixty-two years earlier when he and Sarah left Haran. To underline the point, Scripture employs the same language. *"Lech l'chah"*—Go forth— "from your land, from your birthplace, and from your father's house," God told Abraham then.[76] He says to him now, *"V'lech l'chah"*—And go forth— "to the Land of Moriah. Bring [Isaac] up as an offering on one of the mountains that I shall tell you."[77] In Maimonides' counting of the ten trials, the couple's departure from Mesopotamia was the patriarch's first trial, and this was his last. (For Rashi, it's also the tenth trial.) These two moments in Abraham's life make perfect bookends for that life.

If the beginning of Abraham's spiritual journey was his realization of the truth of a certain uncomplicated monotheism, and if the Akedah is the climax of that journey, then it stands to reason that his understanding of God also reached a climax at that event.

A similar conclusion—that the Akedah is the climax, giving the ultimate meaning of Abraham's life of spiritual discovery—may be drawn from the pattern of events in that life which we saw with assistance from the biblical interpreter Devora Steinmetz. The point is made by the doubled motifs that characterize the Abraham narrative. We discussed four of those motifs. Here is the fifth pair. At the beginning of Abraham's mission to the Holy Land, there was the command to "Go!" from Haran. The pattern was completed with the command to "Go!" to the Akedah. Steinmetz helped us see that the pivot point of the Abraham narrative is Genesis 16, which tells of Hagar's pregnancies, her departure from his household, and the birth of Ishmael. Let's recall how the pivot worked. Before Ishmael's birth, Abraham understood clearly that a child he was destined to have through Sarah would assure the first patriarch's destiny as the father of monotheism. However, after Ishmael's birth, he lost this spiritual vision. Ishmael was in a sense a test that Abraham failed. He regained the vision at the time of Hagar's second departure from his community, when he heeded Sarah's words and expelled the Egyptian woman. At the Akedah, his vision was tested a final time, and God found conclusively that it had been restored. For when Abraham was commanded to slaughter "your son, your only one, whom you love," before the Lord indicated which son was meant, he knew that the son to whom God referred, the "only one," was Isaac, not Ishmael.

So it was that the enlightened patriarch "returned [from Mt. Moriah] to his lads, and they rose up and went together to Beersheba, and Abraham dwelled at Beersheba."[78] The second act of the drama of Abraham's life was concluded—the identity of his successor had been securely established. Isaac, not Ishmael, would lead the movement of nascent monotheism. At the beginning of the *parshah* of *Vayera,* this had been in doubt. Back then, thirty-eight years earlier, Abraham had only one son, the problematic Ishmael, who almost died in the wilderness after Sarah had rejected him along with the boy's mother. As *Vayera* ends, Abraham faces a new crisis, one that will become the focus of his energies as he approaches the end of his life. Isaac is the heir, but what is an heir worth who cannot pass on the master's vision to his own children? At the Akedah, Isaac was already thirty-seven years old and still a bachelor—not an encouraging situation. Abraham could not know that he still had four decdes of life in which to find a wife for the young man. At age 137, it was reasonable for him to assume that this matter must be attended to immediately, so that it should not be left undone when he died. Finding a mate for Isaac is the great quest at the heart of the next *parshah* in Genesis, that of *Chayei Sarah.*

However, even now in the last verses of *Vayera* the seeds of Isaac's redemption from bachelorhood had been sown. Scripture concludes the story of the Akedah with some news that reached Abraham: back in Haran, his brother Nachor's son Bethuel, and the latter's unnamed wife, had had a child, Rebecca. She, it will soon become clear, would make a fine wife for Isaac.

Sadly Isaac was dead. Fortunately Isaac was not dead. There is no record of this ambiguity troubling Rebecca as, we shall see, it did Isaac's mother.

CHAPTER FIFTEEN

The Life of Sarah

arah died in Hebron, 127 years old, her death narrated in the first verse of the *parshah* titled *Chayei Sarah*, which means "The Life of Sarah." Abraham was still away from home in the land of Moriah. It seems from Rashi's notations that having left the site of the Akedah, he proceeded directly to Beersheba, bypassing Hebron.[1] Thus after he and his son departed for the alleged trip to deposit Isaac with Malchizedek, the patriarch never again saw his wife alive. With this point in mind, a glance at any map of Israel offers a less-than-cheerful commentary on their marriage.

Abraham had just gone through the climactic event of his life. Yet he did not rush home to tell his wife what had happened.

We know this because there is only one logical route from Jerusalem, the site of Mt. Moriah, to Beersheba: the road called Derech Ephratah, the Way to Ephrat. Proceeding south-southwest, it passes more or less in a straight line through Bethlehem, then Hebron, then Beersheba. Either Abraham took the Derech Ephratah and slipped through Hebron without Sarah's noticing, or he took some other, much more roundabout path so as to avoid Hebron and Sarah completely.

Did he feel guilty at having lied to her? Recall that we are talking about transportation not by automobile, but on foot or by donkey, where a detour means additional days and increased danger. Possible guilt feelings can't explain what appears to have been a powerful wish to avoid meeting his wife. Instead, he made his way to the *eshel*, which offered the companionship of travelers and others who required his spiritual ministrations. There would seem to be something wrong with a marriage in which the husband experiences a cataclysm and does not rush to tell his wife. Did Abraham then find solace in his career that he could not find at home?

There is another possibility. As we noted earlier, Sarah's intellect was different from Abraham's, and the difference is expressed in the Hebrew terms *mishpat* and *chesed*, loosely translated as "justice" and "kindness." With her orientation toward *mishpat*, Sarah had a difficult time accepting paradoxes, the curves and knots in the fabric of reality. A modern writer expresses this in the word "contingency," the idea that death and life are separated from each other by a hair's breadth.[2] The narrative of our lives does not proceed along a line as straight as the Derech Ephratah, but rather twists and spins almost as if it had no goal. Often God makes it *appear* as if our fates depended purely on chance. That fact, of which the Akedah was a paradigmatic example, makes a *mishpat* personality deeply uncomfortable.

What Sarah did not find difficult was telling hard truths, under any circumstance, as she did when Abraham needed to be told that Ishmael and Hagar must be expelled. With his personality more oriented toward *chesed*, Abraham could easily wrap his soul around curves and knots. But while he challenged public opinion fearlessly, telling hard truths to individuals—who would be hurt by those truths—did not come easily to him. Abraham was an exceptionally *nice* man. He knew that explaining the Akedah to his wife would be a torment to them both. So he put it off by going first to Beersheba and the *eshel*—a place in one respect like other inns and taverns through history, where everyone knows your name and a person, especially a man, can feel free to express the contradictions in his life.

He was right to fear that the Akedah would unhinge Sarah's mind, even to the point of placing her in mortal danger. The biblical text characteristically leaves blank her cause of death. "Sarah died at Kiryat Arbah, which is Hebron, in the land of Canaan."[3] Rashi speaks of her soul "flying away."[4] Was it a heart attack? A stroke? But *Pirke d'Rabbi Eliezer* notes that her cries and wails in death are reproduced in the sobbing notes of the shofar at Rosh Hashanah, which doesn't sound like a death from natural causes.[5]

Indeed, Rashi explains that the story of the Akedah and that of Sarah's death are juxtaposed, one immediately following the other, because the former *caused* the latter.[6] A midrash gives the details.

Having catalyzed the Akedah itself, Satan considered his work incomplete. About the time that Abraham and Isaac were descending the mountain, the Accuser appeared to Sarah in the form of Isaac. There must have been something ghostly about his appearance, for she said, "My son, what has your father done to you?"

Said Isaac-Satan, "My father took me and brought me up mountains and down into valleys. [Finally] he brought me up to the top of a particular mountain. He built an altar, prepared it, set out the wood, and bound me atop the altar. Then he took the knife to slay me as a sacrifice. Had the Holy One Blessed Be He not said to him, 'Do not stretch out your hand against the lad,' I would already have been slain."

The midrash continues: "He had barely finished speaking when her soul went out," and she died.[7]

Satan is a gossipmonger, and it tends to be the way of gossips not to lie outright, but to twist the truth, casting the object of their malice in the ugliest light. In this case, the Satan—that is, the Satan in Sarah—got the Akedah right but for one detail: namely, that the whole enterprise was at God's direction. There is no lie in the account. Only a fatal omission.

The Bible views the death of a person as a comment on that person's life. Moses, Aaron, and their sister, Miriam, for instance, all died by God's "kiss"—the most exalted exit for a human being that can be imagined. That Sarah should die, wailing and sobbing because she listened to Satan, does not reflect well on her.

In particular, it reflects a tendency not to believe the best of her spouse—

a grave fault in a marriage. Judging her husband unfavorably was her beset-
ting temptation. Kind Abraham had believed the best about Ishmael, and
before that about Hagar, long past the point when he should have reconsidered. After Hagar became pregnant the first time and got into the habit of
belittling her barren mistress, Sarah with her keener eye for human frailty at
last had to demand of her husband that Hagar be knocked down from her
perch as wife no. 2. She blamed Abraham for the "injustice" she had suffered
through Hagar's pride and called on God to set things right: "May the Lord
judge between me and you!"[8]

The Talmud fastens onto that harsh statement as the root cause of Sarah's
early death. We saw that praying for someone else, who needs the same benefit you do, will result in your need being answered first. Judging others before yourself works the same way: "He who calls down [divine] judgment
on his neighbor is himself punished first."[9] For there are three things that attract to a person the attention of God the Judge. The other two are walking in a dangerous place, and praying in such a way that conveys your
expectation that your prayers will be answered. All suggest a certain over-
confidence in your own righteousness. For example, you place yourself in
physical danger and then expect, because you're so terrific, that God will
protect you. Instead, He says, "Ah-hah, you think you're wonderful. Let's
take a closer look, shall we?"

The matriarch now received that closer look. She was tempted one last
time. When Satan presented her with the challenge of finding the best
interpretation of an incomplete narrative of the Akedah, she chose to believe
the worst. Her vulnerability to life's "contingency" was thus laid bare. As
Rashi says, "her son was prepared for slaughter, and was nearly slaughtered."[10] But for God's last-minute interruption, it might have happened—
an intolerable idea for Sarah. God might have saved her then, but He
did not.

In Beersheba, Abraham heard the news. After making the short journey
north to Hebron, he found the body of the matriarch in her tent.[11] Scripture speaks of his "eulogizing" and "bewailing" Sarah. According to tradition, his eulogy is preserved in the twenty-two verses at the end of the

Bible's Book of Proverbs: an ode to wifely virtue, which begins, "Who can find a woman of valor? Her price is far above pearls. Her husband's heart relies on her."[12] Customarily this hymn, called "Aishet Chayl," "A Woman of Valor," is sung by a Jewish husband to his wife on their wedding day, on his knees, and again each Sabbath evening for the rest of their lives.

Abraham also bewailed his *aishet chail*. But in keeping with the ideal of Jewish mourning, which is supposed to be neither showy nor overly lachrymose but rather understated, Abraham cut his own mourning short. We may imagine him on his knees, simply reciting the verses that became "Aishet Chail."

Then "Abraham rose up from the face of his dead."[13] The Midrash notes the extraneousness of Scripture's phrase. Obviously he got up from Sarah's presence! Why bother telling us he did?

Because he might have continued there, kneeling before her. Just then his own Satan assaulted him for the last time. Sometimes the Satan tempts by suggesting to us that we are *less* exalted as human beings than we really are. Sometimes he tempts by suggesting that we are *more* exalted. Abraham's temptation now was to blame himself for Sarah's death. It is a temptation we have all felt—to think that everyone else's fate depends on us. Self-aggrandizing and infantile at the same time, it pictures us at the center of not only our own world but that of every other person we know.

As for Abraham, he knew that Sarah had been grieved by Isaac's departure for Malchizedek's academy. Maybe sadness had overcome and killed her. Thus while he was kneeling, he saw a vision of Satan in the form of the angel of death, taunting him.[14] The angel said he was at fault for what had happened to Sarah.

But Abraham refused to listen. Rising up from his wife, he busied himself with the task of finding an appropriate burial place.

This required him to negotiate with the local worthies, whom the Bible in a usual translation calls Hittites—a problematic identification. Actually in Hebrew they are the Bene Chayt, "the Sons of Chayt"—Chayt, or Heth, being a son of Canaan, who was in turn a son of Noah's son Ham.[15] In the scheme of biblical tradition, all humanity descends from Noah's three sons, Ham, Shem, and Japheth, each associated with a certain wide geographic area: Ham with Africa plus the land of Canaan, Shem with Asia, Japheth with Europe. We should expect to find sons of Chayt in the land of Chayt's Hamitic ancestor, Canaan. We should not expect to find Hittites, who were originally from Anatolia, the Asian part of modern Turkey. The Hittites were descendants of native Anatolians who near the beginning of the second millennium B.C. had been invaded by Indo-Europeans with whom they interbred. Since tradition understands Europeans as being the descendants of Noah's son Japheth, the people known to history as Hittites would not have been, in biblical terms, a Hamitic nation, but rather would have descended from Japheth.

Thus the identification is problematic on the biblical level, but also on the more purely historical. There is no evidence that the historical Hittites—who spoke the earliest known Indo-European tongue and formed an imperial political entity between about 1600 and 1200 B.C.—were ever on the scene in Canaan in Abraham's time. All around it seems best not to call the notable residents of Hebron Hittites at all, but rather, as the Bible itself does, simply Bene Chayt, an indigenous Canaanite group as yet unknown to archaeology, and to leave it at that.[16] It's also possible that the Hebronite population was mixed, containing both Bene Chayt *and* Amorite. Having analyzed the names of the Hebronites given in the Bible, Albright concluded that the population was Amorite with, perhaps reflecting a later historical situation, "Hittite" rulers.[17] Indeed, the Book of Joshua, which describes the conquest of the land of Canaan by the Israelites four centuries after Abraham was there, refers to the king of Hebron in Joshua's day, called Hoham, as one of the "kings of the Amorites" in the land.[18] So then, combining the historical and biblical perspectives, let us adopt the provisional view that most of the citizens were Amorite by ethnicity while the town dignitaries were revered as descendants of Chayt.

Not much of their city survives. On the hill of Tel Roumeidah, in the modern Jewish quarter of Hebron, a small dig reveals the town wall dating from about 2000 B.C. with an equally ancient stepped pavement running alongside. Perhaps in Abraham's day these steps led up to the gates of Hebron, where the patriarch would soon stand before the city elders, pleading for a crypt in which to bury his wife.

From Tel Roumeidah, the tomb he had in mind can be glimpsed today from a concrete path running around the edge of some trailer homes. Jewish people, today a most unwelcome minority, occupy the trailers, which are protected by sandbags.

Elsewhere the Bible speaks of the "valley of Hebron,"[19] and the valley, as opposed to the elevated Tel Roumeidah, seems to be the declivity between hills where Zohar's son Ephron had a field. The "tomb" back then was just an outwardly undistinguished cave, the one Abraham had stumbled on thirty-eight years before when the angels came to announce Isaac's birth. Here, chasing after a stray calf to serve to his three angelic visitors, Abraham entered the cave that smelled of Paradise and that disclosed the resting place of Adam and Eve. Ever since, he had wanted to be buried there himself along with Sarah.

Actually to say that he "wanted" to be buried in Ephron's field is an understatement. He wanted it like he had wanted no possession ever before.

Ephron was unaware of the significance of the cave.[20] The Midrash portrays him as a meager, trifling person.[21] When Abraham, a far more distinguished neighbor, appeared before the council of the city, the councilmen were surprised to hear that he insisted on doing business with Ephron.

The institution of those who sat at the city gate to adjudicate such cases was familiar in the Near East of Abraham's day. At Nuzi, source of the famous cache of legal documents, many tablets were found bearing the phrase, this "was written after the proclamation in the entrance of the gate." The point of going to the "gate" was to assure oneself that the whole city knew of the decision that had been rendered, thus obviating the need for any further legal dealings in the matter.[22] Modest issues, especially having to do with property rights, were litigated here. Typically the assembly would meet in the morning. The councilmen would sit, while the litigants stood.[23]

That morning Abraham began directly with this request: "I am an alien and a resident among you. Give to me a holding of a grave with you that I may bury my dead from before you."[24]

They responded, calling him "Prince of God," for they were aware of Abraham's relationship with the Creator. After all, it was from Hebron that Abraham had gone forth to defeat the four kings who had invaded from the east. Angels would visit him at Hebron, and here the townfolk had seen Abraham and his household undergo the trial of circumcision.

There was a legal difficulty in his acquiring permanent possession of a grave. In Canaan, some localities refused to allow those who were not natives to own land altogether. In Ugarit, up the Mediterranean coast in today's Syria, made famous like Nuzi by the outstanding collection of documents found there, the historical Hittites themselves are known to have banned landownership by foreigners.[25] Nachmanides explains that it was the custom in Hebron for established families to have their designated burial place, while foreigners like Abraham were buried in a potter's field.[26] But the assemblymen at the gate replied that the patriarch, being a prince of God, could certainly bury Sarah in any of the already existing family burial plots he wished, indeed in "the choicest of our burial places."[27]

This was an honor, but Abraham demurred. He had a particular spot in mind, and he requested that Ephron, its owner, hear his offer of purchase. A stir must have passed through the assembled Hebronites. Why was he refusing their offer, which was in effect to spend eternity with them and their families? And what special relationship did he have with Ephron, who was a nobody?

But after all, a prince of God is a prince of God. It happened that Ephron was sitting at the gate himself that day. For the sake of good form, so that Abraham should not suffer the indignity of negotiating with a person of such low status, the assembly at once elevated Ephron to a rank that the Midrash, borrowing a Greek term, calls *archistrategos*—something like chief of the local militia.[28]

The new *archistrategos* quickly realized the position he had just been put in. For reasons unknown, this foreigner seemed determined to secure Ephron's miserable little field. The Midrash comments that Hebron was one of the rockiest places in the Holy Land, most unsuitable for agriculture; and visitors to the somewhat dreary modern town can see for themselves the accuracy of this assessment.[29] So Abraham didn't want it for farming. And Ephron knew that the patriarch had turned down the honor of burying his wife in the best crypt anyone locally possessed. Clearly the so-called prince of God had his reasons, which hardly mattered, actually.

What mattered was that he, Ephron, stood to take some serious advantage of the situation. He had two goals in the sale. First, to get as high a price as he could. Second, to sell not just the cave, which neither Ephron nor his father had ever bothered to explore, but the whole field.

Ephron first offered to give Abraham the land for free—a transparent gesture of false generosity. Rashi comments that little people, like Ephron, tend to be big talkers.[30] Ephron also specified that the property being negotiated was the whole field. But quickly the true asking price was revealed. "My lord," Ephron exclaimed, "listen to me! Land worth 400 shekels of silver—what is it, between me and you? Just bury your dead!"[31] When Abraham immediately took out his purse and began weighing out the price, Ephron knew he had a royal sucker on his hands. He said he meant not four hundred ordinary silver shekels, but a particular type of shekel, designated as *over la'socher,* literally "passing to the merchant" and having the sense of "universally negotiable."[32] That is, a measurement of weight so high such that any merchant anywhere would accept it. An equivalent phrase, in Akkadian, occurs often in Old Babylonian legal documents. This worked out to a very high price. In the biblical Near East, whole towns might be purchased for between one hundred and one thousand shekels.[33] The prophet Jeremiah bought a piece of land for just seventeen shekels.[34] Converting shekels *over la'-socher* to ordinary shekels, Rashi gives the value of Abraham's purchase as forty thousand of the latter, a price that *really* lifted poor Ephron up in the world.[35]

In a revealing scholarly disputation, the antiquity and authenticity of the biblical account of Abraham's purchase has been a focus of attention, pitting supporters of patriarchal historicity against skeptics. The supporters (Lehmann, Wright) thought they had found proof here for their position. An opinion was vouchsafed that what we have in this chapter is a "complete application" of certain laws that are straight out of Hittite jurisprudence from not later than 1200 B.C. In Hittite legal codes, burdensome feudal responsibilities (called *ilku*) attached to a piece of land, which could only be transferred to a buyer if the whole parcel, including all its natural features, like caves and trees, was purchased. If just some of the parcel was sold, for instance a cave in a field, then the owner of the original parcel was still obliged to provide all the *ilku* services.

This would explain the Bible's careful repetition of the details of the purchase: "the field and the cave within it and all the trees that were in the field, which was within its border all around."[36] Ephron, thinking like a Hittite, naturally wanted to ensure he was not left with *ilku*-related responsibilities. The scholarly supporters even claimed to discover in this and the surrounding verses the form of a classic Hittite business document.[37] If true, this would not only prove that the identification of Bene Chayt with the Hittites of Asia Minor—the former evidently being an enclave or colony of the latter—was tenable, after all. It would also beat back the more skeptical scholars who wish to say that the strand of narrative here (attributed to J) reflects a late tradition. In fact, it must reflect a tradition no earlier than 1200 B.C., when the Hittite empire collapsed.

The skeptics (Tucker, Van Seters) hit back with the assertion that there is a legal document embedded in the biblical text, but actually it dates to no earlier than the seventh to fifth centuries B.C., the so-called neo-Babylonian period. What our text most resembles is a neo-Babylonian "dialogue document," so called because it takes the form of a dialogue between interlocutors, recounting the specifics of the deal.[38] In other words, in Abraham's encounter with Ephron we find merely an attempt, from a time long after Abraham's putative lifetime, to give an authentic legal gloss to the story—certainly no indication that the patriarch was a historical character.

The truth is that nowhere in Genesis 23, which tells of Sarah's death and burial, is there embedded any text that a disinterested observer would recognize as a fragment of a real-estate contract. The interpretations of both the supporters and the skeptics are forced. There is no reference at all here to feudal obligations; and it's simply absurd to claim to discover a "dialogue document" because the Bible's account of the sale includes dialogue. That a real-estate negotiation should include reference to price and boundaries, offer of sale and acceptance of the deal, is hardly unique to any time or place. One gets the impression that the scholars involved approached the text wishing, however unconsciously, to defend a previously held belief: either that Abraham was a real person (supporters) or that he's a myth (skeptics).

If not to apprise us of the ways of ancient realtors, why, then, does the Bible devote so much attention to a seemingly trivial matter? Let it say, "And Abraham bought a cave in which to bury Sarah," and be done with it!

According to the Oral Torah, the point is to emphasize Abraham's understanding that, in purchasing the cave called Machpelah for Sarah's burial place, he was initiating a statement to the world. Therefore every detail must be attended to. The question of ownership must be left crystal-clear. Any price that needs to be paid will be paid. The statement has to do with marriage—on which Genesis 23, with its associated oral traditions, can be understood as a meditation.

We have seen that Abraham eulogized Sarah with the hymn "Aishet Chail," encapsulating what it means to be a Jewish wife. Rashi finds the theme of marriage in an alternative name given to Hebron, Kiryat Arbah, literally "the City of Four." It is named "after four couples who were buried there, man and wife: Adam and Eve, Abraham and Sarah, Isaac and Rebecca, [Isaac's son] Jacob and [his first wife] Leah"—the "Hall of Fame of Marriage," as a rabbi I know puts it.[39] The name "Hebron" itself alludes to the ultimate union of mortal souls: the Hebrew root "chet-bet-resh," or HBR, means "to join together." And, significantly, the Talmud's discussion of the laws having to do with the initiation of marriages, in tractate *Kiddushin,* opens with the statement that the very first law of betrothal is crystallized in Abraham's purchase of the Machpelah.[40] The exchange of money for Ephron's field in 1675 B.C. is reproduced each time a couple marries and the groom places a gold ring on his bride's finger. However troubling to modern sensitivities, the groom is literally purchasing the exclusive right to his bride. This is why the modern custom of exchanging wedding bands, where the bride gives the groom a ring as well, renders the traditional concept of a wedding ring essentially meaningless.

Though it sounds like the beginning of a Henny Youngman joke, Torah analogizes marriage with fields—and with burial. The equation of marriage and field isn't hard to understand, nor is it unique to Jewish thinking. The Fifth Dynasty Egyptian vizier Ptah-Hotep (circa 2450 B.C.) advised his son, "Make [your wife's] heart glad as long as you live. She is a profitable field for her lord."[41] He meant simply that a wife brings forth male heirs. Torah, though, goes further with the analogy. Marriage is like a field in that it needs to be nurtured and will bring forth only what has been carefully planted and then diligently tended. This having been done, it nourishes and sustains you. It brings wealth—not just in the form of children, but actual wealth. The Talmud stresses that the riches Abraham acquired in his time came only through the merit of his marriage to Sarah. Finally, contrary to how it might appear from the exchange of money in gold that effects the marriage, the relationship of "owner" to "owned" is very subtle. A person purchases land and in theory "owns" it, but what really owns whom? Anyone who "owns" real estate knows that it is just as accurate to say that the land *owns* the owner. It requires his constant attention, will hardly let him leave its presence if he wants to keep it in satisfactory condition. And the bonds of affection between owner and land famously run deep. So it goes with marriage. A man doesn't "own" his wife in the same way he "owns" a wristwatch. She comes to "own" him no less than the other way around.

Marriage is also like burial, which in turn is like planting in a field. This sounds rather grim, but it's not. The ultimate earthly "belonging" is of the body to the ground from which it sprang. This "belonging" the Torah means to parallel with another belonging: of the husband to the wife. The earth embraces us at death, at the "planting" of the body in the ground. In the traditional view, this leads to the ultimate in spiritual growth. We die, are buried, and are released bodily from the ground to the life after life. A new being has been born. In marriage, we find much the same process. A wife embraces her husband in the act of lovemaking, taking him within her body. He "plants" or "buries" himself as deep as he can. Then, if they are blessed, a new being springs up, released from her womb, and grows into another person, the "fruit" of their union.[42]

Since, as we noted earlier, Sarah was a somewhat difficult wife, it may seem ironic to find such observations about marriage encoded in the story of Abraham's parting from her. An incident recorded in the Talmud underlines the apparent irony. A couple of millennia after Sarah and Abraham were buried in the Machpelah, Rabbi Bana'ah happened by and was astonished to encounter the spirit of Abraham's servant Eliezer, who was guarding the entrance of the cave. They engaged in a rather odd conversation.

Bana'ah: "What is Abraham doing?"

Eliezer: "He is lying in Sarah's arms, and she is gazing at his head."

Bana'ah: "Go and tell [him] that Bana'ah is standing at the entrance [of the cave]."

Eliezer conveyed the news to Abraham, who replied, "Let him enter. It is well known there is no [sexual] inclination in this world [of the life after life]." At which Bana'ah entered, the Talmud recording no exchange between him and the patriarch.[43]

The meaning here is complex. Abraham lies in Sarah's arms—the gesture of female embrace that alludes to the embrace of the ground and of the grave, with all that implies about the process of human reproduction and creativity. In this process, the woman typically falls in love not with her husband's body, but with his head: his dreams, ambitions, and beliefs. Sarah and Abraham are thus pictured, of all the four couples residing in the Machpelah, as the ultimate expression of marital perfection. After all, in the cave at Kiryat Arbah, the Hall of Fame of Marriage, Bana'ah could have encountered Isaac and Rebecca or Jacob and Leah. Instead, he met the servant of Abraham and Sarah.

But their marriage reached this peak of perfection, it seems, only after death: when the dross of physical desire, or the sexual inclination, had been shed.

There are two lessons in the story of Bana'ah. First, that marriage is not a static state. Any given marriage continually develops and perfects itself over decades, as the material inclination burns itself up; and this process is consummated in the eternal life.

Second, a marriage transcends the two partners who create it. It is not just the relationship between husband and wife, but something much greater. Sarah was difficult when she was alive. Yet the Talmud depicts her marriage ultimately as the very paradigm of how a wife relates to her husband. A marriage can be perfect, somehow, mysteriously, even if the individual spouses are not. This is a comfort for those of us who find that, as spouses, we fall well short of the ideal.[44]

An imperfect wife in a perfect marriage, Sarah was buried in the cave in Ephron's field. Presumably Abraham buried her in Canaanite fashion, up to a point. We know a lot about funeral habits in the Middle Bronze Age because tombs—often family tombs like the Machpelah, with a vertical shaft running down into a cave and multiple generations interned within—are disproportionately what survive among archaeological remains. So probably she was buried in sheepskin, on her back with her knees raised, her arms thrown out to her sides. What seems unlikely is that Abraham followed the pagan customs of burying his dead with foodstuffs, scents, and other baggage to accompany her to the netherworld, or of moving her skull to one side of the chamber after the flesh had rotted off.[45] Our assumption is that the oral tradition is right when it says that Abraham intuited a large portion of later Jewish practice, which forbids such things.

The impact of her death was profound on Abraham and Isaac, but not only on them. All the people of Hebron, recalling her perhaps with a fondness they hadn't felt when she was alive, closed the doors of their businesses and came to mourn. They accompanied Abraham to the tomb and tried to repay some of the kindness they had received from him over the years.[46]

The Midrash likens Sarah's death to the destruction of the Temple. One often hears at Jewish Sabbath tables that the home stands in for the fallen Temple, the Sabbath meal taking the place of the sacrifices. Ramban explains that the reverse is true. The Temple stood in for the Jewish home, specifically Sarah's. There were certain features of the home she made for Abraham that find their echoes in the Temple and features of the Temple Mount. When she died, just as when the Temple was destroyed, all these must disappear.

When she was alive, over the door of her tent a cloud hung like the cloud of the divine Presence Abraham saw on Moriah. The doors of the family's tents were all open to greet wanderers, like the doors of the Temple that welcomed Jews and gentiles from the world over. There was a blessing in the bread she made—bread representing (as in English vernacular) the material prosperity that came to Abraham through Sarah. In the Temple, the shewbread, twelve loaves set out each Sabbath, was also associated with riches. Finally there was a light that always burned in the tent, like the fire on the Temple altar that was never extinguished.[47]

All these things returned only when Abraham found a wife for Isaac. The Midrash draws a causal relationship between the Akedah and the patriarch's search for a wife for his son. The patriarch thought to himself, "If [Isaac] had died on Mt. Moriah, he would have died without children [and my legacy would die with him]. Now what should I do?"[48] The answer was to marry him off. But it can't be coincidental that the narrative of the search comes not after the Akedah, but directly after Sarah's death.

The implication is clear. Husbands, unlike wives, don't tend to survive very well after their beloved partners pass away. You meet plenty of widows, but not many widowers (a fact that women in that situation find, to their distress, when they seek to remarry). The grief often kills them. We saw that before Isaac was conceived, God restored the patriarch to something like his youth. Thirty-seven years later, as another midrash notes, the full weight of his years "jumped upon" him.[49] As the biblical text says immediately upon concluding the narrative of Sarah's burial, "And Abraham was old."[50]

He thought—wrongly as it turned out—that he would soon die. Isaac was thirty-seven, when plenty of modern men are just beginning to look for their wives. But the succession of matriarchs no less than that of patriarchs required Abraham's personal intervention. The time to find a bride for his son was now.

CHAPTER SIXTEEN

The Two Faces of Eliezer

fter he had buried Sarah and his 137 years leaped upon him, Abraham concluded that the task of assuring that his heir would have an heir—that Isaac would marry and have children—must fall to someone else. The patriarch was too elderly to do it himself. His servant Eliezer must have been old as well, having accompanied Abraham to rescue Lot from the four kings sixty-two years earlier. But evidently he was spry enough to undertake a trying journey.

Abraham commanded Eliezer to place his hand under the patriarch's "thigh"—a biblical euphemism for the male organ, the place of his circumcision.[1] It was the mark to be shared by the members of Abraham's family, thus an appropriate symbol for endogamy, marrying within the family group, on which Abraham's descendants have insisted down to this day. Abraham then warned him, casting Eliezer under a curse should he let Isaac marry a local girl.[2] "And I will cause you to swear by the Lord, God of the heavens and God of the earth, that you will not take a wife for my son from the daughters of the Canaanites among whom I dwell. Rather to my country [that is, Mesopotamia] and my family shall you go and take a wife for my son, for Isaac."[3] The servant first questioned his master—what if no such woman could be found willing to accompany him back to Canaan?—but then accepted the charge.

For all his commitment to duty, Eliezer is an ambivalent figure, hard to pin down. First of all, we should not see him as any kind of lowly step'n'fetchit slave of modern imagining. In the ancient Near East, a servant need not have been servile. He could own property, even a large estate including other slaves.[4] To be a servant was no mark of shame.

With this, the oral tradition concurs. On one hand, Eliezer is self-effacing. Throughout the chapter (Genesis 24) that recounts the search for Isaac's bride, his proper name is never given; he is identified only as ha'eved, "the slave," or simply ha'ish, "the man." On the other hand, Eliezer is portrayed as second-in-command to Abraham, his spokesman to the world—St. Paul to Abraham's Jesus, one might say—overseeing all the material and spiritual wants of Abraham's community.[5] He is the "elder of his house," with all that the term "elder," zaken, implies by way of acquired wisdom.[6] In his relationship with Abraham, Eliezer thus seems to model the ideal relationship of any person to God: losing yourself in Him, in the purpose on earth He gives you.

Yet the tradition offers another, much less saintly, Eliezer. At Mt. Moriah, Abraham had chosen to leave him behind with Ishmael, dismissing them both as spiritual "donkeys." Now we learn that Eliezer secretly hoped he would find no suitable girl in Haran, that he hoped ultimately to marry off his own daughter to Isaac.[7] Abraham sensed this and warned him to "beware of yourself."[8] As we will see, when he returned with what indeed appeared to be a suitable girl, he was suspected of having ruined her morally. In terms of other biblical characters, the tradition includes some intriguing speculations about who Eliezer truly was. One view says that he was Ham's son Canaan, who had sought to elude his grandfather Noah's curse by apprenticing himself to Abraham.[9] The meaning seems to be not that Eliezer was literally Canaan, but rather that he was a spiritual descendant of Ham's son, having inherited the base tendencies of his ancestor.

The two faces of Eliezer have been plausibly explained as a warning about discipleship. In Rashi's words, he would "draw water and give drink to others from the Teaching of his master"—water, as we have seen, being a metaphor for wisdom. The water was never his own. This is the danger in having a great teacher—or a great father, which ought to be the same thing. Learning from a teacher is essential to spiritual growth, but equally important is learning to think independently of your teacher. Failing to do that, going through life as a puppet or mouthpiece of someone who influenced you, repeating his ideas and never coming up with an idea of your own, twists the spirit of the disciple. So it was with Eliezer.[10]

To this complicated man, Abraham entrusted the fate of his whole mission in life, which could not survive another two generations unless Isaac had a son worthy of him. But the Lord guides the arrangement of marriages. The Talmud even says that since He finished the work of creation, He has done nothing *but* labor to join the right wives with the right husbands—a task as hard as it was to split the Sea of Reeds for the Israelites fleeing Egypt.[11]

There does not appear to have been any such problem with Isaac. His role in the present narrative is totally passive—as befits a son in the ancient Near East, where it was the father who initiated the process of finding his boy a wife, and whose permission was needed for matrimony to take place.[12] Here there were two fathers in control of his destiny, one earthly, the other divine. So resistance truly would have been futile.

The Talmud also says that "40 days before the formation of the embryo, a voice [from Heaven] goes forth and says, 'The daughter of so-and-so is [destined] for so-and-so.' "[13] Therefore, God had already chosen Isaac's wife for him. Eliezer needed only to find her and bring her back. Of course, if he blundered and somehow fastened on the wrong girl, the magnitude of the ensuing disaster would depend on how soon the error was caught—before the marriage or long after.

Abraham had no doubt that Isaac's bride must not be sought among the Canaanites near at hand. Instead, Eliezer would have to travel back to Abraham's ancestral home, north to Haran. This fact should trouble us.

Abraham had spent the past six decades ministering to the people of his adopted land. He sat out before his tent waiting for travelers to pass his door, wishing to feed them and turn their hearts toward God. He built the *eshel,* that forerunner of a Salvation Army soup kitchen. The people of Hebron called him "Prince of God," but we call him the founder of monotheism; and the infant monotheistic movement must have amounted now to a sizable community of followers.

Those followers were Canaanites. Yet among all of them, not one had a daughter to whom he would entrust Isaac. But Abraham declined to give even Eliezer's daughter this honor. What is the Bible telling us about Canaanites? Or more important, what is it telling us about Abraham as a spiritual master? What kind of charismatic religious leader raises up a crowd of disciples, none of them good enough to marry into his family? An unsuccessful charismatic religious leader, one might be tempted to say.

But speaking with Eliezer about finding a match for Isaac, he invoked the name of "the Lord, God of the heavens and God of the earth," on which Rashi notes that when Abraham began his career, the Lord had been only "God of the heavens." Before Abraham started teaching, He was unknown on earth.[14] That hardly makes Abraham sound like a failure.

He developed a way of understanding God which he passed to his son (Isaac), which *he* passed to *his* son (Jacob), which *he* passed to *his* children and to succeeding generations down through our own time. The Midrash understands part of a verse in Isaiah, a reference to "Jacob who redeemed Abraham," as teaching that Abraham was saved from the Fiery Furnace by virtue of his being destined to have a son called Isaac, who was destined to have a son called Jacob.[15] That is, Abraham's greatest merit was in establishing a line of teachers including Jacob, from whom the message of God's unity branched out to the world. That merit saved his life.

But there is no record of his nucleus of disciples surviving as a movement in any form for more than a couple of generations. It would seem that, whatever community might have clustered around the family of Abraham, Isaac, and Jacob, those believers were left behind, to blend back into the surrounding pagan culture, when Jacob took the family to Egypt—where they stayed for two centuries, till the Exodus. When the Israelites returned to Canaan as a conquering army under Joshua, they found no believers in the ideas Abraham had taught.

Shortly before that conquest, God instructed the Israelites to shun "the practice of the land of Canaan to which I bring you, and do not follow their statutes."[16] On this verse, Rashi comments that "the practices of the Egyptians and the Canaanites were the most degenerate of all nations."[17]

This appears to mean that the problem was not Abraham's—that, instead, there was something intransigently perverse about the Canaanites. Their moral deficiency as a nation prevented the seed of Abraham's teaching from growing into a tree strong enough to survive the passage of time. Abraham understood this and feared to entrust his posterity to a Canaanite woman.

We noted some of the unattractive aspects of life among the Canaanites, who seem to have grown more floridly wicked by the time Joshua arrived. Some scholars think Canaanites buried firstborn children alive under the foundations of their newly built homes. In later times, the priests of Baal engaged in bestiality.[18] The Gerarites in particular had a culture that appeared civilized but at closer inspection revealed a deeper stratum of amorality. What was the nature of this ingrained perversity to which the Canaanites were subject?

One answer is hinted at in a midrash: "And what did [the Canaanites] do? A man would marry a man, and a woman would marry a woman."[19] This doesn't necessarily mean they allowed homosexual marriage, or "same-sex domestic partnership" as we would call it nowadays. The point is that their culture was a variation on the one Abraham's nephew Lot had encountered in Sodom. The essential corruption of Sodom was not "sodomy" but selfishness, of which the Bible sees homosexual intercourse as emblematic. When a man and woman make love, they exchange physical pleasure. But, assuming they don't use contraception, there is also the possibility of giving to one another a gift of permanent significance: a child. A man who marries a man, or a woman a woman, gives up on providing that everlasting good to another person. And because the partners in such a union are both men or both women, even their passing pleasure has a narcissistic quality: you are pleasing yourself and someone very much like yourself, rather than being compelled to learn to please a profoundly different sort of creature.

So it was with the Canaanites in general, whose eponymous ancestor, Canaan, was cursed because of the greed of his father, Ham. The Talmud relates that after the Flood, which destroyed humanity, Ham castrated his own father, Noah. This was to ensure that the old man would sire no further potential heirs to compete with Ham in dividing up the postdiluvian world. The Bible sees certain negative cultural traits as tough stains in the cloth of an extended family, persisting through generations. Abraham, who had devoted his life to the virtue of *chesed,* of giving, could not take the chance of seeing Isaac paired with a Canaanite, who carried the opposite tendency almost in her blood.

Or at least this is one answer, not an entirely satisfying one, to the question of what happened to Abraham's followers. Is it not reasonable to assume, given that this man planted the seeds of the religions of half the world's present population, that the patriarch was an electric personality of a kind that would dim the light of any charismatic person we know today? Must not his personality have had the power to change souls? Indeed, the Book of Genesis itself (12:5) credits him with *"making"* souls! (By which the Bible means that he converted them to his faith in the One God—converts in the tens of thousands, as Maimonides says.) Is it not urgent that we ask: no matter what the cultural flaws of the Canaanite peoples, what happened to the very special Canaanites that Abraham attracted or, as a leader and a teacher, created? We shall return to this problem in the conclusion of this book.

Providence aided Eliezer. Before he left, Abraham put in his hand a deed to his possessions, material and spiritual.[20] This was so that Isaac's bride-to-be might be assured that the young man really was the chosen spiritual successor of the great patriarch, while her family would be assured that their daughter would be comfortably taken care of. Accompanied by a caravan of transport animals and attendants, Eliezer set off.

From Beersheba, it promised to be a journey of three or four weeks to what the Bible calls "Nachor's city," that is, Haran—Nachor being Abraham's brother who had remained in Mesopotamia.[21] (The identification is clear because in "Nachor's city," Eliezer meets the crafty Laban, who elsewhere in Genesis is clearly pictured as living at Haran.)[22] Yet something supernatural occurred on the road that cut Eliezer's travel time dramatically. Instead of three weeks, it took him only three hours.[23] This is evidenced from his remark later that he "came today" to Haran, suggesting that he left and arrived on the same day. As Rashi explains, the earth "contracted" or, literally, "jumped to him."[24] We don't need to postulate here a massive violation of the laws of plate tectonics. Rather, God miraculously transported Eliezer so that it *seemed* as if the earth contracted.

Eliezer alighted in Haran. Naturally his precise destination would be a well—where, in a desert, town and country dwellers alike would gather, along with any travelers passing nearby. It was the obvious place to go not only to water yourself and your animals but to hear news about the locals. If Eliezer was to locate whatever remained of Abraham's family in Haran, he must go to the well.

Today the citizens of Haran will point you to the well outside the walls of the ancient city where a wife was procured for Ibrahim's son. Enclosed in a concrete bunker and strewn with trash, it looks more like a latrine. A stairway leads down into a darkness thick with some fetid odor. A few dilapidated houses are nearby, and a couple of Arab children stared at us as we got out of the car to have a look. In 1675 B.C., it would have been more lively, and more hygienic. It was evening, the cool of the day when women go to draw water and to gossip.[25]

Eliezer observed the scene and uttered a prayer to God that He should "cause it to chance," *hakreh,* that Eliezer should find the right woman—an interesting way of phrasing the idea of divine providence. The root of the verb *hakreh* implies randomness, but in grammatical terms the verb appears in its causative form, the conjugation called *hifil* in Hebrew. In other words, God operates in the world through events that *seem* to come about by chance. His interventions in our lives are concealed by the appearance of randomness.

Specifically Eliezer asked the Lord to indicate to him which girl was the one for Isaac. When he asked her for water, if she should then offer refreshment not only to him but to his camels, this would mean that God looked favorably on her as a wife for Isaac. Or so Eliezer prayed. The Talmud and Midrash question him for taking what appears to be a gamble with Isaac's fate. What if the girl that Eliezer approached said the right thing but turned out to be in some way morally impaired? As the Talmud puts it, in this moral sense she might be "lame" or "blind"—handicapped in her inclination to do good, or unable to perceive spiritual truth.[26]

But there was a logic to Eliezer's apparent recklessness, which is why God cooperated with him. The servant wished to test any potential wife for Isaac, looking for the quality of exquisite kindness, *chesed,* that was the hallmark of Abraham's household. The key to his test was the offer to give water to his camels as well as to Eliezer himself. The Torah isn't concerned with thirsty camels per se. Consideration to animals is a fine quality to have, but plenty of nasty people love animals. (Hitler, an ardent animal-fancier, comes to mind.) The test was to have the following significance. The girl would be coming down to the well with a pitcher, which she planned to fill and bring back to her family. Let's say she gives Eliezer a drink from this pitcher. Anyone with a proper concern for hygiene would be concerned about letting some dirty stranger gulp water out of her pitcher and then bringing the same vessel home unwashed. But if she washed the pitcher in front of the stranger, that would hurt his feelings! The really sensitive thing to do would be to give the stranger his drink, then offer water to his animals, bringing the pitcher in close contact with the trough from which animals drank. She would *then* wash the pitcher of any traces of camel spit. This would allow her both to bring home a clean pitcher *and* to save the feelings of the traveler. One of the homelier themes of Torah is God's concern with logistics: he wants us to think ahead. Observance of the Sabbath and of the dietary laws, for instance, both rely heavily on preparing one's needs well ahead of time. Any young woman who planned her kindnesses so many steps in advance, like a chess player, would be an appropriate marriage candidate for Isaac.[27]

Eliezer had barely finished asking God's assistance when a young woman caught his eye. The Bible, with its often expressed appreciation of female beauty, tells us frankly that she was "exceptionally good looking."[28] It does not tell us her age. One tradition says she was only three years old, suggesting that this future matriarch had matured at a supernatural pace! Another opinion, easier to accept, is that she was fourteen, an age at which girls in the ancient Near East commonly were wed.[29] She was Rebecca, daughter of Bethuel, whose father was Abraham's brother Nachor. That is, she was Abraham's grandniece.

But Eliezer didn't know this when he approached her—which he did because God gave him a sign that literally jumped out at him. Or rather, jumped out at Rebecca. When she came close to the well, the water miraculously rose up to meet her.[30] Everyone saw it happen and gasped. In the Abraham story, water once before had risen of itself from a well. When the patriarch was disputing with Avimelech the ownership of a well near Gerar, God proved to everyone that the well was Abraham's by causing the water to rise by itself to water the patriarch's flock. There the meaning was that Torah, represented by water, rose up to spiritually refresh Abraham's flock, his disciples, through the merit of the patriarch himself. Here the meaning is the same. Torah was about to rise up to meet Rebecca.

This midrash about the water from the well may sound outlandish, but it is needed in order to resolve the first of two textual difficulties. Describing Eliezer's meeting with Rebecca, the Bible gives the following sequence of actions. He arrives at the well, looking for a girl who's a member of Abraham's extended family. He prays for the sign whereby he will know he has found the right young lady. Rebecca arrives. Eliezer approaches her and asks for water. She readily agrees and offers to water his animals as well—thus apparently giving the sign he prayed for. Amazed at what seems to be the successful conclusion of his quest, he gives Rebecca gifts of jewelry. This is the bride price, to be paid, according to Near Eastern custom, by the groom's father.[31] The offer of valuables, and their acceptance, apparently seal Rebecca's engagement to Isaac. Then Eliezer asks her, "Whose daughter are you?"[32]

The first problem here is: what made him approach Rebecca in the first place? The answer is: he saw the water rise up for her and knew she must be a special girl.

A second problem in the text likewise requires that we consult the oral tradition: why does he give her the gifts before inquiring about her father? Abraham's strict instructions had been to seek a member of Terach's family in Haran. There were other families in town, obviously, and the miracle of the water, as narrated in the Midrash, proved nothing about Rebecca's lineage. Without this midrash, the problem is still more perplexing. According to the plain text, all he had to go on was her offer of water to the camels. But if that was all the proof he needed, why does he bother to ask her father's name at all?

The text without the tradition simply doesn't make sense. Fortunately the rabbis step in and make clear the esoteric meaning of Eliezer's gifts. The plain text says he gave her "a gold nose ring, its weight a *beka,* and two bracelets on her arms, ten gold shekels their weight."[33] But a rabbinic principle holds that the Torah, being God's own composition, doesn't waste words. Here the word *beka* seems superfluous, being the usual weight of a nose ring, give or take some tenths of an ounce. Why bother telling us the exact weight? The word "two" also serves no obviously significant purpose. Does it really matter if she received one, two, three, or four bracelets?

In fact, what we have here is code. The Bible's hidden point is not to detail any gift of real jewelry. Though scholars have labored to define the exact weight of a *beka*—half a shekel, Speiser affirms, or 6.1 ounces, says Gordon[34]—that word in fact needs to be analyzed for its *gematria*. When converted to their numerical equivalents, the letters that spell it out, "bet-kuf-ayin," add up to 172. This is the number of words in the text of the Ten Commandments. The two bracelets allude to the two tablets of the Ten Commandments, while the ten gold shekels refer to the Ten Commandments themselves.[35] The Ten Commandments are understood to represent, in a most abbreviated form, all the 613 commandments that constitute the body of Torah law. Every one of the 613 can be arranged under the heading of one of the Ten.

In short, what Eliezer gave Rebecca was the gift of God's teaching. He sat her down and began teaching what he had learned from Abraham. In the form of this dusty stranger from the desert, the water of divine Truth came to her.

This was the servant's third test of the girl. Some people respond to Torah the way a thirsty man does to water: they gulp it down. Others will have none of it. Eliezer saw that Rebecca responded with gusto. Having already observed the water rising up to her (test no. 1) and heard her answer to his request for water (test no. 2), he knew it was worth inquiring about her family. This last was to be his fourth and final test.

She said, "I am the daughter of Bethuel, son of Milkah, whom she bore to Nachor."[36] This was indeed the right girl. It remained only to seal the marriage agreement and bring her home.

Rebecca ran to tell her mother, of whom we hear nothing further. Nor do we hear anything more about her father, Bethuel, until after her brother, Laban, has taken the matter of Rebecca's engagement exclusively into his own hands. When Eliezer comes to Laban's home and tells of his quest for a wife for Isaac, the Bible has "Laban and Bethuel" answering, "The matter has come from the Lord. We are unable to say a word to you, either bad or good. Here is Rebecca before you. Take [her] and go. Let her be a wife to the son of your master as the Lord has spoken."[37] Eliezer then ate with the family and slept the night in their house. Apart from these two mentions of Bethuel, the father seems to have been left entirely out of the negotiation. Speiser condescendingly notes that we have here yet another editing blunder, "a marginal gloss on the part of some ancient scribe who did not realize that the father had no place in this narrative."[38] But Rashi explains that Bethuel was secretly plotting to stop the marriage. That night the family and its visitor went to sleep, and Bethuel died, having been slain in bed by an angel.[39] The general nonparticipation of Rebecca's father may also have to do with the institution of fratriarchy, well known now from the Nuzi documents, in which a son might displace his father in certain family leadership functions in relation to his siblings.[40]

Laban wasn't eager to see Rebecca go live in Abraham's community, either. Later, in the story of Jacob's sojourn at Haran, the biblical narrative will clearly reveal Bethuel's son as the scoundrel he was. Here we must rely on the oral tradition to amplify the little notes of tension between Laban and Abraham's representative. When Laban heard Rebecca excitedly telling her mother about the proposal to marry Isaac, he rushed out to meet Eliezer, hailing him as "Blessed of the Lord."[41] The Midrash notes that he mistook the slave for the master: Eliezer had served Abraham so well over the decades that he had actually come to physically resemble the patriarch[42]—just as the human who serves God faithfully will absorb certain godlike personality traits. Laban thought that Abraham himself had come to Haran and greeted him accordingly. We find a hint of Laban's nervousness at the encounter in his invitation, "Why should you stand outside, when I have cleared the house and [set] a place for the camels?"[43] What he had "cleared" from the house was the evidence of idolatry[44]—images of gods that in "Abraham's" presence he was ashamed to admit that he worshiped.

The mistaken identity was shortly cleared up. Before the household and its visitor ate, Eliezer showed Laban the document proving that Abraham had deeded to Isaac the spiritual leadership of the nascent monotheistic faith, as well as the patriarch's riches.[45] He handed out gifts of jewelry, clothing, and food. Everyone then retired for the night.

Next morning the proposal was put formally to Rebecca. By now Bethuel had been found dead, an ominous sign, and the Midrash describes the family as "aggrieved and crushed" at the prospect of losing Rebecca as well.[46] They hoped she would refuse. But in line with the regional custom of the period, a woman had the right to answer such a proposal herself, and Rebecca agreed.[47]

The return trip was likewise abbreviated, three hours instead of three weeks, as had happened on the way to Haran.[48] The Bible says, "Then Rebecca rose up with her handmaidens; they rode upon the camels and they went after the man; and the servant took Rebecca and went."[49] Yet again, as when Eliezer first met her, the narrative seems to mix up the order of events. In this one verse, we find Rebecca "rising up" and "riding," then Eliezer "taking" her and "going." But surely he first *took* her, *then* she rode!

The biblical text alludes to something dark. We noted that Eliezer had been ambivalent about relinquishing the prospect of marrying his own daughter to Isaac. When Rebecca turned up at the site of the well immediately upon his own arrival there, he had been "astonished," in Hebrew *mishtaeh*.[50] About this word, Rashi suggests that its connotation is not entirely positive. There is a note of "desolation," of "shock" at an unfavorable outcome.[51] Eliezer was not happy to find that God had guided his way so definitively. He would have preferred to bring home no girl at all from Haran.

The Bible gives no overt indication that their return journey was at all eventful. But there is a covert hint that Abraham would later suspect Eliezer, during the trip, of seeking to foil the match with Isaac. The Hebrew words normally translated as "and the servant took Rebecca," *va'yikach ha'eved et Rivkah,* could also mean "and the servant consummated a sexual relationship with Rebecca." In English, a man may "take" a woman sexually. So may he do in Hebrew.[52] This would mean that Eliezer had acted upon his Hamite instinct to greedily snatch joy from others—in this case, stealing Isaac's joy at being the first man to know Rebecca. What appears to be a mixed-up retelling of the departure and journey is then an allusion to Abraham's suspicion.

Isaac suspected nothing as yet. Having finished a three-year apprenticeship with Malchizedek, he was now forty years old and living at Beersheba but had come to Hebron, by way of Beer-lahai-roi. He had brought with him none other than Hagar, whom he wished to reunite with his father (of which more later). It was the afternoon, and Isaac had made it a personal custom to pray at a certain time before the sun set, as Abraham made it a custom to pray early in the morning. Thus the Talmud credits Isaac with establishing the afternoon prayer, Minchah, as Abraham established Shacharit—a place to which one may go to speak with God, not unlike a physical sanctuary but created in the dimension of time rather than of space.[53] He liked to pray among a grove of trees, walking about, deep in meditation.[54]

His thoughts were interrupted by the arrival of Eliezer and Rebecca. He looked up, and there they were. We aren't told about Isaac's reaction to his first meeting with Rebecca, but the young lady swooned. A midrash notes that while he was lying upon the altar at Moriah, waiting to be slaughtered by Abraham, Isaac had been covered by a shimmering light. This radiance remained with him even now, and Rebecca caught sight of it. She became dizzy at his radiant beauty and fell from her mount.

After Eliezer had helped her up, she said, "Who is that man, walking in the field to meet us?"

The servant said, "He is my master,"[55] for Abraham had deeded to Isaac his estate, including his servants.

Meanwhile Abraham was concerned. He must have sensed a subtle shiftiness in his servant's face. We have seen that Eliezer's soul was divided between nobility and corruption, that the selfishness and resentfulness of Noah's son Ham ran deep in him. Though it pained Abraham to cause his soon-to-be daughter-in-law any distress, he was haunted by the possibility that Eliezer had been overcome by his dark side and had in some way violated the girl. If so, his compassion would have been powerfully stirred; but there was something more important at stake even than the feelings of an innocent young woman.

In an ordinary marriage, the innocence of the bride need not be a dealbreaking consideration. But this was to be no ordinary marriage. The patriarch knew that the spiritual future of the Jewish people, and by extension that of all believers in the One God, would be influenced by everything he and Isaac would ever do in the world. A small error now might result in disaster even centuries or millennia later. That his son should marry a girl who was sexually untouched was therefore crucially important.

In recounting Eliezer's discovery of Rebecca at the well, the Bible notes that she was "a virgin, and no man had known her"—the redundancy indicating, says Rashi, that she was innocent of every kind of intercourse, vaginal, oral, and anal. For the other girls in Haran were careful about the first of these, but not so much about the other two.[56] However, a midrash indicates that as far as Abraham was concerned, under Eliezer's care Rebecca's maidenhood could not be assumed to have remained intact.

He said to Isaac, "This servant is under suspicion of sin, and deception is in his hand. See that he has not so much as touched her genitals. Take the young woman into the tent and remove her hymen with your finger. If her maidenhood is intact, behold by the will of the Mighty One she is yours."[57] He did as his father asked, and Rebecca submitted to the indignity, for she, too, understood that the family's assurance must be complete.

In most translations, the Bible says that "he brought her into the tent of Sarah his mother," but the Hebrew grammar is strange. The word here meaning "to the tent," *ha'ohelah,* should have been in its construct state— which would have given it the needed possessive sense, "to the tent of Sarah his mother"—but it's not. "Grammatically unmanageable," Speiser sniffs, and leaves it at that, as if the Redactor had been so dim as to be unaware of even the most elementary rules of Hebrew composition.[58] Literally the verse means "he brought her into the tent—Sarah his mother."[59] According to *Pirke d'Rabbi Eliezer,* the intended meaning is that when he brought her into the tent and conducted the necessary gynecological exam, he found her to be just like "Sarah his mother"—pure and innocent. The guilt Abraham had sensed in Eliezer's face was evidently from the desire to thwart the marriage, not from having actually committed a trespass.

They were soon married, perhaps in a ceremony conducted at sunset, as was the custom of the land.[60] The text goes on to say that he "loved her."[61] In traditional societies, long before the elevation of romance in the Middle Ages, love was assumed to be a gift one received after marriage, not its precondition. Yet the Torah is not a book free of romantic sentiment. On the verse about Sarah's tent, Rashi comments about the "unmanageable" grammar that it teaches the way of the world. A young man clings to his mother till he marries. Then when his mother dies, from that time his wife fully displaces his mother as the object of his ultimate affection.[62] This isn't romance of the Harlequin kind, but a compelling insight nevertheless about the romantic attachment of husband to wife, which is as deep, and in much the same way, as that of boy to mother. Isaac brought Rebecca into the tent and in a sense *she became* Sarah his mother.

When Sarah died, the cloud of the Presence disappeared from above her tent, as the light from her candles had done and the blessing from her bread. When Rebecca became Isaac's wife, all these were restored.

A rule of what one might call domestic spiritual economy had been established. The cloud stands for a family's relationship with God. The light stands for the illumination given by religious learning. The bread stands for the fullness of their material prosperity. In Sarah's home, these things depended on Sarah. In Rebecca's home, they depended on Rebecca. In every home, the blessings of spirituality, knowledge, and prosperity depend on the woman of the home more than any other source.

Sarah was dead. But in Rebecca, she lived again.

CHAPTER SEVENTEEN

Abraham's Bones

lassically the difference between tragedy and comedy has been expressed as this: the former ends with death, the latter with marriage. If so, then Abraham's story must be judged a comedy—not in the modern sense of eliciting laughter, but of ending on a note of hope. Although the patriarch's life was drawing to a close, the Bible records his death amid a profusion of marriages and births.

We have already met Isaac's wife. He had waited passively for Eliezer to fetch a bride for him, but his passivity did not extend to observing the loneliness of his father. While Abraham was preparing to send Eliezer away to Haran, the forty-year-old Isaac said to himself, "I am about to take a wife, but my father stands [alone], without a wife."[1]

The Bible notes the seemingly irrelevant detail that on Eliezer's return from Haran, Isaac himself was returning from Beer-lahai-roi. The text doesn't say what he was doing there. However, the last time we heard the name of that place was in the context of Hagar's first encounter with an angel in the desert and the annunciation of Ishmael's birth. In the Bible, according to the oral tradition, there are no irrelevant details. At the mention of Beer-lahai-roi, we are meant to think of Hagar and to understand that Isaac had been there to find her and bring her back. He intended to reunite her with his father.[2]

For Hagar, the thirty-eight years since her final expulsion had constituted a trial of her own. She returned to the worship of the Egyptian gods and, after a failed attempt with the dyspeptic Isa, at last successfully married off Ishmael. The lapse into idolatry was a temporary condition that pained her so much that she gave it up and repented. Her twenty-seven years in Abraham's household had left an indelible mark on her soul. Embracing the worship of the One God once again, she took the new name "Keturah," meaning "Incense," as a sign that she had become a new person whose deeds would from now on be sweet-smelling: fragrant smoke would erase the foulness of her previous idolatry. The name "Keturah" also shares a cognate root with the word *keshurah,* or "closed up." For all the years she had been apart from Abraham, her place of intimacy had been closed up to all other men, like a sealed bottle.[3]

The romance of Hagar and Abraham is a theme that goes undeveloped by the classical Jewish commentators. That Hagar had a great passion for Abraham is, however, clear. She stayed faithful to him even though, according to *Pirke d'Rabbi Eliezer,* he had formally divorced her and she was thus free to become any other man's wife or concubine.[4] Nor did Abraham have any reason to resent Hagar. Although Sarah was greatly vexed by her own relationship with the Egyptian, the handmaiden doesn't seem to have given her master any trouble—unlike Sarah herself, who was capable of seeking to call down on him a divine curse. Expansive, tolerant, and compassionate, the patriarch was probably rather fond of this spirited ex-princess. I imagine him bantering enjoyably with her at family meals. If Rebecca comforted Isaac and took the place of Sarah in his affections, we may imagine that Hagar did the same for Abraham.

So they remarried. The Bible gives the names of the children and grandchildren they subsequently had together, obscure names—Zimran, Jokshan,

Medan, Midian, Ishbak, Shuah, and so on—that scholars identify with tribes or towns that traced a route for incense traders through the Arabian Peninsula. The scholarly assumption is that this "incense route," which had been established by the eighth century B.C., inspired the author of the passage to give Keturah her name, thus explaining the relationship of Arabia to Israel during the reign of King David's descendants. Otherwise, the fragrant name "Keturah" has no parallel among the attested personal names of the ancient Near East.[5] In other words, the text reflects a political situation long after the purported life of Abraham, making its historical accuracy, in scholarly eyes, suspect.

The marriage of Rebecca and Isaac was less fruitful. For twenty years, Rebecca was barren. When Isaac was 60 and Abraham was 160, she finally bore the twins Jacob and Esau. Esau was eventually the cause of five years being shaved off Abraham's life.

The patriarch would have merited a life of 180 years in length—the number 18 being the numerological value of the Hebrew word meaning "life," *chai*. However, when Abraham was 173, God judged that it would be a greater reward to him if he did not see too many of the years following Esau's coming-of-age. Before the twins' thirteenth birthday, says Rashi, "their deeds could not be distinguished and no man could tell what their nature would turn out to be." But after thirteen, the threshold of manhood, each took his separate path, Jacob to the study of divine teaching and Esau to the idolatrous temples.[6]

At first, Esau's progress toward moral dissolution was subtle, and his family may not have noticed. It wasn't till he turned fifteen that he really began to cut loose—that is, in his grandfather Abraham's 175th year. To save the patriarch from witnessing what followed, God decided to take the patriarch's life five years early.[7]

The manner of his death is attested. The Midrash observes that Scripture employs what seems to be a redundant expression, "And Abraham perished and died." But what information does "perish" *(va'yigvah)* convey that "die" *(va'yamat)* doesn't? The former refers to a sickness that preceded his death. Some ten or twenty days before their death, the righteous of old, including

Abraham, would suffer from a certain affliction of the bowels. God's purpose was to cleanse them of any remaining sins, just as diarrhea empties the digestive system of any remaining food. Eating is thus compared with the whole range of our daily activities, which mostly are wasted, just as most of the food we eat is turned into waste. In preparation for separating from life, the saint is cleansed of all such dross. In the Talmud, Rabbi Yose, a second-century sage, is even quoted as praying, "May my lot be among those who die of an affliction of the bowels."[8]

Did Abraham sin? Nachmanides regarded the patriarch as a mortal with mortal failings. Rashi may be understood as saying otherwise. When the Torah notes that Abraham lived a total of "a hundred years and seventy years and five years," or 175, Rashi explains the awkward diction: "At 100 years of age, he was like a 70-year-old; and at 70 years of age he was like a 5-year-old, without sin."[9] This is generally taken to mean that Rashi thinks Abraham remained innocent throughout his life. More likely it means that Abraham was innocent till his seventieth year, just before his move to Canaan and the real beginning of his mission to bring the worship of the One God to the world. A public life, one that achieves permanent relevance, cannot be free of sin. A consequence of having an impact on others is that one must mix himself up with humanity, which necessarily leaves him open to unwholesome influences. The price of perfection is irrelevance. Though Abraham was not perfect, some days or weeks of agony erased his imperfections.

According to the grammatical analysis of Rabbi Samson Raphael Hirsch, the three-letter Hebrew root that means "to perish" (gimel-vav-ayin) is a variant of the root that means "to groan" or "moo" like an animal (gimel-ayin-heh). We can hear Abraham's moans as his insides flushed themselves out again and again, gradually starving and dehydrating him.

Another benefit of this extended illness was that it gave Abraham time to put his affairs in order. In intermissions between waves of sickness, the patriarch composed himself and confirmed his gift to Isaac of "all that he had"—meaning his entire estate, the leadership of nascent monotheism, and a mysterious power to give blessings.[10] Abraham had received from God the ability to heal the sick and to cause barren women to conceive. Isaac inherited this ability.

The scriptural text notes that to Keturah/Hagar's children the patriarch likewise gave "gifts" and sent these young men off, "while he was still alive, eastward to the land of the east."[11] Rashi raises the obvious difficulty. If Abraham had already given "all that he had" to Isaac, what did he have left to give to Keturah's children? The answer is that he bestowed upon them certain spiritual "gifts" of a surprising, rather dark kind. In the cryptic language of the Talmud, they were the gifts of an "impure name."[12]

The end when it came was fast, and in contrast to what had come before, painless.[13] In the year 1637 B.C., Abraham inhaled the air of his God's world for the last time. Not only Isaac and Rebecca but Ishmael was at his side, the latter having followed the example of his mother and returned to the obedient monotheism in which he had been raised.

The Bible says that after Abraham died, "His sons Isaac and Ishmael buried him in the cave of Machpelah in the field of Ephron son of Zohar the Hittite."[14] From the placement of Isaac in front of Ishmael in the verse, the Talmud understands that Ishmael had undergone the spiritual evolution called *teshuvah,* "return": he had returned to Abraham's fold, accepting Isaac in the role assigned to him by their father. The rivalrous brothers were, for now, reconciled. Conspicuously Isaac and Ishmael are designated equally as Abraham's "sons." Genesis didn't need to tell us that—the apparently superfluous expression indicates Ishmael's repentance and the consequent affirmation of his status as a full "son" of Abraham.

Malchizedek attended the funeral and walked ahead of the bier, inspecting the interior of the cave before Abraham was laid to rest in it. Also in attendance was every Hebronite who thirty-eight years before had paid honor to Sarah at her funeral. Through their kindness to her, they all, old and young, merited to escape death long enough to offer the same respect to Abraham.[15]

The Bible concludes its narrative of the patriarch's life with the customary phrase—used elsewhere in Scripture to describe the death of the righteous—that Abraham was "gathered to his people."[16] The commentator Sforno notes the difficulty in reading this verse as other than a pious and meaningless cliché. If he really was "gathered to his people," what people do we mean? His family was buried not in the Machpelah, but back in Haran. And they were all pagans. Is it not an insult to Abraham to suggest that he joined them in their eternal reward? The early Christians, notably the author of the Letter to the Hebrews, argued that Abraham's true "people," his authentic "seed," was not defined by blood, including the blood of the ethnic group called Jews, but was rather the community of the faithful of all races.[17] In this view, the definition of Abraham's "people" transcends blood. Sforno says something not entirely dissimilar: "He was gathered within the bonds of life, of the life eternal, with the righteous of [all] the generations, who [truly] are his people in that they resemble him [spiritually]."[18]

Scripture thus ends the story of Abraham's life with the great truth that his teaching was not confined to a single bloodline. Abraham's God is not the exclusive possession of any race or family. This is why it is a mistake to understand the religion of Torah, called Judaism, as merely the ethnic folkways of a particular racial group. Admittedly there is a racial element to the definition of what it means to belong to the people Israel: anyone born of a Jewish mother belongs to Israel without being required to undergo a ritual of conversion. But the collectivity is open equally to all who commit themselves to upholding Truth, regardless of who their mother was. To join, one is required to affirm before a rabbinical court that Torah is Truth. But having done so, the convert is spiritually and legally indistinguishable from any other person in Israel.

The Jewish people was born when the Torah was given at Mt. Sinai, some 325 years after Abraham's death. Before that, there was a family of Abraham, Isaac, and Jacob, but there were no "Jews." That fact may help explain the confusion and rivalry among his descendants, each claiming to be his true heir, which continues down to our own time. Abraham named an heir, Isaac, but Isaac was only a man who himself died and, like his father, left behind more than one son vying for the right to call himself the heir of his father and grandfather.

The Bible wants us to understand that this rivalry, never to be resolved till the promised redemption of humankind when God will answer all of mankind's questions, was woven into the fabric of history from early on. It also wishes us to see that the truth Abraham discovered about God was dispersed, in forms that might be pure or mixed with other elements, through several branches of civilization spanning Europe, Asia, and Africa.

In Scripture's terse genealogy of Abraham and his sons and grandsons, we have a capsule history of the world's great religious cultures. Isaac was the father of Jacob, who received the name "Israel" and gave that name to his descendants. At Sinai, they became the Jewish people, the "great nation" promised to Abraham.[19]

Ishmael is claimed by the Arab peoples as their forefather, and in this, Jewish tradition concurs. Immediately following Abraham's death, the plain text of Scripture merely names Ishmael's twelve sons, who founded the twelve tribes of the Ishmaelites: Nebaioth, Kedar, Adbeel, Mibsam, Mishma, Dumah, Massa, Hadad, Tema, Jetur, Naphish, and Kedem. Their number suggests an analogy to the twelve sons of Jacob who founded the twelve tribes of Israel. Modern scholarship observes that Ishmael's sons appear to correspond with various Arabian tribes or towns, attested from Assyrian and other sources of the eighth to sixth centuries B.C. and later. The name "Ishmael" itself seems to match the name of a confederation of bedouin tribes, called Sumu'il, that alternately fought for or against the Assyrians. The Sumu'il were loosely organized and politically unstable, tending to battle among each other when they weren't battling outsiders—a fact that would explain the Bible's references to Ishmael, "a wild ass of a man, his hand in everything and everyone's hand against him."[20] One pair of scholars concludes that because these tribes are known to have been active only long after Abraham's presumed lifetime, "there seems little doubt that these genealogical passages were crafted between the late eighth and sixth centuries B.C.E."[21] An equally plausible view was offered by the medieval commentator Radak. He explains that the sons of Ishmael gave their names to eponymous tribes: "Each of those mentioned was the chief and leader of a numerous family from whom there went forth that tribe which was called by his name."[22] These tribes naturally would have appeared late on the historical stage. For a single person to become a whole tribe great enough to fight wars would require the passage of time.

As always, the scholars bring to their analysis of the text the assumption that it cannot possibly be a communication from God. Thus whenever Scripture speaks prophetically, naming tribes that will not be unveiled in history till much later, what we really have is an attempt to project back into the mid-second millennium B.C. events that were current at the time of the writing, in the mid-first millennium.

In any event, says the tradition, Ishmael's descendants were these early Arabs, who became the first disciples of the Abrahamic faith called Islam. In the culture of Islam, therefore, we see the struggle of two natures. There is the "wild ass" of Ishmael, the violent, reckless inheritance of pre-Islamic

Arabs. And there is the pure faith of Abraham, whose memory Ishmael's descendants retained in their traditions. In Muslim civilization at its best, the Abrahamic inheritance is ascendant over the Ishmaelite.

Much the same pattern holds true among the descendants of Abraham's other sons and grandsons. Scholars identify several of the sixteen named descendants of Keturah with other Arabian or Aramean tribes or towns, which they again adduce as evidence that the text was written much later than Abraham's time, and which again may be explained as Radak suggests. As for the children of Keturah who have not yet been identified, they, too, went off "eastward to the land of the east."

An intriguing rabbinic speculation asserts that they migrated as far as India, where they brought the Abrahamic idea into the culture that became Hinduism. This is the story as reported by the seventeenth-century Dutch sage Rabbi Menashe ben Israel. The history of the Hindu faith extends back four thousand years, and from early on its priests were called Brahmans—a name that ben Israel explains as a reference to their ancestor, Abraham. If the first Brahmans retained some memory of Hebrew, then the name of the oldest Hindu scripture, called *Veda* in Sanskrit, meaning "knowledge," could be a derivation of the Hebrew root *yedah,* which also means "knowledge." It is interesting, if hardly conclusive, to note other linguistic parallels. What of the "impure name" Abraham entrusted to his sons? A Hindu term that refers to a kind of impurity, *tamas,* sounds like the Hebrew term that means roughly the same thing, *tumah.* Scholars will assert that any such similarity can only be attributed to coincidence. (Hebrew and Sanskrit belong to separate language families, respectively the Hamito-Semitic and the Indo-European, though Jewish tradition suggests that all languages ultimately derive from Hebrew, the language Adam and Eve spoke.)[23]

Rashi explains that Abraham gave to Keturah's children a knowledge of sorcery having to do with *shedim,* or demons.[24] If we are prepared to credit the existence of such harmful disembodied spirits, we may speculate that in India at the time, a sorcery was practiced from which Abraham thought his sons required protection, which in turn required that they themselves have a command of the black powers. His protection failed them. Like Kurtz in *The Heart of Darkness,* they were swallowed up by the native culture. Anyone who has spent time looking at Hindu art, full of horrendous images of demonic creatures, knows that this venerable culture continues to wrestle with *shedim.* On the other hand, the number of Westerners who report finding enlightenment in the teaching of the East—including Buddhism, which spun off from the religion of the Brahmans—must suggest even to faithful monotheists that Hinduism is not without an element of truth even as Abraham might define it.

Did that truth come from Abraham? Do his sons really lie buried on the banks of the Ganges? The thought must remain a tantalizing possibility, without solid grounding in the traditions that have guided our way in this book.

By contrast, the identification of Abraham's grandson Esau and his descendants is widely attested in rabbinic literature. Esau is Rome: the Roman Empire and by extension the dominant culture of the West into modern times.

The Roman Empire did not end once and for all in A.D. 476, when Goths deposed the last Western emperor. It was revived in the Holy Roman Empire, of which there was a nominal sovereign as late as 1806. At Constantinople, the Eastern Empire, which called itself Roman, persisted until the triumph of the Turks and the final sack of the city in 1453. But even then the influence of Rome was not extinguished. The founding of the United States was partly inspired by Roman republican ideals. Much of the official architecture of the American capital is meant to evoke Rome in its glory.

The rabbis understood Esau specifically as the embodiment of destructive tendencies in Western culture. At first, Esau kept those tendencies in check, but they bloomed in full horrid color when he was fifteen. As the Talmud explains, he committed five grievous transgressions. He engaged in an adulterous sexual relationship. He murdered. He denied the very existence of God, as well as the doctrine of the afterlife, particularly the resurrection of the dead. And he belittled the special role of the firstborn who were originally meant to serve in the priestly role later assumed by a caste drawn from the tribe of Abraham's great-grandson Levi.[25] In short, he committed the worst possible indecencies against other people and against God.

Esau was the firstborn, having emerged first from his mother's womb. When he sold his birthright to his brother, Jacob, all he asked in return was a serving of the red lentil stew Jacob was cooking. Lentils were the dish served to mourners upon the death of a close relative. Jacob was cooking his stew to serve to their father, Isaac, who was mourning Abraham's death that very day.[26]

Since Esau is identified with Rome, and since nowadays the principal distinction of the city is that it includes the headquarters of the Roman Catholic Church, the relationship of Esau to Christianity needs to be clarified. When Christians have persecuted Jews, an accustomed Jewish response has been to attribute such persecution to the influence of Esau, whose hatred of the house of Jacob has never dimmed. In this connection, we may point out that most of the violence against Jews by anti-Semitic Christians has been committed not by Protestants, but by Roman Catholic and Eastern Orthodox Christians. Perhaps this is because Protestant Christianity is unified in its utter rejection of Rome. The Eastern Church, on the other hand, has merely split from Roman authority, while maintaining Roman practices in many instances more punctiliously than the Roman Church itself. While Protestants, starting with Martin Luther, have written and said hateful things about Jews, we find no record of pogroms in Protestant countries. Nor is it a coincidence that America and other Anglo nations—all historically Protestant—have a far better record of tolerating, gently nurturing, even indulging Jewish communities than any countries have compiled in the history of the Diaspora.[27]

Esau represents an aspect of Western culture against which the Abrahamic element in Christianity struggles.[28] At some times and in some churches, the spirit of Esau has gained ascendancy. Then the face of the church turned against whatever descendants of Jacob were near at hand. At other times, the spirit of Abraham rules, and the Christian attitude toward Jews ranges from tolerant to affectionate. In the historical moment we occupy today, it would seem that both the Catholic and the Protestant churches are aligned more with Abraham than with Esau.

Rashi observed that this pattern had already been set when Esau and Jacob were born. Jacob emerged from the womb grasping Esau's heel, an indication that the brothers can never both be dominant at the same time. When one falls, the other rises up. "It is a sign," says Rashi, "that this one will not have the chance to end his rule before this one stands and takes it from him."[29] So it would seem to be in the case of Ishmael and Keturah's spiritual descendants. At times, the spirit of Abraham rules among them; at other times, that of Ishmael, or of the "impure name."

The Talmud offers another tragic perspective on Esau's legacy, and Abraham's. Jewish tradition depicts the unfolding of history in terms of interactions among biblical personalities and their spiritual descendants: Jacob/

Israel, Ishmael, Esau. To these three, add the figure of Amalek, a thoroughly sinister desert tribe that plays a role in the Pentateuch, descended from a man by the same name, a grandson of Esau. The Jews associate this name with the wickedest, most anti-Semitic regimes in history. In regarding the Nazis, for instance, as a manifestation of Amalek, it isn't meant that Hitler was himself a biological heir of Amalek. Rather that a spirit of ultimate evil is somehow passed down and inherited by various groups at various times.

Amalek himself was the son of a woman named Timna. Genesis mentions her fleetingly, irrelevantly, as the sister of a certain tribal chieftain, Lotan. The Talmud explains that before she had had any children she was stirred to join Abraham's household, his community of disciples. We don't know when or why, but Abraham turned her away. So did Isaac, in his role as patriarch. So did Jacob. Devastated by the successive rejections, she resolved to join a branch of the patriarchal family as the concubine of Esau's son Eliphaz. She explained, "Better to be a maidservant to this people, than to be a princess to another people." To Eliphaz she bore a child who would bedevil the Jewish nation and the world with violence and hate for millennia to come: Amalek.[30] Under the worst anti-Jewish Christian and Muslim regimes, it has apparently been not merely the spirit of Esau or Ishmael at work but that of Amalek. Again, the seeds of history were planted in Abraham's day, by Abraham himself.

So the excruciating tension remains between faiths that should regard each other as brothers. If in the future there is to be peace between Ishmael's seed and Isaac's, what's needed is a reconciliation as profound as the one the Bible hints at in its description of Abraham's burial. The prospect would seem dim except that just such an unlikely reconciliation has been under way between Jacob's children and the children of Esau, providing a model of the hoped-for peace between Abraham's sons. Taken together, the evolving Catholic Church and the philo-Semitism of American Christianity, which we noted in chapter 14, alert us that Esau is not locked forever in opposition to Jacob.

Just as the Book of Genesis includes a scene of reconciliation between Ishmael and Isaac, it includes a reunion between Esau and Jacob. Fearing fratricide, Jacob had fled from Canaan. After decades of exile, he returned and was met at the frontier by Esau and a band of ruffians. The brothers threw off their enmity: "Esau ran to greet him, embraced him and fell upon his neck and kissed him; and they wept."[31] On this verse, Rashi cites a midrashic tradition that Esau (meaning Christianity) will always hate Jacob (meaning the Jews)—this has the status of nothing less than a *halachah,* a "law" of history. But a revered nineteenth-century sage, Rabbi Naftali Zvi Yehudah Berlin (called Netziv; Russian, 1817–93), writes in his commentary *Haamek Davar,* "This [verse] comes to teach that at this time there was also aroused in Jacob a love for Esau. Thus in future generations when the seed of Esau is roused by a spirit of purity to recognize the seed of Israel . . . , then we should rouse ourselves to recognize Esau, for he is our brother."[32] The Netziv was advising us, amid Russian pogroms, that there would come a time when Esau acknowledges the role God set out for Jacob to play in world history and will embrace him. When that happens, it will be time for the Jewish people to respond in kind, embracing Christians as their long-lost brothers.

There is no tradition of a *halachah* that Ishmael hates Isaac. If Esau and Jacob can throw their arms around each other and weep, sincerely, in love and mutual acceptance, it stands to reason that the same can happen in the presently tormented relationship of Ishmael and Isaac. In fact, the sweep of history, as tradition gives us to understand, would seem to demand it, to guarantee it. The same tradition that illuminates the bare narrative of Abraham's life as recorded in Genesis also views history as a process of reconciliation between all men and the One God.

History has an end point, and by that time Abraham's mission must succeed. The Hebrew prophets assure us that it will. The Torah declares, "The Lord shall reign forever!"[33] The prophet Zechariah exults, "So shall the Lord be King over all the earth. On that day, the Lord will be One and His Name will be One."[34]

On the day of Abraham's burial, all this lay in the future. As Scripture notes, "the Lord had blessed Abraham with everything,"[35] including the comforting illusion that his legacy was safe in the hands of Isaac, never to be seriously challenged or assaulted by others of the patriarch's children.[36]

No location on earth better illustrates what a fragile illusion that was than the place of his burial, the Machpelah. Its more recent history has been almost unremittingly violent.

For the first millennium after the patriarchal family had been buried in Ephron's field, there was no grand structure to mark the spot. Only a tradition was passed down through the generations, indicating the location. In the first century B.C., King Herod built the imposing fortresslike edifice one sees today, intending it as a smaller replica of the Temple Mount enclosure that was his greatest architectural achievement. The Machpelah building was constructed with precisely the same proportions, of the same masonry in the same style. Anyone who has visited the Western Wall will remember the huge Herodian stones, recognizable by the elegant frame of hewn stone around a central boss. The enclosure at Hebron is made of such ashlars (one measuring twenty-four feet in length!), which could have been lifted directly from the wall.

Just as Jews, Christians, and Muslims have struggled desperately among themselves for mastery of the Temple Mount, so have they for the Machpelah. At first, Herod's enclosure was just a wall guarding the cave. In the fifth or sixth century, Byzantine Christians built a church inside the wall. After Muslims invaded the Holy Land, they tore down the church and built a mosque that included six cenotaphs, memorials to the patriarchs and their wives. Those that can be seen today range in provenance from the ninth to fourteenth centuries.

Crusaders drove the Muslims out in A.D. 1100, and turned the mosque into a church. Muslim forces under Saladin reconquered Hebron in 1188 and reconverted the church into a mosque. For a brief interlude afterward, not only Muslims but Jews and Christians could enter the Machpelah. This liberal allowance lasted for less than a century, after which only Muslims were permitted inside, all nonbelievers being limited to the first seven steps along the southeastern wall. Through a crack in the wall next to the seventh step, one might peer inside.

In 1836, the American traveler John Lloyd Stephens visited. He wrote warmly of the "chief rabbi of the Jews" there who led him up on the roof of the synagogue, where they gazed "out as by stealth upon the sacred mosque containing the hallowed ashes of [the rabbi's] patriarch fathers." Palestine was Ottoman land then, and Stephens describes the seven hundred to eight hundred Arab families living under the Turks in Hebron as "the wildest, most lawless, and desperate people in the Holy Land." The rabbi took him for a closer inspection of the Machpelah, and Stephens recalls stopping "for a moment to look up at the long marble staircase leading to the tomb of Abraham." Just then "a Turk came out from the bazaars, and, with furious gesticulations, gathered a crowd around us; and a Jew and a Christian were driven with contempt from the sepulchre of the patriarch whom they both revered."[37]

Today Muslims pray in the mosque, Jews in the courtyard within the enclosure, and Israeli soldiers stand guard lest one come into contact with the other and violence ensue. Nor may a Christian pay his respects to the patriarchs in safety.

As I learned when I went there, for a non-Arab to get to Hebron has become complicated. Our bulletproof public bus, no. 160 from Jerusalem, descended a steep hill to a barren concrete plaza surmounted by steps leading to Herod's structure. Entering these cyclopean walls, then proceeding through the main synagogue area, we found a small chapel with massive green doors and paved in two-thousand-year-old flagstones. In the back wall was a black iron gate, behind which loomed in the dark a tall cenotaph from the ninth century, covered in dusty green silk bedecked with Arabic formulations, memorializing the burial place of Abraham.

In the grottoes underneath, the wind of Abraham's spirit blows. In the literature of those who have sought to enter the tomb over the centuries, a theme persists of a supernatural force that haunts the place. Not long after Herod built these walls, Rabbi Bana'ah met the soul of Eliezer guarding the entrance of the cave, where Abraham and Sarah lay in each other's arms within.

Muslims and Christians have had other experiences. By their own account, the former—who call the place Haram el Khalil, "the enclosure of the friend [of God, namely Abraham]"—have been made to feel somewhat less welcome than Rabbi Bana'ah. One Islamic story tells of a man who on entering the cave fell paralyzed to the floor. Another recounts the experience of Ali of Herat, who in 1192 descended and felt the breeze gusting about that others have reported. He encountered "the extended body of Abraham—peace be on him!—clothed in green garments, and the wind as it blew tossed about his white beard." A supernatural voice rang out: "Beware, for it is the Haram!" Tales from the fourteenth and fifteenth centuries speak of a certain Abou Abu Bakr al Askafy who explored with a guide, Sa'luk. The two collapsed on the ground after hearing a voice from nowhere call out, "Depart ye from the Haram, and God have mercy on you!"[38] They got out, but soon died anyway. When a party of four Muslim spelunkers were unspeakably terrorized, three dying on the spot and one emerging mute, religious authorities sought to ban all further entry except once a year by the grand mufti.[39]

Christians, during their periods of control, have descended and brought back detailed descriptions of what lies beneath. In 1119 a monk felt an unexpected breeze blowing from a crack in the flagstones near Isaac's cenotaph. Some colleagues helped him pull up the stones and a monk called Arnoul was lowered by rope down a seventeen-foot shaft. He found masonry-lined rooms leading to a cave, which he entered, holding a candle in one hand, crossing himself with the other, and singing the Kyrie Eleison to fend off terror. Here and in a second grotto he found bones which he identified as those of Abraham, Isaac, and Jacob. The Jewish traveler Benjamin of Tudela claimed, in 1163, to have found six sarcophagi with inscriptions, apparently in Latin: "This is the grave of Abraham," "This is the grave of Isaac," and so on.[40]

In the long history of struggle for possession of the Machpelah, most recently the State of Israel captured it from the Kingdom of Jordan. Hebron entered Israeli jurisdiction on June 8, 1967. Access to the entire Herodian compound had been denied to Jews for precisely seven centuries, since 1267. Upon victory, the Israeli defense minister, General Moshe Dayan, an amateur archaeologist, wasted no time in planning to explore. The night of October 9, 1968, a skinny twelve-year-old girl, Michal Arbel, was lowered on a rope through an eleven-inch aperture in the floor.

Was she spooked at the thought of entering a tomb? Not at all. A "bright and courageous" child, as Dayan later wrote of her, she feared neither "ghosts" nor "spirits," for "their existence was not proven."[41]

Ghosts and spirits notwithstanding, she entered a subterranean chamber empty but for three stone slabs. The tallest, in the middle, stood six feet high and revealed a chipped, faded verse from the Quran asserting that Allah neither slumbers not sleeps. Before Michal had a chance to explore further, she was recalled to the earth's surface. As an adult, Michal was asked whether she had expected to find Abraham's bones in the tomb. "No," she replied, "I was under no illusions."

The Muslim keepers of the tomb would view any further attempt as an intolerable desecration. Not that Jews haven't tried. The most recent exploration was conducted hastily one night in 1981, after the Muslim guards had gone home to sleep. Under the cover of saying penitential prayers before

Rosh Hashanah, a party of Jews from nearby Kiryat Arbah pulled up some prayer rugs from the floor of the mosque and chiseled a hole among the paving stones. They, too, felt the strange wind, but otherwise encountered no overt supernatural presence. They retrieved some bone fragments from the inner cave, which were analyzed and found to be ancient but not old enough to belong to the patriarchs. The photos they took, the only such images of the grotto of which I'm aware, can be seen on the Internet site of the Hebron Jewish community. One shows a stone in the wall of the outer cave bearing a rough inscription in Roman letters: "ABRAHAM."

Michal's word, the "illusion" of Abraham's bones, is an apt description of a question that haunts all modern discussions of the patriarch's legacy. Did he live, a real man in a certain time and place? Or to quote a recent popular writer on the subject, is he something more like "a compendium—a crystallization" of various personalities, real and imagined, that filtered through the minds of ancient Israelites?[42] The upshot of the latter view, itself the crystallization of modern scholarly opinion, is that Abraham the man is an illusion not far removed from the ghosts and spirits that smart, lively Michal knew she would not encounter in the tomb because "their existence was not proven."

Who was buried in Abraham's tomb? For those of us with an ear willing to listen to the voice of orally transmitted data, one answer is: the discoverer of God. Another answer, which amounts to the same thing, is: your father.

"Patriarch" literally *means* "high father." Abraham is *my* father because like all converts to Judaism I acquired upon my conversion the patronymic "ben Avraham," son of Abraham. When I think of this father of mine, I often turn to the letter that Maimonides wrote from Fostat, Egypt, in the twelfth century to another convert to Judaism, presumably a former Muslim, called Obadiah. The man had written to Maimonides because he was concerned about certain formulations in Jewish prayer that speak in the person of the historical Jewish people who descend by blood from the biblical Hebrews, ultimately from Abraham. Obadiah worried that in uttering these formulations himself, he was giving voice to an untruth, for he could not claim such descent. To this, Maimonides replied comfortingly that membership in the people Israel is not like belonging to some tribe where blood is what really matters:

> Whoever adopts Judaism and confesses the unity of the Divine Name, as it is prescribed in the Torah, is counted among the disciples of Abraham our Father, peace be upon him. These men are Abraham's household, and he it is who converted them to righteousness.
>
> In the same way as he converted his contemporaries through his words and teachings, he converts future generations through the testament he left to his children and household after him. Thus Abraham our Father, peace be upon him, is the father of his pious posterity who keep his ways, and the father of his disciples and of all proselytes who adopt Judaism.[43]

I want to suggest that by the very criteria set out in the Torah, Maimonides' words apply not only to Jews.

Judaism has a rather supple definition of fatherhood. There is, of course, the base, material sort of fatherhood that depends exclusively on whose sperm fertilized which egg. In this sense, even animals have fathers. Abraham himself introduced another understanding of fatherhood, mixing the biological and spiritual. In this view, the father may be the man who contributed half the child's DNA, but what's really important about him is that he gave the child his spiritual outlook, teaching his son or daughter what he knows about God.

This definition of fatherhood needn't have anything at all to do with blood. The Talmud cites a passage in the Book of Numbers where the sons of Aaron, Moses' brother, are named, and described as "the offspring of Moses and Aaron."[44] Is this—yet again!—an instance of our Redactor paying less attention than he should to the simple meaning of the words? No, the intent here is that Moses was reckoned as the father of those younger men solely because he taught them about God. For the Talmud insists that a man who teaches the Truth to someone else's son is given by Scripture the status of father to his student. That is why, reverting to the personal, I regard my adoptive father as my father, for he taught me what he had been taught. It is also why I regard my rabbi as my father.

To be reckoned as a father like this, you don't need to have been alive to personally teach your child. Jewish tradition speaks of Moses as "our rabbi," meaning "our teacher." And your "child" doesn't need to be the perfect representation or receptacle of your teaching. I am certainly not the perfect representation of Moses' or Abraham's teaching; nor is anyone I know. So Abraham is my father. He is *your* father, too. The patriarch stands in a unique relationship to the Jewish people, but it is clear that Christians and Muslims have been taught through a chain of transmission that also originated with him. This makes Abraham their teacher and, in Scripture's own terms, their father. Or, rather, I should say that this is clear for Christians and Muslims, and for Jews, if and only if we accept the claims of tradition.

Without tradition, Abraham and His God fade to nothingness. Without tradition—without Abraham—we are all orphans.

CONCLUSION

Israel and Humanity

n February 25, 1994, Baruch Goldstein, an American-born physician, entered the courtyard over the Machpelah tomb during dawn prayers of the Muslim holy month, Ramadan. Dressed in the uniform of the Israeli Defense Force, he opened fire on the crowd of praying Muslims, killing twenty-nine. The Israeli soldiers who guarded the tomb thought a riot had begun, sealed off the courtyard, and shot at fleeing Arabs.

Blood was flowing in Hebron long before 1994. In 1929, during riots that began in Jerusalem and spread across British Palestine, Hebron's Arabs rose against their Jewish neighbors, who had lived side by side with them for centuries. The Arabs slaughtered sixty-seven Jews.

Political solutions have not succeeded in pacifying Abraham's children. What, then, of religion as an agent of peace? Or is religion, the monotheism Abraham bequeathed to the world, the very problem itself? Would the world be better off without him?

Rejecting this patriarch as our spiritual father is not an option. Rejecting him would mean rejecting God. Is there, however, a way to reimagine his legacy, to reconceive what it means to be his spiritual descendants that could—maybe, someday—give comfort to the troubled world of monotheism?

We are concerned with finding a paradigm of mutual understanding to reconcile Muslims with Jews and Christians. Perhaps the household of Abraham is that paradigm.

What became of Abraham's disciples? They were called the Masters of the Covenant of Abraham, as Genesis says (14:13). Perhaps his household never really disbanded or dissolved, but only appeared to do so, fading from written history. Perhaps it is more than just a paradigm.

We know what happened to Abraham's direct lineal descendants through Isaac and Isaac's son Jacob: they became the Jewish people. Then there entered into the world the teachings of Jesus and of Muhammad. What of those peoples, pagan in Abraham's time, whose ancestors became Christians and Muslims, accepting on themselves the ideology of a monotheism centered on the God of Israel? When the seeds of the Hebrew Bible were sown in Europe and western Asia, had the field not been prepared ahead of time?

Writing a century ago and drawing on kabbalah, Rabbi Elijah Benamozegh offers an intriguing speculation. In his book *Israel and Humanity,* he points out that in ancient societies, notably Greece and Rome, from about a thousand years after Abraham died we find records of what are called mystery cults. Individuals seeking enlightenment and not finding it in the conventional pagan rites would join societies that promised occult knowledge of spiritual matters. This knowledge, typically conveyed in sacred dramas performed before the initiated, was kept secret from outsiders. Benamozegh suggests that Abraham's monotheism was not lost from among the gentile peoples after his and his successors' death but was conveyed as occult knowledge, circulated as an underground freemasonry, a kabbalah among the nations of the world. There is no record of these Abrahamic mysteries, but there would not be. The field was being prepared quietly, the peoples introduced by imperceptible degrees to the radical idea our patriarch had preached openly. Initiates of the mysteries influenced the cultural atmosphere of their societies without openly propagandizing. The process may have been deliberate and conscious, or it may have been organic and unplanned.

Either way, when followers of Jesus and Paul, or Muhammad, began to teach their version of Abrahamism, the idea was a match set to kindling. The world still burns, and as Christianity continues to penetrate Africa and East Asia, the conflagration grows.

A century ago, there arose a movement of liberal Catholic intellectuals and clergy called Modernism. Before being suppressed by the Vatican, it was celebrated by Benamozegh's student, Aimé Pallière, in striking terms. He wrote, "All the reforms at present within Christianity are really tending toward Judaism. The dogmas which are decidedly crumbling after having been considered during the centuries as impregnable fortresses, without which no Christian faith was possible, are precisely those which Israel stubbornly denied for nineteen hundred years."[1] He didn't mean that Christians were becoming Jews—that is not what God wants. Rather, Christians, specifically Catholics, were moving closer to accepting the role of Judaism in the world as Judaism itself conceives that role: Judaism as a living covenant rather than a dead weight, with Christianity in the role of "younger brother" rather than triumphant successor. In the church of John Paul II, and before that in the church of Paul XXIII, radical reforms have been carried out. Catholic teaching now holds the Jewish and Christian relationships with God to be separate but equally valid—a remarkable departure from older doctrine. The 1965 document *Nostra Aetate* spelled out this new teaching, which has continued to be articulated and allowed to unfold.

It is not only the Catholic Church that has helped to transform, however subtly, the face of Christianity in relationship to Judaism. Much more important has been the rise of the United States.

America is a Christian nation, the most enthusiastically so in the world, but its Christianity is special. America has long displayed a deeply philo-Semitic streak, seeing in its own history a replaying of the sacred history of the people Israel.[2] This was evident even before the country was founded.

Just as Israel fled from Egypt to establish a godly society in Canaan, the first Americans fled from England to establish a godly society in Massachusetts. Both groups were called separatists—as the word "Hebrews," Ivrim, can fairly be translated. When they celebrated Thanksgiving for the first time, in 1621, the Pilgrims imagined it as a kind of Yom Kippur, a day of repentance, prayer, and fasting. William Bradford, second governor of the Plymouth colony, observing that Hebrew was the Lord's own language, introduced his *History of the Plymouth Plantation* with passages in Hebrew. Early American preachers Increase Mather (1639–1723) and Cotton Mather (1663–1728) were students of Hebrew and used it in their writings, citing learned Jewish sources including the Talmud and Midrash, Rashi and Maimonides. The legal codes of colonial Massachusetts and Connecticut were based explicitly on the legal framework of the Five Books of Moses. American towns were often named for Old Testament localities: Bethel, Goshen, Pisgah, Hebron, Jericho, Salem, Zion. Benjamin Franklin recommended as the seal of the United States a portrait of the Israelites crossing the Red Sea, with the motto "Rebellion to Tyrants Is Obedience to God." The Liberty Bell at Philadelphia's Independence Hall is inscribed with a quotation from Leviticus: "Proclaim liberty throughout all the land unto all the inhabitants thereof" (25:10).

The scholar Michael Novak describes what he calls the "Jewish metaphysics" of the American founding. The founders conceived of God as Creator, King, Judge, Providence—in short, Abraham's God, conveyed in terms that are more Jewish than Christian. Like the Pilgrims, they sought to establish "God's American Israel," and that idea has shaped the soul of the nation ever since.[3] That is why Americans today circumcise our baby boys at a rate that is, outside of Israel, higher than anywhere on earth. It is why American Christians support Israel, demanding that our government stand by her, no matter what the rest of the world may say about the Jewish state.

Abraham's household may well be here, though not only here. It may be all around us in our own country, America—not a Jewish land, but very much Abrahamic. America's non-Jewish religion, the unique faith of American Christianity, is melded with Jewish metaphysics, hinting at the reconciliation of peoples that could be. If so, then the future prospects for the idea Abraham introduced to the world may be observed, however imperfectly represented, in our houses of worship, our government, and the more traditional aspects of our culture. The best hope for peace among Abraham's children may lie in a model like the one we find in the United States.

In Benamozegh's terms, God's plan is evident in history: Judaism for the Jews, the kingdom of priests, and "the religion of the patriarchs for the gentiles,"[4] to whom the Jews are to minister. As yet the form of that ministration has been mainly to provide Scripture, knowledge of the One God, to the nations. Benamozegh insists that Christianity and Islam are not ideal expressions of Abrahamic religion. The former has its trinity of divine personalities, its assertion that God became incarnate in a man—problematic ideas in the context of Abraham's faith as tradition gives us to understand it. The latter denies the Torah as a witness to God's will—also a problem. Christians and Muslims will, of course, disagree with this analysis. However, history is not finished, and the religions are not static.

Tracking the post-Abrahamic career of the monotheistic idea down to our own day, one is left bewildered and dismayed by the present moment's configuration of warring faiths: radical Muslims breathing hatred of the Jewish people and of the world's leading Christian nation. The conception offered here—of a grand if fractured Abrahamic civilization resting on its three foundations of Judaism, Christianity, and Islam, moving toward reconciliation—is, I realize, not easy to accept. Today the more natural interpretation may seem to be of a war of civilizations, that of the Quran confronting that of the Bible. In such a reading, Abraham is afflicted by a split personality: the Ibrahim of the Quran at the throat of the patriarch as he appears in the Bible.

God's plan, the plan initiated by Abraham, is still being worked out.

Not tomorrow. Nor the day after. But eventually, inevitably.

NOTES

ABBREVIATIONS

ABD 1–6	*Anchor Bible Dictionary (6 vols.; New York, 1995)*
ANET	*Ancient Near Eastern Texts Relating to the Old Testament (Princeton, N.J., 1969)*
BA	*Biblical Archaeologist*
BARev	*Biblical Archaeology Review*
BASOR	*Bulletin of the American Schools of Oriental Research*
IEJ	*Israel Exploration Journal*
JBL	*Journal of Biblical Literature*
JNES	*Journal of Near Eastern Studies*
JSS	*Journal of Semitic Studies*
OEA 1–5	*Oxford Encyclopedia of Archaeology in the Ancient Near East (5 vols.; Oxford, 1997)*
PRE	*Pirke d'Rabbi Eliezer*

INTRODUCTION: Bus No. 160

1. Albright 1961:52.

2. Rabbi Daniel Lapin helped me understand this.

3. Gen. 1:28.

4. See, for instance, *Shabbat* 10a; also Benamozegh 1995:190–204, where this point is laid out in detail.

5. *Genesis Rabbah* 43:7.

6. Gen. 12:1–17:27, 18:1–22:24, and 23:1–25:18.

7. Maimonides, *Mishneh Torah, Hilchot Avodat Kochavim* 1:2.

CHAPTER ONE: A Palace in Flames

1. Ginzberg 1:188–200, 5:212–13.

2. Rashi on Gen. 10:9.

3. Secular scholars deny the attribution.

4. *PRE* 26.

5. See Maimonides 1956:315; Ramban on Gen. 11:28; Firestone 1990:25.

6. Saggs 1962:310.

7. See Sarna 1995:82; Albright 1957:150; Gordon and Rendsburg 1997:112.

8. Nachmanides, Rashi, and the Midrash all hint at this. For a discussion of these traditional Jewish sources in the light of modern science, see Schroeder 1997.

9. Saggs 1962:18.

10. See Saggs 1962:31 and Gen. 10:10.

11. Maimonides, *Mishneh Torah, Hilchot Avodat Kochavim* 1:1–2.

12. Speiser 1964:10.

13. Rashi on Gen. 24:7.

14. Ibid. on Gen. 11:32.

15. Jacobsen 1976:3–7.

16. Ibid.

17. Radak on Gen. 10:8.

18. Woolley 1965:125.

19. Gen. 10:26; *Genesis Rabbah* 37:8.

20. Benamozegh 1995:100.

21. *Pirke Avot* 5:8.

22. Liverani 1978:105–6.

23. De Vaux 1978:59.

24. Bright 1972:77; de Vaux 1978:196.

25. Cassuto 1964:298.

26. Rashi on Gen. 20:12.

27. Saggs 1962:314.

28. Josh. 24:2.

29. Maimonides, *Mishneh Torah, Hilchot Avodat Kochavim* 1:2.

30. *Genesis Rabbah* 39:8.

31. Bright 1972:77, 98.

32. Weinberg 1999:48.

33. Cassuto 1964:267.

34. See Gen. 10:10, which also credits Nimrod with founding "Calneh," whose identification remains uncertain.

35. Saggs 1962:347.

36. *Baba Batra* 91a.

37. *Genesis Rabbah* 39:1.

38. Zornberg 1995:76.

39. For interpretations of the parable, see Heschel 1955:112, 367, and Sacks 2000:54–60.

CHAPTER TWO: Let There Be Light

1. Gen. 11:28.

2. *Baba Batra* 91a.

3. *Genesis Rabbah* 38:13.

4. Saggs 1962:305, 308.

5. Rashi on Gen. 11:28.

6. See Rashi on Gen. 19:28.

7. *Pesachim* 118a.

8. Rashi on Gen. 24:7.

9. Ibid. on Gen. 11:28.

10. *Genesis Rabbah* 38:13.

11. Maimonides, *Mishneh Torah, Hilchot Avodat Kochavim* 1:2–3. For the sake of clarity, I have omitted Rambam's references to Ur Kasdim, which here he seems to present, at its level of surface meaning, as if it were a city.

12. *Nedarim* 32a; *Genesis Rabbah* 64:4.

13. Maimonides, *Mishneh Torah, Hilchot Avodat Kochavim* 1:3.

14. Ibid.

15. Bloom 1991:195.

16. *Genesis Rabbah* 38:13.

17. *Baba Batra* 91a; and see the translation of Onkelos on Gen. 8:4.

18. Ramban on Gen. 11:28.

19. Ibid.

20. Maimonides, *Mishneh Torah, Hilchot Avodat Kochavim* 1:2.

21. *Shabbat* 36a.

22. Rashi on *Pesachim* 94b.

23. Sforno on Gen. 11:6.

24. *PRE* 24, quoting Ps. 55:10.

25. Christie 1977:376–77.

26. See Finkelstein and Silberman 2001.

27. Radak on Gen. 11:28.

28. Gen. 22:22.

29. Gen. 14:7.

30. Gen. 14:14.

31. Gen. 21:14.

32. Leibowitz 1996:273.

33. See Prov. 31:24.

34. See Gen. 37:25, 27. In this passage, a caravan of Midianites are called Ishmaelites.

35. See Deut. 26:5. In this passage, the patriarch Jacob is called an Aramean, meaning that he worked as a shepherd.

36. See Dan. 2:2, where Kasdim are listed among several classes of occultists.

37. *Megillah* 14a.

38. Vermes 1998:454.

39. *Genesis Rabbah* 40:5.

40. See *Yebamot* 64a–b with *Tosafot;* also 81a; and *Baba Batra* 126b.

41. Weinberg 1999:86, 92.

42. Maharsha on *Yebamot* 64b.

43. Gen. 11:30.

44. *Yebamot* 64b.

45. Woolley 1965:101.

46. Saggs 1962:214.

47. Gordon 1963:82–83.

48. Cahill 1998:58.

49. De Vaux 1978:195; Parrot 1968:40–41.

50. Maimonides, *Mishneh Torah, Hilchot Avodat Kochavim* 1:3.

51. Gen. 12:5.

52. Rashi on Gen. 12:5.

53. *Sanhedrin* 99b.

54. *Genesis Rabbah* 39:14.

55. Maimonides, *Mishneh Torah, Hilchot Avodat Kochavim* 1:3.

56. Isa. 41:8.

57. *Yoma* 86a.

58. *Sefer Hamitzyot,* positive commandment no. 3.

59. See Twersky 1972:406.

60. Maimonides, *Mishneh Torah, Hilchot Melachim* 8:10.

61. Sforno on Exod. 19:6.

62. The phrase is used by Rabbi Lawrence Keleman in an excellent book of the same name.

63. Maimonides, *Mishneh Torah, Hilchot Avodat Kochavim* 1:3.

64. Ibid.

65. *Avodah Zarah* 14b.

66. *Kiddushin* 32b; *Baba Batra* 16b.

67. Anyway, it encapsulates teachings that Abram originated. Its written form probably dates to between A.D. 200 and 400.

68. See Kaplan 1997:xii–xiv.

69. Prov. 3:18.

70. The Talmud's scheme of three two-thousand-year epochs appears in *Avodah Zarah* 9a and *Sanhedrin* 97a–b. Ramban on Gen. 2:3 explains the correspondence of each millennium to a day of creation. For those keeping track, the third two-thousand-year epoch began in A.D. 240, shortly after the completion of the Mishnah. This was the

first time the Jews had committed part of their oral tradition to writing, concerned they would forget it if they did not, and was considered an ominous occasion. So commenced the slow, two-thousand-year lead-up to the coming of the Messiah, whose deadline for arrival would thus be the year 6000 in Jewish reckoning, or A.D. 2240.

71. De Vaux 1978:225–30.

72. Maimonides, *Mishneh Torah, Hilchot Avodat Kochavim* 1:3.

73. *Pirke Avot* 5:3.

74. *Pirke Avot* 5:1.

75. Maimonides 1956:304.

76. Gen. 22:12.

77. *Genesis Rabbah* 56:7.

78. Augustine 1950:555.

79. Ramban on Gen. 22:1.

CHAPTER THREE: Did Abraham Live?

1. "Hashem," literally meaning "the Name," will be used here where the Bible uses the ineffable four-letter Hebrew name of God. The latter, called the tetragrammaton, is by a strong convention never pronounced, or even written out except in holy books. By the same convention, other divine names are pronounced differently from how they are written. Thus "Elohim" is pronounced "Elokim," and "El" is pronounced "Kel."

2. For a lively summary of the latest version of Wellhausen's thinking, see Friedman 1987.

3. Glueck 1959:31.

4. Respectively, *The Historicity of the Patriarchal Narratives* and *Abraham in History and Tradition*.

5. Fieler 2001:74.

6. Auerbach 1953:14–15.

7. Heschel 1955:236.

8. See Auerbach 1953:9–12; Kugel 1997:17–36.

9. Bloom 1991:26.

10. For an intellectual genealogy of the sages, showing the precise line of transmission, see the first chapter of the Mishnaic tractate *Pirke Avot*.

11. *Menachot* 29b.

12. Skeptics will point out that if Abraham is a historical memory, then so must be the six days of creation and Noah's flood. It would seem so, but deciphering those two memories, conveyed in still more cryptic formulations than the Abraham story, would require two additional books. In the first chapters of Genesis, little is as it seems.

CHAPTER FOUR: The Unknown Land

1. Ramban on Gen. 12:6.

2. Maimonides 1956:240–44.

3. *Nedarim* 38a; *Shabbat* 92a.

4. Maimonides, *Mishneh Torah, Hilchot Yesodei HaTorah* 7:1–4.

5. Gen. 12:1–3.

6. Rashi on Gen. 12:2; *Genesis Rabbah* 39:11.

7. Ramban on Gen. 12:1.

8. Rashi on Gen. 12:9.

9. *Rosh Hashanah* 16b.

10. Gen. 22:18.

11. Gordis 1997:42.

12. Parrot 1968:60.

13. Aharoni et al. 1993:map 43.

14. Wiseman 1983:143.

15. Ramban on Gen. 12:1.

16. *ANET* 19.

17. *Genesis Rabbah* 39:8.

18. Gen. 12:6.

19. Rashi on Gen. 12:6.

20. Gen. 13:7.

21. Ramban on Gen. 13:7.

22. Gen. 14:7.

23. Deut. 7:1. One might object here that in Gen. 15:19–21, in a vision of Abram, God refers to no fewer than ten peoples of the land of Canaan—apparently a contradiction of this verse in Deuteronomy, which counts only seven such groups. But Rashi (on 15:19) understands the ten nations of Canaan as pointing to a distant future time, even the Messianic era. Sages also see here an allusion to the ten mystical levels of spiritual impurity—which may have something to do with the "secret" that Ibn Ezra has in mind.

24. See Bright 1972:43, 54–55.

25. Liverani 1978:108, 124.

26. Lev. 18:25.

27. Albright 1968:111.

28. Ibid., p. 112.

29. Albright 1957:175–78.

30. Gray 1964:76.

31. Ibid., p. 116.

32. Albright 1946:93; Gordon and Rendsburg 1997:94.

33. Gray 1964:136.

34. Lev. 18:3.

35. Gen. 15:16.

36. Gen. 12:6.

37. Stephens 1996:420, 424.

38. *Sanhedrin* 102a.

39. Rashi on Gen. 12:6.

40. De Vaux 1965:406.

41. Ramban on Gen. 12:6.

42. Speiser 1964:267.

43. Freedman and Campbell 1961:258.

44. Maimonides 1956:235.

45. Gen. 12:7.

46. Ibid.

47. Bright 1972:81.

48. Gray 1964:46.

49. *ABD* 1:712.

50. Gray 1964:57–59.

51. Cassuto 1964:331.

52. Sforno on Gen. 12:8.

53. Rashi on Gen. 12:8.

54. This point is made well by Gordis 1997:45.

55. Rashi on Gen. 12:10.

56. Maimonides, *Mishneh Torah, Hilchot Ishut* 15:2.

CHAPTER FIVE: Into the Spiral

1. Cf. *ANET* 21.

2. *Genesis Rabbah* 40:5.

3. Ramban on Gen. 12:10.

4. Rashi on Gen. 12:10.

5. Wilson 1951:258.

6. Ibid., p. 11; Glueck 1959:67.

7. Glueck 1959:88.

8. Rashi on Gen. 13:3.

9. Wilson 1951:23.

10. *Genesis Rabbah* 40:4.

11. Gen. 12:11.

12. Rashi on Gen. 12:11.

13. See Rohl 1995.

14. *PRE* 26.

15. Wilson 1951:120.

16. Ibid., pp. 58–59, 114, 118–120.

17. Frankfort 1946:75–77.

18. *Tanchuma, Lech L'chah* 5.

19. *ANET* 22.

20. Gen. 12:16.

21. *Baba Metzia* 59a.

22. Radak on Gen. 12:12; *Shabbat* 32a.

23. Ramban on Gen. 12:1.

24. Bloom 1991:200.

25. *PRE* 26.

26. *Ketubot* 77b.

27. Rashi on Gen. 12:17.

28. *Genesis Rabbah* 41:2.

29. Gen. 12:18–19.

30. Cassuto 1964:357–58.

31. *Genesis Rabbah* 45:1.

32. Gordon and Rendsburg 1997:67.

33. Actually one difference between the early and later skeptical Bible critics is that while the former saw only five or so writers whose work the Redactor had combined, some recent opinions favor a hypothesis in which the Torah was stitched together from innumerable shards of text. For the sake of simplicity, in this book I engage with the classic and more streamlined theory of the earlier skeptics.

34. Gen. 20:18.

35. Speiser 1964:150.

36. Bloom 1991:200.

37. Speiser 1964:91ff.

38. Shanks 1975:22–26.

39. I heard this explanation from Rabbi Daniel Lapin.

40. See Free 1944.

41. Ramban on 12:10.

42. *Exodus Rabbah* 1:22.

43. Exod. 12:33.

44. Exod. 12:35–36.

45. Rashi on Gen. 13:3.

46. Gen. 13:5.

47. Gen. 12:16.

48. Rashi on Gen. 19:29.

49. *Genesis Rabbah* 41:8.

50. *Genesis Rabbah* 41:5.

51. Rashi on Gen. 13:8.

52. Ibid.

53. Gordon 1935:227.

54. Rashi on Gen. 13:9.

55. Gen. 13:8–9.

56. Gen. 13:10.

57. See Num. 15:39; Deut. 6:4.

58. Radak on Gen. 13:11.

59. Gen. 13:10.

60. Harland 1961:47; Sarna 1995:139.

61. Gen. 13:11.

62. Rashi on Gen. 13:11.

63. Gen. 3:24.

64. Ps. 89:21; *Genesis Rabbah* 41:4.

65. The Talmud, in *Sanhedrin* 91b, recounts a debate between sages as to how radically the Messiah's appearance will transform history. One view indicates that the change will elevate mankind to a new, supernatural level of existence. The other says it will amount only to the establishment of universal peace and justice and the end of oppression by the world's nations so that humans can pursue their relationship with God unhindered by violence and coercion. Either way, as the Hebrew prophets made clear, there will be no mistaking that history as we know it has ended. There follows the resurrection of the dead and the reward of the righteous of all peoples in a heavenly Garden of Eden, the World of Souls, where they live in the Presence of God forever after.

66. Gen. 13:17.

CHAPTER SIX: The Fugitive

1. Josephus 1981:276.

2. *Yoma* 28b.

3. Gen. 14:13–14.

4. *Yoma* 28b.

5. Ibn Ezra on Gen. 14:5.

6. Gordon and Rendsburg 1997:91–92.

7. Deut. 3:11.

8. *Genesis Rabbah* 18:6.

9. De Vaux 1978:218–19; Speiser 1964:106–7.

10. Rashi on Gen. 14:4.

11. Speiser 1964:109.

12. 2 Chron. 20:2.

13. Glueck 1955:7–8.

14. *Genesis Rabbah* 42:7.

15. *Tanchuma, Lech L'chah* 6.

16. *Genesis Rabbah* 42:8.

17. Gordon 1963:81.

18. Ps. 112:7.

19. *Genesis Rabbah* 43:1; *Berachot* 60a.

20. Gen. 14:14.

21. De Vaux 1978:217.

22. Speiser 1964:101–8.

23. Maimonides, *Mishneh Torah, Hilchot Yesodei HaTorah* 2:2.

24. Ibid., *Mishneh Torah, Hilchot Teshuvah* 10:6.
25. Gen. 14:13.
26. *Genesis Rabbah* 43:2.
27. *Nedarim* 32a.
28. *Genesis Rabbah* 43:2.
29. *Sanhedrin* 96a.
30. 1 Kings 12:28–29.
31. *Tanchuma, Lech L'chah* 13.
32. *Genesis Rabbah* 43:2.
33. Rashi on Gen. 14:24.
34. *Sanhedrin* 108b.
35. Gen. 14:15.
36. *PRE* 27.
37. Ibid.
38. 2 Sam. 18:18.
39. *ABD* 3:751.
40. Gen. 14:18 with Ibn Ezra's comments; cf. Ps. 76:3.
41. Rashi on Gen. 14:17.
42. Gen. 14:21; Rashi on Gen. 14:24.
43. *PRE* 27.
44. May 1941:114–15.
45. Della Vida 1944:2–6.
46. Exod. 15:11.
47. Ramban on Gen. 14:18.
48. Rashi on Gen. 14:18.
49. Sforno on Gen. 14:18.
50. Ps. 110:4 with commentary of Hebrews 8.
51. Heb. 7:2–3.
52. Heb. 7:7.
53. *Baba Batra* 121b.
54. *Nedarim* 32b.
55. Exod. 19:6.
56. *PRE* 40.
57. Benamozegh 1995:325–26.
58. *Tanchuma, Vayera* 22.
59. *Megillah* 16b.
60. Gen. 10:22.
61. *Genesis Rabbah* 44:7.
62. *Genesis Rabbah* 43:6.
63. Prov. 9:5.
64. *Genesis Rabbah* 42:4.
65. *Genesis Rabbah* 43:6.

CHAPTER SEVEN: What the Stars Said

1. Bloom 1991:201.
2. Gen. 15:1.
3. See *Genesis Rabbah* 44:4–5 and Ramban on Gen. 15:1.
4. Ramban on Gen. 15:1.
5. Maimonides, *Mishneh Torah, Hilchot Yesodei HaTorah* 7:31.
6. *Moed Katan* 28a.
7. Rashi on Gen. 15:1.
8. Gen. 15:1.
9. Gen. 15:2.
10. Bright 1972:78.
11. Gen. 15:3.
12. Gen. 15:4.
13. Gen. 15:5.
14. Gen. 15:12.
15. *Shabbat* 156a; *Genesis Rabbah* 44:10.
16. Rashi on Gen. 15:5.
17. Ibid.
18. *Genesis Rabbah* 44:12.
19. Gal. 3:6.
20. Malbim on Gen. 15:6–8.
21. Sarna 1995:126.
22. Speiser 1964:112–13.
23. Rashi on Gen. 15:10.
24. Ibid.
25. *Megillah* 31b.
26. Kaplan 1997:33–35.
27. *Megillah* 31b.
28. Malbim on Gen. 15:9.
29. *Genesis Rabbah* 44:16.
30. Maimonides 1956:245.
31. Gen. 15:12.
32. *Genesis Rabbah* 44:15.
33. *Genesis Rabbah* 44:17.
34. See Maimonides, *Mishneh Torah, Hilchot Melachim* 10–11, based on the prophecies contained in the Torah and the Hebrew prophets.
35. Gen. 15:13.
36. Gen. 15:16.
37. Exod. 12:40.
38. *Genesis Rabbah* 91:2; Rashi on Gen. 15:13, 42:2.
39. Ibn Ezra on Gen. 15:13.

40. *Avodah Zarah* 9a.

41. Exod. 12:40.

42. Gen. 15:17–18.

43. *Genesis Rabbah* 44:21.

44. *Genesis Rabbah* 44:22.

CHAPTER EIGHT: The Handmaiden's Tale

1. *Genesis Rabbah* 60:5.

2. *Genesis Rabbah* 45:3.

3. Sforno on Gen. 16:8.

4. *Genesis Rabbah* 45:7.

5. Maimonides 1956:162.

6. Gen. 12:2.

7. Malbim on Ps. 27:13.

8. *Yebamot* 64a.

9. *Genesis Rabbah* 45:2.

10. *Sanhedrin* 106b.

11. *Genesis Rabbah* 45:4.

12. Ibid.

13. Rashi on Gen. 16:3.

14. Woolley 1965:100.

15. Gordon and Rendsburg 1997:111.

16. *ANET* 220; Gordon 1940:3.

17. Speiser 1964:120–21.

18. Gen. 16:2.

19. Sarna 1995:128; Ramban on Gen. 16:2.

20. Kardimon 1958:123–26.

21. Rashi on Gen. 16:2.

22. Maimonides, *Mishneh Torah, Hilchot Yesodei HaTorah* 7:4.

23. *Genesis Rabbah* 45:5.

24. *Genesis Rabbah* 47:1.

25. *Genesis Rabbah* 45:3.

26. Rabbi David Silber makes this point in a taped lecture.

27. Maimonides, *Commentary on Pirke Avot* 5:3.

28. Rashi on Gen. 16:4.

29. *Yebamot* 34a.

30. *Genesis Rabbah* 45:4.

31. Rashi on Gen. 23:1, 25:7.

32. Ramban on Gen. 16:6.

33. For this understanding of patriarchal "sin," I am indebted to Rabbi Daniel Lapin.

34. *ANET* 220.
35. Ibid., 172.
36. Ibid., 525.
37. Gen. 16:5.
38. *Genesis Rabbah* 45:5.
39. *Rosh Hashanah* 16b.
40. *Baba Kamma* 93a.
41. Gen. 16:6.
42. *Genesis Rabbah* 45:6.
43. Rashi on Lev. 25:39.
44. Ibid. on Gen. 16:5.
45. Gen. 16:6.
46. Radak on Gen. 16:7.
47. *ABD* 1:676.
48. *Chagigah* 11b.
49. Maimonides 1956:66.
50. *ABD* 1:250.
51. *Genesis Rabbah* 10:6.
52. Luzzatto 1988:75.
53. Ibid., pp. 87, 147.
54. *Genesis Rabbah* 50:2.
55. *Genesis Rabbah* 1:3.
56. *Sotah* 33a.
57. *Chagigah* 16a.
58. Maimonides, *Mishneh Torah, Hilchot Yesodei HaTorah* 2:7.
59. Rashi on Gen. 14:10.
60. Rashi on Gen. 16:13.
61. *Genesis Rabbah* 45:7.
62. Gen. 16:11–12.
63. *Targum Onkelos* on Gen. 16:12.
64. Rashi on Gen. 16:12.
65. Sura 19:54–55.
66. See Firestone 1990:41–46.
67. Ramban on Gen. 16:11.
68. Rashi on Gen. 16:15.
69. Steinmetz 1991:63ff.

CHAPTER NINE: The Kindest Cut

1. Ramban on Gen. 17:26.
2. *Genesis Rabbah* 47:7.
3. *Genesis Rabbah* 49:2.

4. Sforno on Gen. 17:1.

5. Gen. 17:1–2.

6. Gen. 17:4–8.

7. Speiser 1964:xxiv, 125.

8. Gen. 17:16.

9. Rashi and Ramban on Gen. 17:18.

10. Gen. 17:18.

11. Gen. 17:21.

12. Gen. 12:7.

13. Gen. 13:15.

14. Gen. 15:18.

15. Gen. 17:8.

16. Ramban on Gen. 15:17.

17. De Vaux 1978:197; Speiser 1964:124; Sarna 1995:130.

18. Rashi on Gen. 17:5.

19. *Genesis Rabbah* 63:3.

20. *Genesis Rabbah* 47:1.

21. Gen. 17:7–8.

22. Gal. 3:16–29.

23. De Vaux 1978:198.

24. Gen. 17:10–12.

25. Gollaher 2000:2.

26. *ANET* 326.

27. Sasson 1966:473–76.

28. Maimonides 1956:378.

29. See Gollaher 2000.

30. *Genesis Rabbah* 46:2.

31. *Genesis Rabbah* 46:3.

32. Gen. 18:1.

33. *Genesis Rabbah* 42:8.

34. *Tanchuma, Vayera* 3.

35. Malbim on Gen. 18:1.

36. Gen. 17:23.

37. Rashi on Gen. 2:15, 12:5.

38. Ibid. on Gen. 17:23.

39. Maimonides 1956:378.

40. Ibid.

41. *Genesis Rabbah* 47:7.

42. *Genesis Rabbah* 46:9.

43. Rashi on Gen. 17:1.

44. Gen. 26:5; *Yoma* 28b; *Genesis Rabbah* 64:4. Also see Rashi on Gen. 26:5.

45. For this analogy, I'm indebted to Rabbi Daniel Lapin.

46. Rom. 4:11.

47. Delaney 1998:152.

48. Siker 1991:166–67.

CHAPTER TEN: Annunciation

1. Malbim on Gen. 18:1.

2. *Baba Metzia* 86b.

3. Gen. 35:19.

4. Feiler 2001:51.

5. Rashi on Gen. 20:1.

6. *Genesis Rabbah* 48:8.

7. Firestone 1990:54.

8. Ibid., p. 8.

9. Ramban on Gen. 18:1.

10. *Genesis Rabbah* 48:2; Malbim on Gen. 17:10, 18:1.

11. Gen. 18:1–2.

12. *Baba Metzia* 86b.

13. Rashi on Gen. 18:1.

14. Malbim on Gen. 18:2.

15. Ramban on Gen. 18:1.

16. Quran 11:69–70.

17. Gen. 18:3 as interpreted in Rashi's second explanation.

18. Rashi on Gen. 18:4.

19. *Baba Metzia* 86b.

20. Gen. 18:4–5.

21. Gen. 18:11, 24:1.

22. *Genesis Rabbah* 48:16.

23. Gen. 18:6.

24. Speiser 1964:130.

25. *Baba Metzia* 86b–87a.

26. Rashi on Gen. 18:7.

27. Delaney 1998:177.

28. *PRE* 36.

29. Rashi on Gen. 18:2; *Baba Metzia* 86b; *Yoma* 37a.

30. Rashi on Gen. 18:16; Ramban on Gen. 18:3.

31. Maimonides 1956:238.

32. Ramban on Gen. 18:1.

33. *PRE* 36; *Genesis Rabbah* 48:14.

34. Malbim on Gen. 18:9.

35. *Baba Metzia* 86b; *Genesis Rabbah* 48:14.

36. Rashi on Gen. 18:5.

37. Malbim on Gen. 18:9.

38. Rashi on Gen. 18:10.

39. *Genesis Rabbah* 48:16.

40. Rashi on Gen. 18:12.

41. Gen. 18:12.

42. Rashi on Gen. 18:12.

43. Gen. 18:13.

44. Radak on Gen. 18:13.

45. Gen. 18:22.

46. Gen. 18:14; Rashi on Gen. 21:2.

47. Gen. 18:17.

48. *Baba Kamma* 60a.

49. *Genesis Rabbah* 49:6.

50. Gen. 18:16.

51. Rashi on Gen. 18:16.

CHAPTER ELEVEN: Sin Cities

1. *Genesis Rabbah* 49:14.

2. *Genesis Rabbah* 50:2.

3. Gen. 19:2.

4. Gen. 13:12.

5. *Genesis Rabbah* 50:9.

6. *Targum Onkelos* on Gen. 19:15.

7. Rashi on Gen. 19:1.

8. Ibid. on Gen. 19:3.

9. Ibid. on Gen. 19:1.

10. Gen. 13:10.

11. Harland 1961:73.

12. Ibid.

13. Ibid., p. 56.

14. Shanks 1980:33.

15. *Sanhedrin* 109a.

16. Gen. 13:13.

17. *Sanhedrin* 109a.

18. Bloom 1991:204.

19. *Genesis Rabbah* 50:7.

20. *Sanhedrin* 109a.

21. For these insights, I am grateful to Rabbi Daniel Lapin.

22. Gen. 18:20–21.

23. Speiser 1964:134.

24. *PRE* 25.

25. Gen. 19:3.

26. Sforno on Gen. 19:3.

27. Or HaChaim on Gen. 19:3.

28. *Genesis Rabbah* 50:4.

29. *Genesis Rabbah* 51:5.

30. Rashi on Gen. 19:4.

31. Gen. 19:8.

32. *Genesis Rabbah* 50:5.

33. *Genesis Rabbah* 50:9.

34. Gen. 19:14.

35. *Genesis Rabbah* 50:9.

36. Gen. 19:15.

37. Rashi on Gen. 19:17.

38. *Genesis Rabbah* 50:11.

39. Eccles. 5:12.

40. Gen. 19:17.

41. *Genesis Rabbah* 49:7.

42. Harland 1961:48–50.

43. Gen. 12:8, 13:3; Rashi on Gen. 19:17.

44. *Genesis Rabbah* 39:16; also see Joshua 7.

45. Gen. 19:19.

46. *Berachot* 26b.

47. Gen. 19:28.

48. Bloom 1991:205.

49. Rashi on Gen. 19:24.

50. *Genesis Rabbah* 49:5.

51. Rashi on Gen. 19:24.

52. Gen. 19:25.

53. *Genesis Rabbah* 51:4.

54. Harland 1961:59.

55. Radak on Gen. 19:30.

56. Gen. 19:31–32.

57. *Genesis Rabbah* 51:9.

58. Finkelstein and Silberman 2001:39.

59. Rashi on Gen. 19:33.

60. *Genesis Rabbah* 51:8.

61. *Genesis Rabbah* 50:10; Ps. 89:21.

CHAPTER TWELVE: Thy Neighbor's Wife

1. Rashi on Gen. 20:1.

2. Speiser 1964:150.

3. Rashi on Gen. 12:19.
4. Radak on Gen. 20:11.
5. Malbim on Gen. 20:11.
6. *Baba Kamma* 92a.
7. Rashi on Gen. 20:2.
8. Gray 1964:85.
9. *Baba Kamma* 92a.
10. Gen. 20:2
11. *ABD* 2:989.
12. Aharoni 1956:31; Kenyon 1979:164–66.
13. *OEA* 2:474.
14. Gen. 21:32, 34.
15. Gen. 26:1.
16. Finkelstein and Silberman 2001:38.
17. *ABD* 5:333.
18. Jer. 47:4 Gen. 10:14; *ABD* 1:869.
19. Wiseman 1983:150–51; Kenyon 1979:187.
20. Gordon and Rendsburg 1997:118.
21. Gen. 20:5.
22. Maimonides, *Mishneh Torah, Hilchot Ishut* 1:1.
23. *Genesis Rabbah* 52:12; Ramban on Gen. 20:17.
24. *Genesis Rabbah* 52:13.
25. Gen. 20:18.
26. Rashi on Gen. 20:9.
27. Gen. 20:5–6.
28. Rashi on Gen. 20:6.
29. *Genesis Rabbah* 52:9.
30. Gen. 20:3.
31. Gen. 20:6–7.
32. Gen. 20:9.
33. Gen. 20:12.
34. Rashi on Gen. 20:12.
35. Gen. 20:13.
36. Rashi on Gen. 21:14.
37. Ramban on Gen. 12:10.
38. Radak on Gen. 20:1.
39. Gen. 20:17.
40. *Genesis Rabbah* 52:13.
41. *Baba Kamma* 92a.
42. Ramban on Gen. 20:16.
43. Gen. 20:16.
44. Rashi on Gen. 20:16.

CHAPTER THIRTEEN: Birth of a Nation

1. *PRE* 30.
2. Gen. 21:14.
3. Speiser 1964:154–55.
4. Rashi on Gen. 21:14–15.
5. *Genesis Rabbah* 53:10.
6. Van Seters 1975:111.
7. See De Vaux 1978:229–30.
8. Gen. 20:14.
9. Matthews 1986:120.
10. Gen. 20:15; *Genesis Rabbah* 54:2, 6.
11. Rashi on Num. 5:28.
12. Gen. 21:1.
13. *Genesis Rabbah* 53:6.
14. *Rosh Hashanah* 11a.
15. *Genesis Rabbah* 53:7.
16. *Genesis Rabbah* 53:8.
17. Rashi on Gen. 21:7.
18. *Genesis Rabbah* 53:6.
19. Rashi on Gen. 21:8.
20. Gen. 21:7.
21. Rashi on Gen. 21:8.
22. *Baba Metzia* 87a.
23. Rashi on Gen. 21:6.
24. *Genesis Rabbah* 53:11; Gen. 21:10.
25. *ANET* 173.
26. Gen. 21:12.
27. *Genesis Rabbah* 53:12.
28. Gen. 21:10, 12.
29. Rashi on Gen. 21:12.
30. Gordon 1940:3; Gordon and Rendsburg 1997:120.
31. *ANET* 160.
32. *Genesis Rabbah* 53:11; *PRE* 30.
33. For this insight I am, as always, indebted to Rabbi Daniel Lapin.
34. Rashi on Gen. 22:2.
35. Ibid. on Gen. 21:14.
36. *PRE* 30.
37. Gen. 21:14–15.
38. *PRE* 30.
39. Rashi on Gen. 21:15.
40. Ibid. on Gen. 21:17.

41. Ibid.
42. *Rosh Hashanah* 16b.
43. Gen. 21:19.
44. Speiser 1964:156.
45. *PRE* 30.
46. Quran 2:127.
47. Firestone 1990:63–68.
48. *Genesis Rabbah* 56:1.
49. *PRE* 31.
50. Delaney 1998:176–77.
51. Firestone 1990:80–100.
52. *Exodus Rabbah* 28:6; *Tanchuma,* Buber ed., *Netzavim* 8.
53. Gen. 21:26.
54. Gen. 21:33.
55. See Benamozegh 1995:101.
56. Matthews 1986:134.
57. Wiseman 1983:49.
58. De Vaux 1978:285; Deut. 12:2.
59. Speiser 1964:160.
60. *Genesis Rabbah* 54:5.
61. Rashi on *Sotah* 10a.
62. *Tanchuma, Noah* 14.
63. *Genesis Rabbah* 54:6.
64. Gen. 21:33.
65. *Sotah* 10a.

CHAPTER FOURTEEN: The Slaughter of Isaac

1. See Maimonides, *Mishneh Torah, Hilchot Bait Habechirah* 2:1–2; *PRE* 31.
2. Gen. 22:9.
3. Speiser 1964:165.
4. Gen. 22:9–10.
5. Rashi on Gen. 22:9 and *Shabbat* 54a.
6. *Genesis Rabbah* 56:8; *PRE* 31.
7. Maimonides 1956:244.
8. Rashi on Gen. 22:12; *Genesis Rabbah* 56:7.
9. Gen. 22:18.
10. Gen. 12:3.
11. Sforno on Gen. 22:18.
12. Gen. 22:19.
13. See Ramban and Ibn Ezra on Exod. 33:11, where Joshua, Moses' fifty-six-year-old subordinate, is called a lad.

14. Delaney 1998:139.

15. Quran 37:100–9.

16. Firestone 1990:135.

17. Delaney 1998:180.

18. Kierkegaard 1983:66.

19. Anati 1963:427; Finegan 1959:147–48; Eliade 1974:109; Gray 1964:66–67. For a dissenting view, see Finkelstein 1959:345.

20. See Num. 3:11–13 with Sforno's commentary.

21. *Sanhedrin* 89b.

22. Rashi on Gen. 21:34.

23. *Genesis Rabbah* 58:5, 38:12.

24. *Baba Batra* 16a.

25. *Genesis Rabbah* 55:4.

26. Gen. 22:1–2.

27. Bloom 1991:206.

28. Exod. 32:13.

29. Rashi on Exod. 32:13.

30. *Sotah* 12a.

31. *Sanhedrin* 87a. Ordinary theft is prohibited elsewhere, in Lev. 19:11.

32. Zornberg 1995:97.

33. Weinberg 1999:83.

34. *Sanhedrin* 89b.

35. Gen. 22:3.

36. *Genesis Rabbah* 55:8.

37. *Tanchuma, Vayera* 23.

38. Radak on Gen. 22:3.

39. Zornberg 1995:136.

40. Gen. 22:3; *Genesis Rabbah* 55:8.

41. Ramban on Gen. 22:2.

42. Rashi on Gen. 22:2.

43. Eccles. 4:12.

44. Skinner 1969:328.

45. Finkelstein 1959:347.

46. Glueck 1959:63–64.

47. Ramban on Gen. 23:2.

48. *Genesis Rabbah* 56:3.

49. *ABD* 1:1207–9.

50. *Tanchuma, Vayera* 22.

51. *PRE* 31.

52. *Genesis Rabbah* 56:1; *PRE* 31.

53. *Tanchuma, Vayera* 23; Gen. 22:5.

54. Gen. 11:3–4.

55. For this insight, I am indebted to Rabbi Daniel Lapin.

56. Gen. 22:7–8.

57. Speiser 1964:165.

58. Rashi on Gen. 22:6, 8.

59. Gen. 22:2.

60. Speiser 1964:166.

61. 1 Chron. 21:15.

62. *Berachot* 62b.

63. *Zevachim* 62a.

64. *Tanchuma, Vayera* 23.

65. Rashi on Gen. 22:14.

66. Ibn Ezra on Gen. 22:19.

67. Spiegel 1993:33–37.

68. *Pirke Avot* 5:8.

69. Spiegel 1993:57.

70. *Tanchuma, Vayera* 23.

71. Maimonides, *Mishneh Torah, Hilchot Yesodei HaTorah* 1:1.

72. Ibid., 1:7.

73. Ps. 145:13.

74. This title is invoked each Sabbath before the Torah reading.

75. Deutsch 1997:288, 291.

76. Gen. 12:1.

77. Gen. 22:2.

78. Gen. 22:19.

CHAPTER FIFTEEN: The Life of Sarah

1. Rashi on Gen. 23:2.

2. For a full and illuminating discussion of this idea, see Zornberg 1995:127.

3. Gen. 23:2.

4. Rashi on Gen. 23:2.

5. *PRE* 32; Zornberg 1995:124.

6. Rashi on Gen. 23:2.

7. *Tanchuma, Vayera* 23.

8. Gen. 16:5.

9. *Rosh Hashanah* 16b.

10. Rashi on Gen. 23:2.

11. Ramban on Gen. 23:2.

12. Prov. 31:10–31.

13. Gen. 23:3.

14. *Genesis Rabbah* 58:6. For the identification of the angel of death with Satan, see *Baba Batra* 16a.

15. Radak on Gen. 23:3.

16. Though the opinion of the great Cyrus H. Gordon, a brave modern scholar who upheld the identification between Hittites and Bene Chayt, is not to be scorned entirely; see Gordon and Rendsburg 1997:80.

17. Albright 1961:48.

18. Josh. 10:3–5.

19. Gen. 37:14. Thanks to David Wilder for explaining this reference to me.

20. Ramban on Gen. 23:9.

21. *Genesis Rabbah* 58:7.

22. Sarna 1995:169.

23. Kohler 1953:130–41.

24. Gen. 23:4.

25. Gordon and Rendsburg 1997:114.

26. Ramban on Gen. 23:4–6.

27. Gen. 23:6.

28. *Genesis Rabbah* 58:7.

29. *Genesis Rabbah* 58:4.

30. Rashi on Gen. 23:16.

31. Gen. 23:15.

32. Gen. 23:16.

33. Speiser 1964:171.

34. Jer. 32:9.

35. Rashi on Gen. 23:16.

36. Gen. 23:17.

37. Lehmann 1953:15–18; Wright 1962:51.

38. Tucker 1966:79–84; Van Seters 1975:98–99.

39. Rashi on Gen. 23:2. Thanks to Rabbi Daniel Lapin for his memorable phrase.

40. *Kiddushin* 2a.

41. *ANET* 413.

42. Rabbi Daniel Lapin explained to me all the meaning packed so tightly into the opening phrases of *Kiddushin* 2a.

43. *Baba Batra* 58a.

44. Again, thanks to Rabbi Lapin for explaining to me the Talmud's true meaning.

45. See *ANET* 21; Kenyon 197:66–68, 172–73.

46. *Genesis Rabbah* 58:7.

47. *Genesis Rabbah* 60:16; Lev. 6:6.

48. *Genesis Rabbah* 57:3.

49. *Tanchuma, Chayei Sarah* 4.

50. Gen. 24:1.

CHAPTER SIXTEEN: The Two Faces of Eliezer

1. Rashi on Gen. 24:2.
2. Sforno on Gen. 24:3.
3. Gen. 24:3–4; for the translation of the phrase rendered "my country and my family," see Ramban on 24:7.
4. Speiser 1964:183.
5. Rashi on Gen. 15:2.
6. Gen. 24:2.
7. Rashi on Gen. 24:39.
8. Gen. 24:6.
9. *Genesis Rabbah* 60:7.
10. See Eisen 1993.
11. *Sotah* 2a.
12. Sarna 1995:172; *ABD* 4:562.
13. *Sotah* 2a.
14. Rashi on Gen. 24:7.
15. Isa. 29:22; *Genesis Rabbah* 63:2.
16. Lev. 18:3.
17. Rashi on Lev. 18:3.
18. Gordon and Rendsburg 1997:93–94.
19. *Sifra* on Lev. 18:3.
20. Rashi on Gen. 24:10.
21. Gen. 24:10.
22. Gen. 27:43, 28:10, 29:4.
23. *PRE* 16.
24. Rashi on 24:42.
25. *Genesis Rabbah* 59:12.
26. *Taanit* 4a.
27. I heard this interpretation in a lecture by Rabbi David Lapin.
28. Gen. 24:16.
29. See Tosafot on *Yebamot* 61a; *ABD* 4:562.
30. *Genesis Rabbah* 60:5.
31. *ABD* 4:562.
32. Gen. 24:23.
33. Gen. 24:22.
34. Speiser 1964:175; Gordon and Rendsburg 1997:121.
35. See Rashi on Gen. 24:22.
36. Gen. 24:24.
37. Gen. 24:50–51.
38. Speiser 1964:181–82.
39. Rashi on Gen. 24:55.

40. Gordon 1935:226.
41. Gen. 24:31.
42. *Genesis Rabbah* 60:7.
43. Gen. 24:31.
44. *Genesis Rabbah* 60:7.
45. *PRE* 16.
46. *Genesis Rabbah* 60:13.
47. Sarna 1995:175.
48. *PRE* 16.
49. Gen. 24:61.
50. Gen. 24:21.
51. Rashi on Gen. 24:21.
52. See, e.g., Deut. 20:7, 24:1.
53. *Berachot* 26b.
54. Radak on Gen. 24:63.
55. Gen. 24:65.
56. Rashi on Gen. 24:16.
57. *PRE* 16.
58. Speiser 1964:182.
59. Gen. 24:67.
60. Gray 1964:114.
61. Gen. 24:67.
62. Rashi on Gen. 24:67.

CHAPTER SEVENTEEN: **Abraham's Bones**

1. *Tanchuma, Chayei Sarah* 8.
2. Rashi on Gen. 24:62.
3. *Genesis Rabbah* 61:4.
4. *PRE* 30.
5. *ABD* 4:31.
6. Rashi on Gen. 25:27.
7. Rashi on Gen. 25:30.
8. *Shabbat* 118b.
9. Rashi on Gen. 25:7.
10. Ibid. on Gen. 25:5.
11. Gen. 25:6
12. *Sanhedrin* 91a.
13. *Eruvin* 41b; Ibn Ezra and Radak on Gen. 25:8.
14. Gen. 25:9.
15. *Genesis Rabbah* 62:3.
16. Gen. 25:8.

17. Delaney 1998:153.
18. Sforno on Gen. 25:8.
19. *Tanchuma, Lech L'chah* 3.
20. Gen. 16:12.
21. Finkelstein and Silberman 2001:42.
22. Radak on Gen. 25:16.
23. *Tanchuma, Noach* 19.
24. Rashi on *Sanhedrin* 91a.
25. *Baba Batra* 16b.
26. Rashi on Gen. 25:30.
27. It's true that Germany was largely a Protestant nation when it embraced Nazism, but Hitler himself was raised a Catholic and the Nazi belief system was viciously anti-Christian.
28. Thanks to Rabbi Daniel Lapin for explaining this subtle point to me.
29. Rashi on Gen. 25:26.
30. *Sanhedrin* 99b; see Gen. 36:12, 22; though cf. 1 Chron. 1:36, which seems to identify her along with Amalek as *children* of Eliphaz. Radak on this verse explains, based on subtleties of biblical narrative patterns, that she was indeed only the concubine of Eliphaz, not his daughter.
31. Gen. 33:4.
32. *Haamek Davar* on Gen. 33:4.
33. Exod. 15:18.
34. Zech. 14:9.
35. Gen. 24:1.
36. *Baba Batra* 16b.
37. Stephens 1996:308–20.
38. Miller 1985:41.
39. Parrot 1968:138.
40. Miller 1985:41.
41. Dayan 1978:48.
42. Feiler 2001:28.
43. Twersky 1972:475–76.
44. Num. 3:1; *Sanhedrin* 19b.

CONCLUSION: Israel and Humanity

1. Pallière 1985:182.
2. For a celebration of America's Jewish spiritual heritage, see Lapin 1999 passim.
3. See Novak 2002:5–24.
4. Quoted in Pallière 1985:136.

GLOSSARY

Akedah: "Binding" of Isaac.

ayin ha'rah: "Evil eye"; Neither evil nor an eye, but rather a destructive spiritual force attracted to the kind of immodesty where a person hurts others by flaunting his gifts. Typically the prideful person is robbed of precisely the gift in which he most glories.

brit: Covenant; also shorthand for *brit milah,* the Covenant of Circumcision.

Chayei Sarah: Portion of the Torah (Gen. 23:1–25:18), third of three that constitute Abraham's biography as told in Hebrew Scripture.

chen: Very loosely translated "grace," means something more like sociability or personal interactivity.

chesed: Kindness.

Documentary Hypothesis: Theory that the Torah was woven together at a late date by a redactor from earlier source documents, as opposed to having been set down in writing by Moses, as tradition has it.

gematria: Numerological system for analyzing Hebrew words in which each letter of the alphabet is assigned a number value and these values are added up to illuminate deeper meanings of the word.

Genesis Rabbah: Midrash covering the Book of Genesis.

Ghor: Sunken plane of the Dead Sea, now bone-dry and salt-poisoned, once green and populous.

hadith: Muslim traditional literature, comparable to midrash, fills in blanks in the narrative left by the Quran.

halachah: Jewish law.

Hashem: "The Name"; a euphemism for God's four-letter name, which is not spoken aloud; typically translated as "the Lord."

Ibn Ezra: Rabbi Abraham Ibn Ezra, Spanish sage (c. 1089–1164).

Ka'bah: The ancient, revered cubic structure in the middle of the Great Mosque at Mecca, said to have been built by Abraham and Ishmael.

kabbalah: Jewish mystical tradition.

Lech L'chah: Portion of the Torah (Gen. 12:1–17:27), first of three that constitute Abraham's biography as told in Hebrew Scripture.

Machpelah: Tomb complex including the burial places of Abraham, Isaac, and Jacob.

Maharal: Acronym of Rabbi Yehudah Loewe ben Bezalel of Prague (1526–1609).

Maimonides: See Rambam.

mareh: A prophetic vision.

Midrash: Biblical interpolation, filling in the gaps in the scriptural narrative. "A midrash" is a narrative drawn from a midrashic collection; "the Midrash," as I use the term, is *Genesis Rabbah.*

Mishnah: A fundamental crystallization of Oral Torah, edited by Rabbi Judah the Prince about A.D. 200.

Mishneh Torah: Maimonides' summation of Jewish teaching.

mishpat: Justice.

mishteh: A drinking feast.

Mitzrayim: Egypt.

mitzvah: Religiously ordained commandment.

Nachmanides: See Ramban.

Oral Torah: Orally transmitted explanation of the Written Torah, ultimately committed to writing in the Mishnah, Talmud, Midrash, and other rabbinic writings.

parshah: Portion of the Torah, of which one (sometimes two) is read in synagogues each week to complete a cycle in which the whole Torah is completed in a year.

Pentateuch: Torah; Five Books of Moses.

Pirke Avot: "Chapters of the Fathers"; a tractate of the Mishnah dealing primarily with ethical matters.

Pirke d'Rabbi Eliezer: Midrashic collection attributed to the first-century-A.D. sage Rabbi Eliezer.

Radak: Acronym of Rabbi David Kimchi (Provençal, 1160–1235).

Rambam (sometimes "the Rambam"): Acronym of Rabbi Moses ben Maimon (Maimonides; Spanish, 1135–1204).

Ramban (sometimes "the Ramban"): Acronym of Rabbi Moses ben Nachman (Nachmanides; Spanish, 1194–1270).

Rashi: Acronym of Rabbi Solomon bar Isaac (Shlomo Yitzchaki; French, 1040–1105).

Redactor: Editor who wove together the strands of the source documents to produce the text of the Written Torah, according to believers in the Documentary Hypothesis; thought perhaps to have been Ezra the Scribe.

Sefer Yetzirah: Mystical text attributed to Abraham, probably composed in its present form between A.D. 200 and 400.

Sforno: Rabbi Ovadiah Sforno (Italian, 1470–1550).

Shacharit: Jewish morning prayer service.

shed (pl. *shedim*): Demon.

Talmud: Fundamentally a commentary on the Mishnah but including much else in the way of Oral Torah that goes far beyond the Mishnah's more limited scope, including commentary on law and midrashic explanation of scriptural narratives, as well as accounts of sayings and doings of the rabbinic sages.

Tanchuma: Midrashic collection attributed to the students of the late-fourth-century sage Rabbi Tanchuma bar Abba.

tetragrammaton: The unspoken four-letter name of God.

Torah: First five books of the Bible, attributed to Moses: Genesis, Exodus, Leviticus, Numbers, and Deuteronomy.

tumtum: Sexually ambiguous person, born with concealed genitals.

tzedakah: Righteousness.

Vayera: Portion of the Torah (Gen. 18:1–22:24), second of three that constitute Abraham's biography as told in Hebrew Scripture.

BIBLIOGRAPHY

JEWISH TRADITIONAL SOURCES

Targum Onkelos
Babylonian Talmud
Genesis Rabbah
Exodus Rabbah
Tanchuma
Pirke d'Rabbi Eliezer (PRE)
Sifra
Mishneh Torah
Sefer Hamitzvot

JEWISH MEDIEVAL AND LATER COMMENTATORS

Rashi
Tosafot
Radak
Rambam
Ramban
Ibn Ezra
Sforno
Maharsha
Sfas Emes
Malbim
Netziv
Samson Raphael Hirsch

SOURCES IN ENGLISH

Aharoni, Yohanan. 1956. "The Land of Gerar." *IEJ* 6:26–32.

Aharoni, Yohanan, et al. 1993. *The Macmillan Bible Atlas*. 3rd ed. New York: Macmillan.

Albright, W. F. 1946. *Archaeology and the Religion of Israel*. Baltimore, Md.: Johns Hopkins University Press.

———. 1957. *From the Stone Age to Christianity: Monotheism and the Historical Process*. Baltimore, Md.: Johns Hopkins University Press.

———. 1961. "Abram the Hebrew: A New Archaeological Interpretation." *BASOR* 163:36–54.

———. 1968. *Y-hweh and the Gods of Canaan*. London: Athlone Press.

Anati, Emmanuel. 1963. *Palestine Before the Hebrews*. New York: Knopf.

Auerbach, Erich. 1953. *Mimesis: The Representation of Reality in Western Literature*. Translated by Willard R. Trask. Princeton, N.J.: Princeton University Press.

Augustine. 1950. *The City of God*. Translated by Marcus Dods. New York: Modern Library.

Benamozegh, Elijah. 1995. (First published in 1914.) *Israel and Humanity*. Translated by Maxwell Luria. New York: Paulist Press.

Bloom, Harold. 1991. *The Book of J*, including a translation by David Rosenberg. New York: Vintage.

Bright, John. 1972. *A History of Israel*. 2nd ed. Philadelphia: Westminster Press.

Cahill, Thomas. 1998. *The Gifts of the Jews*. New York: Doubleday.

Cassuto, Umberto. 1964. *A Commentary on the Book of Genesis*. Translated by Israel Abraham. Jerusalem: Magnes.

Christie, Agatha. 1977. *An Autobiography*. London: Collins.

Dayan, Moshe. 1978. *Living with the Bible*. New York: William Morrow.

Delaney, Carol. 1998. *Abraham on Trial*. Princeton, N.J.: Princeton University Press.

Della Vida, G. Levi. 1944. "El Elyon in Genesis 14:18–20." *JBL* 63:1–9.

Deutsch, David. 1997. *The Fabric of Reality*. New York: Viking.

Dodds, E. R. 1951. *The Greeks and the Irrational*. Berkeley: University of California.

Eisen, Chaim. 1993. "Unmasking Avraham's Slave: A Midrashic Analysis of Eliezer." In *The 1993 Book of Jewish Thought*, edited by Chaim Eisen and Moshe Sosevsky. New York: Orthodox Union/Yeshivat Ohr Yerushalayim.

Eliade, Mircea. 1974. *The Myth of the Eternal Return*. Translated by Willard R. Trask. Reprint, Princeton, N.J.: Princeton University Press.

Feiler, Bruce. 2001. *Walking the Bible: A Journey by Land through the Five Books of Moses*. New York: William Morrow.

Finegan, Jack. 1959. *Light from the Ancient Past*. Princeton, N.J.: Princeton University Press.

Finkelstein, Israel, and Silberman, Neal Asher. 2001. *The Bible Unearthed: Archaeology's New Vision of Ancient Israel and the Origins of Its Sacred Texts*. New York: Free Press.

Finkelstein, Jacob J. 1959. "The Bible, Archaeology, and History: Have the Excavations Corroborated Scripture?" *Commentary* 27:341–49.

Firestone, Reuven. 1990. *Journeys in Holy Lands: The Evolution of the Abraham-Ishmael Legends in Islamic Exegesis.* Albany, N.Y.: State University of New York Press.

Frankfort, H., et al. 1946. *The Intellectual Adventure of Ancient Man.* Chicago: University of Chicago Press.

Free, Joseph P. 1944. "Abraham's Camels." *JNES* 3:187–93.

Freedman, David Noel, and Campbell, Edward F., Jr., eds. 1961. *The Biblical Archaeologist Reader.* Vol. 2. Garden City, N.Y.: Anchor.

Friedman, Richard Elliott. 1987. *Who Wrote the Bible?* New York: Summit Books.

Ginzberg, Louis. 1998. *The Legends of the Jews.* 7 vols. Translated by Henrietta Szold. Reprint, Baltimore, Md.: Johns Hopkins University Press.

Glazerson, M. 1984. *From Hinduism Back to Judaism.* Jerusalem: Himelsein Glazerson Publishers.

Glueck, Nelson. 1955. "The Age of Abraham in the Negev." *BA* 18:2–9.

———. 1959. *Rivers in the Desert: A History of the Negev.* New York: Farrar, Straus & Cuddahy.

Gollaher, David L. 2000. *Circumcision: A History of the World's Most Controversial Surgery.* New York: Basic.

Gordis, Daniel. 1997. *Does the World Need the Jews? Rethinking Chosenness and American Jewish Identity.* New York: Scribners.

Gordon, Cyrus. 1935. "Fratriarchy in the Bible." *JBL* 54:223–31.

———. 1940. "Biblical Customs and the Nuzu Tablets." *BA* 3:1–12.

———. 1963. "Abraham of Ur." In *Hebrew and Semitic Studies Presented to G. R. Driver.* Oxford: Oxford University Press.

Gordon, Cyrus, and Rendsburg, Gary A. 1997. *The Bible and the Ancient Near East.* New York: Norton.

Gray, John. 1964. *The Canaanites.* New York: Frederick A. Praeger.

Harland, J. Penrose. 1961. "Sodom and Gomorrah." In *The Biblical Archaeologist Reader.* Vol. 1. Garden City, N.Y.: Anchor.

Heschel, Abraham Joshua. 1955. *God in Search of Man: A Philosophy of Judaism.* New York: Noonday.

Hogarth, David G., ed. 1899. *Authority and Archaeology: Sacred and Profane: Essays on the Relation of Monuments to Biblical and Classical Literature.* London: John Murray.

Jacobsen, Thorkil. 1976. *The Treasures of Darkness: A History of Mesopotamian Religion.* New Haven, Conn.: Yale University Press.

Jaynes, Julian. 2000. *The Origins of Consciousness in the Breakdown of the Bicameral Mind.* New York: Mariner Books.

Josephus. 1981. *The Jewish War.* London: Penguin.

Kaplan, Aryeh. 1997. *Sefer Yetzirah: The Book of Creation.* York Beach, Maine: Samuel Weiser.

Kardimon, Samson. 1958. "Adoption as a Remedy for Infertility in the Period of the Patriarchs." *JSS* 3:123–26.

Kenyon, Kathleen. 1979. *Archaeology in the Holy Land*. New York: Norton.

Kierkegaard, Soren. 1983. *Fear and Trembling*. Translated by Howard V. and Edna H. Hong. Princeton, N.J.: Princeton University Press.

Kohler, Ludwig. 1953. *Hebrew Man*. Translated by Peter R. Ackroyd. New York: Abingdon Press.

Kugel, James. 1997. *The Bible as It Was*. Cambridge, Mass.: Belknap.

Lapin, Rabbi Daniel. 1999. *America's Real War*. Sisters, Ore.: Multnomah.

———. 2000. *Buried Treasures: Hidden Wisdom from the Hebrew Language*. Sisters, Ore.: Multnomah.

Lehmann, Manfred R. 1953. "Abraham's Purchase of Machpelah and Hittite Law." *BASOR* 129:15–18.

Leibowitz, Nehama. 1996. *Studies in Devarim*. Brooklyn: Lambda Publishers.

Liverani, M. 1978. "The Amorites." In *Peoples of Old Testament Times*, edited by D. J. Wiseman. Oxford: Oxford University Press.

Luzzatto, Moshe Chayim. 1988. *The Way of God*. Translated by Aryeh Kaplan. New York: Feldheim.

Maimonides. 1956. *The Guide for the Perplexed*. Translated by M. Friedlander. Reprint, New York: Dover.

Matthews, Victor H. 1986. "The Wells of Gerar." *BA* 49:118–26.

May, Herbert Gordon. 1941. "The Patriarchal Idea of God." *JBL* 60:115–18.

Miller, Nancy. 1985. "Patriarchal Burial Site Explored for First Time in 700 Years." *BARev* 9, no. 3:26–43.

Novak, Michael. 2002. *On Two Wings: Humble Faith and Common Sense at the American Founding*. San Francisco: Encounter.

Pallière, Aimé. 1985. (First published in 1926.) *The Unknown Sanctuary: A Pilgrimage from Rome to Israel*. Translated by Louise Waterman Wise. New York: Bloch Publishing Co.

Parrot, Andre. 1968. *Abraham and His Times*. Translated by James H. Farley. Philadelphia: Fortress Press.

Rohl, David. 1995. *Pharaohs and Kings: A Biblical Quest*. New York: Crown.

Sacks, Jonathan. 2000. *A Letter in the Scroll*. New York: Free Press.

Saggs, H. W. F. 1962. *The Greatness That Was Babylon: A Survey of the Ancient Civilizations of the Tigris-Euphrates Valley*. New York: Praeger.

Sarna, Nahum M. 1977. "Abraham in History." *BARev* 3, no. 12:5–9.

———. 1995. (First published in 1966.) *Understanding Genesis: The World of the Bible in the Light of History*. New York: Schocken.

Sasson, Jack M. 1966. "Circumcision in the Ancient Near East." *JBL* 85:473–76.

Schroeder, Gerald. 1997. *The Science of God: The Convergence of Scientific and Biblical Wisdom*. New York: Free Press.

Shanks, Hershel. 1975. "The Patriarchs' Wives as Sisters: Is the Anchor Bible Wrong?" *BARev* 1, no. 3:22–26.

———. 1980. "Have Sodom and Gomorrah Been Found?" *BARev* 6, no. 5:26–36.

Siker, Jeffrey S. 1991. *Disinheriting the Jews: Abraham in Christian Controversy.* Louisville, Ky.: Westminster/John Knox Press.

Skinner, John. 1969. *A Critical and Exegetical Commentary on Genesis.* Reprint, Edinburgh: T.&T. Clark.

Speiser, E. A. 1964. *Genesis: A New Translation with Introduction and Commentary.* New York: Doubleday.

Spiegel, Shalom. 1993. *The Last Trial: On the Legends and Lore of the Command to Offer Isaac as a Sacrifice.* Translated by Judah Goldin. Reprint, Woodstock, Vt.: Jewish Lights.

Steinmetz, Devora. 1991. *From Father to Son: Kinship, Conflict, and Continuity in Genesis.* Louisville, Ky.: Westminster/John Knox Press.

Stephens, John Lloyd. 1996. *Incidents of Travel in Egypt, Arabia Petraea, and the Holy Land.* Reprint, New York: Dover.

Thompson, Thomas L. 1974. *The Historicity of the Patriarchal Narratives.* Berlin: de Gruyter.

Tucker, Gene M. 1966. "The Legal Background of Genesis 23." *JBL* 85:77–84.

Twersky, Isadore, ed. 1972. *A Maimonides Reader.* West Orange, N.J.: Behrman House.

Van Seters, John. 1975. *Abraham in History and Tradition.* New Haven, Conn.: Yale University Press.

Vaux, Roland de. 1965. *Ancient Israel.* Vol. 2, *Religious Institutions.* New York: McGraw-Hill.

———. 1978. *The Early History of Israel: To the Exodus and the Covenant of Sinai.* Translated by David Smith. London: Darton, Longman & Todd.

Vermes, Geza. 1998. *The Complete Dead Sea Scrolls in English.* London: Penguin.

Weinberg, Matis. 1999. *FrameWorks: Bereishit-Genesis, Parashot II–XII.* Boston: Foundation for Jewish Publications.

Wilson, John A. 1951. *The Culture of Ancient Egypt.* Chicago: University of Chicago Press.

Wiseman, D. J. 1983. "Abraham Reassessed." In *Essays on the Patriarchal Narratives,* edited by A. R. Millard and D. J. Wiseman. Winona Lake, Ind.: Eisenbrauns.

Woolley, C. Leonard. 1965. (First published in 1928.) *The Sumerians.* New York: Norton.

Wright, Ernest G. 1962. *Biblical Archaeology.* Philadelphia: Westminster Press.

Zornberg, Aviva Gottlieb. 1995. *The Beginning of Desire: Reflections on Genesis.* New York: Image.

INDEX

© Cris Rapp

DAVID KLINGHOFFER is the author of the spiritual memoir *The Lord Will Gather Me In*, a finalist for the National Jewish Book Award. Formerly the literary editor of *National Review*, he has contributed articles to the *New York Times, Los Angeles Times, Washington Post, Commentary,* and other publications. He lives on Mercer Island, Washington.